Persian Gulf 2013

Persian Gulf 2013

India's Relations with the Region

Edited by
P. R. Kumaraswamy

SAGE www.sagepublications.com
Los Angeles • London • New Delhi • Singapore • Washington DC

First published in 2014 by

SAGE Publications India Pvt Ltd
B1/I-1 Mohan Cooperative Industrial Area
Mathura Road, New Delhi 110 044, India
www.sagepub.in

SAGE Publications Inc
2455 Teller Road
Thousand Oaks, California 91320, USA

SAGE Publications Ltd
1 Oliver's Yard, 55 City Road
London EC1Y 1SP, United Kingdom

SAGE Publications Asia-Pacific Pte Ltd
3 Church Street
#10-04 Samsung Hub
Singapore 049483

Published by Vivek Mehra for SAGE Publications India Pvt Ltd, Phototypeset in 10/13pt Berkeley by Diligent Typesetter, Delhi and printed at Saurabh Printers Pvt Ltd, New Delhi.

Library of Congress Cataloging-in-Publication Data
Persian Gulf 2013 : India's relations with the region / edited by P. R. Kumaraswamy.
    pages cm
Includes bibliographical references and index.
    1. Persian Gulf Region—Foreign relations—India. 2. India—Foreign relations—Persian Gulf Region. 3. Kumaraswamy, P. R., editor of compilation.
    DS326.P435   327.53054—dc23   2013   2013039090

ISBN: 978-81-321-1352-2 (HB)

The SAGE Team: Rudra Narayan, Alekha Chandra Jena, Rajib Chatterjee and Dally Verghese

To
The Friend of MEI@ND
With respect, admiration and gratitude

Thank you for choosing a SAGE product! If you have any comment,
observation or feedback, I would like to personally hear from you.
Please write to me at <u>contactceo@sagepub.in</u>

—Vivek Mehra, Managing Director and CEO,
SAGE Publications India Pvt Ltd, New Delhi

Bulk Sales

SAGE India offers special discounts for purchase of books in bulk.
We also make available special imprints and excerpts from our
books on demand.

For orders and enquiries, write to us at

Marketing Department
SAGE Publications India Pvt Ltd
B1/I-1, Mohan Cooperative Industrial Area
Mathura Road, Post Bag 7
New Delhi 110044, India
E-mail us at <u>marketing@sagepub.in</u>

Get to know more about SAGE, be invited to SAGE events, get on
our mailing list. Write today to <u>marketing@sagepub.in</u>

This book is also available as an e-book.

Contents

List of Tables and Figures

Tables

Figures

List of Abbreviations

AABEX	Arab Asian Business and Exhibition Centre
ABS	American Bureau of Shipping
ACD	Asian Cooperation Dialogue
ACU	Asian Clearing Union
ADACH	Abu Dhabi Authority for Culture and Heritage
ADIA	Abu Dhabi Investment Authority
AQAP	Al-Qaeda in the Arab peninsula
ASSOCHAM	Associated Chambers of Commerce and Industry of India
BAE	British Aerospace
BCCI	Bahrain Chamber of Commerce and Industry
BDF	Bahrain Defence Force
BICI	Bahrain Independent Commission of Inquiry
BIS	Bahrain-India Society
BITS	Birla Institute of Technology and Science
BORL	Bharat Oman Refineries Ltd.
BPCL	Bharat Petroleum Corporation Limited
bpd	barrels per day
BSE	Bombay Stock Exchange
CBD	Convention on Bio-diversity
CBEC	Central Bureau of Excise Control
CBSE	Central Board of Secondary Education
CECA	Comprehensive Economic Cooperation Agreement
CERD	Committee on the Elimination of Racial Discrimination
CII	Confederation of Indian Industry
CLS	Cable Landing Station
CMACM	Co-operation and Mutual Assistance on Custom Matters
CVE	Countering Violent Extremism

DFAT	Department of Foreign Affairs and Trade
DGCA	Directorate General of Civil Aviation
DMIC	Delhi–Mumbai Industrial Corridor
DP World	Dubai Ports World
DP	Delhi Police
DTAA	Double Taxation Avoidance Agreement
FDI	Foreign Direct Investment
FICCI	Federation of Indian Chambers of Commerce and Industry
FIEO	Federation of Indian Export Organisations
FIFA	Fédération Internationale de Football Association
FNC	Federal National Council
FTA	Free Trade Agreement
GCC	Gulf Cooperation Council
GCSS	General Cultural Scholarship Scheme
GCTF	Global Counter-Terrorism Forum
GEP	Global Economic Prospects
GJEPC	Gems & Jewellery Export Promotion Council
GPC	General People's Congress
HLMM	High Level Monitoring Mechanism
HMEL	HPCL-Mittal Energy Ltd.
IAEA	International Atomic Energy Agency
IAF	Iranian Artists Forum
IBLF	Indian Business Leaders Forum
IBC	Iraq Body Count
IBPN	Indian Business and Professionals Network
ICAI	Institute of Chartered Accountants of India
ICC	Indian Cultural Centre
ICCR	Indian Council for Cultural Relations
ICT	Information and Communication Technology
ICWA	Indian Council of World Affairs
IDEX	International Defence Exhibition
IEA	International Energy Agency
IEI	Institution of Engineers India
IITC	International Information Technology Company
ILSA	Iran–Libya Sanctions Act
IMA	Indian Medical Association

INSTC	International North South Transport Corridor
IOC	Indian Oil Corporation
IOR-ARC	Indian Ocean Rim Association for Regional Cooperation
IOSCG	India and Oman Strategic Consultative Group Meetings
IPI	Iran–Pakistan–India pipeline
IPS	Indian Police Service
IDRO	Industrial Development and Renovation Organisation
IT	Information Technology
ITPC	Iraqi Telecommunications and Post Company
ITPO	India Trade Promotion Organisation
ITUC	International Trade Union Confederation
JCM	Joint Commission Meeting
JDCC	Joint Defence Cooperation Committee
JMP	Joint Meeting Parties
JSL	Jyoti Structures Ltd.
KNPC	Kuwait National Petroleum Company
KPI	Kuwait Petroleum International
KPTL	Kalpataru Power Transmission Ltd.
KRG	Kurdistan Regional Government
KV	Kendriya Vidyalaya
L&T MFY	Larsen & Toubro Modular Fabrication Yard
L&T	Larsen & Toubro
LANCI	Lanco Infratech Limited
LNG	Liquefied Natural Gas
MHA	Ministry of Home Affairs
mmBtu	million metric British thermal unit
MMCFD	million cubic feet per day
MMTPA	million metric tonnes per annum
MNNA	major non-NATO ally
MOIA	Ministry of Overseas Indian Affairs
MoU	Memorandum of Understanding
MP	Member of Parliament
MRPL	Mangalore Refinery and Petrochemicals Ltd.
NAM	Non-Aligned Movement
NATO	North Atlantic Treaty Organization
NDC	National Dialogue Conference
NHAI	National Highway Authority of India

NIOC	National Iranian Oil Company
NSA	National Security Advisor
OCL	Oman Container Lines Inc.
OHI	Oman Holdings International
OIC	Organisation of Islamic Cooperation
OMIFCO	Oman–India Fertilizer Company
OMPL	ONGC Mangalore Petrochemicals Limited
ONGC	Oil and Natural Gas Corporation
OPAL	ONGC Petro Additions Limited
OPEC	Organization of Petroleum Exporting Countries
PBD	Pravasi Bhartiya Divas
PDO	Petroleum Development Oman
PDRY	People's Democratic Republic of Yemen
POL	petroleum, oil and lubricants
RAK	Ras al-Khaimah
SAGE	South Asian Gas Enterprises
SAGIA	Saudi Arabian General Investment Authority
SAMA	Saudi Arabian Monetary Agency
SBI	State Bank of India
SCF	Strategic Cooperation Forum
SCSS	Sheba Centre for Strategic Studies
SFAAI	State Financial and Administrative Audit Institution
SGS	Societe Generale de Surveillance
SIBC	Saudi-India Business Council
SIBN	Saudi India Business Network
SLOC	Sea Lines of Communication
TCS	Tata Consultancy Services
TDAP	Trade Development Authority of Pakistan
TERC	Trade and Economic Relations Committee
UAE	United Arab Emirates
UNGA	United Nations General Assembly
UNSC	United Nations Security Council
UNSCOP	United Nations Special Committee on Palestine
UPF	United Principalist Front
USSR	Union of Soviet Socialist Republics
WB	World Bank
WHO	World Health Organization
YAR	Yemen Arab Republic

1
Introduction

P. R. Kumaraswamy

The wider Middle East, stretching from Morocco in the West to Iran in the East, is perhaps the most important region than it is commonly recognized and understood. Unlike other parts of the world, the Middle East not only provides opportunities but also presents challenges to India's ability to play a leadership role in the world. Indeed, India's willingness to shoulder greater responsibility, both political and diplomatic, would be tested by its ability to manage some of the sensitive issues that dominate the Middle East. The region that encompasses the Arab world as well as three prominent non-Arab states, namely, Iran, Israel and Turkey, would play a pivotal role in India's political, economic, cultural, religious and, above all, strategic interests and policies. The region offers India the wherewithal to pursue aspirations for leadership role while simultaneously presenting severe challenges to its diplomatic acumen. Some of the vexed problems that dominate the current global political agenda are located in or could be traced to the Middle East. Diverse issues such as popular disenchantment with the existing political order, demands for good and transparent governance, accountable leadership and empowerment of women and youth have dominated the Middle Eastern landscape. These issues have overshadowed, if not diluted, traditional global agendas such as inter-state conflicts and tensions, minority rights and nuclear proliferation.

The primacy of the Middle East for India, however, is not reflected in New Delhi's attitudes and policies towards it. The region continues to evoke public attention only for controversies and unpleasant developments: recurring wars and conflicts; violent political upheavals; periodic interference and intervention by extra-regional powers; proxy wars by prominent countries; elusive and futile peace processes; frequent bouts of terrorism and other forms of political violence; resurgent piracy against international shipping; political instability in Lebanon; civil war situations in Iraq, Yemen and of late in Syria; marginalization of ethnic and religious minorities; political tension and competition between Iran and Saudi Arabia over leadership of the Islamic world; great power rivalry for regional hegemony; extra-regional ambitions of prominent Middle Eastern countries; concerns over weapons of mass destruction; nascent fears over the emergence of various Islamist parties; and the never-ending controversies over Iran's nuclear ambitions.

If these long-standing problems were insufficient, since January 2011 the Arab world has been witnessing a series of popular protests against its rulers and the established political order. What began as an individual protest by Mohamed Bouazizi, a marginalized vegetable vender in Sidi Bouzid in central Tunisia, soon engulfed the entire Arab world. With the sole exception of Qatar, a country with world's highest per capita income, no Arab country remained immune to widespread public disenchantment with the political status quo. While political road map, let alone the end result, remains unclear, at least in the medium-term political uncertainty would be the most prominent hallmark of the Arab Spring.[1]

These developments clearly indicate that India has to take cognizance of the region, its challenges and, in the process, carve out a niche for itself. Fortunately, India merely has to look at its recent past to reorient its Middle East policy.

Historic Links

Civilizational Links! This expression is common in any discussion on the Indo–Iranian relations. This, however, is true for India's relations with most countries of the Middle East; for Arab and non-Arab countries or for Islamic and non-Islamic societies. Centuries before Christ, there were strong trade relations between the two regions. Centuries before the birth of Islam, the Arabian Peninsula was a major trading centre for Indian merchants and the importance of Mecca as a major trading destination for Indian merchants was enhanced in the seventh century following the ushering in of the Hajj pilgrimage. India had close cultural ties with all the three monotheistic religions that emerged in the Middle East, namely, Judaism, Christianity and Islam.

Over centuries, it had also become home to a number of Islamic sects such as Ahmadiyyas and Bohras as well as the Baha'i faith, which branched out of Islam. The followers of the pre-Islamic Zoroastrian faith from Persia, the Parsis, can also be found in India. As its leaders periodically harp, India is also home to the world's third largest Shia community after Iran. According to a 2012 study by *PEW Center*, India currently has the second largest Muslim population after Indonesia.[2] However, during the British rule, India had the largest Muslim population in the world and this influenced, and at times dictated, the British policy towards the Middle East.[3] This was most apparent in its Palestine policy whereby a section of the British officials were highly opposed to the Balfour Declaration due its adverse impact upon the Indian Muslims.[4]

During the British Raj, the Middle East, especially the Persian Gulf region, was of paramount importance. Long before the discovery of oil and resultant strategic importance, imperial policies and interests in the Gulf were determined, pursued and administered from the Bombay Presidency. The British policy towards the emerging protectorates in the Gulf, which subsequently became independent sovereign entities, was pursued from New Delhi.[5] These imperial connections with, and advantages in, the Gulf region, however, were not adequately leveraged following India's independence. The earlier linkages with the region were abhorred as vestiges of colonialism and imperial legacies and India thus shunned from building its post-1947 relations upon them. Free India was pursuing a foreign policy under the banner of anti-imperialism and anti-colonialism and Jawaharlal Nehru and his colleagues failed to appreciate the unique advantages offered by linkages with the Persian Gulf that the British had built. India's penchant for secular Arab nationalism and progressive Arab socialism passed over most countries along the Gulf and their monarchical political order and pro-Western conservatism.

As a result, until the oil crisis of 1973 and the resultant economic capital and clout acquired by the oil-rich Arab countries, the Gulf region did not figure prominently in the Indian foreign policy calculations. For long its political orientation towards the Middle East was centred around Cairo, and following Gamal Abdul Nasser's defeat in the June war of 1967, gradually shifted to Baghdad. The energy resources of Iraq added an economic dimension to the political ties between the two countries whose ruling parties, the Congress and Ba'ath, officially espoused secularism. This trend continued until the 1980s when a host of controversial policies pursued by Iraq under the leadership of Saddam Hussein strained the bilateral relations.

The Arab–Israeli Conflict

The most salient feature of the Middle East has been the prolonged Arab–Israeli conflict, which naturally had a profound impact upon India's approach towards this region and its developments. Since the early 1920s, the Indian nationalists found a common cause with the Arabs of Palestine and adopted an unsympathetic attitude towards Jewish aspirations for a homeland in Palestine. The Zionist proximity with the British and domestic political compulsions resulted in them adopting an overtly pro-Arab position. In early 1947, when the newly formed United Nations (UN) took cognizance of the Palestine question, India sided with the Arabs. While a majority of the UN Committee recommended partition as the solution, India came out with a federal plan.[6] Thus, when the partition plan came before the General Assembly on 29 November 1947, India was one of the three non-Arab and non-Muslim countries to vote against the UN plan for Palestine.[7]

The formation of Israel in May 1948 and its recognition by major powers did not dilute the Indian position and in May 1949, it voted against Israel's admission into the UN. Gradually, India came around to accepting Israel and granted it recognition on 17 September 1950,[8] which, however, was not followed by the establishment of diplomatic relations. Initial explanation of absence of personnel and resources gradually became complicated and India's Israel policy was sucked into a host of conflicts and tensions in the Middle East as well as India's growing friendship with Gamal Abdul Nasser of Egypt. Thus, for over four decades, non-relations became the hallmark of India's Israel policy. This was reversed in January 1992 following the end of the Cold War and the systemic transformation in the international political order.[9]

Thus, until 1992, support for the Arabs of Palestine and non-relations with Israel served as effective diplomatic instrument to further India's interests in the wider Middle East. These were expressed within the context of prevailing mood of anti-colonialism and anti-imperialism. These also figured prominently in its responses to various developments in the region, especially the Suez War of 1956 and the June war of 1967. Nehru's acquiescence to Arab pressures resulted in Israel's non-invitation for the Afro-Asian Conference in Bandung in April 1955 and its subsequent exclusion from the Non-aligned Movement.

Non-relations with Israel and support for the Palestinians, the twin plank used by India to further its interests ironically reflected India's limitations. During the Cold War years, India's ability to influence the global events could be accomplished only through political statements and positions. The moral high ground that India sought to acquire was severely undermined by its stands during some of the developments pertaining to the Eastern bloc countries; its position on crises in Hungary and Czechoslovakia proved to be controversial and less principled.

They also camouflaged a much larger problem: the absence of non-political instruments available to India. During the Cold War era, India was an economically weak power and was dependent upon financial help and assistance from the outside world. Its political leverage was severely dented following the Sino-Indian war which exposed its inability to defend itself. In the following decade, as its political leverage, especially in the Non-aligned Movement, was waning, India had to confront an economic shock in the form of the 1973 oil crisis. Thus, despite its large population, India remained a marginal player in Asia and beyond largely because of its weak economic basis. Under these circumstances, anti-Israeli and pro-Arab political rhetoric remained the only means available to India to further its interests in the Middle East.

The Pakistan Factor

The Middle East, however, remained important for India for one other consideration, namely, Pakistan and its roots can be traced to the early part of the twentieth century and located within India's struggle for independence. The formation of the Muslim League in 1906 and its gradual emergence as the voice of a powerful section of Indian Muslims challenged the homogenizing post-British political entity that the Congress and its leaders sought to project. Due to historical and social reasons, the initial participation of the Muslim masses in the Congress-led freedom movement was limited. The British policies, as well as Muslim fears of a Hindu-dominated Congress replacing the colonial rule, were responsible for the lukewarm Muslim attitude towards the Congress. Partly to address the Muslim concerns and partly to enhance its all-inclusive identity, in the early 1920s the Congress party embraced the Khilafat struggle (1919–24).[10] The possible dismemberment of the Ottoman Empire, whose ruler was also the temporal head of the Sunni Muslims, angered the Indian Muslim community, which sought to rally around the beleaguered Sultan-cum-Caliph. This bonhomie initiated by Mahatma Gandhi did not endure and gradually the Muslim League gathered strength. It sought to champion the cause of the Muslims of the subcontinent as a distinct religious and, hence, separate political entity. This process culminated in the partition of the subcontinent and the formation of Pakistan.

The Congress–Muslim League tussles for the support and loyalty of the Indian Muslims, however, did not remain within the subcontinent but also affected their respective policies towards the Middle East since 1947. The rivalry more clearly manifested in the position adopted by the Indian nationalist leaders towards the Jewish political aspirations in Palestine and their demand for a Jewish homeland.[11] If the League supported the Arabs of Palestine due to its solidarity with the Muslims, the Congress party viewed the issue as a means of expanding its support base among the Indian Muslims. Besides making a common cause with the Arabs in their struggle against imperialism, the Congress also viewed the Jewish nationalism as a replica of the demands for a separate state pursued by the Muslim League. Thus, its internal opposition to the religion-based nationalistic demands of the Muslim League was manifested in its equal opposition to similar demands by Jews vis-à-vis Palestine. Both these demands, the Congress leaders felt, were against democratic principles but supported separatism and religion-based nationalism. Thus, the Congress party's opposition to the two-nation theory in the subcontinent was accompanied by its vehement opposition to the idea of a Jewish state in Palestine.

The partition of the subcontinent and the emergence of Israel as a sovereign entity forced India to be pragmatic and adopt a less dogmatic view towards partitions in the subcontinent and Palestine. The process was relatively shorter towards the geographically closer Pakistan than politically complicated Middle East. The erstwhile Congress–League rivalry transformed into an Indo-Pakistan competition for Arab and Islamic support in the Middle East. This competition was a principal reason for the prolonged absence of diplomatic relations between India and Israel; while its recognition came in September 1950 the normalization had to wait until January 1992. The controversial observation of Yosef Hassin, the Israeli Consul in Mumbai in 1982, aptly summed up the reality: India was competing with Pakistan for political and diplomatic favours from the Middle East.[12]

The traditional Arab support for Pakistan, especially during its conflicts with India, did not influence the attitude of the latter. Cognizant of the Middle Eastern support for a fellow Islamic country, India never insisted on reciprocity when dealing with the Arab and Islamic countries of the region. Indian leaders understood and explained the pro-Pakistan bias of the Middle East even when Pakistan remained the most dominant foreign policy preoccupation in New Delhi. This trend could not be changed until the end of the Cold War and India's newly found great power aspirations.

Post-Cold War Transformation

A meaningful, albeit minimalist, Middle East policy of India began with the end of the Cold War and the resultant transformation of the global order. The sudden disappearance of its long-term friend, the Union of Soviet Socialist Republics (USSR), and the absence of bloc politics forced India to re-evaluate its understanding of and response to new international order. It was also compelled to find ways to coexist with a world dominated by the United States (US). These meant India adopting policies driven by hard-nosed realism than erstwhile political rhetoric. Furthermore, global changes were accompanied by a severe internal economic crisis. Prolonged mismanagement of the Soviet-style state-controlled economy forced India to seek international aid and assistance. The situation was so precarious that the Reserve Bank of India airlifted and mortgaged 200 tonnes of gold to pay for the import of essential food items.[13]

Forced to act by these changes, Prime Minister Narasimha Rao (1991–96) brought about changes that transformed not only India's policy towards the Middle East but also its fortunes in the turbulent region. At the political level, he abandoned the four-decade-long hesitation towards Israel and established full diplomatic relations. The ongoing Middle East peace process and the Arab willingness to seek a negotiated political settlement largely enabled India to overcome the past blinkers and move closer to Israel. The marginalization of the Palestine Liberation Organization (PLO) in the wake of Yasser Arafat's support for Iraqi President Saddam Hussein during the 1990–91 Kuwait crisis meant that the support for the Palestinians largely lost its regional diplomatic relevance. This in turn facilitated the Indian move. Since January 1992, India's bilateral relations with Israel have grown considerably and encompass wide range of political, economic, cultural and, above all, security co-operation.[14]

More importantly, Rao's decision on Israel established a balance in India's Middle East policy. In the past India squarely blamed Israel for almost every upheaval in the Arab–Israeli conflict and was not prepared to understand, let alone accommodate the concerns of the Jewish State. Normalization altered this partisanship and since 1992, there has been a marked shift in this stance towards Israel, the conflict and the region. New Delhi has been less vocal and more nuanced and balanced in reacting to the periodic outbreak of violence. It is no longer in the forefront of anti-Israeli resolutions in the UN and other international forums. Much to the consternation of Israel, India continues to vote with the Arab countries in the UN, but it has been less sermonizing. Above all, there is a noticeable shift in India's understanding of the importance of the bilateral relations and its differences over various aspects of the peace process. By delinking one from the other, India has been pursuing fruitful bilateral relations with Israel while simultaneously maintaining its political support for the Palestinians. This is manifested in the security arena where Israel has emerged as a principal arms supplier and India as the largest destination for Israel's defence exports. This would not have been possible if India had not delinked the bilateral relations from the multilateral issues.

This delinking and the new balance have their dividends. Unlike the past, India's relations with other countries of the Middle East have not become hostage to its Israel policy. Despite some initial differences, the Arab and Islamic countries have come to terms with the Indo–Israeli relations and the strategic rationale for India seeking closer friendship with Israel. Even a rabidly anti-Israeli country like the Islamic Republic of Iran has not made Israel an issue in its bilateral relations with India. Rapid growth of political and economic ties between India and the countries of the Middle East indeed happened after India's normalization of relations with Israel rather than before.

This is vividly demonstrated in the spate of state visits to and from the Middle East region during the post-1992 period. Some of the most notable state visits include those by Iranian Presidents Hashemi Rafsanjani (1993) and Mohammed Khatami (2003), King Abdullah of Saudi Arabia (2006), Syrian President Bashar al-Assad (June 2008), Egyptian President Hosni Mubarak (November 2008), the Emir of Kuwait al-Ahmad al-Jabar al-Sabah (June 2006), the Crown Prince of Bahrain Salman bin Hamad al-Khalifa (March 2007 and May 2012), Algerian President Abdelaziz Bouteflika (January 2001) and the Emir of Qatar Hamad bin-Khalifa al-Thani (April 1999, May 2005 and April 2012). Three of these leaders, namely, Khatami, Abdullah and Bouteflika, were given the honour of being chief guests at India's Republic Day celebrations while the Sultan of Oman narrowly missed this honour in January 2013. Indeed, within months of Khatami's visit, India hosted Israeli Prime Minister Ariel Sharon in September 2003. There were a host of reciprocal visits from India to countries of the region.

If Israel did not impede Indo-Middle East relations, what pushed the countries of this region to seek greater interactions with India?

The answer to this puzzle has to be located in India's economic growth since reforms were introduced in 1991. From being a major recipient of international aid and assistance, it has emerged as one of the major economies of the world. During the Cold War years, the vulnerability of its non-alignment was most visible in its economic dependency; it received large quantities of food subsidy from the US under its PL-480 Programme and resorted to Rupee–Rouble arrangement to pay for its large defence imports from the USSR. The economic reforms presided over by Rao, along with his then Finance Minister Manmohan Singh, dramatically changed that image. More than two decades later, the economic reforms continue to face problems and challenges and economic prosperity has not percolated widely and benefits are cornered by a few creamy layers. Much of the social tensions in different parts of the country are the direct result of the lopsided economic reforms, mismanagement of priorities, misuse and misappropriation of funds and marginalization of the masses from the benefits of economic reforms.

Important as they are, it is not possible to ignore the significant strides made by the Indian economy since 1991. Not as impressive as the Chinese economy, India's growth has nevertheless been consistent and has enabled it to overtake all but two of the Western economies. More importantly, currently India's economy is larger than all other European countries, including its former colonial ruler, the Great Britain. In 2006 India became the fourth largest economy in the world after the US, China and Japan. Notwithstanding the initial concerns, India has successfully weathered the global economic crisis and continues to register a lower but positive growth, something that most Western countries could not even imagine. With the Japanese economy struggling to make a sustainable recovery, India is poised to be become the third largest economy after the US and China.[15]

Persian Gulf

India's economic story means two things for the countries of the Middle East, especially those along the Persian Gulf: a guaranteed market for their energy resources, and a potential alternate destination for investments. The latter is yet to take a concrete course and investments from oil-rich Middle Eastern countries continue to remain in the realm of potentials than a reality. The former has manifested in the form of growing Indian import of crude oil from the region and their role in expanding energy trade of India.

The phenomenal economic growth of India is reflected in its trade with the Middle East. During 1995–96, its bilateral trade with the Middle East stood at a meagre amount of US$6.2 billion while this rose to

US$205.1 billion in 2011–12, and this is more acute in the case of the Persian Gulf (Tables 1.1 and 1.2 and Figures 1.1 and 1.2). The region has overtaken the US and European Union (EU) as India's most favourable destination for foreign trade. From about one-sixth in the mid-1990s the share of the Middle East in its total foreign trade has gone up close to 30 per cent by 2011–12.

Some of India's prominent trade partners can be found in the region, especially the Persian Gulf. For example, as Table 1.3 and Figure 1.3 indicate, among India's top 25 trading partners in 2011–12, six belong to the Gulf region, namely, the UAE, Saudi Arabia, Iraq, Kuwait, Iran and Qatar. During 2009–10, the UAE was India's largest trading partner,

Table 1.1
Persian Gulf Share in India's Total Imports (in US$ Million)

Year	Total imports	Imports from Persian Gulf	Share per cent
1996–97	39,132.41	5,225.60	13.35
1997–98	41,484.49	5,182.19	12.49
1998–99	42,388.71	6,252.67	14.75
1999–2000	49,738.06	7,708.73	15.50
2000–01	50,536.45	1,914.12	3.79
2001–02	51,413.28	2,018.62	3.93
2002–03	61,412.14	2,189.82	3.57
2003–04	78,149.11	3,549.26	4.54
2004–05	111,517.43	7,505.67	6.73
2005–06	149,165.73	8,519.55	5.71
2006–07	185,735.24	46,131.24	24.84
2007–08	251,654.01	64,328.98	25.56
2008–09	303,696.31	80,292.24	26.44
2009–10	288,372.88	73,640.76	25.54
2010–11	369,769.13	96,595.68	26.12
2011–12	489,319.49	133,825.28	27.35

Source: Adapted from Director General of Foreign Trade, New Delhi, http://www.dgft.gov.in
Note: Between 2000–01 and 2005–06, the Director General of Foreign Trade did not publish a country-wise break down of petroleum imports.

Table 1.2
Persian Gulf Share in India's Total Exports (in US$ Million)

Year	Total exports	Exports to Persian Gulf	Share in per cent
1996–97	33,469.95	2,720.03	8.13
1997–98	34,784.98	2,952.81	8.49
1998–99	33,218.72	3,280.56	9.88
1999–2000	36,822.49	3,539.78	9.61
2000–01	44,560.29	4,376.42	9.82
2001–02	43,826.72	4,405.61	10.05
2002–03	52,719.43	5,946.79	11.28
2003–04	63,842.55	8,277.87	12.97
2004–05	83,535.94	11,423.92	13.68
2005–06	103,090.53	13,398.41	13.00
2006–07	126,414.05	19,209.10	15.20
2007–08	163,132.18	25,997.08	15.94
2008–09	185,295.36	35,104.98	18.95
2009–10	178,751.43	33,537.55	18.76
2010–11	251,136.19	50,076.90	19.94
2011–12	305,963.92	48,882.30	15.98

Source: Adapted from Director General of Foreign Trade, New Delhi, http://www.dgft.gov.in

marginally overtaking the Chinese mainland. Though it had dropped to second place in 2011–12, the UAE remains the most favourite destination for Indian exports accounting for over US$35 billion.

The tension in their ties with the US following the September 11 attacks fuelled speculations that countries like Saudi Arabia are adopting a Look East policy and looking to Asia for long-term economic partnership. Political engagements between the Gulf countries and China and India were seen and interpreted through this paradigm. There are signs that India is looking towards the oil-rich Arab countries for its infrastructure development plans. According to estimates by the Paris-based International Energy Agency (IEA) between 2006 and 2030, India would require US$1.25 trillion in energy-related infrastructure

Figure 1.1
Persian Gulf's Share in India's Total Imports

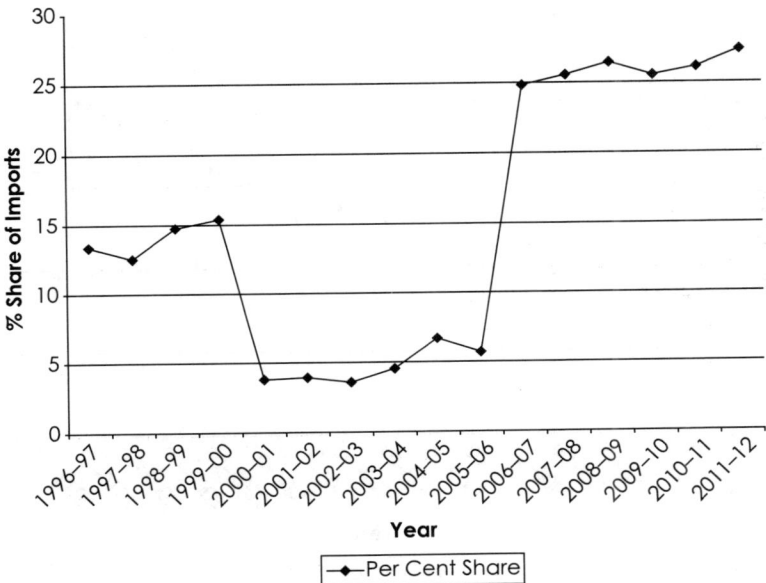

Source: Adapted from Director General of Foreign Trade, New Delhi, http://www.dgft.gov.in
Note: Between 2000–01 and 2005–06, the Director General of Foreign Trade did not publish a country-wise breakdown of petroleum imports.

development.[16] During his visit to Saudi Arabia in April 2008, the then Foreign Minister Pranab Mukherjee reminded King Abdullah of India's infrastructure plan which 'requires huge investments' and could attract 'US$500–600 billion'.[17]

Energy Security

The economic growth witnessed since the early 1990s was accompanied by a galloping demand for energy, especially hydrocarbon, resources. As economic liberalization accelerated demands for oil and gas, domestic supplies remained static, thereby forcing India to rely heavily on imports, especially from the countries along the Persian Gulf. The prognosis

Figure 1.2
Persian Gulf's Share in India's Total Exports

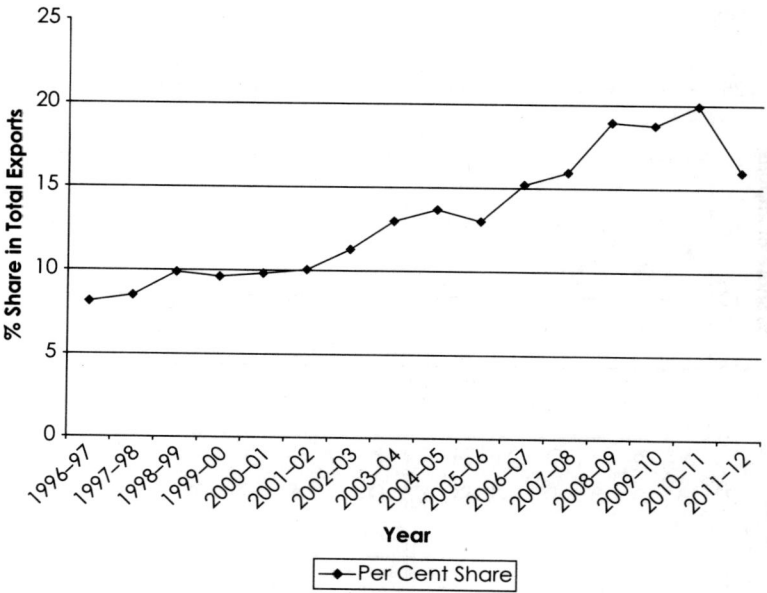

Source: Adapted from Director General of Foreign Trade, New Delhi, http://www.dgft.gov.in

Table 1.3
Place of Middle Eastern Countries among the Top 25 Trading Partners of India during 2011–12

Country	Ranking	Imports from	Exports to	Total trade	Per cent of total trade
UAE	Two	35,790.39	35,925.52	71,715.91	9.02
Saudi Arabia	Four	31,060.10	5,683.29	36,743.40	4.62
Iraq	Ten	18,939.63	763.97	19,703.60	2.48
Kuwait	Thirteen	16,375.37	1,181.41	17,556.78	2.21
Iran	Nineteen	13,556.71	2,411.33	15,968.03	2.01
Qatar	Twenty-one	12,923.82	807.95	13,731.77	1.73

Source: Adapted from Director General of Foreign Trade, New Delhi, http://www.dgft.gov.in

Figure 1.3
Exports, Imports and Ranking of Persian Gulf Countries in India's Total Trade (2011–12)

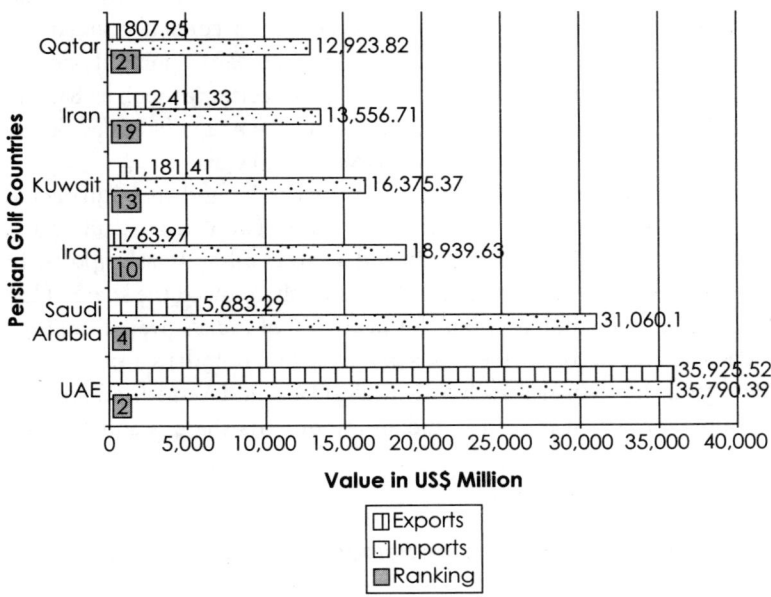

Source: Adapted from Director General of Foreign Trade, New Delhi, http://www.dgft.gov.in

on hydrocarbon self-sufficiency is rather bleak. Various national and international estimates suggest that India's import dependency would only increase in the coming years.

According to *India Hydrocarbon Vision 2025*, a document published by India's Planning Commission, 'The gap between supply and availability of crude oil, petroleum products as well as gas from indigenous sources is likely to increase over the years.'[18] Likewise, the IEA estimates that 90 per cent of India's crude oil need would have to be met through imports by 2030.[19] It also estimates that by 2024 India would overtake Japan as world's third largest oil importer after the US and China.[20]

The growing dependency upon energy imports enhanced the importance of oil-rich Gulf countries for India. As rentier states that rely heavily on the revenue from energy resources, these countries need stable and assured markets to continue their welfare state model. Their cradle-to-grave subsidy model would require guaranteed markets without which the political stability of these states would be in serious doubt. As the ongoing popular upheavals in many Arab countries remind, the ability of these countries, especially the energy-rich countries, to contain popular demands for political reforms depends equally upon partial political opening and continued economic largess. In this regard, countries such as Bahrain and Oman are less endowed than others and have had to be bailed out by their oil-rich neighbours such as Saudi Arabia and Qatar.

The energy-dominated relations between India and the Gulf region are highlighted by Table 1.4 and Figure 1.4. The Persian Gulf region accounts for a substantial share in India's total oil and gas imports. In recent years, diversification efforts have slightly reduced the share of the Gulf region, but still it accounts for nearly 60 of India's overall imports. Indeed, energy accounts for a substantial portion of India's imports from the region. In countries such as Kuwait, Qatar and Yemen, oil and gas accounts for almost the entire Indian imports. Its share is equally high

Table 1.4

India's Energy Imports from the Persian Gulf Region (in US$ Million)

Country	2007–08	2008–09	2009–10	2010–11	2011–12
Bahrain	599.46	1,215.37	248.34	219.19	591.76
Iran	10,048,97	11,248.63	10,362.04	9,377.88	11,528.97
Iraq	6,834.57	7,660.78	6,981.32	8,954.66	18,848.26
Kuwait	7,289.51	9,193.78	7,909.80	9,729.09	15,667.11
Oman	688.68	624.70	2,904.41	3,293.14	2,081.05
Qatar	1,897.18	2,890.14	4,101.68	6,060.95	11,702.89
Saudi Arabia	17,755.00	18,386.52	15,390.04	17,932.31	27,940.11
UAE	7,806.25	10,317.90	6,443.36	9,398.23	14,599.83
Yemen	1,445.39	745.07	1,563.15	1,722.95	955.26
Total Gulf	54,365.01	62,282.89	55,904.14	66,688.4	103,915.24
Total imports	86,384.04	103,933.77	96,321.16	115,929.06	172,753.97
Percentage	62.93	59.93	58.04	57.53	60.15

Source: Adapted from Director General of Foreign Trade, New Delhi, http://www.dgft.gov.in

Figure 1.4
India's Energy Imports from the Persian Gulf Region

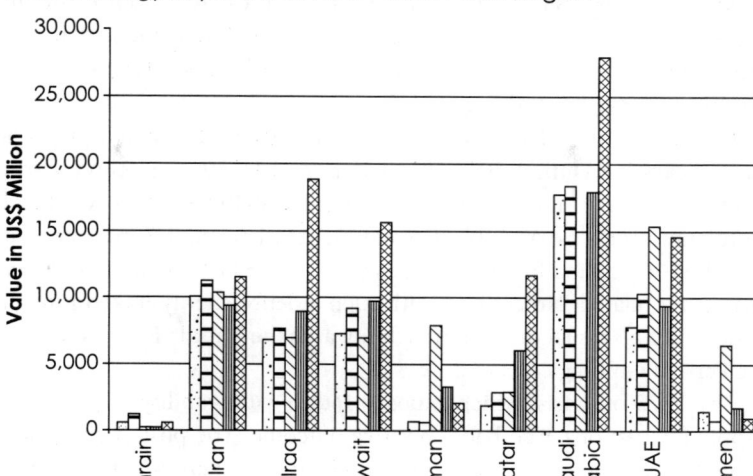

Source: Adapted from Director General of Foreign Trade, New Delhi, http://www.dgft.gov.in

in other countries and only the UAE has a more diversified trade with India, where energy constitutes less than 50 per cent of India's imports.

The rapid growth in India's energy imports is not exclusively driven by increasing domestic consumption as a significant portion is processed into petroleum products and exported. According to IEA, India 'is geographically well placed, close to both Middle Eastern crude oil suppliers and to rapidly expanding refined products markets in Asia and the Middle East'.[21] The privatization of the oil sector and resultant mega projects have contributed to the rapid increase of crude oil imports. The Reliance-run Jamnagar refinery, which became operational in July 1999, is today the largest in the world with an installed capacity of 1.24 mbd.[22] Since 2000–01, oil products have emerged as an important component of India's exports and were among the top five export commodities, and their share has been increasing since then. In 2000–01, India exported US$1.9 billion worth of oil products and this accounted for about 4.3 per cent of its total exports. During 2011–12, it exported over US$29 billion worth of oil products, which made up about 16 per cent of its overall exports. Until India buckled under American pressure in 2009, Iran was a principal market for petroleum products (Table 1.5 and Figure 1.5).

In other words, oil accounts for a major portion of India's imports as well as exports. During 2011–12, it imported US$96.32 billion worth of oil; during the same period, it exported US$29.04 billion worth of petroleum products. As Table 1.6 and Figures 1.6 and 1.7 indicate, out of its US$467 billion foreign trade, as much as US$125 billion, or 26 per cent, is oil related. No country with such a dense energy-linked foreign trade could be casual in its approach towards the Middle East, especially the Persian Gulf region.

The 1973 oil crisis, which exposed India's vulnerability to price and supply fluctuations, also had a positive outcome. The post-crisis period unleashed a massive construction boom in the energy-rich countries along the Gulf and paved the way for large-scale labour migration from India to the Arab countries along the Persian Gulf. This was different from the earlier waves of Indian migration to different parts of the world, especially during the colonial era. This wave is voluntary and is driven by economic incentives and opportunities in the Gulf. While there are a significant number of professionals and managerial class workers, a vast majority of the Indian migrants in the Gulf belong to unskilled and

Table 1.5
Share of Oil-related Exports to Iran (in US$ Million)

Year	Oil exports to Iran	Total oil exports	Iran's share in total oil exports	Exports to Iran	Per cent of oil in exports to Iran
2007–08	845.12	29,085.48	2.91	1,943.92	43.48
2008–09	1,056.17	28,437.14	3.71	2,534.01	41.68
2009–10	180.80	29,036.29	0.62	1,853.17	9.76
2010–11	30.28	42,610.74	0.07	2,492.90	1.25
2011–12	49.77	57,391.93	0.09	2,411.33	2.06

Source: Adapted from Director General of Foreign Trade, New Delhi, http://www.dgft.gov.in

Figure 1.5
Share of India's Oil-related Exports to Iran (in US$ Million)

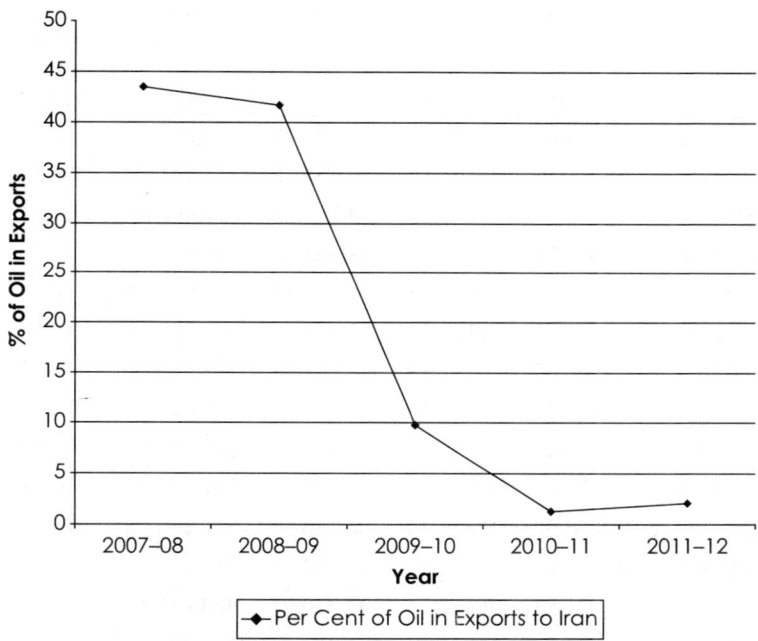

Source: Adapted from Director General of Foreign Trade, New Delhi, http://www.dgft.gov.in

semi-skilled categories. Although official figures of Indian workers are not accurate, 2013 estimates put them at 6.5 million.[23]

These unskilled, semi-skilled, professional and managerial workers provide significant financial gains to India. The labour migration partly mitigates the unemployment situation in India and the migrants repatriate large amounts of foreign exchange earnings to their families. Once again there are no accurate estimates of Gulf remittances but one can infer the trend. In 2001–02, overseas workers remitted US$15.8 billion to India, and during 2010–11 that figure rose to US$55.9 billion.[24] As the government admits, '[A] significant proportion of remittances are contributed by the increasing number of unskilled and semi-skilled Indian workers employed in the Gulf countries.'[25] In certain countries, the Indian migrants also constitute the largest expatriate community. With a population of 1.6

Table 1.6
India's Total Oil Trade (in US$ Million)

Year	Oil imports	Oil exports	Total oil trade	Total trade	Oil as percentage of total trade
1996–97	11,464.60	516.43	11,981.03	72,602.35	6.06
1997–98	10,067.75	394.52	10,462.27	76,141.43	13.74
1998–99	8,043.19	141.08	8,184.27	75,448.63	10.85
1999–2000	14,350.19	90.87	14,441.06	86,499.29	16.70
2000–01	17,545.14	1,930.99	19,476.13	95,016.43	20.50
2001–02	15,771.75	2,182.94	17,954.69	95,167.08	18.87
2002–03	19,680.60	2,707.24	22,387.84	114,040.40	19.63
2003–04	22,700.20	3,734.32	26,434.52	141,882.53	18.63
2004–05	34,818.66	7,140.39	41,959.05	190,646.40	22.00
2005–06	50,310.06	11,866.60	62,176.66	232,739.35	26.71
2006–07	61,778.90	18,859.48	80,638.38	312,140.55	25.83
2007–08	86,384.07	29,085.48	115,469.55	414,751.34	27.84
2008–09	103,933.81	28,437.14	132,370.95	488,981.25	27.07
2009–10	96,321.16	29,036.29	125,357.45	467,098.71	26.84
2010–11	115,929.06	42,610.74	158,539.80	620,905.32	25.53
2011–12	172,753.97	57,391.93	230,145.90	795,283.41	28.94

Source: Adapted from Director General of Foreign Trade, New Delhi, http://www.dgft.gov.in

million, the Indian expatriate community is the largest in Saudi Arabia.[26] It also forms a significant portion of the total resident population of Bahrain.

Challenges

The Middle East has its share of problems; perhaps more than other regions of the world. Nonetheless, the region also offers a number of challenges and opportunities for the outside world, including India. While the oil wealth of some of these countries is critical for the global

Figure 1.6
Share of Oil in India's Total Trade

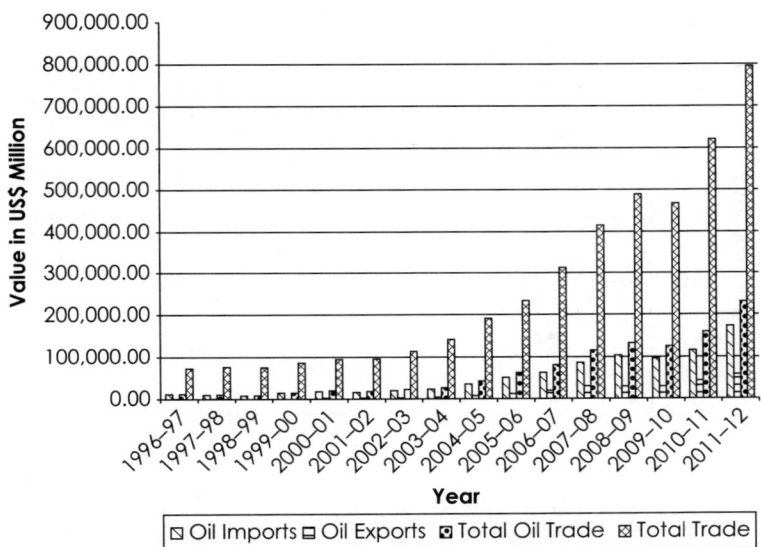

Source: Adapted from Director General of Foreign Trade, New Delhi, http://www.dgft.gov.in

economy, the popular protests in many Arab countries highlight the difficulties of co-opting public discontent through wealth. The welfare model adopted by various rentier economies of the region has proved to be insufficient in meeting rising popular expectations. Regimes could no longer secure the loyalty of their citizens only through generous state subsidy or tax-free economic structure. While some countries do not have the resources for such a welfare arrangement with its citizenry, those who have are finding it difficult to manage the rising political expectations of the youth. While the final road map is still elusive, the Arab Spring appears to have irreversibly changed the political landscape of the Middle East.

Some of the world's major political battles are to be fought in the Middle East. This was true during the Cold War; it has held true since. The withdrawal of American combat soldiers from Afghanistan by 2014 would have far-reaching consequences for not only the region, but also for American influence in the Middle East and beyond. Political issues

Figure 1.7
Share of Oil in India's Total Trade (in Per Cent)

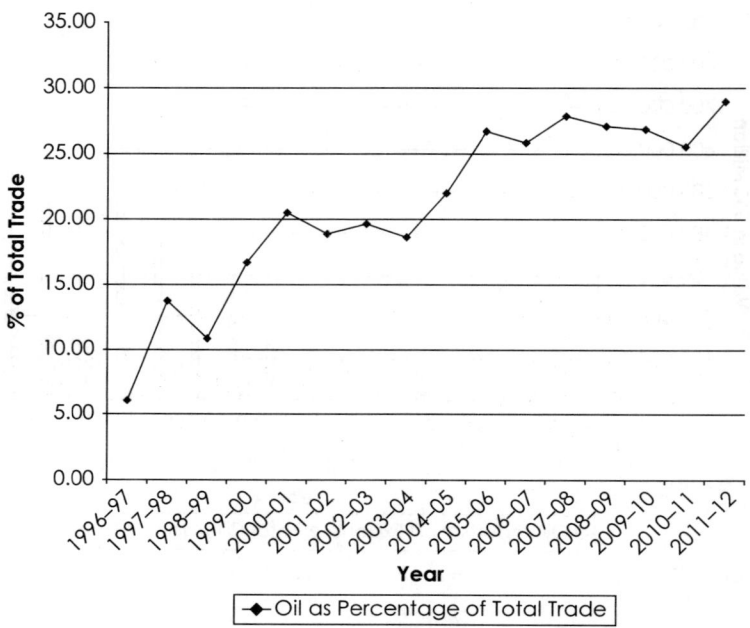

Source: Adapted from Director General of Foreign Trade, New Delhi, http://www.dgft.gov.in

in the Middle East have strong emotional and theological underpinnings among the followers of the three monotheistic religions. Debates of war or peace invariably bring in religious sentiments and inclinations. No country can thus ignore the Middle East, even if it wishes to.

While it seeks closer ties with all the countries of the Middle East, India would have to consider inter-state rivalries of the region. Its desire to pursue closer political and economic ties with Iran has come into conflict with the Indo–US relations. This has manifested in American pressures over India's positions regarding Iran's nuclear ambitions as well as procurement of Iranian oil. Its bonhomie with Israel since the normalization of relations in January 1992 did not go down well with Egypt as improvements in Indo-Israeli ties were accompanied by cold winds from Cairo.[27] The Arab Spring has partially revived the historic Arab–Turkish rivalry while the nuclear controversy has ignited traditional Arab fears over Iranian hegemony. India would not be able to ignore these internal cleavages, tensions and fears while seeking closer ties with the Middle Eastern countries. Its energy security calculations vis-à-vis the region would have to consider growing Chinese presence and competition in the oil-rich Persian Gulf region. It is not accidental that Iran has been using the China angle to force India's hands on the never-ending negotiations over the Iran–Pakistan–India gas pipeline.[28] Likewise, its closer military ties with the Jewish State would have a bearing on India's political ties with such diverse actors as the Palestinians, Egypt, Iran and, of late, Turkey.

Besides these political considerations and geographic proximity, the Middle East is important for a host of reasons and one could classify them as political and economic issues and challenges; there are also some country-specific issues that India would find difficult to ignore.

Political Issues

First, India's great power aspirations would be tested not in the immediate neighbourhood of South Asia but in the ever complex and more challenging Middle East. In the coming years, much of the great power rivalry involving the US, Russia, China and Japan would play out in this region, especially over its energy resources. The region would figure prominently in India's persisting disagreements with the administration of US President Barack Obama over issues such as non-proliferation and energy security. The Sino-Indian political co-operation would be tested by how both countries manage their competition for the Gulf energy. Likewise, the maturity of India's foreign policy establishment would be measured by how it handles the India–Iran–Israel[29] and India–Iran–US triangles.

Two, lack of substantial political contacts and interactions between India and the Gulf region is a cause for concern. With the sole exception of Prime Minister Manmohan Singh's visit to Tehran to attend the 16th Summit meeting of the Non-Aligned Movement, there was no state visit from India to the Persian Gulf region in 2012. Indeed, there was no presidential visit to the region since Pratibha Patil's visit to the UAE in November 2010 and the last visit by the Vice President to the

Gulf took place in April 2009 when Hamid Ansari visited Kuwait. Like-wise, Manmohan Singh's visit to Saudi Arabia took place in February 2010. In short, there were no high-level political visits to the Gulf region since the outbreak of the Arab Spring. This trend was scrupulously maintained during 2012.

The continuing neglect of this region raises question about India's readiness to recognize the importance of the Gulf region and its willingness to politically engage with its leaders. The ongoing Arab Spring and the political turmoil partly account for this indifference, but there has been a traditional Indian reluctance for high-level political contacts with the Gulf. This indifference towards the Gulf region has become the norm ever since the Congress-led UPA government came to power in 2004. Despite the lack of initiatives from New Delhi, Gulf leaders were more active during 2012. As discussed elsewhere, the Emir of Qatar and Crown Prince of Bahrain visited India during the same period. India also saw a separate visit of Princess Mozah bint Nasser al-Missned, wife of the Qatari Emir, in October 2012.

Three, the neglect of the Gulf was clearly manifested in the political mishap over the visit of Omani Sultan. The prestigious Jawaharlal Nehru Award for International Peace for 2004 was to be given to Sultan Qaboos. The highest honour that can be given to a foreign leader was meant to recognize and appreciate the role played by Sultan Qaboos in promoting the bilateral relations between the two countries. In some ways, India hoped that Oman would play a positive role to further its interest in the Gulf region, similar to the role played by Singapore since the early 1990s in promoting India's interest in South-east Asia and ASEAN. The visit of the Sultan to India to personally receive the honour was delayed partly to create an occasion and partly to increase the profile of the event. Thus, India was hoping to invite the Sultan as the chief guest of the Republic Day celebrations in January 2013. Once again, this is the highest Indian honour to a foreign head of state. In recent years, Algerian President Bouteflika, Iranian President Khatami and Saudi King Abdullah have been given such honours. At one time, it was suggested that Egyptian President Hosni Mubarak demanded such an honour to visit India to accept the Jawaharlal Nehru Award bestowed upon in 1995.[30] India's decision to bestow the double honour, Nehru award and Chief Guest for the Republic Day, upon Sultan Qaboos, however, floundered and in late December, it was announced that King of Bhutan and not Qaboos would be the chief guest.[31] New Delhi offered no formal explanation for this diplomatic embarrassment.

Four, despite its diminishing influence, especially in the Persian Gulf region, the US would continue to play a dominant role. In some cases this role is harmful to India, while in others it is helpful. Following its 2003 invasion, the US tried to induce India into bestowing legitimacy to its occupation by joining the reconstruction of post-Saddam Iraq.[32] The controversial nature of the American invasion and the sectarian violence that followed largely dampened the initial Indian enthusiasm.

A far more intense pressure is now being waged over Iran. India's relations with Iran have become hostage to the US and its policies. India's ability to pursue a host of energy-related relations with Iran and thus to consolidate political ties with Tehran have been hampered by the US.[33] Indian oil companies could not invest in energy explorations because of the American sanctions under the Iran Sanctions Act (ISA). Its long-term LNG deal could not materialize because the US is not ready to part with the technology. The Iran–Pakistan–India gas pipeline could not take off because of continued American opposition and resistance. Since 2010, even commercial energy transactions have become a problem because of the American opposition to payment mechanism. In December 2010, the Reserve Bank of India had to cancel the Tehran-based Asian Clearing Union arrangement under pressures from the US, and its subsequent efforts to secure alternative payment routes through banks in Germany[34] and Turkey[35] have also fallen through. In early 2012, both countries reached an agreement whereby India would settle a part of its energy dues to Iran through rupee payment. This arrangement, however, can only be temporary as the bilateral trade is heavily skewed in favour of Iran and the rupee payment would cover only 45 per cent of the total payment dues.

Regarding the Arab uprising and protests in the Gulf region, the US has been less interventionist, than, say, in Egypt or Libya. This has enabled India to seek closer ties with the existing regimes. Bahrain and Saudi Arabia, for example, sent senior emissaries to New Delhi shortly after the Gulf Cooperation Council (GCC) forces entered Bahrain in defence of the beleaguered rulers. India had also welcomed the change of ruler in Yemen and was quick to extend an official invitation to

President Abd Rabbuh Mansur al-Hadi shortly after he assumed office in February 2012.

Five, since the end of the Cold War, the role of Pakistan in India's Middle East policy has considerably diminished. Greater self-confidence and growing economic clout has enabled India to pursue closer ties with the countries of the Middle East without worrying about Pakistan. Indeed, even on Israel it is not unduly worried about Pakistan. Speaking to reporters in Israel in January 2012, Indian Foreign Minister S. M. Krishna admitted that Israel–Pakistan relations were a bilateral matter and India was not unduly concerned.[36] This delinking is more clearly manifested in the manner in which India has sought to further its ties with Saudi Arabia, a country believed to be closer to Pakistan because of the Islamic factor.

Emergence of economic co-operation as the principal platform for closer ties with the Gulf has meant that India's political differences and competition with Pakistan have lost their erstwhile pre-eminence. Focus on Pakistan only limits India's ability to forge closer ties with the Islamic countries of the region and would result in these countries trying to seek a balance between the two South Asian neighbours. Indeed, the re-emergence of Pakistan factor following the 26 November terror attacks in Mumbai did not last long and by freeing itself from the Pakistani baggage, India has managed to seek, and in the process secure, more stable bilateral relations with the Islamic and non-Islamic countries of the Middle East.

Six, in recent years, China has replaced Pakistan as India's major foreign policy preoccupation. The emergence of China as the world's second largest economy and its growing political influence across the globe weighs heavily on India's strategic calculations. This is more acutely felt in the energy sector; Chinese search of energy security often puts that country at severe competition with India. Although there is occasional co-operation in countries such as Sudan[37] and Syria,[38] on the energy front both are competing intensively, which at times has resulted in price escalations. India's ability to seek investment opportunities in Iraq, for example, would be severely limited by the Chinese presence in that country and its successes in outbidding India's efforts.[39] The story is similar in Iran; while India's energy deals with the Islamic Republic have become problematic, China has made political gains from similar deals with Tehran.[40]

This is largely because of the greater political profile and influence enjoyed by China. Moving away from its traditional indifference, China has shrewdly capitalized on its international stature and permanent membership in the United Nations Security Council (UNSC). These came into the open when it forced the US to accommodate its concerns and interests over issues such as Iranian nuclear controversy and popular unrests in Libya and Syria.[41] By conditioning its support to issues such as peaceful resolution of dispute and non-interference, China not only increased its international profile but also sought to befriend countries of the Middle East. The political use of its economic resources would mean that new regimes in Libya and Syria would not be able to ignore the role of China and its importance in national reconstruction efforts.

Last, India would not be able to ignore the intensifying sectarian divide in the region. The Shia–Sunni divide is as old as Islam that surfaced shortly after the death of Prophet Mohammed. In recent decades this divide has assumed greater political colour. The willingness of countries like Iran and Saudi Arabia to project themselves as the leader of the Shia and Sunni Muslims, respectively, has accentuated the traditional theological cleavages. Political tensions and violence in countries such as Bahrain, Iraq and Lebanon are often played out along sectarian lines. Minority Shia groups in countries like Saudi Arabia are often accused of being sympathetic to Iran. The fall of Saddam Hussein had also caused Iraq to emerge as the first Shia Arab country in the political sense of the term and there are apprehensions in the Gulf that possible overthrow of King Hamad al-Khalifa's regime could lead Bahrain into a similar situation. Indian officials claim that the country has the third largest Shia population after Iran and hence it would not be able remain indifferent to ongoing sectarian violence in some of the Middle Eastern countries.

Economic Interests

First and foremost, the Middle East has emerged as the most important trading partner of India. During 2011–12, it accounted for nearly 25.58 per cent of India's total trade; exports to this region stood at US$56.8 billion, while imports stood at US$105.8 billion. Although the economic recession has slightly dented the volume of trade from the previous year, which stood at US$120.75 billion, the Middle East is still India's largest trading partner, larger than the EU.

Two, the picture is much starker on the energy front where the region meets the bulk of India's energy imports. Out of the US$172.7 billion worth of hydrocarbon imports in 2010–11, as much as US$105.6 billion came from the energy-rich countries such as Saudi Arabia, Iraq, Kuwait, the UAE, Qatar and Iran. Incidentally during 2010–11, Iran occupied fourth position. In recent years, the Persian Gulf region alone has accounted for close to 60 per cent of India's total hydrocarbon imports. India's bilateral ties with most of the countries along the Persian Gulf such as Iraq, Kuwait, Saudi Arabia and Yemen have been dominated by energy imports. Various Indian and international estimates suggests that India's dependence on hydrocarbon imports would reach close to 90 per cent by 2025. This is bound to increase India's reliance upon the Middle East in the coming years.

Three, partly because of the growing volume of oil trade, the six countries along the Persian Gulf are among the top 25 trading partners of India. In 2012, the UAE has emerged as the largest destination for India's exports and bilateral trade stood at US$71.71 billion, including US$35.92 billion worth of Indian exports. Indeed during 2010–11, the UAE was India's largest trading partner, a status acquired by China during 2011–12.

Four, Islam plays an important role in India's ties with the Middle East. Even though most of the global Muslim population lives outside the region, it has become coterminous with the expression 'the Islamic world'. India now has the second largest Muslim community after Indonesia. One of the largest numbers of hajj pilgrims come from India. Progress or upheaval in the Middle East naturally reverberates worldwide. If al-Qaida promoted negative stereotypes about Islam, the interfaith dialogues initiated by countries in the region, especially Qatar and Saudi Arabia, highlight the growing awareness in the Middle East for a better and nuanced understanding of other faiths. The willingness of some Islamic countries to allow open worship of non-Islamic religions is reflection of tolerance induced by globalization. Despite the September 11 attacks on the US and growing Shia–Sunni cleavages, the mainstream in the Middle East is still moderate and needs to be befriended, encouraged and cultivated.

Five, during 2012, some of India's strategic economic decisions have caused concern among the Gulf investors, especially from the UAE. The cancellation of the 2G spectrum allocation by the Supreme Court in February has resulted in the withdrawal of the Emirati firm Etisalat from the Indian market. Among the biggest losers following the court verdict, the company wrote off US$827 million investment in India[42] and decided against taking part in the revised bidding held in November 2012. Likewise, the interest of Etihaad to invest in private Indian airliners such as Jet Airways was also dampened by similar concerns over investment security. These concerns figured prominently when Commerce Minister Anand Sharma visited Abu Dhabi in March 2013 to entice the UAE to invest in the US$90 billion Delhi–Mumbai Industrial Corridor project.[43] The Indian government, therefore, needs to fine-tune its policies and provide political support to the Gulf countries if it were to attract investments for its infrastructure projects. While sovereign guarantees may not be feasible, especially in the light of judicial interventions, India would have to find ways to minimize the fears and apprehensions of the potential investors from the region.

Six, India's bilateral trade relations with the countries of the Middle East, especially those from the Persian Gulf, are skewed in the latter's favour. This is more visible in the case of Iran and Saudi Arabia, where India's exports form a fraction of the imports from these countries. New Delhi would not be able to sustain such a huge imbalance, especially when its oil bill is increasing rapidly, due to rising demand for crude and increasing oil prices. This trade imbalance became a political problem when India sought to settle its oil dues with Iran in currencies other than Euros and dollars due to Western sanctions. Currently, its exports to Iran are about 10 per cent of its total imports. India needs to find ways of bridging its mounting trade imbalance with the region. A more balanced trade with Iran could have enabled India to opt for barter trade or to adjust its oil bill with construction projects in Iran, as China does.

Seven, Indian expatriate population in the Gulf has played an important role. While there are no clear numbers, current estimates suggest the presence of at least 6.5 million Indian expatriates in the Gulf region.[44] They are engaged in productive employment in the oil-rich Arab countries and contribute immensely to the social and economic development of the oil economies. In the process, they also earn their livelihood and contribute a substantial amount to their families back in India. The continued presence of Indian workers is critical for Bahrain. Their contribution to the economy has been acknowledged by Bahraini leadership through their participation in the national dialogue initiated by al-Khalifa. Any large-scale exodus of Indians would undermine the Bahraini stability and result in its economic undermining. The expatriate community also becomes a challenge following the Arab Spring when India repatriated 750 persons from Egypt, 17,927 from Libya and 846 from Yemen during 2011.[45] The presence of Indian community was a deterrent against India making any statements in response to events in Bahrain since 14 February 2011. Their safety, security and continued employment are vital for India and hence, it refrained from making any public comments about Bahrain other than expressing its concern for the safety of Indians.[46]

At the same time, the expatriate population also has a flip side. There are no accurate figures regarding the size of the Indian expatriate community in the Gulf country and actual figures are available only for the ECR-linked émigrés, that is, émigrés who require special clearance for going abroad. Persons who do not have higher secondary education were issued passports that clearly stated that they should require ECR (Table 1.7 and Figures 1.8 and 1.9). At one time 153 countries were listed under this category which was reduced to 18 in December 2006 and to 17 in August 2008.[47] Emigration of certain category of workers to all the six GCC countries and Iraq and Yemen require special clearance. Thus, all figures about the size of Indian expatriate labourers in the Gulf region are only educated guesses or estimates. If the frequent cases of 'illegal workers' are an indication, most go to the region on a tourist or visitor's visa and decide to stay on to work illegally.[48]

A large portion of Indian emigrant workers are unskilled labourers. If one were to accept 6.5 million as the size of the Indian expatriates in the Gulf region, the ECR category accounts for about 10 per cent. Until recently, Kerala accounted for a large portion of this category but as has been argued by various scholars, the profile is changing in favour of states such as Uttar Pradesh, Tamil Nadu and others. This shift is attributed to higher educational qualification obtained by the Kerala émigrés and their skilled and professional nature. The space vacated by Keralite émigrés are now filled by unskilled workforce from other states. Emigration from Kerala was studied by Thiruvananthapuram-based Centre for

Table 1.7
ECR Issued

Country	2009	2010	2011
Bahrain	17,541	15,101	14,323
Iraq	—	390	1,177
Kuwait	42,091	37,667	45,149
Oman	74,963	105,807	73,819
Qatar	46,292	45,752	41,710
Saudi Arabia	281,110	275,172	289,297
UAE	130,302	130,910	138,861
Yemen	421	208	29
Total Gulf	592,720	611,007	604,365
Total Gulf as per cent	97.13	95.27	96.46
Total ECR	**610,272**	**641,356**	**626,565**

Source: Ministry of Overseas Indian Affairs, *Annual Report 2011–12*, 58.

Figure 1.8
Number of ECR Issued

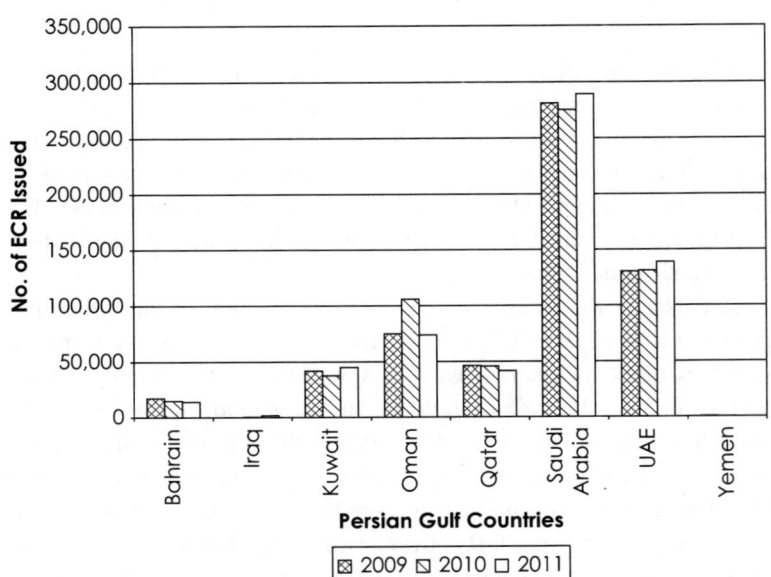

Source: Ministry of Overseas Indian Affairs, *Annual Report 2011–12*, 58.

Figure 1.9
Per Cent of ECR Issued to Persian Gulf Countries in 2011

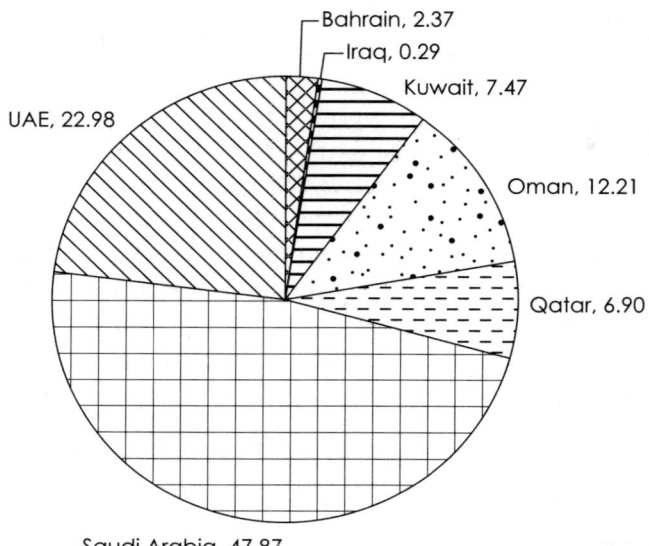

Saudi Arabia, 47.87

Source: Ministry of Overseas Indian Affairs, *Annual Report 2011–12*, 58.

Development Studies (CDS) and others. Similar studies by new entrant states such as Tamil Nadu and Uttar Pradesh do not exist and would take considerable effort to establish. Over the years, emigration has become coterminous with Kerala émigrés who at one point accounted for more than half the number of Indian expatriates in the Gulf region. The ECR-linked emigration from other states would require greater dedication and sustained efforts.

The state of Kerala makes up significant segment of the Indian migrant workers in the Gulf. Though the number of migrants from the state seeking ECR clearance has been slowly falling, the state still makes up for much of the Indian workforce in the region. According to one estimate for 2009, out of the 5,050,000 Indians in the Gulf, as much as 2,191,412 came from Kerala; in other words, over 43 per cent of the Indian migrant workers in the Gulf were Keralites.[49] The acuteness of the migrant-dependency becomes obvious, especially during crisis times. As a study warns, because Kerala 'relied heavily on migration to the Gulf and remittances from the migrant workers, any return of migrants in large numbers will create serious economic consequences'.[50] This becomes more acute if one looks at the larger problem of most of the migrant workers being temporary contract workers.

Their heavy dependence upon the migrant labourers has skewed the demography of the Gulf countries. According to a UN report published in 2009, as of 2005, the migrants make up 71.4 per cent of the population of UAE, 62.1 per cent in Kuwait, 25.9 per cent in Saudi Arabia and 25.9 per cent in Oman.[51] The share of the migrants in the labour market is ever higher. As of 2008, the migrant workers make up 94 per cent of the labour force in Qatar, 92 per cent in UAE, 84 per cent in Kuwait, 74 per cent in Bahrain, 68 per cent in Oman and 51 per cent in Saudi Arabia. Correspondingly, only six per cent of the labour force in Qatar is made up of the citizens and the figure is eight per cent in the UAE.[52] In 2005, for example, Indians accounted for about 42.5 per cent of the total labour force in the UAE.[53]

Country-specific Concerns

Following the trend of recent years, during 2012 Iran continued to remain the most serious challenge facing India not just in the Persian Gulf region but also with regard to its overall foreign policy. It has to manage its energy-driven political relations within the context of the nuclear controversy and the resultant Iranian isolations. Growing concerns over the Iranian nuclear ambitions have given rise to regional tensions not only between Iran and Israel[54] but also between the Islamic republic and its Arab neighbours.[55] India's desire to pursue energy security through Iran has come into conflict with its desire to move closer to the US. The three-decade-long tension between Tehran and Washington considerably limits India's ability to maintain closer ties with both these countries.

There is a perceptible shift in the attitude of some of the Gulf countries regarding India's fight against terrorism. In the past some of these countries have been indifferent and unconcerned about its request to extradite some of the key figures accused of various terror offenses in India. In a significant move in June 2012 Saudi Arabia deported Zabiuddin Ansari to India to face charges related to 2008 Mumbai terror attacks.

This was followed by the deportation of A. Rayees and Fasih Mohammad, wanted in connection with other terror-related charges.

Iraq offers both serious opportunities and challenges to India. The ill-conceived US-led invasion opened the past sectarian divisions and plunged that country into a civil war. The ushering in of democracy, installation of popularly elected government and the withdrawal of American combat troops have not resulted in political stability or abetment of violence. At the same time, the reconstruction of the country, building of political institutions and revival of its oil industry offer enormous opportunity for India to share its expertise and meet its needs. The continuation of violence, however, could impede India from capitalizing on the opportunities in Iraq. At the same during 2012, Iraq has emerged as the second largest supplier of crude oil from the Gulf region after Saudi Arabia, and the bilateral trade more than doubled than the previous year. From US$9.68 billion during 2010–11 it rose to US$19.7 billion in 2011–12, largely contributed by a surge in energy imports from that country.

Saudi Arabia has been undergoing a major transformation ever since King Abdullah assumed full powers in 2005. Opposition from within the al-Saud family and the conservative clergy have severely restricted Abdullah's pace of reforms. The kingdom, however, faces the much larger problem of succession. All the principal figures in the al-Saud are septuagenarians and sooner or later the al-Saud will have to skip a generation and look for a king among the grandsons or great grandsons of the founder Abdul-Aziz. This move could face resistance, especially from those who would be left out of the process. Besides confronting domestic unrests especially from women and Shia minority, Saudi Arabia also faces external tensions vis-à-vis Iran. Its 2011 proposal to expand the GCC with the inclusion of Jordan and Morocco has not made any headway as there was little enthusiasm among other members to make the GCC into a monarchical club. Thus, the stability of the world's largest oil producer and the custodian of the two sites holy to Islam would be of critical importance not only for the region but also for India. The succession issue would also haunt Oman after the demise of the current heirless ruler, Sultan Qaboos. Historically, Oman has been India's closest country in the Gulf and both have shared political, economic and cultural ties. In recent years, however, there has been a slack in bilateral relations, which it would be in India's interest to consolidate.

Looking Forward

Despite its vast importance, the Middle East has not received adequate importance in India's foreign policy agenda. The region continues to be ignored in favour of the immediate South Asian neighbourhood and its myriad problems.

Indeed, the strategic importance of the Middle East for India is inversely proportionate to the expertise within the country. This disjoint is manifested in the common and official nomenclature, *West Asia*. Its usage disregards the common expression used not only by the international community but also by the concerned countries of the region. Those harping on the imperial and colonial origins of the expression 'Middle East' too conveniently ignore that the expression 'India', meaning the land across River Indus, was given by the outsiders. Moreover, even in academic discourses the Persian Gulf, recognized by the UN, is discouraged and one is advised to refer to the body of waters between Iran and the Arabian Peninsula merely as the Gulf. Those unfamiliar with India might mistake the term for the Gulf of Mexico.

The political and strategic importance of this region is not reflected in the priority accorded to the Middle East by various think tanks. The same holds true for various educational institutions; the exceptions being the three Central Universities—Jawaharlal Nehru University, Jamia Millia Islamia and Aligarh Muslim University—and a few others. This disjoint is accompanied by the lack of interest and expertise on the region. One could easily identify a dozen or so scholars for whom the Middle East is a lifelong passion, while the rest have only a nodding acquaintance with the region and its complexities. The latter's body of knowledge is often confined to a few years when they served or looked after the ever dynamic Middle East. Thus, much of the debates on the Middle East are either uninformed or ill-informed. Its nature is also often cursory, emotional and opinionated.

Understanding the complexities of the region is essential not only for the pursuit of knowledge but also for the evolution of meaningful policy options. Time has come for a serious, nuanced and non-partisan understanding of the Middle East and its complexities. Erstwhile platitudes, historic bonhomie and civilizational rhetoric are important but insufficient to meet the present dynamics and future challenges. Through publications such as these, the Middle East Institute at New Delhi (MEI@ND) is taking small steps in this direction. While the India and the Persian Gulf Series was inaugurated as a Kindle version last year, *Persian Gulf 2013* is the first print version under the SAGE (India) imprint.

While the wider Middle East is important, the core Indian interests lie in the Persian Gulf region. Under this Series, therefore, the MEI@ND seeks to focus on India's bilateral relations with the Gulf region. Given the region's political, strategic, economic, energy, cultural and social importance, the MEI@ND has initiated this Series to closely follow, detail and assess bilateral relations annually. Each issue of India and the Persian Gulf would examine the bilateral developments in the previous year.

On terminologies, the MEI@ND prefers Persian Gulf to other nomenclature because of its historic nature. It admits that like Arabian Sea, Indian Ocean and South China Sea, the term Persian Gulf does not denote Iranian ownership of the said waters.

A note of caution is needed for trade figures put out by the Director General of Foreign Trade in India. The trade figures for a current year are often revised in the following year and hence there could be a slight discrepancy. For example, the trade figures for 2010–11 would be different in 2011 and in 2012.

This print version of the Series has become possible because of the active support of Vivek Mehra of SAGE, with whom the MEI is establishing a partnership.

Persian Gulf 2013 is the result of the team of young researchers who are associated with the MEI@ND. As the editor of this Series and as the Honorary Director of the MEI@ND, I register my sincere thanks and gratitude to them. Special thanks are reserved for Atul Mishra, Mushtaq Hussain and Md. Muddassir Quamar for their delicate skills in improving the earlier drafts. Figures and diagrams are the handiwork of Manjari Singh. During the critical moments, Dipanwita has been a great source of help and inspiration.

I am dedicating our second volume in the Series and the first print version to the True Friend of the MEI@ND, who shall remain anonymous, with great personal respect, admiration and gratitude. All omissions and commissions are mine. And mine alone.

P. R. Kumaraswamy
20 April 2013

Notes

1. Some have taken exception to the expression Arab Spring, some depicting it as an orientalist term. Other expressions used to describe the popular protests in the Arab world include Revolution, Awakening, Uprising, Social Revolution, Protests Movement, etc. Some of them carried the prefix 'Arab' and some did not.

2. Pew Research Center, 'The Global Religious Landscape', Pew Research Center, 18 December 2012, http://www.pewforum.org/global-religious-landscape-muslim.aspx

3. PEW Research Center, *Mapping the Global Muslim Population: A Report on the Size and Distribution of the World's Muslim Population* (Washington, DC: PEW Research Center, October 2009), http://www.pewforum.org/newas-sets/images/reports/Muslimpopulation/Muslimpopulation.pdf

4. Among others, see Leonard Stein, *The Balfour Declaration* (London: Simon and Schuster, 1961); and Saad Omar Khan, 'The "Caliphate Question": British Views and Policies toward Pan-Islamic Politics and the End of the Ottoman Caliphate', *The American Journal of Islamic Social Sciences* 24 (2007): 4, http://i-epistemology.net/attachments/922_ajiss24-4-stripped%20-%20 Khan%20-%20The%20Caliphate%20Question.pdf

5. For a recent and detailed study, see James Onley, *Britain and the Gulf Shaikhdoms, 1820–1971: The Politics of Protection, CIRS Occasional Paper No. 4* (Doha: Center for International and Regional Studies, Georgetown University School of Foreign Service in Qatar, 2009).

6. In this endeavour, India was supported by Iran and erstwhile Yugoslavia. For a discussion, see B. N. Mehrish, 'Recognition of the Palestine Liberation Organization (PLO): An Appraisal of India's Policy', *Indian Journal of Political Science* 36, no. 2 (April–June 1975): 137–60. Despite the title, the article largely discusses only the United Nations Special Committee on Palestine (UNSCOP) and offers no critical evaluation of the Indian plan. Nor does it explain the underlying reasons for its rejection not only by the Jews but also by the Arabs.

7. The other two were Cuba and Greece.

8. P. R. Kumaraswamy, 'India's Recognition of Israel, September 1950', *Middle Eastern Studies* (London), 31, no. 1 (January 1995): 124–38.

9. P. R. Kumaraswamy, 'India and Israel: Prelude to Normalization', *Journal of South Asian and Middle Eastern Studies* 19, no. 2 (Winter 1995): 53–73.

10. For detailed discussions on the Khilafat struggle, see A. C. Neimeijer. *The Khilafat Movement in India, 1919–1924* (The Hague: Martinus Nijhoff, 1972), and Gail Minault, *The Khilafat Movement: Religious Symbolism and Political Mobilization in India* (New Delhi: Oxford University Press, 1999).

11. For a discussion see, P. R. Kumaraswamy, *India's Israel Policy* (New York: Columbia University Press, 2010): 68–84.

12. This remark resulted in him being declared a persona non grata in June 1982.

13. Nirupam Bajpai, 'Economic Crisis, Structural Reforms, and the Prospects of Growth in India', Center for International Development, Harvard Kennedy School, 1996; http://www.cid.harvard.edu/archive/india/pdfs/530.pdf

14. P. R. Kumaraswamy, 'The Maturization of Indo-Israeli Ties: New Delhi Moves toward a Closer Friendship with Israel', Middle East Quarterly 20, no. 2 (Spring 2013): 39–48.

15. 'India Will Be Third Largest Economy by 2030', The Economic Times, 28 February 2012, http://articles.economictimes.indiatimes.com/2012-02-28/news/31104962_1_demand-growth-energy-demand-largest-economy

16. International Energy Agency, World Energy Outlook, 2007 (Paris: IEA, 2007), 489.

17. 'Briefing Points by Official Spokesperson on External Affair Minister's Visit to Saudi Arabia', Press Briefings, MEA website, 19 April 2008, http://meaindia.nic.in/mystart.php?id=530313820

18. The complete text of the report of the Group on India Hydrocarbon Vision 2025 can be found in Jasjit Singh, Oil and Gas in India's Security (New Delhi: Knowledge World and Institute for Defence Studies and Analysis, 2001), 131–230.

19. International Energy Agency, World Energy Outlook, 2007 (Paris: IEA, 2007), 495.

20. Ibid., 496.

21. Ibid.

22. 'Reliance Commissions World's Biggest Refinery', The Indian Express, 26 December 2008, New Delhi, http://www.indianexpress.com/news/reliance-commissions-world-s-biggest-refinery/402999/

23. Address of Defence Minister A. K. Antony at the 15th Asian Security Conference, 13 February 2013, www.idsa.in/keyspeeches/DefenceMinister AKAntony_15ASC

24. Ministry of Overseas Indian Affairs, Annual Report, 2010–11.

25. Ministry of Overseas Affairs, Annual Report, 2009–10, 28–29, http://meaindia.nic.in/mystart.php?id=500415660

26. MEA, 'Briefing Points by Official Spokesperson on External Affairs Minister's Visit to Saudi Arabia', Press Briefings, MEA website, 19 April 2008, http://meaindia.nic.in/mystart.php?id=530313820

27. Kumaraswamy, India's Israel Policy, 261.

28. P. R. Kumaraswamy, 'India Should Focus on the Middle East', The New Indian Express, 26 November 2009, http://expressbuzz.com/search/india-should-focus-on-the-middle-east/124903.html

29. P. R. Kumaraswamy, 'Israel: The Non-Parallel Player', Strategic Analysis 36, no. 6 (November–December 2012): 976–86.

30. After a gap of 15 years, Mubarak came to India in 2008 and received the award. For the discussion on the delay, see P. R. Kumaraswamy, '"Mubarak's

Chutzpah": Cairo Treating India with Contempt', *The New Indian Express*, 14 April 2008, Chennai.

31. Pranab Dhal Samanta, 'R-Day: Bhutan King Steps in after Oman Sultan Says No', *The Indian Express*, 29 December 2012, http://www.indianexpress.com/news/rday-bhutan-king-steps-in-after-oman-sultan-says-no/1051706/0

32. Sudha Ramachandran, 'India Dithers over Iraq Dilemma', *Asia Times*, 19 June 2003, http://www.atimes.com/atimes/South_Asia/EF19Df01.html

33. P. R. Kumaraswamy, 'India's Energy Dilemma with Iran', *South Asia*, Monash, forthcoming.

34. Amitav Ranjan, 'Germany Stops Helping India Pay Iran for Oil', *The Indian Express*, 6 April 2011, http://www.indianexpress.com/news/germany-stops-helping-india-pay-iran-for-oil/772261/

35. 'Turkey Refuses to Open BPCL Account for Iran Oil Sources', *Reuters*, 15 December 2011, http://in.reuters.com/article/2011/12/15/india-iran-turkey-idINL3E7NF1XO20111215?type=companyNews

36. 'Counterweight: India Won't Oppose Pakistan–Israel Ties', *The Express Tribune*, 11 January 2012, Karachi, http://tribune.com.pk/story/319700/counterweight-india-wont-oppose-pakistan-israel-ties/

37. 'ONGC Hopeful of Sudan Project Stake', *The Financial Express*, 3 January 2003, http://www.financialexpress.com/news/ongc-hopeful-of-sudan-project-stake/69256/2

38. 'ONGC-CNPAC JV Acquires Syrian Field for $750m', *The Financial Express*, 21 December 2005, http://www.financialexpress.com/news/ongccnpc-jv-acquires-syrian-field-for-750-m/155006/

39. 'India Way behind China in Securing Oil Supplies', *The Economic Times*, 6 June 2010, http://articles.economictimes.indiatimes.com/2010-07-06/news/27574061_1_oil-import-bill-oil-india-nm-borah

40. Tamsin Carlisle, 'China Signs $10bn of Deals with Iran Petrochemicals Firms', *The National*, 2 August 2010, http://www.thenational.ae/business/energy/china-signs-10bn-of-deals-with-iran-petrochemicals-firms

41. Keith B. Richburg, 'China Notes Rift with US on Global Issues ahead of Xi Jinping Visit', *The Washington Post*, 9 February 2012, http://www.washingtonpost.com/world/asia_pacific/china-us-clash-on-syria-other-global-issues-ahead-of-xi-visit/2012/02/09/gIQAGWNa0Q_story.html

42. 'Etisalat Takes $827m Hit on India Operations', *The Times of India*, 10 February 2012, http://articles.timesofindia.indiatimes.com/2012-02-10/india-business/31045992_1_etisalat-db-swan-telecom-india-operations; and Beryl Menezes, 'Etisalat First to Pull Out of 2G Auction', 6 September 2012, *DNA* (Daily News & Analysis), Mumbai, http://www.dnaindia.com/money/1737267/report-etisalat-first-to-pull-out-of-2g-auction

43. 'Cold Shoulder', *The Indian Express*, 9 March 2013, http://www.indianexpress.com/news/false-claim/1085433/

44. Ministry of Overseas Indian Affairs, Government of India, *Annual Report 2011–12*, http://moia.gov.in/writereaddata/pdf/Annual_Report_2011-2012.pdf

45. Ibid., 37.

46. For a discussion on India's response to the Arab Spring, see *Reading the Silence: India and the Arab Spring* (Jerusalem: Leonard Davis Institute for International Relations, 2012), http://www.dmag.co.il/pub/huji/ReadingtheSilence/view_book.html

47. Ministry of Overseas Indian Affairs, *Annual Report 2011–12*, 36.

48. Emigration clearance to Libya and Yemen were suspended in 2011 because of 'domestic turmoil' in these countries. Ministry of Overseas Indian Affairs, *Annual Report 2011–12*, 35.

49. S. Irudaya Rajan and D. Narayana, 'The Financial Crisis in the Gulf and its Impact on South Asian Migration and Remittances', in *India Migration Report 2012: Global Financial Crisis, Migration and Remittances*, ed. S Irudaya Rajan (New Delhi: Routledge, 2012), 86.

50. S. Irudaya Rajan and B. A. Prakash, 'Migration and Development Linkages Re-examined in the Context of the Global Economic Crisis', in *India Migration Report 2012: Global Financial Crisis, Migration and Remittances*, ed. S Irudaya Rajan (New Delhi: Routledge, 2012), 16.

51. Quoted in Irudaya Rajan and Prakash, 'Migration and Development Linkages Re-examined', 15.

52. Olga Marzovilla, 'The Effect of the Global Economic Imbalance on Migrant Workers and Economies of the Gulf Cooperation Council', in *India Migration Report 2012: Global Financial Crisis, Migration and Remittances*, ed. S Irudaya Rajan (New Delhi: Routledge, 2012), 55.

53. Quoted in Irudaya Rajan and Prakash, 'Migration and Development Linkages Re-examined', 15.

54. P. R. Kumaraswamy, *Israel Confronts Iran: Rationale, Responses and Fallouts, Monograph No. 8* (New Delhi: Institute for Defence Studies and Analysis, 2012), http://www.idsa.in/monograph/IsraelConfrontsIran_PRKumaraswamy

55. Shibley Telhami, 'The Israeli and Arab Dimensions of Iran's Nuclear Program', *Brookings*, 10 April 2012, http://www.brookings.edu/research/papers/2012/04/10-iran-telhami

2

Bahrain

Mushtaq Hussain

Key Indicators

Area: 760 sq km; **Population:** 1.28 million; **Native:** 46 per cent; **Expats:** 54 per cent; **Youth:** 15.9 per cent; **Population growth rate:** 2.65 per cent; **Life expectancy at birth:** 75.2 years; **GDP:** US$32.44 billion; **Per capita income:** US$28,200; **Foreign trade:** US$35.9 billion; **Oil reserves:** 107.2 million bbl (2013); **Gas reserves:** 92.03 billion m³; **Ruling family:** al-Khalifa; **Ruler:** King Hamad bin Isa al-Khalifa (since 6 March 1999); **National Day:** 16 December; **Defence budget:** 4.8 per cent of GDP; **HDI rank:** 48; **Literacy rate:** 94.6 per cent; **UN education index:** 0.748; **Gender inequality index:** 0.258.

Source: CIA, *The World Factbook,* https://www.cia.gov/library/publications/the-world-factbook/index.html; *UN Human Development Report,* Statistics, http://hdr.undp.org/en/statistics/
Note: All data for 2012.

Since 1783, the al-Khalifa family has ruled Bahrain, which subsequently came under the British protection in the nineteenth century. Bahrain achieved independence in August 1971 following a UN-sponsored referendum in which a significant majority of the population, including Shiites, supported independence and creation of an 'Arab Bahrain'.[1] Since then, though, the political situation has been perceived by many, mostly Shias, as increasingly discriminatory in favour of the minority Sunni population. After he came to power in March 1999, King Hamad bin Isa al-Khalifa brought about significant reforms, including a referendum on 14 February 2002 on a 'National Action Charter'. This became the basis for the return of the elected assembly, suspended since 1975, and the Charter was also proclaimed as the new constitution.[2] However, the Shias who constitute about 65–70 per cent of the Bahraini population[3] were not satisfied with the reforms, especially with the perceived lack of adequate representation in government and other important offices. The dilution of the promise of elected representation with the setting up of an all-appointed upper house of equal strength was seen as a retrograde step. Failure to satisfy the aspirations of the Shia population and growing socio-economic grievances eventually led to the protests of 14 February 2011, bandwagoning on the momentum generated by the region-wide uprisings.

As a result, India's relations with Bahrain have proved to be among the most challenging in the Persian Gulf region since 2011. The widespread popular demands for reforms that gradually turned into a protest against the al-Khalifa rule have tested the endurance of bilateral relations. The presence of a large number of expatriate Indian workers in the island Kingdom and the socio-economic linkages meant that New Delhi had to handle the issue rather delicately.

Domestic Developments

Bahrain has been in the grip of popular protests since 14 February 2011. With protesters occupying the landmark Pearl Monument in Manama and initial offers of dialogue being rejected by the opposition groups including the Shia political parties, Bahraini security forces were able to control the situation only with the help of Saudi-led armed intervention and crackdown. Although the uprising has not come close to toppling the al-Khalifa regime, it has nonetheless defied resolution. When the report of the Bahrain Independent Commission of Inquiry (BICI), released on 23 November 2011, criticized the government's action against the protesters, hopes were raised for a peaceful resolution of the crisis.[4] The government asserted that it has implemented most of the 26 recommendations made by the Commission, but some human rights groups termed these as modest and incomplete.[5] After the constitution of the BICI, the government had initiated a 'National

Dialogue' and based on the recommendations, amendments to the constitution were brought about. However, the situation remained grim because amendments and other changes promised by the al-Khalifa government failed to satisfy the opposition. Further complicating the situation, Saudi Arabia continues to back the hard-line faction within the regime that opposes any compromise with the protesters. Similarly, some members of the ruling family hold more hard-liner position than the King; the Prime Minister and the King's uncle Khalifa bin Salman al-Khalifa and the commander of Bahrain Defence Force (BDF) Khalifa bin Ahmed al-Khalifa who has been known to be sceptical of political accommodation of the Shias.[6]

Following the first round of 'National Dialogue' during 2–30 July 2011, King Hamad appointed a committee to implement the consensus recommendations, headed by Deputy Prime Minister Mohammad Mubarak al-Khalifa.[7] Amendments to the Bahraini constitution, drafted by the committee to implement these recommendations, were announced by the King on 16 January 2012 and adopted by the National Assembly. These amendments were finally ratified by the King on 3 May 2012.[8] Among others, these amendments limit the power of the King to appoint members to the Shoura Council, the upper, non-elected house of National Assembly. They give the power of drafting legislation or constitutional amendments to both houses, thereby giving the Council of Representatives (the Lower House) the power to veto the government's work plan without the concurrence of the Shoura Council.[9] However, the opposition parties, including the most influential al-Wefaq party, immediately rejected the amendments and took to protests, claiming that the reforms fell short of their demands and offered no 'fundamental changes'.[10]

More than a year after the BICI recommendations and two major commissions appointed to oversee their implementation, significant political issues remain unaddressed. In the absence of any serious process of political dialogue, the population of Bahrain became increasingly fragmented and violence started escalating throughout 2012.[11] A report by the Project on Middle East Democracy, a pro-democracy American NGO, and the Bahrain Human Rights Observatory has concluded that in a year since the publication of BICI report only three out of its 26 recommendations have been fully implemented.[12]

The three recommendations on which there is broad agreement on full implementation includes stripping the National Security Agency of law enforcement powers and limiting it to only intelligence gathering; drafting and providing training on a code of conduct for the police, based on best international practices; and training judiciary employees and prosecutors on preventing and eradicating torture and ill-treatment.[13] An amendment to the 2002 decree establishing the National Security Agency was enacted to bring about the necessary change. Further, the head of the organization was removed and was replaced by a non-royal personality. Towards reforming the security forces, the government hired former Miami Police Chief John Timoney and former Chief of Scotland Yard John Yates. They would teach and train Bahraini police tactics and techniques that conform to international standards of human rights practices.[14] The government implemented another major recommendation regarding the reinstatement of the nearly 4,600 workers who were sacked during the protests. On 21 November 2012, King Hamad ordered the reinstatement of all those who were not convicted or charged with criminal cases, making up almost 98 per cent of the sacked workers.[15] The government established a National Fund, with a budget of Bahraini Dinar (BD) 2.3 billion (US$6.1 billion), to compensate families of those who died during the unrest or were tortured.[16]

However, there were no significant moves regarding the implementation of other major recommendations of BICI. These include some of the principal demands of the opposition, such as the abolition of military court system, holding security officials accountable for abuses during the protests, and referral of all cases against security personnel to the public prosecutor.[17]

Outside the purview of the BICI, the government continued to promote dialogue with the moderate opposition. On 30 August 2012, Deputy Prime Minister Mohammad Mubarak al-Khalifa held a meeting with al-Wefaq representatives.[18] The efforts did not bring the desired results immediately. All the steps taken by the government, including the BICI recommendations and commissions to implement them, did not succeed in putting an end to the demonstrations or satisfying the opposition parties. With continued reports of bombings and protesters and police officers being killed during protests, on 30 October 2012, the government imposed a ban on all public rallies and demonstrations in an effort to 'calm things down'.[19] On 7 November 2012, the government revoked the citizenship of 31 dissidents for 'damaging national security'.[20]

While protests and demonstrations and the ensuing violent crackdowns continued, efforts to resolve the crisis seemed ill-fated due to the political deadlock. In October 2012, an effort was made at the highest level when the King 'rejected a grave escalation on the streets' and said that the 'door for dialogue is open'.[21] The call was reiterated by the Crown Prince Salman bin Hamad al-Khalifa in December 2012 during a conference where he said that 'only through face-to-face dialogue will any real progress be made'.[22] The opposition's response was immediate, with al-Wefaq welcoming the call for dialogue and expressing its desire for coexistence and 'readiness to engage in dialogue'.[23] As a show of good intentions, the ban on demonstrations and rallies was lifted to allow the opposition groups to organize their activities legally.[24] Throughout the last months of 2012 protests continued along with the growing calls for a national dialogue. Finally, in January 2013, following another invitation by King Hamad, al-Wefaq and a coalition of five other parties accepted the invitation for talks and dialogue began on 10 February 2013.[25]

On the economic front, despite the troubles in the social and political front, Bahrain showed an impressive growth in 2011 and 2012. During 2011, the economy grew by 2.2 per cent which was significantly higher than the estimates which, owing to the troubled global economy, pegged growth at 1.5 per cent.[26] For the first three quarters of 2012, the rate of economic growth was 4.4 per cent, fuelled by the strong performance of non-oil sectors, leading to an overall growth for the year 2012 at an estimated 3.9 per cent.[27] In contrast to the grim political scenario, there were many positive developments in the economic sector. Bahrain continued to be among the freest economies in the region and the world. According to a study by the Vancouver-based Fraser Institute, Bahrain is the most economically free country in the Middle East and North Africa (MENA) region and the seventh freest economy in the world.[28] The 2012 *The Wall Street Journal/Heritage Foundation Economic Freedom* Index ranked Bahrain first in the Middle East region and 12th in the world.[29]

With continued promotion of its economic sector by the government, many new organizations and businesses chose Bahrain as the destination to tap the Gulf Cooperation Council (GCC) market. In October 2012, a new global Islamic finance knowledge hub was opened in Bahrain.[30] In keeping with the efforts to project Bahrain as an attractive destination for business, the government organized the seventh Spring of Culture Festival from March till mid-April 2012. It was one of the most important events in Bahrain, attracting international business and tourism alike, both playing a key role in achieving the ambitions of the Kingdom's Vision 2030 and National Economic Strategy.[31] Another such initiative aimed at harnessing the country's economic potential to address the social issues was the organization of Social Business Week 2012. Organized in collaboration with the 2006 Nobel Peace Prize winner Muhmmad Yusuf's Grameen Bank its focus was on Islamic microfinance. Commenting on the aims of the event, the Minister of Social Development Fatima al-Balooshi said, 'The Social Business Week 2012 marks an important step towards promoting awareness of social issues, and the development of solutions to help alleviate the difficult economic conditions that many in the region face.'[32] Towards refurbishing its international image, the Bahraini government decided to go ahead with the Bahrain Formula 1 Grand Prix. The race which was originally scheduled for March 2011 was held on 22 April 2012 amidst tight security.[33]

Faced by continued political crisis and uncertainty, the Bahrain government has taken steps to assuage the opposition groups, while at the same time, it has strived to ensure that the benefits of continued economic growth reaches more sections of the population. With a new National Dialogue starting in February 2013, hopes have been renewed for speedy political reform that would accommodate the aspiration of the majority Shia population. With the pragmatic approach adopted by the regime and the Shia opposition parties towards dialogue, prospects for a negotiated end to the political unrest seem bright.

Bilateral Relations

India's relations with Bahrain date back to 3,000 BC. Based on archaeological findings, it has been established that there were extensive ties between the cities of ancient Harappan civilization and Dilmun, identified with present-day Bahrain.[34] Trade was the predominant link between the two ancient lands, with Dilmun being an important outpost for traders plying between India and Mesopotamia. In more recent times, Indian merchant communities established trading posts in Bahrain in the nine-teenth century, which thrived under British protection.[35] Most of the merchant families came from the Indian provinces of Sindh (present-day Pakistan) and Kathiawad (Gujarat). By 1925, the number of Indian families settled in Bahrain had risen to 2,500.[36] After the discovery of oil in 1934–35, labour immigration from the Indian subcontinent started in large numbers. Presently, the Indian community constitutes the largest expatriate community in Bahrain.[37]

Political Relations

There is a great convergence of political interests between India and Bahrain. The favourable climate is manifested by the presence of a large number of Indian expatriate workers. There are about 400,000 expatriate Indians accounting for more than a third of the total population of the country.[38] Bahrain supported India's candidacy for the non-permanent membership of the United Nations Security Council (UNSC) during 2011–12 and, in return, New Delhi has expressed its commitment to support Bahraini membership during 2026–27.[39] The latter has also pledged its support for India's bid for a permanent membership of the UNSC. Both countries have a number of bilateral agreements covering issues such as extradition, aviation, media, culture, and labour.

Diplomatic relations between the two countries were established at the ambassadorial level on 12 October 1971.[40] Political visits between the two countries have, however, been limited until recently. The senior-most state visit took place in March 2007 when Crown Prince Salman bin Hamad al-Khalifa visited India and met Indian leaders, including President A. P. J. Abdul Kalam, Vice President Bhairon Singh Shekhawat and Prime Minister Manmohan Singh.[41] Bahrain's Foreign Minister Shaikh Khalid bin Ahmed bin Mohamed al-Khalifa, who accompanied the Crown Prince made a separate visit in March 2011, shortly after the outbreak of unrest in his country.[42] The visit of King Hamad has been on the cards since October 2009 and both sides are working towards realizing this visit 'at the earliest possible mutually convenient dates'.[43]

The absence of similar high-level visits from India is conspicuous. There were, however, other ministerial level visits from India and they

include visits by Ministers of State for External Affairs E. Ahamed
(January 2009) and Shashi Tharoor (October 2009); Minister of Overseas Indian Affairs Vayalar Ravi (October 2009, January and November
2011); and Minister of Human Resource Development Kapil Sibal
(October 2010). Indeed, three out of these four Ministers hail from the
state of Kerala, which accounts for the largest portion of the Indian expatriates in Bahrain.

On 29–31 March 2011, Bahraini Foreign Minister Shaikh Khalid
bin Ahmed bin Mohammed al-Khalifa visited India and met Indian
officials.[44] The visit took place amid popular protests and unrest in
Bahrain and both sides 'had detailed discussions on issues of mutual interest including recent developments in Bahrain and the region'. Shaikh
Khalid conveyed 'the firm assurance of the Bahraini leadership' towards
ensuring the 'safety and security of the Indian community numbering
well over 350,000'. The Bahraini Minister referred to his 26 March 2011
meeting with more than 200 members of the Indian community towards
reassuring their concerns.[45] For his part, External Affairs Minister S. M.
Krishna took the opportunity to convey India's gratitude to 'the Government and the people of Bahrain for extending a warm welcome to the
sizeable Indian community there who in turn have contributed through
their dedication and hard work to Bahrain's development'. He also admitted that the contribution of the Indian community had been 'recognized by the Bahraini leadership and we thank them for their continued
support to the Indian community'.[46] Deputy National Security Advisor
Vijaya Latha Reddy called on the Bahraini Foreign Minister to discuss
issues of bilateral importance.[47] As part of the institutional mechanism
between the two ministers, Foreign Office Consultations between India
and Bahrain were held on 23 October 2011 in Manama.[48] Latha Reddy
met the Bahraini Foreign Minister and the Bahraini National Security Adviser again in December 2012 on the sidelines of the 'Manama Dialogue'
which took place in Bahrain from 7 to 9 December 2012.[49]

The bilateral relations got a boost with the visit of the Crown Prince
and Deputy Supreme Commander of the Kingdom of Bahrain Salman
bin Hamad al-Khalifa during 30–31 May 2012 at the invitation of the
Vice President of India.[50] The Crown Prince was accompanied by a
high level business delegation during his visits to Mumbai and Delhi.
In Mumbai, he met with some of the leading Indian industrialists. During his stay in New Delhi, the Crown Prince called on the President

and met other Indian leaders including the Prime Minister and Minster for External Affairs. Both sides agreed on the importance of maintaining high-level contacts and increasing the frequency of interactions in order to broaden and deepen bilateral ties. The Indian leadership expressed its appreciation to the Kingdom of Bahrain in ensuring the safety and well-being of the Indian community during the recent turmoil in Bahrain.[51] During the exchanges, the importance attached by India to peace and stability in the entire region was emphasized. Both sides also underlined the need to resolve all differences through peaceful dialogue and without recourse to violence.[52]

Towards the last quarter of 2012, the unrest in Bahrain took an ugly turn in the form of bombings, some of which seemed to target expatriates. After one such attack which left six Asian expatriates including one Indian national injured, Bahrain's Interior Minister Rashid bin Abdullah al-Khalifa criticized the attacks and vowed to protect expatriates against terror acts.[53] In another incident, an Indian was killed in a bomb blast following which the Indian government condemned the violence and conveyed its concerns to the Bahraini authorities. India expressed hopes and confidence that 'the authorities in Bahrain will ensure security of our citizens living and working in Bahrain'.[54] This confidence is reflected in the fact that, unlike other major countries, India refrained from issuing an adverse travel advisory during the period of turmoil in Bahrain.

Ever since the political crisis of 2011 erupted, India has been in constant touch with the Bahraini authorities regarding the peaceful resolution of the crisis. In an appreciation of the special stake India has in the situation, on 24 November 2012, the Bahraini Ambassador to India Mohammed Ghassan Shaikhu presented the Indian government with a copy of the follow-up report detailing the steps taken by the Bahraini Government to implement the recommendations of the Bahrain Independent Commission of Inquiry.[55] This commission was set up to look into the 2011 unrest and suggest suitable amendments to the laws of the country to meet the demands of the protesters.

Economic Relations

India and Bahrain have had economic and trade relations for over several centuries. Bahrain has been a favoured trading destination for Indian traders since historic times. These relations received fresh impetus from the oil boom of the early 1970s. This brought about prosperity and a higher standard of living in Bahrain and created a demand for global imports of goods and services, including from India. Economic co-operation with India was enhanced with the drive for industrial diversification initiated by the Bahraini Government in the 1990s. New job opportunities attracted a large number of Indian expatriates to Bahrain, who contribute billions of dollars in remittances to Indian economy.

India has significant bilateral trade with Bahrain, which hovers over a billion dollars annually. It is only the second country in the Persian Gulf region (the other being Yemen) with which it has a favourable balance of trade. India's bilateral trade with Bahrain reached US$1.31 billion in 2011–12 which is a slight increase from the previous year (Table 2.1 and Figure 2.1).

The Bahraini economy is the most diverse of all the Gulf States and 75 per cent of its GDP is accounted for by the aluminium, financial and tourism sectors. At the same time, the oil industry is crucial to Bahrain's economy as it accounts for more than 60 per cent of its exports and is the main source of revenue.[56] India's trade relations with Bahrain have been on a strong footing owing to India's oil imports since the 1970s. However, as Table 2.2 and Figure 2.2 highlight, bilateral trade is relatively diverse and the share of crude oil has marginally increased.

However, the depth of the Indo-Bahrain economic relations should not be narrowed down to trade. India is one of Bahrain's leading trading partners, especially for the export of oil. At the same time, the deteriorating political situation in the country has affected economic relations.

Table 2.1
India–Bahrain Bilateral Trade (in US$ Million)

	2009–10	2010–11	2011–12
India's total exports to Bahrain	250.21	651.83	439.99
India's total imports from Bahrain	502.86	641.25	876.30
Total trade	753.07	1,293.08	1,316.28
Share of Bahrain in total trade	0.16	0.21	0.17

Source: Adapted from Director General of Foreign Trade, New Delhi, http://www.dgft.gov.in

Figure 2.1
India–Bahrain Bilateral Trade

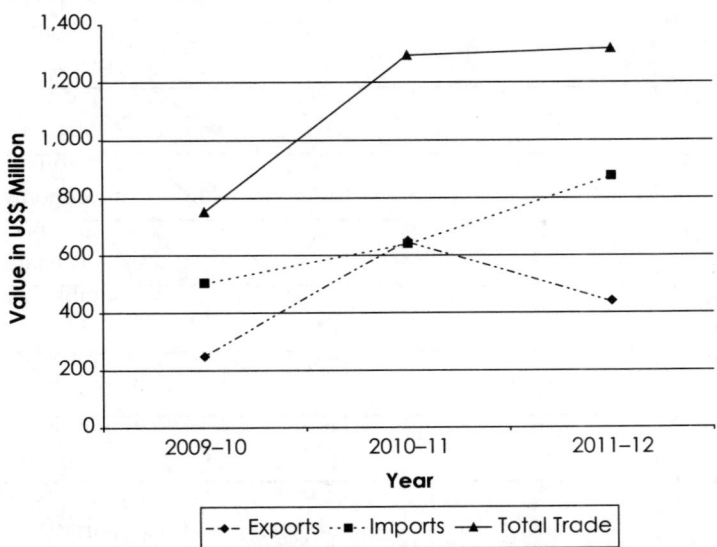

Source: Adapted from Director General of Foreign Trade, New Delhi, http://www.dgft.gov.in

Table 2.2
Share of Oil in India's Imports from Bahrain (in US$ Million)

Year	Oil imports from Bahrain	Total oil imports	Bahraini share in total oil imports	Imports from Bahrain	Per cent of oil in imports from Bahrain
2009–10	248.34	96,321.16	0.26	502.86	49.39
2010–11	219.19	115,929.06	0.19	641.25	34.18
2011–12	591.76	172,753.97	0.34	876.30	67.53

Source: Adapted from Director General of Foreign Trade, New Delhi, http://www.dgft.gov.in

Following the unrest and violence in March 2011, a number of Indian companies, especially information technology giants such as Wipro, Infosys and Tata Consultancy Services (TCS), which had a substantial presence in Bahrain, decided to evacuate their employees.[57] The following month, many Indian banks either withdrew from Bahrain or delayed

Figure 2.2

Share of Oil in India's Total Imports from Bahrain

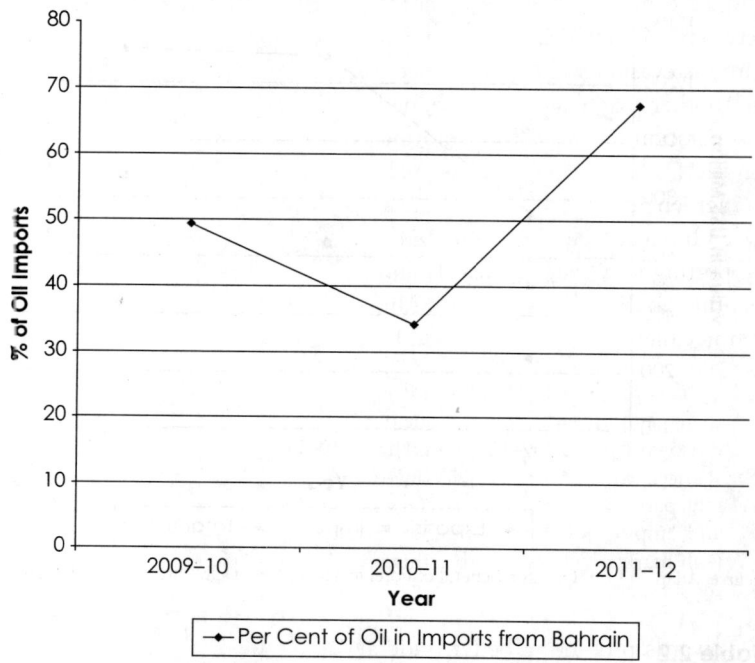

Source: Adapted from Director General of Foreign Trade, New Delhi, http://www.dgft.gov.in

their plans to open branches in that country. However, as an exception, the year 2011 also witnessed the completion of five years of the State Bank of India (SBI) which has been operating since the 1970s.[58] SBI's support for Bahrain came despite having had to relocate some of its employees due to the unstable political situation in the country.

To intensify bilateral economic ties, business community in Bahrain had called for a double taxation avoidance agreement (DTAA) with India. In October 2011, the powerful business organization Bahrain-India Society (BIS), which seeks closer economic co-operation between the two countries, called for a double taxation avoidance agreement similar to the one India has with many other countries in the region.[59] This bore fruit during the May 2012 visit of Crown Prince Salman bin Hamad al-Khalifa to India when both countries signed a Tax Information Exchange

Agreement to promote economic and joint investment between them.[60] This Agreement is designed to enable effective exchange of information between the concerned authorities in both countries which will help curb tax evasion and tax avoidance.[61]

Another major agreement signed during the visit was the MoU on co-operation in the field of Information and Communication Technology (ICT). Its objective was to make a sustained effort to develop and strengthen industrial, technological and commercial co-operation between India and Bahrain in the ICT sector by promoting, facilitating and supporting joint ventures, R&D and markets of the ICT sector.[62] Commenting on the MoU, Kamal bin Ahmed, Minster for Transportation and Acting Chief Executive of Bahrain Economic Development Board, said:

> India is renowned worldwide for its expertise in ICT. So we are delighted to be gaining the expertise of one of the world's best as we look to build on our own ICT sector in Bahrain. High-value industries like ICT or financial services, which require a skilled workforce in order to thrive, are an important part of our economic strategy to create sustainable economic growth and employment. We hope that Indian businesses looking to access the Gulf market will benefit from this partnership as much as we benefit from their expertise.[63]

Towards promoting better trade and investment relations, the Bahrain Chamber of Commerce and Industry (BCCI) and the Federation of Indian Chambers of Commerce and Industry (FICCI) and the Associated Chambers of Commerce and Industry in India signed an agreement for the formation of the Bahrain India Business Council to develop economic, trade and technical relations between the two countries.[64]

It is essential to recognize that India's trade with Bahrain is a miniscule part of the total Indian trade with the GCC, which was estimated to be US$145 billion in the period 2011–12.[65] Even though the political turmoil dampened the investment and trade climate since 2011, there exists untapped potential for enhancing bilateral trade. Since Bahraini economy is more diverse than other Gulf States, there exist more avenues to diversify and increase bilateral trade. In the period 2005–10, India's share of Bahrain's total foreign trade was only 4.1 per cent.[66] The range of products presenting potential for export to Bahrain could include machinery and transport equipment; cotton and woven fabrics; food, petroleum, pharmaceutical, ceramic and aluminium products; and articles made of iron and steel. At the same time, focus sectors for investment could include information technology (IT) and telecommunications, education and training, tourism, health care, financial services and downstream industries.[67] One avenue where India can tap is the Foreign Direct Investment (FDI). Between 2000 and 2009, the total FDI flow into India from the GCC region was US$1.64 billion; of this, Bahrain accounted for only US$25.85 million[68] and Bahrain ranked fourth, after the United Arab Emirates (UAE), Oman and Saudi Arabia. This is one area where India needs to pay more attention.

Bahrain is being positioned as a gateway to the US$1 trillion GCC market and the government is showcasing the Kingdom's business-friendly credentials to attract the Indian business community. During his visit in May 2012, Khaled Ali Alamin, Chairman of the Bahrain India Business Council said:

> The countries of the GCC alone represent a market of well over one trillion US dollars, a market which is set to reach two trillion dollars by 2020. Bahrain's position as a gateway to the region and its strong historic ties with India mean that it is an ideal strategic partner from which Indian businesses can access this market and its opportunities.[69]

Reflecting this interest in Indian economy, the Ahlia University of Bahrain organized a conference on 'Emerging Trends in the Indian Economy and Prospects for Sustainable Growth' on 5 November 2012 with the Indian Ambassador delivering the keynote address.[70]

Energy Relations

Energy supplies have been central to Indo–Bahrain relations since the oil boom of the 1970s and Bahrain contributes about 0.19 per cent of India's total energy imports and around 0.57 per cent of imports from the Persian Gulf region (Table 2.3). In 2011–12, India imported US$591 million worth of crude oil from Bahrain. As highlighted in Figure 2.2, oil accounts for the bulk of India's total imports from Bahrain. Although oil has been one of the major items imported by India from Bahrain since the 1970s, it has seen a decline since 2008.

Table 2.3
India's Oil Imports from Bahrain (in US$ Million)

	2009–10	2010–11	2011–12
Oil imports from Bahrain	248.34	219.19	591.76
Total oil imports	96,321.16	115,929.06	172,753.97
Total imports from Persian Gulf	55,904.14	66,688.4	103,915.24
Share in total imports	0.26	0.19	0.34
Share in imports from Persian Gulf	0.44	0.33	0.57

Source: Adapted from Director General of Foreign Trade, New Delhi, http://www.dgft.gov.in

Cultural Relations

Cultural relations between the two countries have been strengthened by the presence of one of the largest Indian expatriate communities. The Indian presence in Bahrain is seen as essential to the functioning of the country by the Bahraini establishment. The official support has helped the Indian community thrive in Bahrain. Ramon Magsaysay Award winner Indian social activist and retired Indian Police Service (IPS) officer Kiran Bedi visited Bahrain in May 2012 to take part in 'NRIs and India-Building Bridges', organized by the Arab Asian Business and Exhibition Centre (AABEX).[71] Indian culture was also showcased at the 'Irresistible India Gala Dinner' held under the patronage of the Indian Embassy on 15 November 2012.[72]

The Indian expatriate community enjoys great goodwill from the Bahraini authorities and the employers alike. It is no secret that Indians are preferred over other expatriates from the subcontinent. The main reasons for this are trust factor, strong work ethics and the 'apolitical' orientation of Indian expatriates. Despite the serious unrest in Bahrain since 2011, it is noteworthy that there was no 'targeting' of Indians by the opposition activists and the safety and security was ensured by the Bahraini authorities.[73]

External Players

The US: The unrest in Bahrain presented the US with a peculiar dilemma. Unlike other protest-ravaged countries such as Tunisia, Libya and

Syria, the US has deep security relations with Bahrain. The US Navy's Fifth Fleet and the naval component of US Central Command are based in Bahrain. Owing to its continued support in US involvements in Iraq, Iran and Afghanistan, Bahrain has been designated as a 'major non-NATO ally' (MNNA), a status that allows Bahrain to purchase all the US defence systems that are available to NATO allies.[74] These factors and other considerations, like the threat of increased Iranian influence, put the US in a bind regarding its response to the developments in Bahrain. Under domestic and international pressure to use its leverage with the Bahraini establishment in actively promoting political reform, the US suspended most of the security assistance programmes pending genuine reform.[75]

After the Bahraini Crown Prince stated his government's 'commitment to reform, both political and economic', during his visit to the US in May 2012, the Obama administration expressed support for the upcoming National Dialogue and agreed to restart arms sales.[76] However, US–Bahrain relations continued to be strained, when during the 'Manama Dialogue', an annual security conference held in Bahrain, the Crown Prince did not name the US among the allies that had provided critical support during the political disturbances.[77] While the US continues to assert that support for reforms are not incompatible with continued security relationship with Bahrain, it is nonetheless threatened by the prospect of Iran gaining from the situation. While publically supporting the need for upholding human rights and ensuring religious freedom, the US is wary of the instability in Bahrain as it could unleash Shia–Sunni conflict across the region, thereby strengthening Iran and weakening US allies, particularly Saudi Arabia.

China: China's response to the outburst of public protests in Bahrain has been one of wait-and-watch. In contrast to the much-publicized role in the case of Libya and Syria, China maintained a studied silence over the Bahrain issue, quite akin to the policy pursued by India. China is the third largest non-GCC market for Bahrain's exports and the second largest import destination. Owing to the strong trade and economic ties with Bahrain and the GCC as a whole, China chose to support Bahrain's ruling regime during the trying times of widespread protests. Throughout 2012, China continued to call on involved parties to resolve the dispute through dialogue and 'peaceful approach'.[78] China welcomed the resumption of the National Dialogue in Bahrain. Chinese Foreign Ministry spokesperson expressed hope that 'Bahrain's relevant parties maintain peaceful ways, including dialogue, to properly solve disparities so as to realize national long-term stability and development'.[79]

Pakistan: Bilateral ties between Pakistan and Bahrain are extremely cordial as evident from a recent statement of King Hamad where he referred to Pakistan as his 'second home'.[80] This show of camaraderie was on display during the meeting between the King and the Pakistani Prime Minister Raja Parvez Ashraf on the sidelines of the Asian Cooperation Dialogue (ACD) Summit in Kuwait in October 2012. The King also acknowledged the role of 65,000 strong Pakistanis in the development and progress of Bahrain. The Pakistani Prime Minister commended King Hamad's endeavour to promote understanding among various segments of society and resolve the 'problems of his people through dialogue'.[81]

The two countries enjoy close defence ties. During the visit of the Pakistani Deputy Chief of Naval Staff to Bahrain, the Commander-in-Chief of Bahrain Defence Force reiterated the need to find ways of bolstering military co-operation.[82] In October 2012, Pakistan Air Force took part in air exercises in Bahrain, in which the US also participated.[83] But the security co-operation has another side as well. At the height of the political unrest in 2011, the al-Khalifa government was hiring retired soldiers and police by the thousands in Pakistan's Baluchistan province for its National Guard and the Bahrain Defence Force—the regular army.[84] In an embarrassing development, five such Pakistani policemen were put on trial for allegedly torturing and killing two Shia men during protests.[85] However, this issue was not given too much importance by both sides and Pakistani security personnel continue to serve in Bahrain.

This was characteristic of the approach long espoused by the Bahraini establishment. Despite its confluence of interests with the other GCC states, Bahrain has been unwilling to depend solely on the GCC for security provisions. Instead it has hedged its bets through the development of a *peripheral balancing mechanism*; a string of bilateral alliances based on the mutual interest of curtailing Iran's domination.[86] Bahrain's relationship with India is also a part of this peripheral balancing, and Pakistan's role is a major factor influencing this aspect of relationship. There have been sentiments that India has, at times, preferred Bahrain over Iran, owing to the large population of expatriate Indians living in Bahrain and the Kingdom's overt support for UNSC reform to allow for an Indian permanent seat.

Saudi Arabia: Political unrest in Bahrain fuelled fears among the GCC states, especially in Saudi Arabia, of its possible spread to other countries of the Gulf region. The Saudis were also wary of an Iranian intervention in Shia-dominated Bahrain, a nightmarish situation given the significant Shia population in its Eastern provinces. To counter the threat, Saudi Arabia backed the hard-line, anti-compromise faction of the royal family. In a show of unstinted support, in May 2012, Saudi Arabia and Bahrain announced plans to form a closer political and military union among the GCC states.[87] Although the move was opposed by other member states, it nonetheless showed unqualified Saudi support for the ruling family in Bahrain.

Conclusion

While India's relations with Bahrain were considerably strained during the political upheaval of 2011, desire to pursue a political dialogue towards seeking a peaceful resolution to the unrest has helped calm India's anxiety. The assurances provided by the government regarding the safety of expatriates and almost non-existent cases of harassment against foreigners eased the pressure on India. With about 400,000 Indian migrant workers in that country, India's options were in any case limited. Even while organizing the evacuation of its citizens from Egypt and Libya following the outbreak of popular protests in those countries, India had been cautious towards Bahrain. Mass-scale evacuation was not only problematic, but would have had severe economic consequences also for Bahrain. While continuing to express its concern over the welfare of its citizens, India refrained from making any public statement concerning the developments in Bahrain. Its high-level political contacts with Bahrain indicated its willingness to support political stability in Bahrain and orderly reforms.

Notes

1. *The Bahrain Situation: Assessment Report*, Arab Centre for Research and Policy Studies, March 2011, http://english.dohainstitute.org/file/get/c88f7ee8-2ad0-4851-8d3b-23a700fd6745.pdf
2. Kristian Coates Ulrichsen, 'Bahrain's Aborted Revolution', *LSE Ideas*, 2011, http://www2.lse.ac.uk/IDEAS/publications/reports/pdf/SR011/FINAL_LSE_IDEAS__BahrainsAbortedRevolution_Ulrichsen.pdf
3. Graham Fuller, 'Bahrain Blowback', *The New York Times,* 16 February 2011, http://www.nytimes.com/2011/02/17/opinion/17iht-edfuller17.html. Also see, Kenneth Katzman, 'Bahrain: Reform, Security and U.S. Policy', *Congressional Research Service Report for Congress*, 12 February 2013, 1. http://www.fas.org/sgp/crs/mideast/95-1013.pdf
4. The full report of the BICI is available at http://www.bici.org.bh/
5. Katzman, 'Bahrain', 1.
6. Ibid.
7. 'Committee to Execute Dialogue Outcomes', *Gulf Daily News*, 1 August 2011, http://www.gulf-daily-news.com/NewsDetails.aspx?storyid=310911
8. 'Turning Point in Bahrain's History', *Gulf Daily News*, 4 May 2012, http://www.gulf-daily-news.com/source/XXXV/045/pdf/page02.pdf
9. Katzman, 'Bahrain', 10.
10. 'Bahraini's Rally against Hamad's Constitutional Reforms', *Press TV*, 4 May 2012, http://www.presstv.com/detail/239531.html
11. 'The Outlook for Bahrain', Middle East and North Africa Programme Roundtable Summary, Chatham House, November 2012, http://www.chathamhouse.org/sites/default/files/public/Research/Middle%20East/1112bahrain_summary.pdf
12. 'One Year Later: Assessing Bahrain's Implementation of the BICI Report', Project on Middle East Democracy, 2012, http://pomed.org/blog/2012/11/assessing-bahrains-implementation-of-the-bici-report.html/
13. Katzman, 'Bahrain', 13.
14. 'Hamad Promises Reform to Build Kingdom of Tolerance', *Gulf News,* 14 December 2011, http://gulfnews.com/news/gulf/bahrain/hamad-promises-reform-to-build-kingdom-of-tolerance-1.950503
15. 'Bahrain Making Reforms Progress', *Gulf Daily News*, 22 November 2012, http://www.gulf-daily-news.com/source/XXXV/247/pdf/page06.pdf
16. Ibid.
17. Katzman, 'Bahrain', 13.
18. Ibid., 15.
19. 'Citing Violence, Bahrain Bans All Protests in New Crackdown', *The New York Times,* 30 October 2012, http://www.nytimes.com/2012/10/31/world/middleeast/bahrain-bans-all-protests-in-new-crackdown.html?_r=0

20. 'Bahrain Revokes Nationality of 31 over National Security', *Reuters*, 7 November 2012, http://www.reuters.com/article/2012/11/07/us-bahrain-nationality-idUSBRE8A61RC20121107
21. 'Govt Is Open to Talks, Says Bahrain King', *Khaleej Times*, 15 October 2012, http://www.khaleejtimes.com/kt-article-display-1.asp?xfile=/data/middleeast/2012/October/middleeast_October152.xml&section=middleeast
22. 'Bahrain Crown Prince Calls for Talks with Opposition', *Reuters*, 8 December 2012, http://uk.reuters.com/article/2012/12/08/uk-bahrain-politics-idUKBRE8B706F20121208
23. Website of the Al-Wefaq National Islamic Society, 'Bahraini Opposition Welcomes CP Call to Initiate Dialogue', 8 December 2012, http://www.alwefaq.net/index.php?show=news&action=article&id=7258
24. 'Bahrain Lifts Ban on Rallies Imposed in October', *Xinhua*, 13 December 2012, http://news.xinhuanet.com/english/world/2012-12/13/c_132037163.htm
25. 'Bahrain Holds Talks to End Political Deadlock', *Al Jazeera*, 11 February 2013, http://www.aljazeera.com/video/middleeast/2013/02/20132106950246731.html
26. 'Bahrain's Economy Continued to Grow in 2011', Bahrain Economic Development Board, 22 May 2012, http://www.bahrainedb.com/press-beq-outlook-2012.aspx
27. 'Recovery Gaining Momentum with Growth of over 6 per cent Forecast for 2013', Bahrain Economic Development Board, 12 February 2013, http://www.bahrainedb.com/press-economic-quarterly-2013.aspx
28. Fraser Institute, 'Economic Freedom of the World: 2012 Annual Report', 18 September 2012, http://www.freetheworld.com/2012/EFW2012-complete.pdf
29. Terry Miller, Kim Holmes and Edwin Fuelner, 'Highlights of the 2012 Index of Economic Freedom: Promoting Economic Opportunity and Prosperity', *Heritage Foundation*, 14 January 2013, http://www.google.co.in/url?sa=t&rct=j&q=2012%20wall%20street%20journal%20%2F%20heritage%20foundation%20economic%20freedom%20index.&source=web&cd=9&cad=rja&ved=0CHAQFjAI&url=https%3A%2F%2Fthf_media.s3.amazonaws.com%2Findex%2Fpdf%2F2012%2FIndex2012-Highlights.pdf&ei=gY80UY_wIInRtAbAg4DYDA&usg=AFQjCNHYYq116koPjMjeAI5XScZd4wNlVg&bvm=bv.43148975,d.Yms
30. 'Thomson Reuters Launches Global Islamic Hub in Bahrain', Bahrain Economic Development Board, 4 October 2012, http://www.bahrainedb.com/press-reuters-finance-hub.aspx
31. 'Bahrain Announces Seventh Spring of Culture Festival', Bahrain Economic Development Board, 20 February 2012, http://www.bahrainedb.com/press-spring-of-cultures-2012.aspx
32. 'Bahrain Harnesses Financial Leadership to Boost Social Enterprise', Bahrain Economic Development Board, 16 September 2012, http://www.bahrainedb.com/press-social-enterprise.aspx

33. 'Bahrain Stages F1 Grand Prix Despite Protests', *BBC News*, 22 April 2012, http://www.bbc.co.uk/news/world-middle-east-17803310
34. Lakshmi Chatterjee, *Heritage of Harappa*, Vol. 1 (New Delhi: Global Vision Publishing House, 2005), 162.
35. James Onley, 'Britain's Native Agents in Arabia and Persia in the Nineteenth Century', *Comparative Studies of South Asia, Africa and Middle East* 24, no. 1(2004): 129–37.
36. Ministry of Overseas Indian Affairs, 'Country Profile—Bahrain,' Ministry of Overseas Indian Affairs, New Delhi, http://moia.gov.in/pdf/Bahrain.pdf
37. Ibid.
38. The Gulf, West Asia and North Africa, Ministry of External Affairs, *Annual Report Ministry of External Affairs, 2011–12* (hereafer MEA AR, 2011–12), 41, http://www.mea.gov.in/mystart.php?id=500419226
39. Government of India, 'India–Bahrain Relations, February 2012', Ministry of External Affairs, New Delhi, http://meaindia.nic.in/mystart. php?id=50042438
40. 'Bahrain–Indo Relations', The Embassy of the Kingdom of Bahrain in India, New Delhi, http://www.bahrainembassyindia.com/relation-with-india.html
41. 'India–Bahrain Joint Statement on the Occasion of the Official Visit to India by His Highness Shaikh Salman bin Hamad Al Khalifa, Crown Prince and Commander in Chief of the Bahrain Defence Force (19–22 March 2007)', *Statements*, Ministry of External Affairs, New Delhi, http://meaindia.nic.in/mystart.php?id=530212547
42. 'Visit of Foreign Minister of Bahrain to India', Press Releases, 30 March 2011, Ministry of External Affairs, New Delhi, http://meaindia.nic.in/mystart.php?id=530217486
43. Ministry of External Affairs, 'India–Bahrain Relations, February 2012'.
44. Ministry of External Affairs, 'Visit of Foreign Minister of Bahrain to India'.
45. Ibid.
46. 'Opening Remarks by External Affairs Minister Mr. S. M. Krishna during Visit of Foreign Minister of Bahrain', *Speeches & Statements*, 30 March 2011, Ministry of External Affairs, New Delhi, http://meaindia.nic.in/mystart.php?id=530117485
47. Ibid.
48. Ministry of External Affairs, 'India–Bahrain Relations, February 2012'.
49. Ministry of External Affairs, Government of India, 'Briefs on India's Bilateral Relations—Bahrain', Ministry of External Affairs, New Delhi, http://www.mea.gov.in/Portal/ForeignRelation/Bahrain_Bilateral_brief.pdf
50. Ibid.
51. Ibid.
52. 'Official Visit of Crow Prince of Bahrain to India', Press Release, Embassy of India, Kingdom of Bahrain, Ghudaibiya, 1 June 2012, http://www.indianembassybahrain.com/cp_bah_visits_india.html

53. 'Bahrain Vows to Protect Expatriates from Terror Acts', *Xinhua*, 9 October 2012, http://news.xinhuanet.com/english/world/2012-10/09/c_131893928. htm

54. 'Bomb Blasts in Bahrain', *Media Briefings*, 5 November 2012, Ministry of External Affairs, New Delhi, http://www.mea.gov.in/media-briefings. htm?dtl/20772/Bomb+blasts+in+Bahrain

55. 'Indian Official Presented with BICI Follow-up Report', Bahrain News Agency, 24 November 2012, http://www.bna.bh/portal/en/news/534568

56. 'Monthly Economic and Commercial Report for the Month of June 2011', Embassy of India, Kingdom of Bahrain, Ghudaibiya, http://www.bombaychamber.com/uploads/Bahrain%20-%20June%202011.pdf, 5.

57. 'Wipro, Infosys, TCS Recall Staff from Bahrain', *The Times of India*, 21 March 2011, http://timesofindia.indiatimes.com/tech/careers/job-trends/Wipro-Infosys-TCS-recall-staff-from-Bahrain/articleshow/7751778.cms

58. 'State Bank of India Celebrates Five Years of Retail Banking in Bahrain', *AME Info*, 17 December 2011, http://www.ameinfo.com/284537.html

59. Currently India has similar agreements with Turkey, Libya, Egypt, Israel, Jordan, Syria, Morocco, Saudi Arabia, Kuwait, Qatar, Oman and the UAE.

60. 'HRH The Crown Prince Leads Bahrain Business Delegation to India', *eNewsletter*, Bahrain Economic Development Board, http://www.bahrainedb.com/enewsletter/en/default.asp?action=article&id=130

61. 'Documents Signed during the Official Visit of the Crown Prince of Bahrain to India', *Bilateral/Multilateral Documents*, Ministry of External Affairs, New Delhi, http://www.mea.gov.in/bilateral-documents.htm?dtl/19905/Docum ents+signed+during+the+Official+Visit+of+the+Crown+Prince+of+Bahrain +to+India

62. Ibid.

63. 'Bahrain Signs Agreement with India to Boost Bilateral Ties', *Bahrain News Agency*, 31 May 2012, http://bna.bh/portal/en/news/511057

64. 'Bahrain Signs Agreements to Boost Bilateral Ties with India', *The Economic Times*, 1 June 2012, http://articles.economictimes.indiatimes.com/2012-06-01/news/31959458_1_india-and-bahrain-bahrain-economic-development-board-bahrain-chamber

65. 'Gulf Cooperation Council', Ministry of External Affairs, New Delhi, http://www.mea.gov.in/staticfile/gccmarch2011.pdf

66. 'HRH The Crown Prince Leads Bahrain Business Delegation to India'.

67. Shaliesh Tripathi and Surendar Singh, 'India's Trade and Investment Relation with GCC Countries in WTO Era', *Pragyaan Journal of Management* 7, no. 1 (2009): 86–92.

68. 'FDI Synopsis on Countries: Gulf Countries', Department of Industrial Policy and Promotion, Government of India, http://dipp.nic.in/English/Publications/SIA_NewsLetter/Annualreport2009/chapter6.1.D.pdf

69. 'Bahrain Signs Agreement with India to Boost Bilateral Ties', *Bahrain News Agency*, 31 May 2012, http://bna.bh/portal/en/news/511057

70. Embassy of India, Bahrain 'Monthly Economic and Commercial Report for the Month of November 2012', Bombay Chamber of Commerce and Industry, http://www.bombaychamber.com/uploads/0000000765-Bahrain%20Nov%202012.pdf

71. 'Kiran Bedi in Bahrain', *The Daily Tribune*, 29 May 2013, http://www.dt.bh/newsdetails.php?newsid=280512175104&key=301110213450

72. Embassy of India, Bahrain 'Monthly Economic and Commercial Report'.

73. Ministry of External Affairs, 'Briefs on India's Bilateral Relations—Bahrain'.

74. Katzman, 'Bahrain', 23.

75. 'U.S. Must Bring Pressure to Bear on Bahrain', *The Washington Post*, 6 February 2012, http://articles.washingtonpost.com/2012-02-06/opinions/35442679_1_shiite-opposition-bahrain-obama-administration

76. 'Bahrain Crown Prince Visits US', *Al Jazeera*, 11 May 2012, http://www.aljazeera.com/news/americas/2011/06/201167212647437406.html

77. The Washington Institute, Simon Henderson, 'U.S. Differences with Bahrain Playing Out in Public', The Washington Institute, 10 December 2012, http://www.washingtoninstitute.org/policy-analysis/view/u.s.-differences-with-bahrain-playing-out-in-public

78. 'China Condemns Bahrain Bombings', *Xinhua*, 8 November 2012, http://news.xinhuanet.com/english/china/2012-11/08/c_131960625.htm

79. 'China Welcomes Resumption of National Talks: FM', *Xinhua*, 8 February 2013, http://news.xinhuanet.com/english/china/2013-02/08/c_132160523.htm

80. 'Pakistan Keen to Strengthen Relations with Bahrain: PM', *The Nation*, 17 October 2012, http://www.nation.com.pk/pakistan-news-newspaper-daily-english-online/national/17-Oct-2012/pakistan-keen-to-strengthen-relations-with-bahrain-pm

81. Ibid.

82. 'Bahrain–Pakistani Military Cooperation Discussed', *Bahrain News Agency*, 16 July 2012, http://www.bna.bh/portal/en/news/517194

83. Sehar Kamran, 'Pak–Gulf Defense and Security Cooperation', *Center for Pakistan and Gulf Studies*, 2013, http://cpakgulf.org/documents/Pak-Gulf-Security-Ties-final.pdf, 14

84. Bruce Riedel, 'The New Bahrain–Pakistan Alliance', *The National Interest*, 2 August 2011, http://nationalinterest.org/commentary/bahrain-calls-mercenaries-silence-protestors-5689

85. 'Bahrain Puts Pakistani Policemen on Trial for Using "Excessive Force"', *The Tribune*, 12 January 2012, http://tribune.com.pk/story/320235/bahrain-puts-pakistani-policemen-on-trial-for-using-excessive-force/

86. Mitchell A. Belfer, 'Bahrain in Context', *Central European Journal of International and Security Studies (CEJISS)*, 2012, http://cejiss.org/editors-desk/bahrain-context

87. Katzman, 'Bahrain', 8.

3

Iran

Alvite Singh Ningthoujam

Key Indicators

Area: 1,648,195 sq km; **Population:** 79.85 million; **Youth population:** 19.8 per cent; **Population growth rate:** 1.247 per cent; **Life expectancy at birth:** 73.2 years; **GDP:** US$997.40 billion; **Per capita income:** US$13,100; **Foreign trade:** US$133.34 billion; **Oil reserves:** 151.2 billion bbl; **Gas reserves:** 33.07 trillion m³; **Ruling party:** Abadgaran; **Ruler:** President Mahmoud Ahmedinejad (since 3 August 2005); **National Day:** 1 April; **Defence budget:** 2.5 per cent of GDP; **HDI rank:** 76; **Literacy rate:** 77 per cent; **UN education index:** 0.707; **Gender inequality index:** 0.496.

Source: CIA, *The World Factbook*, https://www.cia.gov/library/publications/the-world-factbook/index.html; UN Human Development Report, Statistics, http://hdr.undp.org/en/statistics/
Note: All data for 2012.

The Indo–Iranian relations date back to thousands of years and could be traced to migration from Persia centuries before Christ.[1] One of the main binding forces for these ties was the common proto-language shared by Sanskrit and Persian.[2] While the diplomatic relations were established in March 1950, the framework for this was laid during the visit of the Iranian delegation to the Asian Relations Conference held in March 1947 in New Delhi.[3] There was a period of lull between the two countries. This was well-attributed to the Cold War calculations when Iran closely aligned with the West while India adhered to its nonalignment policy.[4] Iran and Pakistan joining the Baghdad Pact further complicated the Indo–Iranian relations. However, since the end of the Cold War, the Indo–Iranian relations have become the most controversial and complex aspect of India's foreign policy.

Domestic Developments

Since the 1979 Islamic revolution, Iran has been ruled by a highly conservative clerical elite but began to witness some political and social changes after liberals emerged victorious in the 2000 parliamentary election.[5] The reformation of the Iranian society began visibly after the moderate cleric Mohammad Khatami won the 1997 presidential election. However, an opposite result was witnessed during the 2004 parliamentary elections when the conservative forces secured victory.[6] Since then, elections have been engulfed by controversies, including the 2009 presidential election.[7]

On the economic front, during early 2007, there was a bitter rivalry between President Mahmoud Ahmedinejad and elderly influential opponent such as Hashemi Rajsanjani over the control of economic policy.[8] Ahmedinejad was severely criticized for requesting supplementary budget in the past years due to which country's foreign currency reserves were drained. Simultaneously, inflation and unemployment were on the rise. Considering the escalating political and economic crisis in the country since late 2000, some were of the view that words such as 'Islamic' and 'Republic' in the Islamic Republic of Iran were no longer applicable.[9] This was particularly due to the controversial result of the 2009 election and the ill-treatment of the protestors during the time. What added to this economic plight is its nuclear programme due to which the US, in 2010, imposed unilateral sanctions to squeeze Iran's energy and banking sectors.[10] Alongside this, women also figured in Iranian domestic issues. Many of them, in 2009, voiced their resentment about discrimination, especially from joining politics. Many demanded that there should be women cabinets in the ministry.[11] In 2010, nearly 1,200 women signed a statement against a bill that could significantly curb women's rights.[12] This said bill would give rights to men to take additional wives without even informing the current wives 'under certain conditions and would impose restrictions on alimony for women'.[13] Despite these attempts, brutality towards women still continues, and in some instances, they used social media to express their plights.[14]

Likewise, in 2012, Iran had witnessed a number of major events as many government officials and politicians were accused of corruption charges. The situation had become so worse that President Mahmoud Ahmedinejad even threatened to reveal the involvement of Supreme Leader Ali Khamenei's son Mojtaba in 'terrible' corruption affairs.[15] There was also a split between the conservative groups headed by Ahmedinejad and the Supreme Leader. Furthermore, the reformist faction led by the former President Mohammad Khatami boycotted the 2012 election and such internal developments had dominated other issues such as the threat of Israeli attack on Iran for its nuclear programme or the tightening US-led sanctions.

The year began with the preparation for the March parliamentary elections which was considered as one of the most 'consequential electoral events in the 32-year history' of the Islamic republic.[16] The Iranians keenly observed this election not only because it would draw a new political map but it was likely to determine the political legacy that would be left behind by Ahmedinejad when he finishes his term in 2013. On 2 March 2012, 48 million Iranians went to the polls to elect their representatives to the 290-seat Majlis (Parliament). Iran's Guardian Council approved the candidacy of 3,454 persons.[17] The voter turnout was high (about 66.4 per cent) compared to the previous ones. With the announcement of the result, it was clear that the support for Ahmedinejad in Iran's parliament had crumbled. The United Principalist Front (UPF), the party that was backed by Khamenei won majority of the seats and was seen as a humiliation for the president.[18] The results also indicated that Ahmedinejad might face a more belligerent parliament till his term ends in August 2013. Even at this juncture, the outgoing parliament and Ahmedinejad were at loggerheads over the means to solve the economic crisis, particularly food crisis and energy subsidies. In the words of Parliamentary speaker Ali Larijani, 'the parliament won't allow him to quickly end the remaining subsidies because it would cause wild inflation and public dissatisfaction'.[19] In short, this election was a battle fought by the factions within the establishment for a greater share of power. In March, the Supreme Leader appointed members of the Expediency Council for a five-year period with Ayatollah Hashemi Rafsanjani being reinstated as its chairman.[20]

The role of women in society also received some attention. In August many universities across Iran had announced that about 80 subjects in liberal arts and sciences would be off limits to the female scholars.[21] As it is well known, women in Iran are subject to many cultural restrictions and the new move could be seen as an attempt to subdue Iran's nascent feminist movements. Ironically, the Iranian women were in the forefront during the protests in 2009 over the disputed presidential elections.

Considering their contribution for the betterment of the society, Iranian women still take a back seat when it comes to politics. One of the most prominent incidents was the sacking of the Health Minister Marziyeh Vahid Dastjerdi, only female minister in the Ahmedinejad's cabinet in December 2012.[22] She was the first woman minister in the 30-year-old history of the Islamic Republic. It was believed that she was removed for her protests against the price-rise of drugs caused by the sanctions. In November, the Iranian lawmakers were considering to implement a law that prevents single women under the age of 40 to obtain a passport and travel abroad without permission from her father or a male guardian.[23]

Throughout 2012, Iran continued to strive to defy Western efforts at international isolation. In August, it hosted the 16th Summit of the Non-Aligned Movement (NAM) where more than 100 countries participated. Iran used this forum to exhibit international solidarity and peaceful coexistence, especially 'in the face of imperialist aggression and threat of all-out world war'.[24] The high international attendance was also considered by Iran as a 'diplomatic triumph' against Israel which was believed to have asked some NAM members not to attend the summit or to scale down their participation.[25]

The nuclear programme, which has continued to receive international attention, was one of the agendas of the NAM Summit. During his inaugural address the Supreme Leader declared that Iran considered the use of chemical, nuclear and other weapons to be a 'great and unforgiveable sin'.[26] The Iranian leaders also criticized the manoeuvres of Israel and the United States (US) to isolate Iran over its nuclear programme. The final communiqué of the summit expressed support for Iran's nuclear programme, and rejected the US sanctions against the country.

Economy

During 2012, the Iranian economy was severely hit by the continued Western sanctions over its nuclear programme. Some of the important sanctions imposed against Iran include:

- Iran–Iraq Arms Proliferation Act, 1992, of the US[27]—that sanctions any person or entity that assists Iran in weapons development or acquisition of 'chemical, biological, nuclear, or destabilizing numbers and types of advanced conventional weapons'.
- Iran–Libya Sanctions Act (ILSA), 1996, of the US[28]—that imposes sanctions on foreign firms investing more than $20 million a year in Iran's energy sector.
- United Nations Security Council (UNSC) Resolution 1696, 2006,[29] that demanded Iran to halt its uranium enrichment programme.
- UNSC Resolution 1737, 2006,[30] that imposed sanctions on Iran for its failure to halt the uranium enrichment programme and to co-operate in International Atomic Energy Agency (IAEA).
- UNSC Resolution 1747, 2007,[31] that imposed an arms embargo and expanded the freeze on Iranian assets.
- UNSC Resolution 1803, 2008,[32] extended freeze on assets, and to monitor the activities of Iranian banks, inspect Iranian ships and aircraft, and to monitor movement of individuals involved with the nuclear programme.
- UNSC Resolution 1929, 2010,[33] imposed additional sanctions on Iran from participating in any activities related to ballistic missiles, expanding an arms embargo and tightening restrictions on financial and shipping enterprises related to 'proliferation-sensitive activities'.
- UNSC Resolution 2049, 2012,[34] that renewed the mandate of the Iran Sanctions Committee's Panel of Experts for 13 months.

In addition to its difficulty in carrying out trade with other countries, particularly its energy exports, there were several limitations within the country. The year began on a positive note when the World Bank's (WB) Global Economic Prospects (GEP) 2012 predicted a favourable Iranian economy despite the sanctions.[35] What made the WB to adopt a positive view was the subsidy reform plan that came into effect in Iran since December 2010. To overcome the sanctions, the WB said, 'Iran made efforts to reform its income support system away from subsidies and toward better targeted social safety nets, and this has brought down the pace of prices.'[36] On a similar note, President Ahmedinejad, while presenting his annual budget to the parliament, said that the economy would see a growth of eight per cent during 2012. The president set out a US$416 billion or €316.6 billion state budget for 2012–13 fiscal year.[37]

However, with the tightening of the sanctions, Iran's economy began to limp with its inflation soaring high and currency getting eroded. For instance, the Iranian Rial slipped sharply against the dollar since the late 2011 as sanctions made Iran more vulnerable. As an immediate effect of the sanctions and the related payment difficulties, Iranian ships could no longer import grains from Ukraine, and the United Arab Emirates (UAE) asked its banks to stop financing Iran's trade with Dubai.[38] In the recent years, many Iranian companies had opened their branches in Dubai. Iranian citizens began facing problems while obtaining hard currency for travelling abroad. Tellingly, with Iranian oil business providing about one-third of its government's revenues, the sanctions would further undermine Iran's state finances.

The dwindling economy not only affected the trade but also worsened the conditions of the Iranian workers. For example, during 2011 and early 2012, workers in the textiles plants in cities such as Mazandaran and Qazvin were reported to have not been paid their salaries.[39] Added to the plight was the rising unemployment. In January 2012, it was reported that unemployment in Iran stood at 12.5 per cent, and was 29.1 per cent if those under the age of 25 were included.[40] However, Iran planned to bring down the unemployment rate by seven per cent by the end of 2012. As one of the remedies, in February, the Labour Ministry proposed to send 100,000 labourers abroad by 2015, and believed to have identified 18 host countries.[41] The Members of Parliament (MPs) criticized Labour Minister Abdol-Reza Sheykholeslami on issues such as unemployment rate, doubtable statistics, lacking investment and high-rate loans, low economic growth, etc.[42] However, towards the late 2012, unemployment rate fell by 1.2 per cent as compared to the preceding year as some 400,000 people were employed up to March 2012. Nevertheless, it still remains unclear how successful Iran would be in tackling the unemployment crisis, although the Iranian High Council of Employment, in December 2012, announced a plan for the creation of 2.1 million jobs before March 2013.[43] Despite the economic hardships, several government ministers and officials continued to present a rosy picture. In June 2012, Iran's Minister for Industry Mine and Trade Mehdi Ghazanfari said that the country is no longer dependent on oil. According to him, '21 per cent of the Gross Domestic Product takes place in the industry and mines and another 18 per cent is conducted through trade and services'.[44] This was contrary to the belief that the economy has remained succumbed to the anti-Iran sanctions, mostly on oil-based business. The worst time for Iranian economy came in October 2012 when the currency fell as much as 18 per cent (or approximately 35,000) to a record low against the US dollar.[45] For the countries which imposed sanctions on Iran, this was considered a success of their unrelenting effort to cripple the country's economy over its disputed nuclear programme. Along with this came the harshest criticism for Ahmedinejad for his mismanagement of worsening economic plight. There were accusations that the crisis was deliberately manipulated by him and commenting on the situation, an anonymous Iranian analyst said,

> What is making it worse is that the country is plagued by a power struggle between Ahmadinejad and Khamenei. So instead of handling the crisis the president is preoccupied by the arrest of his press adviser and the central bank seems completely undecided and shifts from one policy to another.[46]

As Meir Javedanfar eloquently puts it,

> Supreme Leader Ayatollah Ali Khamenei has played politics too, perhaps more so than anybody else. Part of the strength of his leadership is based on keeping different political factions divided, so that they don't become strong enough to challenge him. This has encouraged intense infighting, where each faction tries to outmanoeuvre the other with Siyasat Bazee instead of working together collectively to tackle Iran's problems.[47]

However, the Supreme Leader chastised the Western governments for expressing 'joy' over the devaluation of the Iranian currency,[48] and vowed to endure the sanctions with the continuation of the nuclear programme.

Despite all these developments, Ahmedinejad, in December 2012, reiterated his confidence of reviving the Iranian economy. He talked of a 'contingency plans' to counter the 'illegal US-engineered sanctions' that is crippling the Iranian economy.[49] The year ended with a note of condemnation over the West's imposition of sanctions on Iran for its nuclear programme.

Alongside this problem, food items were also affected by the economic sanctions. In February, Iran offered gold bullion in overseas vaults or tanker-loads of oil in return for food.[50] As a result of the sanctions, Iranian import of basic staples such as rice, cooking oil, animal feed and tea had become very difficult. Moreover, the crumbling Iranian currency further shot up the prices of meat, bread and other grains. Unable to meet the rising inflation, Iranians were reported to be giving up chicken, red meat and even sugar. For the first time, Iranian demonstrators took to the streets not for social or political reforms but over the so-called 'chicken crisis',[51] and it had become a symbol for the country's economic malaise. Another essential commodity that faced the problem of spiralling prices during 2012 was medicines. Similar to the food items, prices of basic medicines have been soaring and in some cases reported an average of 15–20 per cent rise.[52] This crisis became so rampant that there were reports of deaths due to shortage or non-availability of life-saving drugs.[53] While a major section of the society blamed the sanctions, there were others, even within the government, who accused the officials of negligence. They targeted the costly economic reforms which were launched at a time of increasing uncertainty and reduced government revenues.[54]

Other Developments

Iran had announced a radical policy change in its population policy. In mid-2012, the Supreme Leader had said that the two-decade-old policy of birth control should be ended to increase its population to 150 to 200 million. Iran's population, according to the 2011 census, has reached 75,149,669.[55] Population control during the 1990s was considered as a 'mistake' by the leader. On 1 August, the health minister announced that the budget allocated for family-planning programmes would be completely scrapped and would request for funds to support 'fertility programmes' that would look after mothers, infants and children.[56]

The above-mentioned programme raised concerns amongst some Iranian citizens. First, more than half of Iran's population is under the age of 35 and formed the base of opposition groups, including those who led the Green Revolution of 2009. Most of the ongoing popular protests in the Arab countries are carried out by the youth. Hence, enhancement of number of upcoming generation carries the risk of feeding a future political dissent.[57] Second, in a country whose economy is in shamble, population growth is a complex subject. Because of this, many Iranian couples are postponing their marriage and are reluctant to have children in an economy blighted by unemployment and inflation.[58]

Finally, in the military-security sector, Iranian Defence Ministry has started to initiate plans for export of arms and military equipment to its neighbouring and friendly countries. It is believed to be exporting military equipments to some 40 countries despite the sanctions imposed against the defence industries.[59] Iran has designed and manufactured semi-heavy and heavy weapons, military tools and equipments.

Showcasing its military might, Iran test-fired many missiles during 2012. One of the earliest tests was conducted in January 2012 when it fired long-range shore-to-sea and surface-to-surface missiles, Qader (Capable) and Nour (Light).[60] In a quick succession, several ballistic missiles were test-fired in July 2012. Further, in August 2012, amidst the growing international concern on its military capabilities, Fateh-110 was successfully test-fired by Iran.[61]

Bilateral Relations

Diplomatic relations between India and Iran were established on 15 March 1950, and were marked by 'centuries of substantive interactions between the Indus Valley and Persian civilizations'.[62] However, during the Cold War period, India–Iran relations lacked warmth as India maintained strong military links with the Union of Soviet Socialist Republics (USSR), while Iran was an ally of the US.[63] It was during this time when Indian Prime Minister Jawaharlal Nehru termed such alliances between Iran and Pakistan as 'wrong, dangerous and harmful approach',[64] and opted for NAM. Furthermore, Iran's close ties with

Pakistan during the Indo-Pakistani wars of 1965 and 1971 estranged its relations with India.

The Islamic revolution temporarily impeded any high-level political interactions but relations began to improve in the 1990s when both India and Iran added a strategic dimension to their ties. They have begun to engage intensively on areas such as commercial co-operation, science, education, infrastructural development, and military and intelligence ties.[65] In September 1993, Prime Minister Narasimha Rao visited Tehran and this was followed by visits by Hashemi Rafsanjani (April 1995), Prime Minister Atal Bihari Vajpayee (April 2001) and Mohammad Khatami (January 2003).[66] Energy remains the key component in India–Iran economic relations until today. Both also initiated the North–South transportation corridor project, with the aim of building new roads and railways in Iran, as well as to develop ports to make this route economical and efficient and an access corridor to Central Asian countries.[67]

However, political relations got a setback due to India's vote in September 2005, as well as in February 2006 and November 2009, against Iran at the IAEA over its nuclear programme. Ever since India–US signed their nuclear framework in 2005, 'Iran has become a litmus test that India has occasionally been asked to pass to satisfy U.S. policymakers.'[68] As a result, consequential issues such as oil-payment imbroglio have undermined India–Iran relations significantly, and remain true till today.

Political Relations

The highlight of the year 2012 was the visit by Prime Minister Manmohan Singh to Iran to attend the 16th summit meeting of the NAM. There were doubts about Singh attending the Tehran Summit. Towards strengthening the bilateral relations, Iranian President Mahmoud Ahmadinejad called the Indian leader and expressed his concerns over drop in India's oil imports from Iran and extended his personal invitation to the Indian leader.[69] Furthermore, in May Foreign Minister Ali Akbar Salehi visited New Delhi and invited the Indian Prime Minister to the NAM Summit. Salehi met his Indian counterpart S. M. Krishna and discussed issues related to the US sanctions on Iran and their impact on the procurement of oil from Iran. During this meeting, the Indian Foreign Minister reiterated that India's stand on the Resolutions of the

Security Council on Iran's nuclear programme should not impact bilateral commercial ties.[70]

Taking advantage of the visit, Krishna observed:

> India has always abided by the United Nation's Security Council resolutions on Iran. As far as other sanctions, those decided unilaterally or regionally, we are aware of such measures. In a globalised world, these actions can have an impact on the markets. Our commercial entities take these into account. Such measures should not impact on legitimate trade interests.[71]

The visiting dignitary acknowledged that India needs to diversify its import sources to meet the growing demands and objectives of energy security. Further, the need to enhance trade between the two countries was also discussed. Interacting with the Indian media, Salehi refuted the allegation of an Iranian hand in the attack against an Israeli diplomat in New Delhi in February 2012.[72]

In August, Indian Prime Minister visited Iran to attend the NAM summit and it was converted into a bilateral visit.[73] This happened at a time when the dust of the attack on Israeli diplomat, in which Iranian involvement was alleged, had not settled. Further, the visit showcased that India did not succumb to the international, especially American, pressures to limit its political contacts with Iran.[74] On the sidelines of the summit, Singh held two high-level meetings with Supreme Leader Ali Khamenei and President Ahmadinejad.[75] During these meetings both sides 'resolved to step up economic ties, especially in stabilising Afghanistan and shoring up Indian exports, which have suffered an imbalance with respect to Iranian exports of oil by a factor of five'.[76] Other significant areas of discussion were the need for international co-operation in combating terrorism; regional and international peace and security, particularly in Afghanistan, Syria and the Middle East.[77] Further, the Indian Prime Minister emphasized on improving the trade imbalance with Iran and both the leaders have agreed to facilitate trilateral and bilateral co-operation on the Iranian port of Chabahar, which would be a significant trade and transit route to Afghanistan and Central Asia.[78] The issue of wheat exports to Iran was on the agenda. The Indian leader also managed to meet the tiny Indian community in Iran and enquired about their well-being.[79]

While touching upon the most controversial issue, that is, the Iranian nuclear programme, the Indian Prime Minister expressed his 'hope that

Iran would work within the parameters of the P5+1 dialogue' which could ultimately yield a positive result in the interest of peace in the region.[80] India's dealings with Iran has become difficult as the latter's nuclear programme has been in a collision course with the West. This forced India to reduce its oil imports from Iran by nearly 40 per cent during mid-2012.[81]

Meanwhile, the meeting between Manmohan Singh and the Iranian Supreme Leader Ayatollah Ali Khamenei on the sideline of the summit captured wider attention. This was a very rare occasion for the Supreme Leader, to meet a foreign let alone non-Muslim dignitary. Apart from discussing bilateral matters and tensions prevailing in the region, the Supreme Leader acknowledged the role played by Mahatma Gandhi in India's freedom struggle and of Jawaharlal Nehru in establishing the NAM.[82]

Along with the Prime Minister, the External Affairs Minister Krishna also visited Tehran. The Indian Foreign Minister and his Iranian counterpart focused on enhancing bilateral trade and economy, and also the payment mechanism for India's oil imports from Iran.[83] Like the Indian leaders, similar forward-looking statements were also made by ministers of the host country. For example, Iranian Economy Minister Shamseddin Hosseini was very positive in saying that India would maintain its energy ties with the Islamic Republic. In his words,

> Iran and India had some economic bilateral meetings during the NAM meeting. India considers Iran as an energy-producing source and it is so vigilant in using Iran as one of its energy sources. The Indian government bravely announced several times that it will constantly continue its energy trade with Iran.[84]

There were a number of other political contacts between the two sides during 2012. In January, Deputy Minister of Road and Urban Development Shahriar Afandizadeh visited India to attend the meeting on the International North South Transport Corridor (INSTC) project, and pitched for 'well develop facilitation for transit of goods in INSTC'.[85] This was followed by the visit of Foreign Minister Ali Akbar Salehi in May to invite the Prime Minister for the NAM summit.

In October, Energy Minister Majid Namjoo was on a four-day visit to New Delhi when the Western sanctions were squeezing the Iranian economy. During the visit, the Minister expressed his desire to establish Indo–Iranian joint ventures in the field of renewable energy, power, pharmaceuticals, agriculture and food processing.[86] He had stressed on the lucrative business opportunities with the Iranian private sectors which he said were unaffected by western sanctions. Furthermore, cooperation between India and Iran in hydroelectric energy sector was well-highlighted by him wherein he mentioned the feasibility of exporting approximately 4,000 megawatts of electricity to India.[87]

During 29 October and 2 November 2012, the 12th session of Indian Ocean Rim Association for Regional Cooperation (IOR-ARC) was held in Gurgaon. Speaking at this forum, the Iranian Deputy Foreign Minister Mohammad Mehdi Akhondzadeh extended his gratitude to the Government of India. He also expressed confidence that such meeting would certainly contribute to the efforts of enhancing regional co-operation and to the promotion of the Association.[88]

The Indian Minister of New and Renewable Energy Farooq Abdullah visited Tehran in March and during his meeting with President Ahmadinejad, both sides discussed the possible enhancement of bilateral economic co-operation, particularly in the field of renewable energy.[89] The Deputy National Security Advisor Latha Reddy visited Iran in May 2012 and had discussions with her Iranian counterpart Ali Bagheri and Iranian officials.[90] Apart from the energy-related talks, the Iranian leaders expressed their desires for co-operation with India for stability in the Persian Gulf region.[91] While one witnessed successful political interactions between India and Iran, an incident in late 2012 somehow undermined the overall relations. The 17th round of Indo–Iranian Joint Commission Meeting which was scheduled for 19 November 2012 in Tehran was postponed as it coincided with the Indian parliament session.[92] The media speculated that possible controversy over Salman Khurshid visiting Iran as his first 'port of call' as Foreign Minister was the reason for the postponement.[93]

Economic Relations

Economic relations have been the mainstay of the Indo–Iranian relations. Items exported by India to Iran included dairy products, coffee, tea, spices, sugar, chemicals, pharmaceutical products, rubber, ceramic products, electrical items, aircrafts parts, etc. Iran's exports included sea products, oil seeds, medicinal plants, beverages, textile flooring coverings, iron and steel, machineries, etc. Significance of this relationship is evidenced by the figures given below for the period 2011–12.

During the period 2011–12, India's export value to Iran was estimated to be about US$2,411.33 million, or 3.27 per cent less than in 2010–11 which was US$2,492.90 million.[94] While imports from Iran for the same period stood at US$13,556.71 million, or growth by 24.05 per cent from US$10,928.21 million during 2010–11. The trend in India–Iran bilateral trade for the last three years is visible from Table 3.1 and Figure 3.1.

In 2012, India and Iran engaged considerably to promote their bilateral trade. To the possible extent, both sides tried to sideline the oil-payment imbroglio, and most importantly the impact of Western sanctions on their energy relations. Constant efforts made were evidenced by the reciprocal visits of the trade delegations between India and Iran during this year. Some of the most important discussions revolved around the exploration of potential trade opportunities in non-oil items. In early March 2012, an Indian trade delegation, led by the Joint Secretary in the Commerce Ministry Arvind Mehta visited Iran to explore avenues for potential trade co-operation. During this visit, India and Iran pledged to raise their bilateral trade figure to US$25 billion by 2014.[95] In a reciprocal visit to further explore trade opportunities, a 56-member Iranian trade delegation visited India in May 2012. Both the countries agreed to intensify their bilateral trade on items which are not under sanctions.

Table 3.1
India–Iran Bilateral Trade (in US$ Million)

	2009–10	2010–11	2011–12
Exports	1,853.17	2,492.90	2,411.33
Imports	11,540.85	10,928.21	13,556.71
Total trade	13,394.01	13,421.12	15,968.03
Share of Iran in total trade	2.87	2.16	2.01

Source: Adapted from Director General of Foreign Trade, New Delhi, http://www.dgft.gov.in

Figure 3.1
India–Iran Bilateral Trade

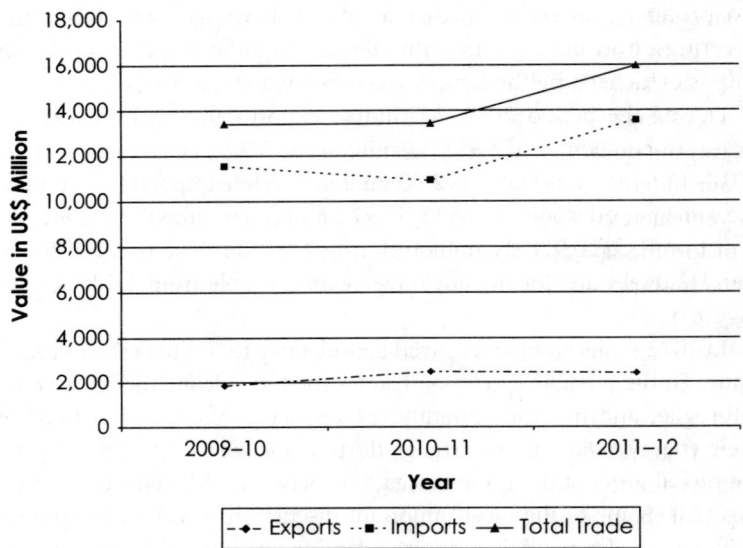

Source: Adapted from Director General of Foreign Trade, New Delhi, http://www.dgft.gov.in

This coincided with the visit of US Secretary of State Hillary Clinton to New Delhi. The visiting Iranian team met with the members from India's Federation of Indian Export Organisations (FIEO), Associated Chambers of Commerce and Industry of India (ASSOCHAM) and Federation of Indian Chambers of Commerce and Industry (FICCI). The meeting focused on exports of items such as agro and allied products, pharmaceuticals, engineering, shipping, banking, petroleum products polymer, textile, as well as e-commerce.[96] Issues related to setting up of branches of Iranian banks in India were also addressed. Such initiative would not only ease Indian export to Iran, mainly to pay for the oil, but also give an opportunity to the latter to approach a wider section of the Indian industry.

In a move to bolster trade with Iran, in April 2012 India offered tax incentives to exporters for sales in rupees to Iran.[97] This was done to avoid difficulties while trading amid the existing US sanctions. These efforts to safeguard non-oil trade against international pressures have succeeded to certain extent as evident from new avenues of trade emerging between the two countries. As a non-oil trade item, in April 2012, Iran enhanced its purchase of soy meal from India, taking up to 275,000 tonnes in various deals signed.[98] India was also planning to export textiles to Iran in addition to the existing opportunities in exporting items such as sugar, rice and wheat. In October, after months of negotiations regarding quality issues, Iran agreed to import 200,000 tonnes of wheat from India.[99] Given the huge potential, export of foodgrains to Iran is a very lucrative field which is being eyed by Indian exporters. Iran is already the largest importer of Indian basmati rice with total exports, mostly shipped through Dubai, reaching about one million tonnes during 2011–12.[100]

Another very important trade item was pharmaceuticals, with India currently exporting about US$51 million worth of drugs to Iran.[101] Sugar and tea were the other major items exported to Iran, and many new export agreements were clinched during 2012.[102] The fact that trade in these commodities was flourishing despite the sanctions barrier augurs well for the bilateral non-oil trade.

Energy Relations

Energy is the main locomotive for the Indo–Iranian relations but considering the current scenario, this has become one of the most important issues that have undermined the bilateral relations. This is well attributed to oil-payment imbroglio, mainly due to the US pressure. During 2011–12, Indian purchased from Iran crude oil worth US$13.5 billion, or 17.5–18 million tonnes[103] (Tables 3.2 and 3.3 and Figure 3.2).

Considering the rising energy demands in the country, India would certainly like to enhance its interactions with the Iranian energy sectors. However, partially due to the aforementioned pressure, India has shelved its plans for further investments. As a result, Iran's efforts to sell extra volumes of oil to Indian refiners on long-term credits have become futile as the Indian government ordered the refineries to reduce import by 10 to 15 per cent.[104] This fluctuation in the supply-and-demand of energy has become a major irritant between India and Iran. On the

Table 3.2
Share of Oil in India's Imports from Iran (in US$ Million)

Year	Oil imports from Iran	Total oil imports	Iranian share in total oil imports	Imports from Iran	Per cent of oil in imports from Iran
2009–10	10,362.04	96,321.16	10.76	11,540.85	89.79
2010–11	9,377.88	115,929.06	8.09	10,928.21	85.81
2011–12	11,528.97	172,753.97	6.67	13,556.71	85.04

Source: Adapted from Director General of Foreign Trade, New Delhi, http://www.dgft.gov.in

Table 3.3
India's Energy Imports from Iran (in US$ Million)

	2009–10	2010–11	2011–12
Energy imports from Iran	10,362.04	9,377.88	11,528.97
Total energy imports	96,321.12	**115,929.02**	172,753.92
Total imports from the Persian Gulf	55,904.14	66,688.4	103,915.24
Share in total imports (in per cent)	10.76	8.09	6.67
Share in imports from Persian Gulf (in per cent)	18.53	14.06	11.09

Source: Adapted from Director General of Foreign Trade, New Delhi, http://www.dgft.gov.in

contrary, in the words of one analyst, 'New Delhi hopes that the gradual steps it is taking to reduce its reliance on Iran will ameliorate some of the concerns in Washington about India's reliability as a partner in managing the issue of Iranian nuclear programme.'[105]

The year 2012 began with the initiatives to solve the oil-payment issue. As the US was tightening the sanctions, India began exploring the possibility of paying for the Iranian oil in Indian rupees. This was believed to have been discussed during the visit of the Indian delegation to Iran during mid-January 2012. Further, Indian National Security Advisor (NSA) Shivshankar Menon monitored the matter of payment constantly. It was also believed that the Indian government made certain moves to get the US administration on board while discussing the supply of crude oil from Iran.[106]

Figure 3.2
Share of Oil in India's Total Imports from Iran

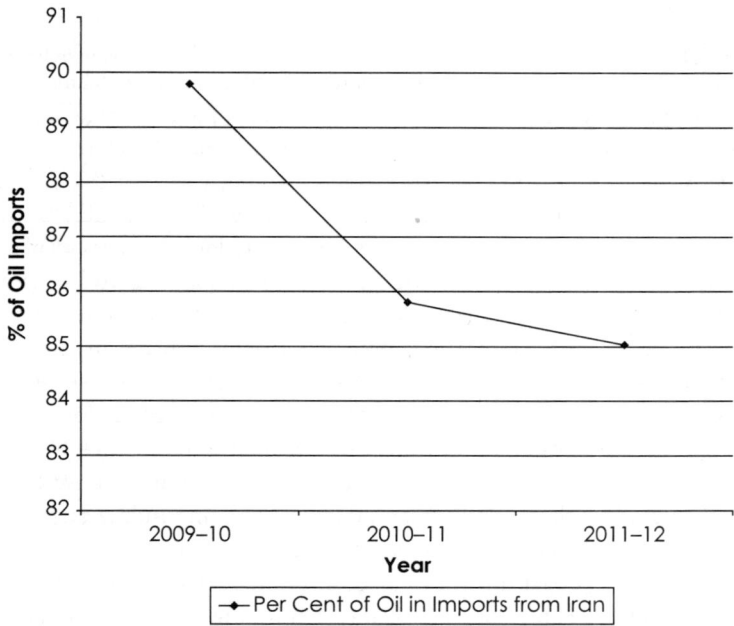

Source: Adapted from Director General of Foreign Trade, New Delhi, http://www.dgft.gov.in

Since late 2010, India has been finding it difficult to settle the payment for its oil imports from Iran. Under US pressure, in December 2010, the Reserve Bank of India cancelled the oil payment to Iran through the Asian Clearing Union (ACU).[107] Subsequently, it tried to settle the payments through Turkey's Hallbank and Germany's EIH Bank.[108] This problem has forced Prime Minister Manmohan Singh to explore the possibility of payments through Russian Rouble during his meeting with the Russian President, Dmitry Medvedev, in December 2011.[109] Numerous alternatives have been suggested since then. One of the initial suggestions was to open a Rupee account for the National Iranian Oil Company (NIOC) in an Indian bank, which would make payments for oil.[110] For its part Iran suggested payments in Yen, as it was not enthusiastic regarding Rupee payments, given the lesser monetary value as compared to the Yen.[111] India also looked at the option of paying for Iranian crude through Gazprombank OJSC of Russia.

While the issue remained intractable, Iran continued to promote oil exports in defiance of the sanctions. In an effort to overcome the sanctions, Iran offered to sell oil to potential customers, including India, at zero per cent interest for six months.[112] Issue of energy trade and US sanctions dominated the course of discussion during Foreign Minister Salehi's visit to India in May 2012. Iran's credibility as a reliable partner for India on matters of energy security was well-highlighted by the Iranian minister. However, the choice for India to look for other available energy sources was also acknowledged during the meeting. In fact, India did finally decide to lessen its dependence on the troublesome Iranian imports and started importing more from other sources in the Gulf region and beyond. Consequently, Iran lost its position as the second largest suppliers of oil to India and imports from Iran came down from 18.5 million tonnes in 2010–11 to 17.44 million tonnes in 2011–12.[113]

While there were more efforts to resolve the payments and sanctions issue, including the use of Iranian tankers[114] or using Indian tankers to circumvent the issue of insurance and indemnity cover,[115] these efforts proved to be stopgap measures at best. From July 2012, Indian companies such as Hindustan Petroleum, Mangalore Refinery and Petrochemicals Ltd. (MRPL) and Essar Oil started using Iranian tankers.[116] However, this route of importing oil from Iran was severely affected with the ban on Irano-Hind Shipping Company, the Indo–Iranian joint venture company involved in oil trade.[117] Similarly, MRPL was also affected by sanctions when the tankers it was utilizing to import Iranian crude failed to get international insurance clearances.[118] Though Indian officials, including Petroleum Minister S. Jaipal Reddy continued to assert that India has not succumbed to US pressure and that India was only following sanctions imposed by the UN and not those of the US/EU,[119] there was a sharp decline in crude imports from Iran. The volume of crude import from Iran was likely to reduce by 12 per cent in 2012 as compared to 2011.[120] On the sidelines of Petrotech 2012 Conference held in New Delhi in October, India's Petroleum Minister made it clear that India was not likely to either reduce or increase crude imports from Iran.[121] Such a statement was taken as 'defying' the sanctions imposed by the Western countries. Further, the Minister also reiterated India's compulsion to rely on Iranian oil to thwart any energy crisis in the country. However, in November 2012, Iran's new Indian client HPCL-Mittal Energy Ltd., known as HMEL, planned to stop importing Iranian oil.[122]

Sanctions were not the only issue to plague Indian import of Iranian crude. The issue of high prices of Iranian oil resurfaced in December 2012. India has planned to reduce the already fluctuating Iranian oil import during 2013, particularly if the prices do not get lowered. The reduction is likely to be about 10 per cent to 15 per cent.[123]

While both the countries were at loggerheads regarding the oil imports, a new opportunity for co-operation was under consideration. In October 2012, Iranian energy minister Namjoo expressed his desire to export 4,000 megawatts of electricity to India. This has been taken as an initiative to expand beyond oil-driven relations,[124] particularly after the Iran–Pakistan–India (IPI) pipeline has been in limbo. A framework for such co-operation was laid out during Farooq Abdullah's visit to Iran in March 2012. Preliminary round of discussion on issues such as industries, oil, gas and green fuels took place during the meeting between Indian Ambassador to Iran D. P. Srivastava and Iran's head of Industrial Development and Renovation Organisation (IDRO) Majid Hedayat, in January 2012. Acknowledging India's excellence in the field of renewable energies, Iran would like to co-operate for the development of similar energy source in its country.

In October 2012, Iranian Deputy Foreign Minister for Asia Abbas Araqchi brought up the issue of the natural gas pipeline which has not been heading anywhere. He was of the view that the pipeline would surely be in India's interest for which New Delhi needs to make up its mind. In his words, '[W]e and Pakistan are working on it and we are serious about it. Our part is almost finished and now we are helping Pakistan in finishing their part as well.'[125]

Given the enormous complexities involved, Indian Foreign Minister Salman Khurshid talked about reviewing India's dependence on Iranian oil for the year 2013. Speaking on the sidelines of a seminar conducted by the Confederation of Indian Industry (CII), in December 2012, he said, 'I think we are well within the structure of US waiver. The bottom line of the conditions of the waiver has been satisfied which is you should not increase dependency on it.'[126] According to him, India was in compliance with the UN sanctions on Iran, and was different from other countries because of the 'principled position' it took. Unsurprisingly, the direct US pressure to reduce India's oil import from Iran was ignored.

Sociocultural Relations

As was the case during 2011, cultural relations between India and Iran were not undermined by the row over oil payment and other political differences due to the sanctions. Both the countries managed to bridge the relations, especially in the field of education, film, art and literature, etc. In a move to expand the bilateral relations, the Iranian Artists Forum (IAF) hosted the India–Iran Cultural week in Tehran between 7 and 12 June 2012. During this event, programmes such as seminars on cultural, literary and architectural commonalities between the two countries were conducted.[127] In August 2012, Indian Prime Minister's wife Gursharan Kaur met the small Indian community in Iran. She also gave grants of 20 million rupees (US$4 million) for the upkeep of Tehran's new Kendriya Vidyalaya (KV), and two million rupees (US$40,000) for running the Gurdwara.[128] What remained to be the most interesting story of her visit was the discussion over the possible connection between Iran and India's Sikhism. Cultural relations have also forayed into the field of cinema. During 2012, many Iranian films were showcased in various Indian film festivals and were well-appreciated.

Issues and Problems

In addition to the energy-related issues, there were other problems that had undermined the Indo–Iranian relations in 2012. Most of these issues were of utmost concerns to both the governments. While on one hand India and Iran are trying unrelentingly to improve civilian interactions, few instances involving Iranian students in India made important headlines throughout the year. As early as in January 2012, a 21-year-old Iranian student, Hussain Afzali, was arrested in Mysore for allegedly committing forgery.[129] Such issues raised eyebrows and created suspicions over foreign students coming to pursue education in India. Shortly after this, in February 2012, four Indian students were expelled from Iran, but no further information was available on this. However, such retaliatory act was also taken as a result of the rupture between India and Iran, apart from the oil issue.[130]

In a similar incident, in April 2012, Hamid Kashkouli, an Iranian doctoral candidate of University of Pune, was deported to Iran as he was reportedly found spying on the Chabad House and other Jewish and Israeli targets in Pune.[131] Another disturbing incident that happened was the arrest of Milad Kharid Shahidi, an Iranian research scholar, by the Delhi Police (DP) after he was found taking photographs near the Israeli Embassy in New Delhi.[132]

Alongside this, illegal activities such as narcotic trade were found to be carried out by Iranian students. In June 2012, a 22-year-old Iranian student, Mohammed Mahmud Azarmehar, was deported to Iran due to alleged links with narcotic trade and for possessing 'objectionable documents'.[133] The Indian community in Iran raised a few concerns during the Prime Minister's visit. One of the most important issues was the difficulty in owning property or getting business licences in Iran.[134] They expressed their fear over the gradual decline in the numbers of the community.

The issue over ban on wheat import also caught attention in April 2012. In a move to facilitate wheat export to Iran, New Delhi had a discussion with Tehran for lifting the 16-year-old ban on importing Indian wheat.[135] While the Iranian authorities are keen on importing the same, they expressed their concerns over the quality of wheat.[136]

Another setback was the decline of the security clearance by India's Ministry of Home Affairs (MHA) for three Iranian banks (Parsian Bank, Bank Pasargad and Eghtesad-e-Novin Bank) which wanted to open branches in India. While these banks could have eased trade relations between India and Iran, there was also fear of using them for money laundering and terror financing.[137] This further added to the payment and other trade-related issues, especially when both the countries aspire to reach the target of 15.5 million tonnes in 2012–13 for Iranian crude oil import. In September 2012, Indian Finance Ministry again declined permission to Parsian Bank to open its branch. Payment-row over Basmati exports to Iran was another issue. In November 2012, reports over reworked Iranian exchange rate raised concerns with the Indian traders. Under the new rate, rice importers in Iran will 'have access to the open market exchange rate with a 2% discount'.[138]

External Players

The US: The US–Iran relations are characterized by the tensions over the latter's nuclear programme and the US leading the international sanctions regime aimed at forcing Iran into complying fully with the IAEA regulations. With the escalating US–Iran disputes, New Delhi 'is caught in the middle'.[139] While Iran is trying to defy the US-led sanctions on its oil exports, the US pressure on Iranian crude importers was having an effect on Iran's bilateral relations as well, including with India. In January 2012, India announced 'Oil for Projects' scheme to continue importing Iranian oil against the US sanctions. Such measures enticed harsh criticisms from the US.[140] Reacting to this indifferent attitude towards sanctions, the US talked of imposing appropriate and harder actions against India that would cripple their bilateral trade. While the sanctions were applicable on strategic items such crude oil, the US, in February 2012, said that rice trade between India and Iran would not be affected.[141] Items such as food, chemicals and medical devices were exempted from American sanctions.

In February India became a major irritant factor for the US in its effort to cripple Iranian economy through sanctions. The news of India continuing with its Iranian crude oil import and that of the business delegation visiting Iran irked the US.[142] Washington's displeasure was exacerbated and could be felt in the words of R. Nicholas Burns,

> India's decision to walk out of step with the international community on Iran isn't just a slap in the face for the U.S.—it raises questions about its ability to lead…the Indian government is now actively impeding the construction of the strategic relationship it says it wants with the United States.[143]

Such statement was an overtone of American anger and frustrations.

Earlier, in March the US Secretary of State Hillary Clinton was reported to have expressed her satisfaction over steps taken by India to reduce Iranian oil imports. However, in March 2012, US did not exempt Iran's two top crude oil importers, India and China, from financial sanctions imposed on other customers. The exempted countries[144] were believed to have drastically reduced their Iranian energy imports. With the unfolding of such events one could always assume the inevitable US pressure that loomed large over India–Iran energy relations.[145] Simultaneously, the

US attempted to efface these talks over their pressure on India. The US Undersecretary of State for Political Affairs, Wendy Sherman, said in New Delhi, 'Washington did not want to jeopardise India's energy security by asking it to reduce its dependence on Iranian oil, but made it clear that New Delhi was expected to join the West's attempts to pressure Tehran into accepting conditions on the nuclear issue.'[146]

In June Indian energy planners felt a relief when the Obama administration announced that India has been exempted from Iranian oil sanctions, along with six other countries.[147] With this, the US hoped that India would scale down its Iranian oil imports in the succeeding years. However, experts have expressed that, despite such flexibility, 'Iran continues to cast a pall over an otherwise brightening US-India relationship.'[148] In August the US closely monitored Indian Prime Minister's visit to Iran to attend the NAM summit. As mentioned above, India was expected to convey the message of international concern to Tehran for its nuclear programme. The same tone was reiterated when the US State Department Deputy Secretary, William Burns, met Indian NSA and Foreign Secretary, in October 2012. This was considered as the first time when the US openly asked New Delhi to intervene with Iran.[149]

Interestingly, India–Iran energy relations also figured during the 2012 US election campaigns. Dov Zakheim, a senior defence advisor to the US presidential candidate, Mitt Romney, criticized the June 2012 exemption granted to India, and said that New Delhi should stop buying Iranian oil.[150] Around this time, there was a fear that new sanctions which could be unleashed after the US presidential election in November might block India's dollar payments to Iran using Turkey's Hallbank.[151] Eventually, 2012 ended on a positive note with regard to the US factor in Indo-Iranian energy ties. The US once again extended the exemptions granted to India, mainly because of its significant decline in the oil import from Iran. This was the second time that India received such waiver from the US under the Iranian Sanctions Act.[152] Considering these developments, one can infer that the US still remains as a major factor in the Indo–Iranian relations.

China: During the year 2012, Sino–Iranian relations did not remain to be a major challenge to India's own engagement with Iran. However, both the countries pledged to expand their bilateral trade. Trade between the two countries is currently concentrated in Iran's energy exports to China, while the main machinery, textiles and consumer goods, are exported from China. Both the countries have set the target of US$100 billion in bilateral trade,[153] which in 2012 was about US$50 billion. An issue for possible concern for India is the Chinese agreement to build a gas pipeline between Iran and Pakistan. The estimated cost for this pipeline on the Pakistani side is about US$1.2 billion.[154] When this project gets through, it could cater to much of Pakistan's energy problems. As it was the case with India, the sanction issue also hit the Iran–China relations during early 2012. In January 2012, China reduced its Iranian oil import by about 285,000 barrels per day.[155] However, with the resolving of payment issue during mid-2012, Iran–China energy relations were believed to have been improved despite the US sanctions.[156]

Pakistan: Iran and Pakistan continued to share cordial relations during the year 2012. Besides their historical, religious and cultural affinity, economic relations remained to be one of the most important drivers of the relations. In 2012, the bilateral trade was estimated to be about US$3 billion.[157] Pakistan's major imports from Iran consisted of petroleum, chemical compounds, chemical material and products, machinery and its parts, and ores, while exports from Pakistan to Iran included rice, fruit, chemical material and products, cotton fabric and manufactures of non-ferrous metals.[158] What remained to be a concern for India in 2012 was the initiative taken up by Pakistan and Iran to expand the natural gas pipeline. As early as March 2012, Pakistani Foreign Minister Hina Rabbani Khar said that construction of such a pipeline would be in the utmost national interest of Pakistan.[159] This project is aimed at exporting approximately 21.5 million cubic metres daily (or 8.7 billion cubic metres per year) of Iranian natural gas to Pakistan.[160] Upon acknowledging the problems between India and Pakistan over gas pipeline, Iran, in October 2012, urged the two nations to settle the differences. Pakistan is very optimistic that the pipeline would begin supplying 750 million cubic feet of gas per day (MMCFD) starting from December 2014.[161]

In the field on non-oil trade, especially wheat, India is likely to be a factor in Iran–Pakistan relations. India, in 2012, planned to entice the Iranian wheat market at a much lower price than Pakistan. For instance,

India, which is world's second-largest wheat producer, was gearing up to export grain to Iran at US$280 a tonne, free on board, as compared to US$290–300 per tonne for Pakistani wheat.[162] However, efforts were underway to enhance their bilateral trade, including wheat and rice, and this could boost if both sign a Free Trade Agreement (FTA). On the political front, Iran was asked to play its part in the settlement of India–Pakistan dispute over Kashmir.[163] Overall, Pakistan did not remain a major obstacle in India–Iran relations in 2012.

Israel: Apart from the aforementioned issues, the attack on the Israeli diplomat, Tal Yehoshua Koren, in New Delhi on 13 February 2012, became the most controversial issue involving India, Iran and Israel. The blame game went for a long time, and India had to walk a tightrope, while maintaining its relations with both the Middle Eastern countries.[164] It was alleged that Iranian hands were behind this ill-fated incident. Right after the incident, Indian Foreign Ministry informed the Iranian Ambassador about these developments and asked for co-operation in bringing to justice those involved in such 'dastardly attack'.[165] India, initially, refrained from siding with the US and Israel that the attack was carried out by Iran[166] and refused to name any country or group. At this juncture, there were also fears of having an impact on Indo–Iranian trade. The president of the All India Rice Exporters' Association said, '[A]ttack on the wife of an Israeli diplomat in New Delhi will damage trade with Iran and may complicate efforts to resolve an impasse over Iranian defaults on payments for rice imports worth around $150 million.'[167] However, the Indian Commerce Minister Anand Sharma, in February 2012, ruled out any negative impact on the bilateral trade.[168] For instance, an 80-member delegation visited Tehran in March 2012 to explore opportunities for business.

In the words of one analyst,

> Tehran's purported role in a bomb attack on an Israeli embassy vehicle in New Delhi and the use of India as a platform for such an attack would further intensify pressure on India to curtail its trade relationship with Iran. Yet given the domestic political situation shaped by the coming state and national elections and growing energy needs, and a looming void in Afghanistan after the US departure, New Delhi isn't in a position to jettison Tehran completely in the immediate future.[169]

In connection with the attack, an Indian journalist, Syed Mohammed Ahmad Kazmi, who was reported to be working for an Iranian publication was arrested in New Delhi in March 2012. Along with him, three more Iranian suspects were identified, namely, Houshang Afshar Irani, Seyed Ali Mahdian and Mohammad Reza Abolghasemi.[170]

To speed up the probe on the attack, New Delhi decided on sending a DP team to Iran where the officials would visit the houses of the three accused, with the help of the Tehran authorities.[171] Amid this attempt, the visiting Iranian Foreign Minister refuted the allegations and remained non-committal on the approval of Indian team going to Iran. However, in early August 2012, a two-member DP team visited Iran but returned empty handed as they could not gather concrete information on the suspected Iranians. It should also be noted that the DP, earlier in July 2012, summed up by saying that the Iranian suspects were members of the Iranian Revolutionary Guard Corps.[172] Till the end of 2012, India and Iran failed to come up with a solution to this problem and it remains as an issue to be sorted out. With this, questions have been raised regarding India's balancing act with Iran and Israel wherein such attacks on Indian soil were highly condemned. There were also concerns as to whether the Middle Eastern conflict between Israel and Iran has spilled over the Indian territory.

Challenges

Since a few years, Indo–Iranian relations have been tangled by various challenges. This is very evident from the aforementioned developments where issues like payment imbroglio, Western sanctions, etc., have undermined the bilateral ties. For the moment, fluctuation in the Iranian energy supply remains as a major challenge to their bilateral relations. These unresolved issues could transform the relations, once described as 'strategic', to an all-time 'new low'.[173] Besides, there are other challenges which could be met effectively by a constant engagement between India and Iran, despite all the odds.

One of the most important challenges is the timely completion of the transportation network, also known as International North–South Corridor. India has been making concerted efforts to reach the Central

Asian nations through Iran. This is a project that would link India's west coast with Bandar Abbas in Iran, and other important ports in Central Asia and Russia. India and Iran have agreed to co-operate by taking up of projects such as constructions of railways and road links. Further, India is believed to be eyeing other similar projects such as Kazakhstan–Turkmenistan Corridor, a 677-km railway line connecting these countries with Iran and the Persian Gulf.[174]

The stalled energy pipeline remains a tremendous challenge between India and Iran. In October 2012, the Vice President of the Islamic Republic of Iran, Mohammad-Javad Mohammadizadeh, expressed Iran's readiness to bring the pipeline project up to the Indian border.[175] He laid emphasis on the fact that India and Iran need to sort out the problems due to which the project has been delayed. Looking into the present deteriorating relations between India and Pakistan, it will be an arduous task for both to come to a viable solution. The rising problem of sea piracy in the Indian Ocean is another challenge where India and Iran can work together effectively. Commander Rear Admiral Habibollah Sayyari, sent out a strong message of protecting against sea piracy in the ocean.[176] As sea is a medium for most of the Indo-Iranian trade, forging a better maritime co-operation should be in their best interests. Besides all these challenges, what remains to be the biggest one is the ability to freely navigate their bilateral relations without any intervention, or interference from 'external powers'.[177]

Notes

1. Seyed Mehdi Nabizadeh, 'India-Iran Relations: Past, Present and Future', *IPCS Special Report, No. 135*, 6 September 2012, http://www.ipcs.org/pdf_file/issue/SR-135-Iranian-Ambassadors-Address.pdf
2. Ibid.
3. C. Christine Fair, 'Indo-Iranian Relations: Prospects for Bilateral Cooperation Post 9-11', in Robert M. Hathaway et al., 'The "Strategic" Partnership between India and Iran', *Asian ProgrammeSpecial Report*, no. 20 (Washington: Woodrow Wilson Centre, 2004), 8, http://www.wilsoncenter.org/publication/the-strategic-partnership-between-india-and-iran-pdf (retrieved on 14 April 2014).
4. Donald L. Berlin, 'India-Iran Relations: A Deepening Entente', *Asia's Bilateral Relations*, Asia-Pacific Centre for Security Studies, 2004, 2, http://www.

apcss.org/Publications/SAS/AsiaBilateralRelations/India-IranRelationsBerlin.pdf (retrieved on 14 April 2014).

5. 'Iran Profile', *BBC*, 9 April 2013, http://www.bbc.co.uk/news/world-middle-east-14541327 (retrieved on 14 April 2014).

6. Inter-parliamentary Union Report of 2004 Election Results, Iran, http://www.ipu.org/parline-e/reports/arc/2149_04.htm (retrieved on 14 April 2014). For an analysis, see, Mahan Abedin, 'Iran after the Elections', *Middle East Intelligence Bulletin* 6, no. 2/3(2004), http://www.meforum.org/meib/articles/0402_iran1.htm (retrieved on 14 April 2014).

7. For the 2009 election results, see, 'The Iranian Election Results, by Province', *The Guardian*, 22 June 2009, http://www.guardian.co.uk/news/datablog/2009/jun/15/iran1 (retrieved on 14 April 2014).

8. 'Ahmedinejad Challenged for Control of Iran's Economy', *The Guardian*, 7 March 2007, http://www.guardian.co.uk/world/2007/mar/07/iran.roberttait (retrieved on 14 April 2014).

9. Hossein Askari, 'Iran on the Edge', *Foreign Policy*, 3 November 2009, http://www.foreignpolicy.com/articles/2009/11/03/iran_on_the_edge (retrieved on 14 April 2014).

10. 'US Imposed Tough Sanctions on Iran', *The Guardian*, 25 June 2010, http://www.guardian.co.uk/world/2010/jun/25/us-imposes-tough-sanctions-iran (retrieved on 14 April 2014).

11. 'Iranian Election Could Be Test for Women's Rights', *CNN*, 11 June 2009. Zahra Rahnavard, wife of reformist candidate Mir Hossein Moussavi, strongly supported women's participation in the Iranian politics alongside men. http://edition.cnn.com/2009/WORLD/meast/06/11/iran.election.women/ (retrieved on 14 April 2014).

12. 'Iranians Protest Bill on Rights of Women', *The New York Times*, 17 February 2010, http://www.nytimes.com/2010/02/18/world/middleeast/18iran.html (retrieved on 14 April 2014).

13. Ibid.

14. 'Social Media Gives Woman a Voice in Iran', *The Guardian*, 22 September 2011, http://www.guardian.co.uk/lifeandstyle/2011/sep/22/social-media-women-iran (retrieved on 14 April 2014).

15. 'In Election-season Iran, Domestic Politics Trump Fear of Israeli Attack', *Haaretz*, 15 February 2012. http://www.haaretz.com/print-edition/features/in-election-season-iran-domestic-politics-trump-fear-of-israeli-attack-1.412949 (retrieved on 14 April 2014).

16. 'Tehran's Domestic Politics Are Torn Ahead of March Election', *The National*, 2 January 2012, http://www.thenational.ae/thenationalconversation/comment/tehrans-domestic-politics-are-torn-ahead-of-march-election (retrieved on 14 April 2014).

17. 'Iran's 9th Majlis Elections Begin', *Press TV*, 2 March 2012, http://www.presstv.ir/detail/229533.html (retrieved on 14 April 2014).

18. For the 2012 election results, see 'Iran Election Watch 2012: Main Principalist Groups Emerge with Weak Majority', *Iran Politik,* The Iran Political Analysis Project, 7 May 2012, http://www.iranpolitik.com/2012/05/07/guide-to-iranian-politics/iran-election-watch-2012-main-principalist-groups-emerge-weak-majority/ (retrieved on 14 April 2014).

19. 'Iran Elections 2012: Ahmadinejad Routed by Rivals', *The Huffington Post,* 5 May 2012, http://www.huffingtonpost.com/2012/05/05/iran-elections-2012-ahmadinejad_n_1483744.html (retrieved on 14 April 2014).

20. 'Reappointing Hashemi Rafsanjani as the Expediency Council presidency', *The Iran Project,* 14 March 2012, http://theiranproject.com/blog/2012/03/14/reappointing-hashemi-rafsanjani-as-the-expediency-council-presidency/ (retrieved on 14 April 2014).

21. 'Iran Universities Reportedly Ban Women', *The Huffington Post,* 21 July 2012, http://www.huffingtonpost.com/2012/08/21/iran-universities-women-en-ban_n_1819281.html (retrieved on 14 April 2014).

22. 'Iran Sacks Sole Female Minister Dastjerdi from Health Post', *BBC News,* 27 December 2012, http://www.bbc.co.uk/news/world-middle-east-20853142 (retrieved on 14 April 2014).

23. 'Iran MPs to Mull Draft Law on Women's Right to Travel', *AzerNews,* 16 November 2012, http://www.azernews.az/region/46323.html (retrieved on 14 April 2014).

24. 'Iran NAM Sends Message of Peace', *Tehran Times,* 25 August 2012, http://www.tehrantimes.com/component/content/article/84-perspectives/100837-iran-nam-summit-sends-message-of-peace (retrieved on 14 April 2014).

25. 'High NAM Presence, Diplomatic Triumph for Iran: Analyst', *Press TV,* 27 August 2012, http://www.presstv.ir/detail/2012/08/27/258371/nam-presence-iran-diplomatic-triumph/ (retrieved on 14 April 2014).

26. 'NAM Showed Israel Isolated, Not Iran', *Press TV,* 31 August 2012, http://www.presstv.ir/detail/2012/08/31/259093/nam-showed-israel-isolated-not-iran/ (retrieved on 14 April 2014).

27. Toni Johnson and Greg Bruno, 'The Lengthening List of Iran Sanctions', *Backgrounder,* Council on Foreign Relations, 31 July 2012, http://www.cfr.org/iran/lengthening-list-iran-sanctions/p20258?cid=ppc-Google-iran_sanctions_backgrounder&gclid=CJqktqqiuLYCFVEf6wodN10Akg (retrieved on 14 April 2014).

28. Kenneth Katzman, 'The Iran-Libya Sanctions Act', *CRS Report for Congress,* 3 April 2006, http://fpc.state.gov/documents/organization/64937.pdf (retrieved on 14 April 2014).

29. United Nations Security Council Resolution 1696, News and Media Division, Security Council, 31 July 2006, http://www.un.org/News/Press/docs/2006/sc8792.doc.htm (retrieved on 14 April 2014).

30. United Nations Security Council Resolution 1737, News and Media Division, Security Council, 23 December 2006, http://www.un.org/News/Press/docs/2006/sc8928.doc.htm (retrieved on 14 April 2014).

31. United Nations Security Council Resolution 1747, News Centre, International Atomic Energy Agency, 24 March 2007, http://www.iaea.org/newscenter/focus/iaeairan/unsc_res1747-2007.pdf (retrieved on 14 April 2014).

32. United Nations Security Council Resolution 1803, News Centre, International Atomic Energy Agency, 3 March 2008, http://www.iaea.org/newscenter/focus/iaeairan/unsc_res1803-2008.pdf (retrieved on 14 April 2014).

33. United Nations Security Council Resolution 1929, Press Release, Security Council, 9 June 2010, http://www.un.org/News/Press/docs/2010/sc9948.doc.htm (retrieved on 14 April 2014).

34. United Nations Security Council Resolution 2049, Iranwatch.org, 7 June 2012, http://www.iranwatch.org/international/UNSC/unsc-res2049-060712.pdf (retrieved on 14 April 2014).

35. 'Iranian Economy Favorable Despite Sanctions: World Bank', Tehran Times, 20 January 2012, http://www.tehrantimes.com/economy-and-business/94731-iranian-economy-favorable-despite-sanctions-world-bank (retrieved on 14 April 2014).

36. 'Iran's Economy to Grow in 2012: WB', Press TV, 23 January 2013, http://www.presstv.ir/detail/222589.html (retrieved on 14 April 2014).

37. 'Iran's Economy to Grow Despite Sanctions: Ahmadinejad', Al-Arabiya, 1 February 2012, http://english.alarabiya.net/articles/2012/02/01/191927.html (retrieved on 14 April 2014).

38. 'Analysis: Iran Economy Could Limp along under Sanctions', Reuters, 6 February 2012. According to this source, if non-oil exports take the same kind of hit as energy shipments, they could decline by about $7 billion from the IMF's estimate for this fiscal year. The combined hit to trade would be around $31 billion, or 6.5 percent of GDP—enough to push the economy, which the IMF has projected will grow 2.5 percent this year in inflation-adjusted terms, into recession.... The official inflation rate has jumped from single digits to around 20 percent in the past 18 months (http://www.reuters.com/article/2012/02/06/us-iran-sanctions-idUSTRE8150MH20120206). (retrieved on 14 April 2014).

39. 'Iran's Economy Feeling the Heat of Sanctions', Haaretz, 21 March 2012, http://www.haaretz.com/print-edition/features/iran-s-economy-feeling-the-heat-of-sanctions-1.419892 (retrieved on 14 April 2014).

40. 'Iran Warned over Mounting Unemployment', The Financial Times, 4 January 2012, http://www.ft.com/intl/cms/s/0/dc9ca060-36c1-11e1-9ca3-00144feabdc0.html#axzz2MBLipm51 (retrieved on 14 April 2014).

41. 'Iran Dec. Unemployment Rate at 11.8 Percent, Tehran Times Says', Bloomberg, 23 February 2012, http://www.bloomberg.com/news/2012-02-23/iran-dec-unemployment-rate-at-11-8-percent-tehran-times-says.html (retrieved on 14 April 2014). See also, 'Unemployment Doubled in the Course of the Year', Iran Labor Report, 6 March 2012. According to Mehdi

Mir Abdollahian, a secretary of Tehran Industries Owners Association, 21 per cent of factories are semi-productive and 16 per cent are on the brink of closure, while 25 per cent have already closed down. Only 38 per cent of the domestic factories remain active, http://iranlaborreport.com/?p=1778 (retrieved on 14 April 2014).

42. 'Iranian MPs Criticize Labor Minister over Unemployment', *Trend*, 22 July 2012, http://en.trend.az/regions/iran/2049184.html (retrieved on 14 April 2014).

43. 'Iran Plans to Create 1.3m Jobs by March 2013', *Tehran Times*, 2 December 2012, http://www.tehrantimes.com/economy-and-business/103728-iran-plans-to-create-13m-jobs-by-march-2013 (retrieved on 14 April 2014).

44. 'Iranian Economy Not Oil Based, Not Affected by Oil Sanctions: Minister', *Press TV*, 12 June 2012. According to the minister, [I]n the past year raw steel production in the country stood at 14 million tonnes, steel products at 17 million tonnes, concrete at 67 million tonnes, tiles at 300 million square meters, automobiles at 1.4 million vehicles, aluminium at 320 thousand tonnes, copper at 235 thousand tonnes and lead at 20 thousand tonnes (http://www.presstv.ir/detail/2012/06/12/245830/iranian-economy-not-oil-based/) (retrieved on 14 April 2014).

45. 'Iran's Rial Hits an All-time-low against the US Dollar', *BBC News*, 1 October 2012, http://www.bbc.co.uk/news/business-19786662 (retrieved on 14 April 2014).

46. 'Mahmoud Ahmadinejad Accused of Causing Iran's Economic Plight', *The Guardian*, 1 October 2012, http://www.guardian.co.uk/world/2012/oct/01/mahmoud-ahmadinejad-iran-economic-plight (retrieved on 14 April 2014).

47. Meir Javedanfar, 'How Politics Nuked Iran's Economy', *The Diplomat*, 6 October 2012. He is an Iranian-born Israeli Middle East expert. He teaches contemporary Iranian Politics course at the Interdisciplinary Centre in Herzliya, Israel, http://thediplomat.com/2012/10/06/how-politics-nuked-irans-economy/ (retrieved on 14 April 2014).

48. 'Iran Economy Seen Worsening', *The Wall Street Journal*, 12 October 2012, http://online.wsj.com/article/SB1000087239639044465780457800508433 18501614.html (retrieved on 14 April 2014).

49. 'West's Pressure Unable to Ruin Iran's Economy: Ahmadinejad', *Press TV*, 23 December 2012, http://www.presstv.ir/detail/2012/12/23/279614/west-could-not-ruin-irans-economy/ (retrieved on 14 April 2014).

50. 'Iran Turns to Barter for Food as Sanctions Cripple Imports', *Reuters*, 9 February 2012, http://www.reuters.com/article/2012/02/09/us-iran-wheat-idUSTRE8180SF20120209 (retrieved on 14 April 2014).

51. 'Iran Lowers Prices as 'Chicken Crisis' Becomes Simmering Political Issue', *Al-Arabiya*, 29 July 2012. According to this source, the price of the chicken reached 80,000 rials ($6.15) a kilo during the mid-2012. http://english.alarabiya.net/articles/2012/07/29/229041.html (retrieved on 14 April 2014).

52. 'Medicine Crisis in Iran Due To Sanctions', *Trend,* 17 October 2012, http://en.trend.az/regions/iran/2077786.html (retrieved on 14 April 2014).
53. 'Haemophiliac Iranian boy "dies after sanctions disrupt medicine supplies"', *The Guardian,* 14 November 2012, http://www.guardian.co.uk/world/2012/nov/14/sanctions-stop-medicines-reaching-sick-iranians (retrieved on 14 April 2014).
54. 'Sanctions, Government Blamed for Iran's Drugs Shortage', *Reuters,* 5 December 2012, http://www.reuters.com/article/2012/12/05/us-iran-medicine-idUSBRE8B40NM20121205 (retrieved on 14 April 2014).
55. 'Iran's Population Reaches 75 Million, National Census Reveals', *Tehran Times,* 24 July 2012, http://www.tehrantimes.com/politics/99936 (retrieved on 14 April 2014) (retrieved on 14 April 2014).
56. 'Khamenei on Population Control: "May God and History Forgive Us"', *Al-Monitor,* 17 October 2012, http://www.al-monitor.com/pulse/originals/2012/al-monitor/iran-population-control.html (retrieved on 14 April 2014).
57. 'Iran Urges Baby Boom with Population Aging', *The Huffington Post,* 27 July 2012, http://www.huffingtonpost.com/2012/07/29/iran-baby-boom_n_1716365.html
58. 'Iran Scraps Birth Control Programme in Baby Boom Bid', *The Telegraph,* 2 August 2012, http://www.telegraph.co.uk/news/worldnews/middleeast/iran/9446882/Iran-scraps-birth-control-programme-in-baby-boom-bid.html
59. 'Iran to Increase Exports of Arms, Military Equipments', *Fars News Agency,* 10 March 2012, http://english.farsnews.com/newstext.php?nn=9012151809
60. 'Iran Tests Fires Missiles in Gulf Exercise', *Reuters,* 2 January 2012, http://www.reuters.com/article/2012/01/02/us-iran-missile-idUSTRE80007E20120102
61. 'Report: Iran "Successfully" Fires Missile Capable of Hitting Targets 185 Miles Away', *CNN,* 5 August 2012, http://edition.cnn.com/2012/08/04/world/meast/iran-missile-test
62. K. Alan Kronstadt, Paul K. Kerr, Michael F. Martin and Bruce Vaughn, 'India: Domestic Issues, Strategic Dynamics, and U.S. Relations', *Congressional Research Service,* 1 September 2011, 34, http://www.fas.org/sgp/crs/row/RL33529.pdf
63. Mushtaq Hussain, 'Indo-Iranian Relations during the Cold War', *Strategic Analysis* 36, no. 6 (2012): 859–70.
64. C. Christine Fair, 'Indo-Iran Ties Thicker than Oil', *The Middle East Review of International Affairs (MERIA)* 11, no. 1(9 March 2007), http://www.gloria-center.org/2007/03/fair-2007-03-09/
65. C. Christine Fair, 'India and Iran: New Delhi's Balancing Act', *The Washington Quarterly* 30, no. 3 (2007): 145.
66. Jalil Roshandel 'The Overdue "Strategic Partnership" between India and Iran', in *Asia Program Special Report No. 120: 'The "Strategic" Partnership*

between India and Iran' (Washington: Woodrow Wilson Centre, 2004), 16, http://www.wilsoncenter.org/publication/the-strategic-partnership-between-india-and-iran-pdf

67. Ibid.

68. Harsh V. Pant, 'India's Relations with Iran: Much Ado about Nothing', *The Washington Quarterly* 34, no. 1 (2011): 61. For an earlier account, please see, P. R. Kumaraswamy 'Nuclear Iran: India Looks through the Energy Prism', *Iran Pulse* (The Alliance Centre for Iranian Studies, Tel Aviv University), no. 12 (27 May 2007), http://humanities.tau.ac.il/iranian/en/previous-reviews/10-iran-pulse-en/115-12

69. 'Iran to Send Foreign Minister to Invite Manmohan Singh to NAM Summit', *The Times of India*, 26 May 2012, http://articles.timesofindia.indiatimes.com/2012-05-26/india/31864241_1_ali-asghar-soltanieh-fordow-ali-akbar-salehi

70. 'Transcript of the Joint Media Interaction of External Affairs Minister of India and Foreign Minister of Iran', *Incoming Visits*, 31 May 2012, Ministry of External Affairs, New Delhi, http://www.mea.gov.in/incoming-visit-detail.htm?19673/Transcript+of+the+Joint+Media+Interaction+of+External+Affairs+Minister+of+India+and+Foreign+Minister+of+Iran

71. 'Iran Remains an Important Source of Oil for India: Krishna', *Business Line*, 31 May 2012, http://www.thehindubusinessline.com/industry-and-economy/iran-remains-an-important-source-of-oil-for-india-krishna/article3477010.ece

72. Ministry of External Affairs, 'Transcript of the Joint Media Interaction of External Affairs Minister of India and Foreign Minister of Iran'.

73. 'PM Likely to Visit Iran for NAM Meet', *The Indian Express*, 25 July 2012. According to this report, The prime minister's decision, however, is rooted in India's close association with the cause of NAM, which was born out of newly-Independent nations' desire to not align with any of the two power blocs—the US-led capitalist bloc and the USSR-led communist bloc—that formed after World War II and immediately engaged in Cold War (http://www.indianexpress.com/news/pm-likely-to-visit-iran-for-nam-meet/979026)

74. 'PM Visit to Be Low-key on India-Iran Engagement', *The Indian Express*, 28 August 2012, http://www.indianexpress.com/news/pm-visit-to-be-lowkey-on-indiairan-engagement/994153

75. 'Transcript of the Media Briefing by Foreign Secretary in Tehran on Prime Minister's Meetings in Iran', *Media Briefings*, Ministry of External Affairs, New Delhi, 30 August 2012. The meeting between Indian Prime Minister and Iranian President was a full-fledged bilateral meeting, whereas that with the Supreme Leader was dominated by the deep-rooted civilizational ties between the two countries, http://www.mea.gov.in/media-briefings.htm?dtl/20439/Transcript+of+the+Media+Briefing+by+Foreign+Secretary+in+Tehran+on+Prime+Ministers+meetings+in+Iran

76. 'India, Iran to Step Up Economic Ties', *The Hindu*, 30 August 2012. According to this source, 'they also agreed that they were on the right track in focusing on enhancing economic and trade relations with Dr. Singh raising the issue of the need for Iran to import more from India and to address the trade imbalance' (http://www.thehindu.com/news/national/article3836935.ece)

77. Ibid.

78. Ibid.

79. 'Indian Community in Iran Meet PM Singh', *Zee News*, 29 August 2012, http://zeenews.india.com/news/nation/indian-community-in-iran-meets-pm-singh_796493.html

80. 'PM Meets Khamenei, Ahmadinejad', *Zee News*, 30 August 2012, http://zeenews.india.com/news/nation/pm-meets-khamenei-ahmadinejad_796402.html

81. 'India Cuts July Iran Oil Imports by over 40 pct y/y-trade Data', *Reuters*, 21 August 2012, http://in.reuters.com/article/2012/08/21/india-irna-imports-idINL4E8JL37120120821

82. 'Khamenei Recalls Mahatma's Contribution', *The Hindu*, 30 August 2012. According to this report, 'Ayatollah Khamenei said he was deeply impressed by Mahatma Gandhi's "brilliant and illustrious visage" and recalled his "heroic" struggle in South Africa which was followed by leadership of the freedom movement, said sources in the government.' The Supreme Leader recalled his meetings with the late Indian prime ministers, namely, Indira Gandhi and P. V. Narasimha Rao, three decades back. http://www.thehindu.com/news/national/article3836933.ece

83. 'India, Iran Firm Up Ties Ahead of NAM Summit', *The Hindu*, 28 August 2012, http://www.thehindu.com/news/india-iran-firm-up-ties-ahead-of-nam-summit/article3830974.ece

84. 'Iranian Economy Minister Says India to Continue Energy Ties', *Bloomberg Businessweek,* 1 September 2012, http://www.businessweek.com/news/2012-09-01/iranian-economy-minister-says-india-to-continue-energy-ties

85. Ministry of External Affairs, Government of India, *Annual Report, 2011–2012, The Gulf, West Asia and North Africa: Iran, Bilateral Trade and Commerce*, 42, http://www.mea.gov.in/Uploads/PublicationDocs/19337_annual-report-2011-2012.pdf. Also see 'Iran for Further Development in International North–South Transport Corridor', *Islamic Republic News Agency,* 20 January 2012, http://www.irna.ir/News/General/Iran-for-further-development-in-International-North-South-Transport-Corridor/30773152

86. 'Iranian Minister Woos Indian Businesses', *Yahoo News,* 10 October 2012, http://news.yahoo.com/iranian-minister-woos-indian-businesses-142926750—finance.html. In order to reduce the impact of the West-imposed sanctions, the Iranian government has begun privatizing the

state-owned companies and a large number have been opened for investments.

87. Ibid.

88. 'Deputy Foreign Minister: Iran Attaches Great Importance to IOR-ARC Countries', *The Iran Project,* 3 November 2012. The 19 member states of the IOR-ARC association are Iran, Australia, Bangladesh, India, Indonesia, Kenya, Madagascar, Malaysia, Mauritius, Mozambique, Oman, Seychelles, Singapore, South Africa, Sri Lanka, Tanzania, Thailand, United Arab Emirates and Yemen. The Association also has five dialogue partners including China, Egypt, France, Japan and the United Kingdom, while the Indian Ocean Tourism Organisation and the Indian Ocean Research Group are observers. http://theiranproject.com/blog/2012/11/03/deputy-foreign-minister-iran-attaches-great-importance-to-ior-arc-countries/

89. Press Information Bureau, Government of India, 'India-Iran to Enhance Cooperation in Renewable Energy', 5 March 2012, http://pib.nic.in/newsite/erelease.aspx?relid=80698

90. 'India-Iran Relations', Embassy of India, Iran, Tehran, August 2012, http://www.indianembassy-tehran.ir/india-iran_relations.php

91. 'Iran's Reserves Guarantee Security of Global Energy Supplies', *Tehran Times,* 9 May 2012, http://tehrantimes.com/politics/97695-irans-reserves-guarantee-security-of-global-energy-supplies-official

92. 'Indo-Iran Joint Commission Meeting Postponed', *Business Standard,* 14 November 2012. The 16th Joint Commission Meeting was held in New Delhi in 2010. Six MoUs, including Air Services Agreement and Agreement on Transfer of Sentenced Persons, were inked. http://www.business-standard.com/generalnews/news/indo-iran-joint-commission-meeting-postponed/79026/

93. 'At Last Minute, Khurshid Calls Off His Visit to Iran', *The Indian Express,* 21 November 2012, http://www.indianexpress.com/news/at-last-minute-khurshid-calls-off-his-visit-to-iran/1033873

94. Exports to Iran, Export Import Data Bank, Department of Commerce, 30 December 2012.

95. 'India, Iran Set Up $25-b Trade Target for Next 4 Years', *Business Line,* 12 March 2012. According to this source, 'the delegation comprised representatives from the public and private sectors including President of the Federation of Indian Export Organisations (FIEO), Mr Rafeeque Ahmed' (http://www.thehindubusinessline.com/industry-and-economy/economy/india-iran-set-up-25b-trade-target-for-next-4-years/article2988140.ece)

96. 'India, Iran Work to Boost Trade in Non-oil Products', *The Hindu,* 8 May 2012, http://www.thehindu.com/business/article3394615.ece

97. 'India Offers Tax Breaks on Iran Exports Despite U.S. Pressure', *Reuters,* 5 April 2012, http://www.reuters.com/article/2012/04/05/us-india-iran-idUSBRE8340JN20120405

98. 'Iran Buys Indian Soymeal at Record Prices', *Reuters*, 13 April 2013, http://in.reuters.com/article/2012/04/13/india-iran-soymeal-idIN-L3E8FD7P120120413

99. 'Iran Lowers Rust Alarm, to Buy 200,000 Tonnes Wheat', *Business Standard*, 23 October 2012, http://www.business-standard.com/india/news/iran-lowers-rust-alarm-to-buy-200000-tonnes-wheat-/192525/on

100. 'Sanctions Set to Hurt Basmati Exports to Iran', *Business Standard*, 21 February 2012, http://business-standard.com/india/news/sanctions-set-to-hurt-basmati-exports-to-iran/465271/

101. 'Iran, India to Boost Pharmaceutical Exports', *Press TV*, 14 December 2012, http://www.presstv.ir/detail/2012/12/14/277927/iran-india-to-boost-pharmaceutical-exports/

102. 'India Exports 176,000 T Sugar to Iran-trade Sources', *Reuters*, 6 September 2012, http://in.reuters.com/article/2012/09/06/india-sugar-idINL4E8K62D220120906. Also see, 'Iran Trade Sanctions Worry India's Tea Exporters', *Business Standard*, 17 February 2012, http://www.business-standard.com/india/news/iran-trade-sanctions-worry-india%5Cs-tea-exporters/464917/

103. 'Iran Wants to Use Rupee Payments from India to Buy Govt Securities', *NDTV Profit*, 12 September 2012, http://profit.ndtv.com/news/international-business/article-iran-wants-to-use-rupee-payments-from-india-to-buy-govt-securities-310719

104. Harsh V. Pant, 'Teheran Stands between Washington and New Delhi', *Business Standard*, 20 May 2012, http://www.business-standard.com/india/news/harsh-v-pant-teheran-stands-between-washingtonnew-delhi/474823/

105. Ibid.

106. 'Team for Iran to Work Out Oil Payment Methods', *The Hindu*, 9 January 2012, http://www.thehindu.com/business/Industry/article2788372.ece

107. 'India, Iran Agree on Payment Mechanism for Trade', *The Hindu*, 7 October 2011, http://www.thehindu.com/business/Economy/india-iran-agree-on-payment-mechanism-for-trade/article2515383.ece

108. 'India Makes First Payment for Iranian Oil in Five Months', *The Economic Times*, 1 August 2011, http://articles.economictimes.indiatimes.com/2011-08-01/news/29838557_1_eih-bank-europisch-iranische-handelsbank-ag-iranian-oil

109. 'Routing Iran Oil Payments on PM's Moscow Agenda', *The Times of India*, 16 December 2011, http://articles.timesofindia.indiatimes.com/2011-12-16/india/30524309_1_iranian-oil-oil-payments-indian-oil

110. 'India Wants to Pay for Iranian Crude in Rupees', *The Economic Times*, 8 January 2012, http://articles.economictimes.indiatimes.com/2012-01-08/news/30604481_1_iranian-crude-eih-bank-iranian-bank

111. 'Iran Said to Seek Yen Payments from India for Oil Amid Sanctions', *Bloomberg Bussinessweek*, 1 February 2012, http://www.businessweek.com/

news/2012-02-01/iran-said-to-seek-yen-payments-from-india-for-oil-amid-sanctions.html
112. 'Iran Offers Oil at Zero-percent Interest', *UPI*, 12 April 2012, http://www. upi.com/Top_News/World-News/2012/04/12/Iran-offers-oil-at-zero-per-cent-interest/UPI-30311334214000/
113. 'India Looks beyond Iran to Boost Its Crude Oil Supplies', *The Hindu*, 16 June 2012. After Saudi Arabia, Kuwait and Iraq, the Iran has become the fourth largest supplier. http://www.thehindu.com/business/Economy/in-dia-looks-beyond-iran-to-boost-its-crude-oil-supplies/article3533839.ece
114. 'Iranian Ships May Ferry Crude Oil', *Business Line*, 22 June 2012, http:// www.thehindubusinessline.com/industry-and-economy/government-and-policy/iranian-ships-may-ferry-crude-oil/article3558287.ece
115. 'Indian Ships Ferrying Iranian Oil to Get Insurance Cover', *The Economic Times*, 29 June 2012, http://articles.economictimes.indiatimes.com/2012-06-29/news/32472493_1_indian-ships-public-sector-insurers-sovereign-guarantee
116. 'India Starts Buying Iranian Oil on a Delivered Basis', *Reuters*, 5 July 2012, http://uk.reuters.com/article/2012/07/05/india-iran-imports-idUK-L3E8I53H820120705
117. 'Sanctions Close Indo-Iranian Shipping Firm', *The Hindu*, 25 July 2012, http://www.thehindu.com/news/national/article3682764.ece
118. 'Iran Sanctions Bite MRPL Crude Imports', *LiveMint*, 27 July 2012, http:// www.livemint.com/Companies/BfmBUAJxo7XXdxr1k1u5tN/Iran-sanc-tions-bite-MRPL-crude-imports.html
119. 'Iran Oil Shipping to Resume as Insurers Step In: Corporate India', *Bloom-berg*, 2 August 2012, http://www.bloomberg.com/news/2012-08-01/iran-oil-shipping-to-resume-as-insurers-step-in-corporate-india.html
120. Ibid.
121. 'India to Keep Oil Import from Iran at Current Level', *Press TV*, 17 Octo-ber 2012, http://presstv.com/detail/2012/10/17/267227/india-to-keep-oil-import-from-iran-at-current-level/
122. 'India HMEL Says to Halt Iran Oil Purchases', *Reuters*, 12 November 2012. According to this report, 'Hindustan Petroleum Corp and Mittal each own 49 percent in the joint venture HMEL' (http://www.reuters.com/ar-ticle/2012/11/12/india-hmel-iran-idUSL3E8MC3RW20121112)
123. 'India to Cut Iran Oil Imports in FY2014', *LiveMint*, 20 December 2012, http://www.livemint.com/Industry/fGWPIrOAnywAW0n4uK8alM/India-to-cut-Iran-oil-imports-in-its-2014-fiscal-year.html
124. 'Iran Plans to Export 6,000 MW of Electricity to India, Pakistan', *Press TV*, 10 October 2012, http://www.presstv.ir/detail/2012/10/10/265846/iran-to-export-6000-mw-to-india-pakistan/
125 'Iran Presses India on Gas Pipeline', *UPI*, 17 October 2012, http://www. upi.com/Business_News/Energy-Resources/2012/10/17/Iran-presses-In-dia-on-gas-pipeline/UPI-51941350480701/

126. 'India to Review Iranian Crude Dependence Issue in New Year: Salman Khurshid, External Affairs Minister', *The Economic Times*, 13 December 2012, http://articles.economictimes.indiatimes.com/2012-12-13/news/35796906_1_crude-imports-oil-imports-iranian-crude

127. 'The Iranian Artists Forum to Host India-Iran Cultural Week', *Press TV*, 26 May 2012, http://www.presstv.ir/detail/2012/05/26/243247/iranian-artists-forum-cultural-festival/

128. 'Iran's Connection to India's Sikhs', *NDTV*, 29 August 2012. As of today, 189 students from LKG to class 12 have enrolled in the KV, and have produced 100 per cent pass results in 10th and 12th standards examinations conducted by Delhi-based Central Board of Secondary Education (CBSE), during the last two years (http://www.ndtv.com/article/india/irans-connection-to-india-s-sikhs-260569). Also see 'Kendriya Vidyalaya Tehran Teaches It All', *Hindu*, 29 August 2012. The origins of the Kendriya Vidyalaya Tehran (KVT) go back to the southeastern province of Zahedan, when the first Indian settlers established a school in the 1930s. It shifted to its present location in Tehran in 1952 and became a Kendriya Vidyalaya in 2004; it currently teaches five languages (http://www.thehindu.com/news/international/article3836836.ece)

129. 'Iranian Student with Fake Documents Arrested', *The Times of India*, 14 January 2012, http://articles.timesofindia.indiatimes.com/2012-01-14/mysore/30627315_1_iranian-student-documents-judicial-custody

130. 'India, Iran in Student Expulsion War', *The Hindustan Times*, 2 February 2012, http://www.hindustantimes.com/India-news/NewDelhi/India-Iran-in-student-expulsion-war/Article1-805417.aspx. Also see 'PM to Take Up Student Issue with Iran at Meet', *Hindustan Times*, 25 August 2012, http://www.hindustantimes.com/India-news/NewDelhi/PM-to-take-up-student-issue-with-Iran-at-meet/Article1-919411.aspx. Four students were Shoebur Rahman from Kanpur (medicine), K. M. Razeen from Kerala (medicine), Rajnish Vij from Varanasi (doctorate, Persian) and Mirza Asif Ali Baig from Jammu & Kashmir (doctorate, architecture).

131. 'Iranian Agent Deported for Spying on Jews in India', *Arutz Sheva7*, 24 April 2012. [T]he topic of Kashkouli's thesis was 'Foreign policy of the Islamic Republic of Iran during the presidency of Khatami' and he had enrolled himself at UoP's Department of Defense and Strategic Studies in 2007. He came to India under the pretext of being a student but was keeping a close eye on the Jewish centres in Pune. He had collected information about visitors' movements at the Chabad House and the Synagogue which he forwarded to intelligence officials in Tehran (http://www.israelnationalnews.com/News/News.aspx/155206#.UQYggb_qnAs)

132. 'Iranian Scholar Held for Taking Photos Near Israel Embassy', *The Times of India*, 23 November 2012, http://articles.timesofindia.indiatimes.com/2012-11-23/delhi/35318126_1_israeli-embassy-israel-embassy-jnu-students-union

133. 'Iranian Student Deported for Links with Narcotics Trade', *The Indian Express*, 7 June 2012. Azarmehar came to Pune on a student visa in 2010. He was currently studying B Com at Bharati Vidyapeeth. He has also been blacklisted by the Pune police so won't be allowed to visit India again.... In 2011, of the 302 foreigners deported or issued Leave India notices by the special branch of Pune police for their alleged undesirable activities, 80 were Iranians. As many as 183 foreigners from 35 countries were issued leave India notices. They included 62 Iranians. Also, 119 foreigners from 37 countries were deported. They included 18 Iranians (http://www.indianexpress.com/news/iranian-student-deported-for-links-with-narcotics-trade/958817/0)

134. 'Iran's Connection to India's Sikhs'.

135. 'India Asks Iran to Lift Wheat Import Ban', *Deccan Herald*, 4 April 2012, http://www.deccanherald.com/content/239721/india-asks-iran-lift-wheat.html

136. Ibid.

137. 'MHA Declines Security Clearance to Three Iranian banks', *The Financial Express*, 22 July 2012. 'The government move follows India accepting international guidelines set by the Financial Action Task Force (FATF), based in Paris. India, which became its member in 2010, is required to follow its international guidelines to check money laundering and terror-financing activities' (http://www.financialexpress.com/news/mha-declines-security-clearance-to-three-iranian-banks/977845)

138. 'Iran's Multiple Exchange Rate to Hit Rice Exports', *The Economic Times*, 26 November 2012. According to this source, Iran functions on a multiple exchange rate system to circumvent the sanctions. First, there is the official exchange rate of 12,500 rial (1,250 toman). Then there is the open market exchange rate which varies between 25,000–28,000 rial (2,500–2,800 toman) and finally the unofficial market rate of 28,000 rial (2,800 toman) (http://economictimes.indiatimes.com/articleshow/17367703.cms)

139. P. R. Kumaraswamy, 'Delhi: Between Tehran and Washington', *Middle East Quarterly* 15, no. 1 (2008): 41–47, http://www.meforum.org/1821/delhi-between-tehran-and-washington

140. 'Senators Irked by India's Iran Ties, Stalled Nuclear Trade', *The Indian Express*, 8 February 2012, http://articles.timesofindia.indiatimes.com/2012-02-08/us/31036869_1_iran-and-india-nuclear-power-sector-nuclear-liability-bill

141. 'Sanctions Won't Affect India-Iran Rice Trade: US State Dept', *Business Line*, 8 February 2012, http://www.thehindubusinessline.com/industry-and-economy/economy/article2871531.ece

142. 'India Defends Oil Purchases *Business Line*, Iran', *The New York Times*, 11 February 2012, http://www.nytimes.com/2012/02/12/world/asia/india-trumpets-ties-with-us-amid-iran-oil-deal.html?_r=0

143. R. Nicholas Burns, 'India Lets U.S Down on Iran', *Diplomat*, 20 February 2012, http://thediplomat.com/2012/02/20/india-lets-u-s-down-on-iran/

144. 'India, China Not Spared from US Sanctions on Iran oil', *Hindustan Times*, 21 March 2012. The eleven countries are Japan, Belgium, Britain, the Czech Republic, France, Germany, Greece, Italy, the Netherlands, Poland and Spain. http://www.hindustantimes.com/business-news/WorldEconomy/India-China-not-spared-from-US-sanctions-on-Iran-oil/Article1-828558.aspx

145. For a detailed analysis, see P. R. Kumaraswamy, 'India's Iran Defiance', *IDSA Comment,* 19 March 2012, http://www.idsa.in/idsacomments/IndiasIranDefiance_prkumaraswamy_190312

146. 'Iran Crucial to India's Energy Needs but Delhi Has Global Obligations, Says U.S. official', *The Hindu,* 3 April 2012, http://www.thehindu.com/news/national/article3273999.ece

147. 'Regarding Significant Reductions of Iranian Crude Oil Purchases', *Press Statement,* U.S. Department of State, 11 June 2012. Six others are Malaysia, Republic of Korea, South Africa, Sri Lanka, Turkey and Taiwan (http://www.state.gov/secretary/rm/2012/06/192078.htm). For a relevant analysis, see Harsh V. Pant, 'The Strategic Tango in Washington', *Indian Express,* 15 June 2012, http://www.indianexpress.com/news/the-strategic-tango-in-washington/962183

148. Brahma Chellaney, 'Troubled US-India-Iran Triangle: India Has to Factor in Its Needs with the US', *The Economic Times,* 22 June 2012, http://articles.economictimes.indiatimes.com/2012-06-22/news/32369070_1_india-and-iran-iran-sanctions-act-purchases-of-iranian-oil

149. 'US Wants India to Sway Iran Join Nuclear Talks', *The Times of India,* 19 October 2012, http://articles.timesofindia.indiatimes.com/2012-10-19/india/34583652_1_nuclear-programme-nuclear-talks-iranian-leadership

150. 'Romney Camp Wants India to Shun Iran Oil', *The Times of India,* 12 October 2012, http://articles.timesofindia.indiatimes.com/2012-10-12/us/34412000_1_iran-oil-romney-camp-nuclear-weapon

151. 'US Barbs May Block India's Pay Path for Iran Oil', *The Times of India,* 7 October 2012, http://timesofindia.indiatimes.com/business/india-business/US-barbs-may-block-Indias-pay-path-for-Iran-oil/articleshow/16705852.cms

152. 'US Extends Exemptions for India, China to Iran Oil Sanctions', *Business Line,* 8 December 2012, http://www.thehindubusinessline.com/news/international/us-extends-exemptions-for-india-china-to-iran-oil-sanctions/article4177763.ece

153. 'Iran Sets China Trade Target of $100 Billion', *Press TV,* 11 September 2012, http://www.presstv.ir/detail/2012/09/11/260925/iran-sets-china-trade-target-of-100bn/

154. 'China to Construct Iran-Pakistan Gas Pipeline Project: Report', *Press TV,* 10 June 2012, http://www.presstv.ir/detail/2012/06/10/245477/china-to-finance-ip-pipeline-project/

155. 'Iran, China Divided over Oil Payment Terms', *Tehran Times*, 6 January 2012, http://www.tehrantimes.com/economy-and-business/94265-iran-china-divided-over-oil-payment-terms

156. 'China Iran Oil Imports Rise as Payment Dispute Resolved', *BBC News*, 22 June 2012, http://www.bbc.co.uk/news/business-18545973

157. 'Iran-Pakistan Trade to Hit $3 Billion', *Daily Times*, 10 October 2012, http://www.dailytimes.com.pk/default.asp?page=2012%5C10%5C10%5C story_10-10-2012_pg5_5

158. 'Iran-Pakistan Trade Rises Despite US Sanctions', *Press TV*, 17 March 2012, http://www.presstv.ir/detail/232200.html

159. 'Pakistan Will Proceed on Pipeline to Iran, Minister Says', *CNN*, 1 March 2012, http://edition.cnn.com/2012/03/01/world/asia/pakistan-iran-pipeline/index.html

160. 'Pakistani PM Urges Boost in Trade with Iran to $10bn', *Press TV*, 9 August 2012, http://presstv.com/detail/2012/08/09/255312/pakistan-eyes-10bn-trade-ties-with-iran/

161. 'Iranian Gas Will Start Flowing from December 2014: Dr Asim Hussain', *The Express Tribune*, 4 September 2012, http://tribune.com.pk/story/430894/iranian-gas-will-start-flowing-from-december-2014-dr-asim-hussain/

162. 'Wheat Exports to Iran: India Pushes to Take Pakistan's Place', *The Express Tribune*, 24 May 2012, http://tribune.com.pk/story/383279/wheat-exports-to-iran-india-pushes-to-take-pakistans-place/

163. 'Iran Urged to Persuade India to Settle Kashmir Dispute', *Pak Tribune*, 5 June 2012, http://paktribune.com/news/Iran-urged-to-persuade-India-to-settle-Kashmir-dispute-250379.html

164. For a detailed analysis, see P. R. Kumaraswamy, 'Israel: The Non-parallel Player', *Strategic Analysis* 36, no. 6 (2012): 976–86. Also see by the same author, 'Indo-Iranian Ties: The Israeli Dimension', in Robert M. Hathaway et al., 'The "Strategic" Partnership between India and Iran', *Asian Programme Special Report*, no. 20 (Washington: Woodrow Wilson Centre, 2004), 27–31, http://www.wilsoncenter.org/publication/the-strategic-partnership-between-india-and-iran-pdf

165. Ministry of External Affairs, Government of India, 'Incident in New Delhi Involving Israeli Diplomat', *Media Briefings*, 16 March 2012, http://www.mea.gov.in/media-briefings.htm?dtl/19098/Incident+in+New+Delhi+involving+Israeli+diplomat

166. 'No Evidence Yet of Iran Hand in Delhi Car Blast: India', *The Tribune*, 14 February 2012, http://www.tribuneindia.com/2012/20120215/main1.htm

167. 'Delhi Bombing Puts India's Trade Ties with Iran to the Test', *Reuters*, 14 February 2012, http://www.reuters.com/article/2012/02/14/india-iran-idUSL4E8DE17V20120214

168. 'India-Iran Trade to Continue despite Bombing', *The Jerusalem Post*, 15 February 2012, http://www.jpost.com/International/Article.aspx?id=257933
169. Harsh V. Pant, 'India's Iran Challenge', *Outlook India*, 17 February 2012, http://www.outlookindia.com/article.aspx?279948
170. 'Blast Lid off, Government Calls Up Iran', *The Times of India*, 17 March 2012, http://articles.timesofindia.indiatimes.com/2012-03-17/delhi/31204517_1_kazmi-mohammed-reza-abolghasemi-israeli-embassy. Also See, 'Delhi Police Team Draws Blank in Iran', *The Times of India*, 16 August 2012. The passport details of these suspects are: Irani (I17287444/issued 9/1/10), Mahdiansadr (J14922614/issued on 25/12/08) and Abolghasemi (F14772374/issued 2/12/08) (http://articles.timesofindia.indiatimes.com/2012-08-16/delhi/33232393_1_mohammad-reza-abolghasemi-houshang-afshar-irani-ali-mahdiansadr)
171. 'Israeli Diplomat Car Blast Probe: Cops Await Tehran Nod for Visit', *The Times of India*, 7 May 2012. This is the first time that an Indian police agency would visit Iran for investigation (http://articles.timesofindia.indiatimes.com/2012-05-07/india/31609965_1_car-blast-israeli-diplomat-tehran)
172. 'Indian Police: Iran behind New Delhi Terror Attack', *IsraelDefense*, 30 July 2012, http://www.israeldefense.com/?CategoryID=484&ArticleID=1497
173. Atul Aneja, 'Oil Payment Row and India-Iran Ties', *The Hindu*, 1 August 2012, http://www.thehindu.com/opinion/lead/article2314031.ece?homepage=true
174. 'India to Spread Tentacles into Central Asia via Iran', *The Times of India*, 13 March 2012, http://articles.timesofindia.indiatimes.com/2012-03-13/india/31159402_1_iranian-oil-oil-imports-rasht
175. 'India, Pakistan Must Sort Out Gas Pipeline Issue, Says Iran', *The Economic Times*, 18 October 2012, http://articles.economictimes.indiatimes.com/2012-10-18/news/34555547_1_indo-iran-india-and-iran-chabahar-port
176. 'Iran Can Ensure Indian Ocean Security against Pirates: Cmdr.', *Press TV*, 30 September 2012, http://www.presstv.ir/detail/2012/09/30/264235/iran-can-ensure-indian-ocean-security/
177. 'Indian and Iran to Expand Trade Engagements Despite Western Sanctions', *The Times of India*, 13 December 2012, http://articles.timesofindia.indiatimes.com/2012-12-13/india/35795645_1_india-and-iran-chahbahar-port-bilateral-trade

4

Iraq

Sonia Roy

Key Indicators

Area: 438,317 sq km; **Population:** 31.85 million; **Youth:** 19.6 per cent; **Population growth rate:** 2.345 per cent; **Life expectancy at birth:** 69.6 years; **GDP:** US$155.4 billion; **Per capita income:** US$4,600; **Foreign trade:** US$145.16 billion; **Oil reserves:** 143.1 billion bbl (2013); **Gas reserves:** 3.171 trillion m³; **Ruling party:** Da'wa Party; **Ruler:** President Jalal Talabani (since 6 April 2005); **National Day:** 14 July; **Defence budget:** 8.6 per cent of GDP; **HDI rank:** 131; **Literacy rate:** 78.2 per cent; **UN education index:** 0.498; **Gender inequality index:** 0.557.

Source: CIA, *The World Factbook*, https://www.cia.gov/library/publications/the-world-factbook/index.html; UN Human Development Report, Statistics, http://hdr.undp.org/en/statistics/
Note: All data for 2012.

During the past three decades, the historical ties between India and Iraq underwent a roller-coaster ride. Ever since Saddam Hussein became president in July 1979, Iraq has seen a series of crisis and conflicts. The eight-year war with Iran during 1980–88 was followed by the ill-fated Iraqi invasion, occupation and annexation of Kuwait in August 1990. This resulted in a United Nations (UN)-backed but US-led international force for the liberation of Kuwait. The Operation Desert Storm was followed by a series of severe sanctions that crippled the Iraqi economy and brought severe problems to its civilian population. The September 11 terror attacks on the US resulted in the Bush Administration accusing Iraq of sponsoring terrorism and possessing weapons of mass destruction. Both were used to organize and justify the US-led invasion of that country in March 2003.

With the fall of Saddam Hussein's regime after the US-led invasion of 2003 and his subsequent execution in November 2006, hopes had run high that a new coalition administration would bring stability along with a new-found freedom for the Iraqi people. Those hopes were dashed in the coming years amidst rising sectarian violence and a US military 'surge' to stabilize the deteriorating situation. Domestic political instability was made worse by rising corruption and economic ruin, with much blame laid on the continued US presence.

Domestic Developments

Even after the complete withdrawal of the US forces in 2011, Iraqi insurgency continued and intensified during 2012. The sectarian tensions have festered into violent outbreaks, and there are Sunni protests against the central government (Shia majority) in the country, added with the presence of al-Qaeda in Iraq.[1] According to the data put out by Iraq Body Count (IBC), there were 4,568 Iraqi casualties in 2012 alone,[2] and this contradicts the official figure of 2,174 deaths.[3] This shows the alarming violence which is faced by the Iraqis in their daily lives. Although the Arab Spring has affected the entire Middle East, it did not find much ground in Iraq; its Kurdistan region did experience what was termed as the 'Kurdish Spring'. The protests were forcefully dealt by the government.[4] As the Human Rights Watch notes, the condition in Iraq has deteriorated significantly after the US withdrawal, with the Iraqi state acting more like a police state. Human rights, freedom of speech and independence of press have undergone a huge setback.

Meanwhile, Iraq hosted the 23rd Arab League Summit in March 2012, after a period of over 20 years. With the sole exception of Syria, which was suspended in the midst of the uprising against the Assad regime, all other members of the Arab League attended the Summit. Several issues were discussed, like the situation in Syria and Iran.

Iraqi Kurdistan is an autonomous region of north-eastern Iraq, which is rich in oil and natural resources. In 2012, Kurdistan Regional Government (KRG) signed an agreement with Turkey, whereby the latter would supply the KRG with refined petroleum products in exchange for crude oil. In an important yet critical development, Jajal Talabani, the President of Iraq, had suffered a stroke and was flown into Germany for his treatment. President Talabani was the main force behind the formation of the coalition government in Iraq in the wake of the 2010 parliamentary elections, which saw competing and destructive forces at play. He is seen as a unifying figure cutting across the Iraqi spectrum, and his absence could mean further uncertainty for a shattered Iraq already divided along sectarian lines.[5]

According to the Human Rights Watch,

> Human rights conditions in Iraq remain poor, particularly for detainees, journalists, activists, and women and girls. Security forces continued to arbitrarily detain and torture detainees, holding some of them outside the custody of the Justice Ministry. The Justice Ministry announced a record number of executions in 2012, but provided little information about the identities of those executed. Iraq security forces continued to respond to peaceful protest with intimidation, threats, violence, and arrests of protesters and journalists. Security forces and pro-government non-state actors harassed journalists and media organizations critical of the government.[6]

This report which narrates the situation of rights and civil liberties in Iraq for the year 2012 is not different from its earlier assessment. The only difference between the two is that the withdrawal of US combat forces was completed by December 2011.

When it comes to public security and stability, the Iraqi situation continues to be precarious. The Transparency International rates Iraq as the third most corrupt country in the world after Sudan and Somalia.[7] When seen along with the Human Right Watch report on the country, Iraq is not only a country which is politically unstable, but it is also high on the corruption index. Both of them put the domestic political situation in Iraq in a very poor light.

The precarious security situation which has prevailed since the US invasion of 2003 has continued unabated. According to the Iraq Body Count Project, a total of at least 110,937 to 121,227 civilian deaths have occurred between March 2003 and 1 January 2013.[8] In 2012 alone, over

4,500 were killed.[9] This shows the alarming violence facing ordinary Iraqis.

On the political front, since 2005, Iraq has had a multiparty parliamentary system of governance at both federal and regional levels. The country is divided along sectarian lines, with the Shia, Sunni and the Kurds being the predominant players. Ethnically, 75 to 80 per cent of the population is Arab, while 15 to 20 per cent is Kurds; while Muslims constitute 97 per cent of the population, Shias constitute 60 to 65 per cent and Sunnis comprise between 32 and 37 per cent of the population.[10] Even with heavy emigration as well as killings that have happened in Iraq since 2003, there is a small percentage of Christian and other minorities present in Iraq. Since the US-led invasion of March 2003, there were widespread migration of Iraqis both within the country as well as to the neighbouring countries like Jordan, Syria and Iran.[11] With the current political turmoil in Syria, Iraq has also received a significant number of refugees from its neighbour. According to the United Nations High Commissioner for Refugees, as of 31 December 2012, Iraq has had 67,625 registered Syrian refugees.[12]

Torn by the sectarian divide, the 7 March 2010 parliamentary elections saw a lot of confusion and controversy. The Iraqi National Movement, led by former Interim Prime Minister Ayad Allawi, won a total of 91 seats in the 325-member parliament, making it the largest bloc. The State of Law Coalition, led by incumbent Prime Minister Nouri al-Maliki, was the second largest with 89 seats.[13] A power-sharing arrangement was finally reached in November 2010 among the political contenders to form a government and maintain domestic stability.[14] President Jalal Talabani has been a significant player who had mediated among Shia, Sunni and Kurdish parties, in ensuring the political stability in Iraq after the 2010 parliamentary elections. As an Iraqi analyst Ibrahim al-Sumaidaie remarked, 'He is the most moderate among Iraqi politicians and the most able to defuse political shocks. I do not think anyone will be able to fill his position as a president and as a politician.'[15] In accordance with the Iraqi constitution, a Kurd has to be nominated as the President, while the two vice-presidential posts are shared by Shia and Sunni candidates, respectively. This is the part of the power-sharing deal worked out in November 2010 to form a stable government amidst growing sectarian strife's in the country.[16] As many political analysts opine, President Talabani's absence would have far-reaching detrimental consequence for

Iraq, as he was seen as the mediator among the three leading sectarian groups in Iraq.[17] Under these circumstances, the health of President Talabani is adding to the political uncertainty in the country. President of the Kurdistan Region Masoud Barzani is increasingly seen as taking up the mantle of mediator in the absence of Iraqi President Talabani[18] who remains hospitalized in Germany due to his health issues.[19]

In 2012, Iraq hosted the 23rd Arab League Summit from 27 March to 29 March. It was the third one held in Iraq till date (earlier ones were held November 1978 and March 1990), and the first one after the Kuwait crisis of 1990–91. The summit enabled acting Kuwait Emir Sabah al-Ahmad al-Jaber al-Sabah to make the first visit to Iraq since 1990. The war-torn Iraq was struggling to re-enter the international environment as a sovereign state and a player in the regional politics. The Arab League Summit was seen as a way to put Iraq back into the glory it has lost after the US invasion in Iraq in 2003 and the fall of Saddam Hussein. This was voiced by Sudan's representative to the League, Kamal Hassan Ali, who said, 'No big decisions are expected from the Baghdad summit, but the biggest gain is the return of convening routine Arab summits after the halt last year, and also the return of Iraq to the Arab arena.'[20] The Summit left a mixed reaction in its aftermath.[21]

Even though the Arab League comprises 22 members, only 10 heads of state attended the Baghdad summit, the rest sending lower level officials. This was seen as an attempt to snub Iraq for having a Shia-led government and for its close ties with Shia Iran, illustrating the strong sectarian split and the rivalry with Iran that has characterized Middle East in this era of Arab Spring. According to Crispin B. Hawes, head of a New York-based risk consultant agency,

> It's no surprise that the Gulf states did not want to give Iraq the prestige that they would by sending heads of state to the summit.... They want Iraq to continue to be a second-rate citizen in the region; they want to keep Iraq inside the box.... They don't want it to be another major regional player.[22]

However, Iraq's newly discovered lucrative oil supply has the potential for making the country a strong competitor in the Persian Gulf.

The Iraqi oil sector is set to see serious boom in the coming years with its cheap alternative in oil and energy production. This would enable it to be in the competing market along with the other Gulf countries, and also Iran. The fact that Iran is undergoing sanctions has had an impact on its own oil and energy exports, a vacuum Iraq is set to fill. As the CIA estimates, 'An improving security environment and foreign investment are helping to spur economic activity, particularly in the energy, construction, and retail sectors.' Iraq is a largely state-run economy, where its oil sector provides more than 90 per cent of government revenue and 80 per cent of foreign exchange earnings. Iraq is looking into energy exports to make up for its GDP.[23] In spite of political instability as well as security concerns in Iraq, its potential has attracted many world players like the US and China to invest in energy imports, foreign direct investment and in other non-traditional sectors like infrastructure and service sector.[24] According to the Bank of America Merrill Lynch, Iraq would emerge as the world's fastest growing economy in 2012–13 and the Wall Street Bank data shows Iraq as the only country that will post a double-digit growth in 2012.[25]

As a World Bank report suggests, doing business in Iraq is becoming more lucrative to the world with Iraq ranking higher in 2013.[26] Iraq is set for Project Iraq 2013 to further profit from this increasing interest as a business venture. As the project flaunts,

> Project Iraq 2013 will be held at the heart of Iraq's business hub, Erbil, from 28 to 31 October 2013 gathering a vast number of cutting-edge exhibitors to represent regional and international companies, and ensuring a meeting place for professionals in the industry. Project Iraq 2013 exhibitors will benefit from massive exposure to premier regional agents, dealers, buyers and distributors, government officials and key decision-makers from all over Iraq and from outside the country.[27]

Project Iraq 2013 would be marked by a host of conferences, exhibitions and other similar events.[28]

Bilateral Relations

The bilateral relations between India and Iraq have been rooted in millennia-old civilizations, with both the countries sharing commonalities of multi-ethnic, multilingual and multi-religious nature.[29] Diplomatic relations were established between the two in 1947 and both were maintaining cordial relations through the years. Iraq is one of the few countries in the Middle East with whom India has a Treaty of Friendship (signed in November 1952). The two countries also signed Cooperation in Cultural Affairs agreement in 1954. Thousands of Indians visit the shrines of Imam Hussein and Imam Abbas in Karbala annually, bringing closer the cultural milieu of the two countries.

The bilateral relations flourished especially after the Ba'athist government came to power in 1958. Secular worldview of the Ba'ath party and their shared opposition to US-led military alliances during the Cold War brought India and Iraq closer. Iraq's support to India over Kashmir[30] and its emergence as a major player in the international oil market since the 1970s added political and economic dynamics to bilateral relations. These were manifested by India's refusal to condemn some of the aggressive foreign policy decisions taken by President Saddam Hussein (in office from 1979 to 2003) since the 1980s. While it adopted a neutral stand over the Iran–Iraq war, it tilted in favour of Iraq and opposed the use of force in 1991 and 2003 to resolve political issues.

At the same time, bilateral relations could not remain immune to the disruption caused by the Iran–Iraq war (1980–88), Kuwait crisis (1990–91) and US-led invasion of Iraq in March 2003. The prolonged conflict and isolation of Iraq considerably weakened bilateral relations. Following the liberation of Kuwait in February 1991, India resumed its trade with Iraq under the UN-mandated oil-for-food-programme that permitted exports of essential food items to Iraq.[31]

Owing to lack of UN approval, India chose to remain neutral during the US-led invasion of Iraq in March 2003. For a brief period, India considered sending a small contingent to post-war Iraq to help maintain security and peace after a unanimous vote in the UN Security Council (1483, adopted on 22 May 2003) over the Coalition's presence in Iraq. This did not materialize owing to strong domestic protest inside India.[32] India normalized its ties with the new democratically elected government of Iraq in 2005, seeking to restart trade and co-operation, though the process has been slow.[33]

Political Relations

There had been a lull in the bilateral relations between India and Iraq since the US-led invasion. After regaining partial sovereignty from the

US occupation authority in 2004, Iraq started to re-engage with the outside world with the appointment of ambassadors to various countries.[34] However, due to internal violence, India's diplomatic presence was scaled down to the level of chargé d'affaires. The deteriorating security situation in the country and a hostage crisis involving the kidnapping of three Indian truck drivers resulted in India's recall of its then ambassador to Iraq, B. B. Tyagi in late 2004.[35] India imposed a travel ban to Iraq, but illegal travel, mainly of economic migrants, continued in spite of such measures.[36] Economic relations between the two states continued, albeit in less frequency in the period between 2004 and 2010.

It was in 2011 that the bilateral relations between the two countries witnessed significant improvement with the appointment in April of S. K. Reddy as India's ambassador to Iraq and he assumed office in May.[37] The Indian ambassador made his first visit to the Kurdistan Region in December 2011 during which he met President of the region Masoud Barzani to discuss economic partnership opportunities with the KRG.[38] The Indian ambassador toured Erbil and met members of the Indian community in Kurdistan and KRG officials.[39]

In December 2012, the Indian Ambassador made his third visit to the region and held discussion with the Minister Falah Mustafa Bakir (Head of the Department of Foreign Relations of the KRG).[40]

From the Iraqi side, a delegation led by the Speaker of the Parliament of Iraq Osama Abdul-Aziz-Mohamed Al-Nujaefi visited India in December 2012 and met the Indian Vice President Hamid Ansari and Lok Sabha Speaker Meira Kumar. The meeting 'focused on enhancing of parliamentary relations to ensure the common interests of the two friendly countries'.[41] Iraq extended an invitation to the Indian vice president to visit Iraq.[42] Speaker Kumar reflected on the need for co-operation between the two countries and stressed for increasing people-to-people contacts between the two and of India's deep commitment in the reconstruction of Iraq. She also offered India's assistance in sharing the expertise in parliamentary practices and procedures with Iraq.[43]

Since the first Gulf War of 1991, there had been no direct flights between India and Iraq for over 20 years. In February 2012, Directorate General of Civil Aviation (DGCA), India's civil aviation regulator approved a proposal by Iraq's national carrier Iraqi Airways to have four direct flights every week to Baghdad, two each from Delhi and

Mumbai.[44] A major reason for resuming the flights, apart from India's efforts in rebuilding Iraq's infrastructure, is religious tourism. Places like Najaf, Karbala, Samarra and Kadhimiya are visited by Shia Muslims from India, which has the second largest Shia population in the world after Iran.[45]

Economic Relations

In recent years, the bilateral trade has accelerated due to increased Indian import of energy resources from Iraq (Table 4.1 and Figure 4.1). Indian exports to Iraq consist of small quantities of agro chemicals, cosmetics, rubber products, paints, gems and jewels, ceramics, manufactures of metals, machine tools, electrical machinery and instruments, transport equipment, electronic goods, handicrafts, cereals, sugar, tea, garments and pharmaceuticals.

Indian Basmati rice has found a good market in Iraq, overtaking US long-grained rice market since 2010.[46] Iraqi government is also looking to import sugar from India for meeting its domestic consumption demands.[47] According to an official, Iraq bought 53,000 tonnes of Basmati from India in April 2010.[48] The market for exporting Basmati rice would increase due to Iraq's preference for the product, as it consumes 1.25 million tonnes of rice a year and Indian market provides a cheaper import option.[49]

An important step to foster stronger economic bilateral ties between the two countries took place in an interactive session on 'Certification

Table 4.1
India–Iraq Bilateral Trade (in US$ Million)

	2009–10	2010–11	2011–12
Exports	477.13	678.14	763.97
Imports	7,026.93	9,008.30	18,939.63
Total trade	7,504.06	9,686.44	19,703.60
Share of Iraq in total trade	1.61	1.56	2.48

Source: Director General of Foreign Trade, http://www.dgft.gov.in

Figure 4.1
India–Iraq Bilateral Trade

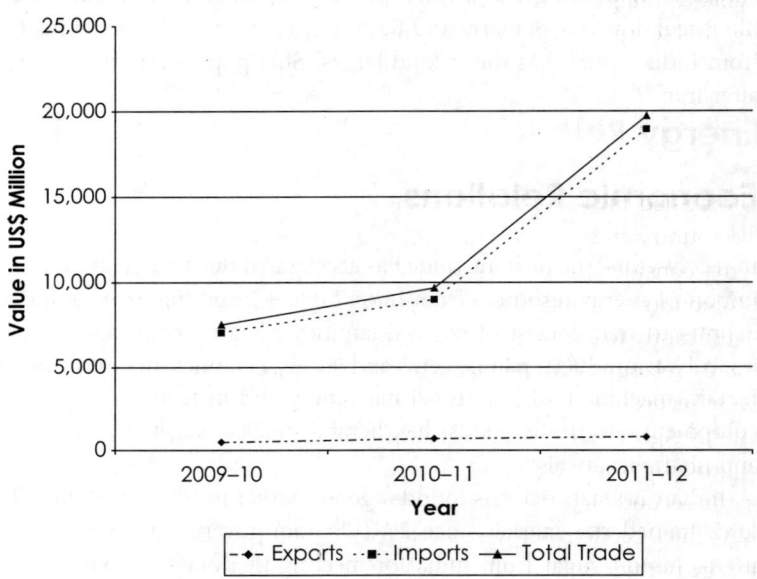

Source: Director General of Foreign Trade, http://www.dgft.gov.in

of Goods and Export Potential of Iraq', organized by the Federation of Indian Export Organisations (FIEO) in April 2012 in New Delhi. Hussein Ali Rajab, the Commercial Councillor, Embassy of Iraq, felt that India's exports to this market should increase from US$750 million to about US$3 billion by 2015. It is directed that all Indian goods imported to Iraq must be certified by their designated inspection agency so that the buyers can release their goods in Iraq.[50] The previous year, Indian tea export suffered a setback as more than 200 containers of Indian Tea that were being exported to Iraq were barred and returned due to quality issues.[51]

Indian steel firm Jindal Saw won a 25-year contract to build and run a factory for manufacturing oil and gas pipelines in south of Iraq.[52] This US$198 million deal was part of Iraq's efforts to revive its long deserted industry sector.[53] As a part of India's effort in infrastructure development in Iraq, Reliance Globalcom, in project collaboration with Iraqi

Telecommunications and Post Company (ITPC), launched the al-Faw Cable Landing Station (CLS) for providing telecom services in the country. It is set to enhance internet speed for Iraqi domestic consumers.[54]

Energy Relations

The US-led invasion of Iraq in 2003, economic sanctions imposed on the country and India's recall of ambassador to Iraq due to security concerns considerably slowed down the economic relations between the two countries. Political equations between the two countries improved significantly from 2011, but the most significant impact has been on the energy relations between India and Iraq (Tables 4.2 and 4.3 and Figure 4.2). According to the *Iraq Energy Outlook* published by the International Energy Agency (IEA) in 2012,[55] the country's oil production is expected to grow by over 5 million barrels a day to 2035. Iraq has replaced Iran as the second largest crude oil supplier to India in 2012.[56] According to IEA Chief Economist Fatih Birol, Iraq is set to become India's strategic energy partner in near future.[57]

At the same time, the political situation in Iran and the western economic sanctions have driven India to look for other energy partners to meet its growing energy requirements.[58] Iraq has risen significantly to the challenge. In 2011, Indian companies signed various deals with the Iraqi government which was seen as a 'welcome development' by the Indian side. Ronen Sen, India's former ambassador to the US, remarked

Table 4.2
Share of Oil in India's Imports from Iraq (in US$ Million)

Year	Oil imports from Iraq	Total oil imports	Iraqi share in total oil imports	Imports from Iraq	Per cent of oil in imports from Iraq
2009–10	6,981.32	96,321.16	7.25	7,026.93 ˙	99.35
2010–11	8,954.66	115,929.06	7.72	9,008.30	99.40
2011–12	18,848.26	172,753.97	10.91	18,939.63	99.52

Source: Adapted from Director General of Foreign Trade, New Delhi, http://www.dgft.gov.in

Table 4.3
India's Energy Imports from Iraq (in US$ Million)

	2009–10	2010–11	2011–12
Energy import from Iraq	6,981.32	8,954.66	18,848.26
Total energy import	96,321.16	115,929.06	172,753.97
Total import from Persian Gulf	55,906.14	66,688.40	103,915.24
Share in total imports (in per cent)	7.25	7.72	10.91
Share in imports from Persian Gulf (in per cent)	12.49	13.43	18.14

Source: Adapted from Director General of Foreign Trade, New Delhi, http://www.dgft.gov.in

Figure 4.2
Share of Oil in India's Total Imports from Iraq

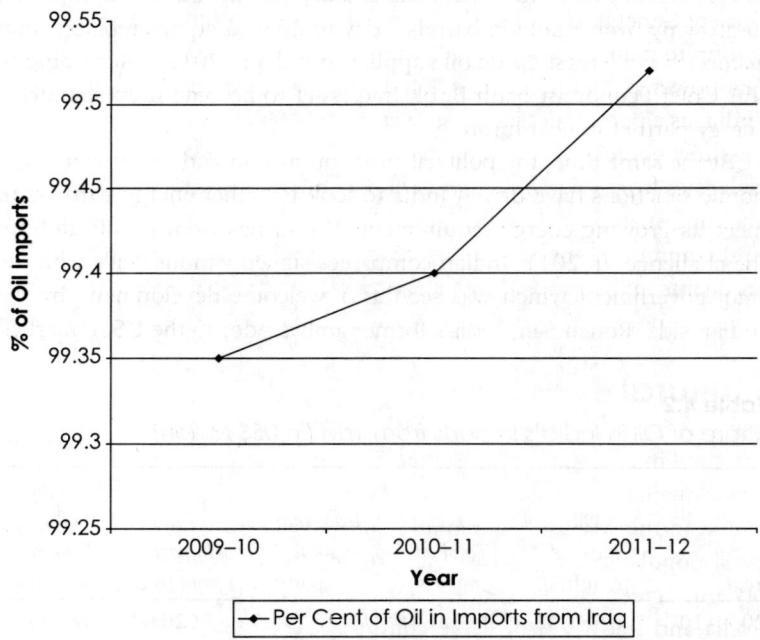

Source: Adapted from Director General of Foreign Trade, New Delhi, http://www.dgft.gov.in

that 'Iraq has been a traditional supplier of oil. We have high stakes in Iraq and we should stay engaged there not only for economic, but also for our energy security. Diversification of supply sources is a very welcome development.'[59]

Even though the Indian government has not officially confirmed reduction of supplies from Iran due to public disdain over the western sanctions, Iran's biggest Indian oil client, Mangalore Refinery and Petrochemicals Limited (MRPL) reduced imports from Iran by more than 20 per cent.[60] To make up for the reduction in Iranian crude supplies, the MRPL signed its first crude oil contract with Iraq.[61] India has been looking at Saudi Arabia and Iraq to diversify its oil purchase keeping the present political realities and market considerations in mind.[62]

India's Lanco Infratech Limited (LANCI) signed a US$81.3 million contract to build a gas-fired, 250 MW power station in western Iraq in 2011. The following year, Swiss inspection and certification company Societe Generale de Surveillance (SGS) has been entrusted by the Lanco Group to manage on-site quality control for the construction of its new gas power plant in al-Anbar, on a three-year agreement.[63] CommLab India, as a part of a turnkey project awarded by Iraqi Oil Ministry, successfully completed a two-month eLearning training programme for 24 delegates from Iraqi Ministry of Oil.[64] The company specializes in implementing methods of learning and training using modern information and communication technology to upgrade the knowledge and skills of its clients in the shortest possible time with minimum effort and cost.

Cultural Relations

Cultural interaction and economic trade between ancient India and Mesopotamia date back to 1800 BC. India has the third largest Shia population in the world after Iran and Pakistan, while Iraq has a significant Shia population of its own, bringing in closer religious–cultural affinity. An agreement of co-operation on cultural affairs in 1954 between India and Iraq reaffirmed the continuation of the ethos. The 'Cultural Exchange Programme (CAP)' and the 'General Cultural Scholarship

Scheme (GCSS)' offered by the Indian Council for Cultural Relations (ICCR) provide scholarships for higher studies to Iraqi students in India.

The Indian Business and Professional Council (IBPC), Kurdistan, which promotes business, economic and cultural co-operation between India and Kurdistan, organized the 66th Indian Independence Celebration, and was attended in large numbers by the Indian community in Kurdistan, as well as by delegates and guests from both countries.[65] Medical tourism in India has attracted Iraqis over the years. The inflow of Iraqi patients was 26,000 in 2011 and has doubled in 2012. Patients come to India for treatment and affordable medical facilities.[66] This year, the Iraqi government allocated 1 billion Iraqi dinars in recruiting Indian physicians and nurses to make up for the country's own shortages in some medical specializations.[67] A leading oncologist from India visited Iraq in April at the Medya Diagnostic Centre, discussing the leading developments in the field in the treatment of cancer.[68]

External Players

The US: The relationship between the US and Iraq has been a strained one following the US-led invasion of the country in 2003. By 2011, all US military forces were withdrawn from the country. The US President Barack Obama promised continued economic and military aid even after the withdrawal. The US voiced displeasure at the Iraqi Grain Board purchasing Indian Basmati Rice against the US fine-grained rice which had a good market in Iraq till 2010.[69] The US had also raised concerns over Iranian arms flying into Syria using Iraqi airspace.[70] However, when the concerns were placed before the Iraqi government, Iraq maintained that they were humanitarian aid, asking the US to bring evidence to the claim.[71] The relationship between the two states has remained fragile at best. The Iraqi government has refused renewed presence of American troops, leaving the US to maintain a large force of mainly private contractors to guard American officials.[72] On the economic side, a Conference on Economic Relations between the US and Iraq was held in 2012 during which Iraqi Finance Minister Rafie al-Issawi said, 'This conference will discuss Iraq's economic relations with the US and ways to strengthen and develop within the strategic agreement framework signed between the two countries.'[73]

China: Diplomatic relations between China and Iraq were established after the revolution of 1958. China has been one of the countries that strongly opposed the US-led invasion of Iraq, calling for withdrawal of all forces from the country. China had also refused to contribute any troops to Iraq without a UN mandate. In the aftermath of the US-led invasion of Iraq, China has benefitted the most in securing a major share of Iraq's oil contracts. In 2008, China National Petroleum Corporation was the first to sign an oil service contract in Iraq under the new US-backed regime to develop the Ahbad Oilfield. By 2010, China had five major oil investments in Iraq, one of which was in Kurdistan.[74] China is one of the major players where the exploration of oilfields and other development ventures in Iraq is concerned.[75] In addition to the oil sector, Chinese companies are also investing in construction, like the Cement Industry, and tourism in Iraq. Iraq is also interested in Chinese arms, signalling future military ties between the two countries.[76]

Pakistan: Diplomatic relations between Iraq and Pakistan were established in 1948, Iraq being the first Arab country to recognize Pakistan. Both countries are members of the Organisation of Islamic Cooperation (OIC). Pakistan strongly supports Iraq's territorial integrity and declines support to Kurdish separatism. Both the countries support the Palestinian cause. Iraq has a good market for Pakistani products such as cement, fruits and vegetables, furniture, handicrafts, rice, poultry and meat. As per Iraq's Grain Board, the country purchased 90,000 tonnes of grain from Pakistan in 2011. Pakistan remained a major rice exporter to Iraq in 2012. Iraq has welcomed Pakistani businessmen to Iraqi markets. Iraq finalized an oil and gas exploration contact with Pakistan Petroleum, signed in Baghdad by Iraqi Deputy Oil Minister Ahmed al-Shammaa and Pakistan Petroleum's Chief Executive Asim Murtaza Khan.[77]

Conclusion

After being held hostage to two decades of war and uncertainty, India's bilateral relations with Iraq are on the upswing again. Re-establishment of full diplomatic presence in 2011 and the political and economic visits since then have provided the bilateral relations with the much needed vigour. There are strong historical ties and cultural affinity between the two countries forming the foundation of present relations. Trade between India and Iraq has started flourishing again, especially in the field of energy supplies where Iraq is playing an increasingly important role, especially in the wake of western sanctions on Iran. Although India is facing stiff competition in this field from China, it has managed to secure significant supplies from Iraq.

Notes

1. Nimrod Raphaeli, 'Culture in Post-Saddam Iraq', *Middle East Forum* 14, no.3 (2007): 33–42, http://www.meforum.org/1707/culture-in-post-saddam-iraq
2. Iraq Body Count, 'Documented Civilian Deaths from Violence', http://www.iraqbodycount.org/database/
3. 'Iraq Government Casualty Figures', Agence France Presse, https://docs.google.com/spreadsheet/ccc?key=0Aia6y6NymliRdEZESktBSWVqNWM1d kZOSGNIVmtFZEE#gid=4
4. Aymenn Jawad Al-Tamimi, 'Spring Comes, but Not for Iraq's Kurds', *Middle East Forum*, 12 August 2011, http://www.meforum.org/3009/iraq-kurds-spring
5. 'Iraq's Jalal Talabani Arrives in Germany for Treatment', *BBC News*, 20 December 2012, http://www.bbc.co.uk/news/world-middle-east-20794273
6. 'World Report 2013: Iraq', Human Rights Watch, http://www.hrw.org/world-report/2013/country-chapters/iraq
7. 'New Report: Transparency International Put Iraq Ranked Third in the List of Most Corrupt Countries', *Iraqi Dinar*, 6 December 2012, http://iraqidinarchat.net/?p=13410
8. 'Documented Civilian Deaths from Violence'.
9. 'Iraq Government Casualty Figures'.
10. 'Iraq', CIA World Factbook, US Central Intelligence Agency, https://www.cia.gov/library/publications/the-world-factbook/geos/iz.html
11. Ibrahim Sirkeci, 'War in Iraq: Environment of Insecurity and International Migration', *International Migration* 43, No. 4 (2005): 197–214.
12. 'Syria Regional Refugee Response–Iraq', United Nations High Commissioner for Refugees, http://data.unhcr.org/syrianrefugees/country.php?id=103
13. 'Allawi Victory in Iraq Sets Up Period of Uncertainty', *The New York Times*, 26 March 2010, http://www.nytimes.com/2010/03/27/world/middleeast/27iraq.html?pagewanted=all&_r=0
14. 'Iraq's Leaders Back Fragile Power-sharing Deal', *The Guardian*, 11 November 2010, http://www.guardian.co.uk/world/2010/nov/11/iraq-leaders-back-fragile

15. 'Iraqi President in Hospital after Suffering Stroke', *Yahoo News,* 18 December 2012, http://uk.news.yahoo.com/iraq-president-hospitalized-suffering-stroke-115422848.html
16. 'Iraq Reaches Power-sharing Deal to Form Government', *The National,* 7 November 2010, http://www.thenational.ae/news/world/middle-east/iraq-reaches-power-sharing-deal-to-form-government
17. 'Iraqi President in Hospital'.
18. 'Is Barzani Assuming Talabani's Role as Mediator in Iraq?', *Al Monitor,* 15 February 2013, http://www.al-monitor.com/pulse/originals/2013/02/barzani-iraq-mediator.html
19. 'Iraq's Jalal Talabani Arrives in Germany for treatment'.
20. 'Iraq Tests Regional Muscle with Arab Summit', *Reuters,* 26 May 2012, http://www.reuters.com/article/2012/03/26/us-iraq-summit-diplomacy-idUSBRE82P0SL20120326
21. 'Arab League Summit Aims to Showcase "The New Iraq"', *CNN,* 27 March 2012, http://edition.cnn.com/2012/03/26/world/meast/iraq-arab-summit
22. Lara Jakes and Hamza Hendawi, 'Arab Summit in Bagdad: Explosions Heard as Meeting Opens', *The Huffington Post,* 29 March 2012, http://www.huffingtonpost.com/2012/03/29/arab-summit-baghdad_n_1387426.html
23. CIA, *The World Factbook,* updated 12 February 2013, https://www.cia.gov/library/publications/the-world-factbook/geos/iz.html
24. The World Bank, 'Doing Business: Economy Profile Iraq 2013', http://www.doingbusiness.org/~/media/giawb/doing%20business/documents/profiles/country/IRQ.pdf
25. 'Iraq to Be World's Fastest Growing Economy 2012/2013', *Iraq Oil Report,* 25 November 2012, http://www.iraqoilreport.com/daily-brief/iraq-to-be-worlds-fastest-growing-economy-20122013-9350/
26. Ibid.
27. Project Iraq 2013, http://www.project-iraq.com/
28. Energy Iraq 2013, http://www.elenex-iraq.com/
29. 'India–Iraq Relations', Ministry of External Affairs, New Delhi, February 2011, http://mea.gov.in/mystart.php?id=50049938
30. 'Iraq Conveys Support to India on Kashmir', *The Economic Times,* 7 July 2002, http://articles.economictimes.indiatimes.com/2002-07-07/news/27332449_1_kashmir-issue-india-and-pakistan-indo-iraq
31. 'Iraq and India Ties Warmed by Oil Deals', *BBC News,* 8 July 2002, http://news.bbc.co.uk/2/hi/business/2115930.stm
32. 'Bihar Assembly Passes Resolution against US on Iraq', *The Times of India,* 25 March 2003, http://articles.timesofindia.indiatimes.com/2003-03-25/patna/27275353_1_resolution-bihar-assembly-iraq-war
33. Ministry of External Affairs, *Annual Report Ministry of External Affairs, 2011–2012,* http://www.mea.gov.in/mystart.php?id=500419226
34. 'Iraq Appoints 43 New Ambassadors', *China Daily,* 20 July 2004, http://www.chinadaily.com.cn/english/doc/2004-07/20/content_349909.htm

35. 'New Delhi Names Envoy to Iraq, First Time since Saddam', *The Indian Express*, 20 February 2011, http://www.indianexpress.com/news/new-delhi-names-envoy-to-iraq-first-time-since-saddam/752372/

36. 'Indians Still Going to Iraq for Jobs despite Ban', *Rediff News*, 1 February 2008, http://www.rediff.com/money/2008/feb/01iraq.htm

37. 'Shri S K Reddy Appointed as Ambassador to Iraq', Press Release, 4 April 2011, Ministry of External Affairs, New Delhi, http://meaindia.nic.in/mystart.php?id=530217514

38. 'India's New Ambassador to Iraq Makes First Visit to Kurdistan', Press Release, Kurdistan Regional Government, 30 December 2011, http://www.krg.org/articles/detail.asp?rnr=223&lngnr=12&smap=02010100&anr=42792

39. Ibid.

40. 'India's Ambassador to Iraq Updates DFR about Establishing Presence in Erbil', Press Release, *Kurdistan Regional Government*, 9 July 2012, http://dfr.krg.org/a/d.aspx?l=12&a=41849

41. 'Nujaifi Looking with Indian Vice President Bilateral Relations', National Iraqi News Agency, 17 December 2012, http://www.ninanews.com/english/News_Details.asp?ar95_VQ=GFDMMJ (Arabic)

42. 'India, Iraq Discuss Bilateral Relations', *Aswat al Iraq*, 17 December 2012, http://en.aswataliraq.info/(S(uymuj1r0xizqzibtyss0boev))/Default1.aspx?page=article_page&id=151785&l=1

43. 'India, Iraq Should Fight the Menace of Terrorism: Meira Kumar', *Zee News*, 17 December 2012, http://zeenews.india.com/news/nation/india-iraq-should-fight-the-menace-of-terrorism-meira-kumar_817351.html

44. '20 Years after the First Gulf War, a Direct Flight to Iraq from India', *The Indian Express*, 9 February 2012, http://www.indianexpress.com/news/20-years-after-the-first-gulf-war-a-direct-flight-to-iraq-from-india/909843/

45. 'Iraqi Airlines Flight to Land at Mumbai Airport after 22 Years', *DNA* 28 April 2012, http://www.dnaindia.com/mumbai/report_iraqi-airlines-flight-to-land-at-mumbai-airport-after-22-years_1681691

46. 'US Upset over Iraq Buying Basmati from India', *Outlook India*, 10 February 2012, http://news.outlookindia.com/items.aspx?artid=752945

47. 'Iraq Looking to Import Rice, Sugar from India', *The Economic Times*, 27 February 2012, http://articles.economictimes.indiatimes.com/2012-02-27/news/31104305_1_oil-imports-import-rice-iraq-exports

48. 'Iraq Seeks to Buy 30,000 Tons of Basmati Rice', *Bloomberg Businessweek*, 11 April 2012, http://www.businessweek.com/news/2012-04-11/iraq-seeks-to-buy-30-000-tons-of-basmati-rice-ministry-says

49. Ibid.

50. 'Exporters Must Tap Iraqi Preference for Indian goods', The Federation of Indian Exports News, September 2012, http://www.fieo.org/uploads/files/file/certification%20of%20goods%20to%20iraq(1).pdf

51. 'Tea Consignment Barred by Iraq on Quality Issues', *The Financial Express*, 11 March 2011, http://www.financialexpress.com/news/tea-consignment-barred-by-iraq-on-quality-issues/760801/0

52. 'India's Jindal Target End-2013 for Iraq Pipe Mill Start', *Arab Steel*, 7 June 2012, http://www.arabsteel.info/total/Long_News_Total_e.asp?ID=1083

53. Ibid.

54. 'Reliance Globalcom Cable Landing Station in Iraq', *The Indian Express*, 2 July 2012, http://www.indianexpress.com/news/reliance-globalcom-cable-landing-station-in-iraq/969381

55. 'Iraq Energy Outlook', International Energy Agency, 9 October 2012, http://www.worldenergyoutlook.org/media/weowebsite/2012/iraqenergyoutlook/Fullreport.pdf

56. 'Iraq Replaces Iran as India's Second Largest Crude Oil Supplier', *The Wall Street Journal*, 16 May 2012, http://online.wsj.com/article/SB10001424052702303448404577407843978018060.html

57. 'Iraq Set to Become India's Strategic Energy Partner: IEA Chief Economist', *The Hindu*, 9 October 2012, http://www.thehindubusinessline.com/industry-and-economy/article3981732.ece?homepage=true&ref=wl_home

58. 'India Must Think Hard to Secure Its Energy Needs', *Financial Chronicle*, 10 January 2012, http://www.mydigitalfc.com/2012/slippery-ground

59. 'BHEL Deal to Deepen India's Commercial Ties with Iraq', *Mint*, 12 May 2011, http://www.livemint.com/Home-Page/qKKvp5Y38MlLHmRWlNGgGN/Bhel-deal-to-deepen-India8217s-commercial-ties-with-Iraq.html

60. 'India's MPRL Plans Hefty Cut in Iran oil Imports', *Reuters*, 5 March 2012, http://uk.reuters.com/article/2012/03/05/uk-mrpl-iran-idUKTRE8240A720120305

61. 'India Seeks Extra Oil from Iraq in FY13', *Reuters*, 29 February 2012, http://in.reuters.com/article/2012/02/29/india-oil-idINDEE81S0DY20120229?type=economicNews

62. 'India Looking at Saudi, Iraq to Diversify Its Oil Sourcing', *The Economic Times*, 18 May 2012, http://articles.economictimes.indiatimes.com/2012-05-18/news/31765500_1_iranian-oil-import-oil-sourcing

63. 'SGS Wins Inspection Contract for Gas Power Plant Project in Iraq', *SGS News*, 26 April 2012, http://www.sgs.com/en/Our-Company/News-and-Media-Center/News-and-Press-Releases/2012/04/SGS-Wins-Inspection-Contract-for-Gas-Power-Plant-Project-in-Iraq.aspx

64. 'CommLab Trains Delegates from Iraqi Oil Ministry', *Iraq Business News*, 5 June 2012, http://www.iraq-businessnews.com/2012/06/05/commlab-trains-delegates-from-iraqi-oil-ministry/

65. 'Indian Independence Day Celebration in Iraq', *Dinamalar*, 31 August 2012, http://www.dinamalar.com/nri/details.asp?id=1604&lang=en

66. 'Iraqi Cancer Patient Finds Hope in India', *Health India*, 23 May 2012, http://health.india.com/diseases-conditions/iraqi-cancer-patient-finds-hope-in-india/

67. 'Indian Physicians and Nurses for Imara Hospital', *Aswat al Iraq*, 23 May 2012, http://en.aswataliraq.info/(S(2w4zhj55vtj2ol55h4ie2k45))/Default1.aspx?page=article_page&id=148715&l=1

68. 'Leading Oncologist from India Visiting Erbil for 3 Days', Press Release, Omega Cancer Hospitals, 23 April 2012, http://www.pr.com/press-release/407409

69. 'US Upset over Iraq Buying Basmati from India', *The Indian Express*, 25 February 2012, http://www.indianexpress.com/news/us-upset-over-iraq-buying-basmati-from-india/916642

70. 'Western Report—Iran Ships Arms, Personnel to Syria via Iraq', *Reuters*, 19 September 2012, http://www.reuters.com/article/2012/09/19/us-syria-crisis-iran-iraq-idUSBRE88I17B20120919

71. 'Iraq's Role in Syria War Poses Problems for US', *Bloomberg Businessweek*, 5 September 2012, http://www.businessweek.com/ap/2012-09-05/iraq-us-must-show-proof-of-iranian-arms-flights

72. Peter Symonds, 'US Pushes for Renewed Military Presence in Iraq', *World Socialist Website*, 2 February 2012, http://www.wsws.org/en/articles/2012/02/iraq-f02.html

73. 'Conference on Economic Relations between US and Iraq', *The Currency Newshound*, 1 July 2012, http://thecurrencynewshound.com/2012/07/01/conference-on-economic-relations-between-us-and-iraq/

74. J. Michael Cole, 'China's Oil Quest Comes to Iraq', *The Diplomat,* 2 December 2012, http://thediplomat.com/2012/12/02/china-introducing-the-middle-easts-future-hegemon/

75. 'How China Won the Iraq War?', *RTE News,* 4 December 2012, http://www.rte.ie/blogs/business/2012/12/04/how-china-won-the-iraq-war/

76. Richard Weitz, 'China-Iraq Ties: Oil, Arms and Influence', *Second Line of Defence,* 25 June 2012, http://www.sldinfo.com/china-iraq-ties-oil-arms-and-influence/

77. 'Iraq Finalizes Petroleum Deal with Pakistan Petroleum', *Kooza,* 5 November 2012, http://www.thekooza.com/iraq-finalizes-exploration-deal-with-pakistan-petroleum/

5

Kuwait

Paulami Sanyal

Key Indicators

Area: 17,818 sq km; **Population:** 2.69 million, **Native:** 45 per cent, **Expats:** 55 per cent; **Youth population:** 15.4 per cent; **Population growth rate:** 1.883 per cent; **Life expectancy at birth:** 74.7 years; **GDP:** US$165.9 billion; **Per capita income:** US$43,800; **Foreign trade:** US$133.5 billion; **Oil reserves:** 101.5 billion bbl (2013); **Gas reserves:** 11.73 billion m^3; **Ruling family:** Al-Sabah; **Ruler:** Emir Sabah al-Ahmad Jabir al-Sabah (since 29 January 2006); **National Day:** 25 February; **Defence budget:** 5.3 per cent of GDP; **HDI rank:** 54; **Literacy rate:** 93.3 per cent; **UN education index:** 0.620; **Gender inequality index:** 0.274.

Source: CIA, *The World Factbook*, https://www.cia.gov/library/publications/the-world-factbook/index.html; UN Human Development Report, Statistics, http://hdr.undp.org/en/statistics/

Note: All data for 2012.

Relations between India and Kuwait started long before the discovery of oil. The discovery of objects like seals, pottery and jewellery on the Kuwaiti Island of Failaka, which was a passage for ships sailing between Mesopotamia and India at that time, proves that Kuwait's relations with India date back to the fourth millennium BC. For centuries sailors from Shatt-al-Arab carried dates and horses to the western ports of India. However, as the horse trade waned after the Second World War, Kuwaitis started trading pearls with India and in exchange took teakwood for ship building. In the colonial era, the British assigned a commissioner to this state from 1906 till 1961.[1] Diplomatic relations between the two countries started in June 1962 with the appointment of Yacoub Abdulaziz al-Rasheed as the first Kuwaiti Ambassador to India following Kuwaiti independence.[2] The discovery of oil led to a much closer relationship between these two countries. Since then, there have been political dialogues and ministerial visits which further strengthened the relationship. The presence of more than 500,000 Indian expatriates in Kuwait and their impact on the economies of both countries also helped in upholding the cordial relations.

Domestic Developments

With a population of around 3.6 million, including expatriates who make up two-thirds, Kuwait is situated at the top of the Persian Gulf between Iraq and Iran in the North West and North East, respectively, and Saudi Arabia in the South.[3] Kuwait's geographic position in between such strong neighbours has created certain hazards and forced the Emirate to lean more heavily on outside powers, especially the United States (US) for protection and survival.

The abundant oil revenue available to Kuwait has provided a high standard of living to its citizens. Oil was discovered in Kuwait in the 1930s and since then it has been the primary source of revenue, with as much as 90 per cent of its export revenues coming from petroleum exports. Kuwait is the fourth biggest producer in the Organization of Petroleum Exporting Countries (OPEC), after Saudi Arabia, Iraq and Iran.[4] Kuwait provides roughly nine per cent of the world's oil supply, and oil accounts for nearly 50 per cent of GDP. Mindful of its over-dependence on oil, from 2010, Kuwait started a five-year plan to diversify the economy, strengthen the private sector and attract foreign investment in other sectors of the economy. However, the country is also facing other institutional problems like the private sector's dependence on government funding and expatriate labour, institutional deficiencies like weak judiciary, corrupt bureaucratic structures. With the spread of Arab Spring in neighbouring countries, these deficiencies became glaring. In an attempt to prevent the effect of Arab spring, last year the Emir gave every citizen 1,000 dinars (US$3,500) in grants and free food coupons.[5]

On 19 June 1961, Kuwait became independent with the end of the British protectorate and in 1963 became the first Arab country in the Gulf region to have an elected parliament. The constitution provides for an independent judiciary, but the Amir appoints all judges. As an Islamic monarchy with the privilege of having a free media and religious liberty, Kuwait has been supporting women's role in politics since May 2005 when parliament granted women the right to vote and stand as candidates in elections for the 50-seat National Assembly. After 2005, there were more developments in this issue. On 22 April 2012, an administrative court cancelled a ministerial order which prohibited women from entry-level jobs at the Ministry of Justice. Moreover, in early June 2012, an administrative court ordered Kuwait University to cancel a policy requiring female students to do better in exams than male students to enrol in certain departments, including colleges of medicine and architecture.[6] But despite these developments, women continue to face certain discrimination in Kuwaiti society. For example, Kuwait's nationality law denies Kuwaiti women who are married to foreign men, the right to pass their nationality on to their children and spouses, a right enjoyed by Kuwaiti men married to foreign women. Kuwait has no laws prohibiting domestic violence, sexual harassment or marital rape.[7]

Kuwait holds first place among the Gulf States with regard to press freedom. But restraints are practised in matters of insulting comments about God and the Prophet, criticism of the Emir, constitution, judiciary and the 'basic convictions of the nation'.[8] In 2012, Kuwaiti lawmakers approved a law with a death penalty for Muslims who curse God, the Koran, all prophets and the wives of Prophet Mohammed. Non-Muslims who commit the same offence face a jail term of not less than 10 years.[9] There are several examples of restrictions on the freedom of expression. The Al-Jazeera was banned in Kuwait for some time. Although authorities lifted the suspension in December 2011, a criminal court suspended *Al Dar* newspaper for three months and sentenced the editor-in-chief Abd al-Hussain al-Sultan to a six-month suspended jail term and fined him 1,000 Kuwaiti Dinars (US$3,500) for allegedly publishing articles that 'raise[d] sectarian strife and incite[d] to violate public order'. The charges arose after the newspaper published three articles containing statements critical and demeaning to the Shia minority in Kuwait. On 5 June 2012, a criminal court sentenced blogger Hamad al-Naqi to 10 years of imprisonment for allegedly posting tweets 'insulting' the Prophet Muhammad and criticising the Kings of Saudi Arabia and Bahrain.[10]

Kuwait shares close links with the US. Kuwait's changing political scenario is monitored by the US which has deployed 13,500 troops in the country to counterweight the threat of Iran's military expansion in the Persian Gulf.[11] Kuwait is under significant influence of its neighbour Saudi Arabia. At the time of Iraq invasion in August 1990, its leaders took refuge in Saudi Arabia, which in turn led to greater Saudi influence in Kuwaiti internal affairs. This can be seen in the role of Salafis in Kuwaiti politics which is leading to several non-liberal developments in the political and social scenario in Kuwait. For example, Salafi lawmakers proposed a 'decency' law in early 2012 banning 'flirtatious behaviour' and 'indecent attire' in public, which would include swimsuits on beaches. A few years ago, Kuwait banned the 'Star Academy' TV talent show for featuring women singing to men, revealing clothes and mixed dancing after complaints from Salafi Members of Parliament (MPs).[12]

Despite the strains on the political and social climate, Kuwait has largely been stable even during the peak of Arab Spring. The citizens were in support of monarchy but there were repetitive demands for an end to corruption. The issue came to the fore in December 2011 when the much media-hyped lawsuit of 'The Parliament of Millions of Payments' took place in which 13 MPs of the 2009 assembly were accused of taking bribes for approval of government plans. Following that another lawsuit, dubbed 'Millions of Transfers', led to the resignation of the Foreign Minister Sheikh Muhammad al-Sabah. However, there were no large-scale violent protests demanding ouster of the regime as witnessed in other Arab countries, although the trend of Islamist ascendancy in Kuwaiti politics continued. In the parliamentary election that took place in February 2012, the opposition led by Islamists gained a majority by winning 34 of the 50 seats in the National Assembly. Kuwaiti opposition is mainly composed of Islamists, liberals and tribal groups and 23 of the 34 seats won by the opposition went to Sunni Islamists. Liberals won nine seats and women did not win any. In contrast, there were four women in the previous parliament.[13] Four months after the elections, constitutional court nullified the election, dissolved the parliament and restored the previous parliament of 2009.[14] This resulted in protests against the government. However, on 7 October 2012, the Emir dissolved the 2009 parliament for the second time and set 1 December 2012 as the election date with certain amendments which according to the opposition were meant to reduce the advantage of the opposition candidates.[15] In the second election held in 2012, the voter turnout was about 40 per cent which was the lowest since the first general election in 1963. The opposition boycotted the election and there was several mass protests calling for people not to take part in the election.[16] However, the differences within the opposition itself earned it a name of 'alliance of convenience'.[17] The liberals within the opposition are demanding wider freedom and western-style openness, whereas the Islamists demand stricter Islamic codes like death sentences for those convicted of insulting the Prophet Muhammad. Tribal groups, on the other hand, want to preserve their influence and fear that the new voting system would reduce their influence.

Although Kuwait did not face the severe turmoil as witnessed in the other Arab states, it was not totally spared from the spillover effects of the Arab Spring. Even before the advent of the Arab Spring, there were opposition forces in Kuwait who were against the government. At the time of Arab Spring, the youth protested against widespread corruption. Opposition leaders supported the youth—under the banner of 'Fifth Fence'[18]—calling for the resignation for the interior minister. With the passage of time, pressure increased on the Prime Minister of Kuwait to take steps against corruption. From 2011 to 2012, there have been several small protests against the government. Demands for dissolution of Parliament and new elections were growing among the Islamist-led opposition which resulted in dissolution of country's parliament on 7 October 2012 and announcement of fresh elections by the Emir Sabah al-Ahmad al-Sabah.[19] Until late 2012, the demonstrations in Kuwait have been relatively small. However, when Sabah regime tried to shape the 1 December 2012 elections to its advantage, a large demonstration took place on 21 October 2012. Oppositionists boycotted the election, lowering the turnout but giving the government an overwhelming majority in the Assembly.[20] When faced with increasing protests, the rulers of the Gulf countries had taken certain appeasement policies for the people. Similarly, economic incentives were announced in Kuwait as well.

Al-Sabah granted all Kuwaiti citizens 1,000 dinars (US$3,500) in aid and announced free distribution of basic food items from February 2011 till March 2013.[21] These were announced as part of the commemoration of the 50th anniversary of the country's independence, 20th anniversary of its liberation from Iraqi occupation and fifth anniversary of Emir's coming to power. Moreover, basic salary of the servicemen was also raised by up to 115 per cent.

Apart from the protests from its citizens, Kuwait is also facing protests from the Bidun communities. At least 106,000 Bidun live in Kuwait and the authorities claim that most Bidun are 'illegal residents' who deliberately destroyed evidence of other nationality to get the benefits that the state provides to its citizens. The Biduns have been protesting throughout 2011 and although the protests are peaceful, authorities are taking harsh measures under Article 12 of the 1979 Public Gatherings law which bars non-Kuwaitis from participating in public gatherings. In April 2012, the United Nation's Committee on the Elimination of Racial Discrimination (CERD) called upon the Kuwaiti government to provide a 'just, humane and comprehensive solution to the situation' of Bidun.[22] Some steps have been taken by the Kuwaiti government to address the issues of the 'stateless' Bidun, including a recent law to naturalize a small number.[23] As Kuwait has the oldest and relatively vocal parliament in the Gulf, the situation would be closely watched by other Gulf countries struggling with their own political pressures. Kuwait's parliament has significant powers compared to its counterparts in other Gulf countries but some have lamented that the MPs only have 'ability, inclination and incentives to block government legislation, question ministers and flag corruption than to produce positive progress on policy'.[24]

The problems faced by the expatriate labour in Kuwait, most important being human trafficking, exploitation and lack of legal regulations, remained contentious in 2012. Kuwaiti households employ more than 600,000 domestic workers, primarily from Asia and East Africa.[25] Public sector in Kuwait depends heavily on the expatriate labourers. But labour laws concerning domestic workers like family cooks, housemaids, nannies, drivers, farmers, guards, shepherds and stablemen who account for roughly eight per cent of Kuwait's 3.1 million populations are pending for years in the parliament without any progress. At present, any problems pertinent with domestic labour issues are referred to the Ministry of Interior. The proposed changes to the labour law recommend the creation of a separate department to deal with the domestic labour affairs or to be later called as the Domestic Labour Department. The existing situation causes heavy hardship to the labourers and the expatriate labourers are sometimes being trafficked to other countries, facing physical and sexual harassments.

The US, in its 2012 State Department report on Trafficking in Persons, classified Kuwait as Tier 3—among the most problematic countries—for the sixth year in a row. The report cited Kuwait's 'failure to enact comprehensive anti-trafficking legislation, weak victim protection measures, and lack of coordination between various governmental institutions focusing on anti-trafficking issues'.[26] This is even straining Kuwait's relation with other countries. For example, Indonesia has stopped sending household workers to Kuwait since 2009.[27] For their part, the Kuwaiti authorities are trying to resolve the problem. Emir Sheikh Sabah al-Ahmad al-Jaber al-Sabah signed a memorandum of understanding (MoU) with the Philippines on the recruitment of household workers during his visit in March 2012 to Manila because the Philippines threatened to stop sending domestic workers to Kuwait unless the MoU was signed.[28]

Bilateral Relations

Political relations between the two countries started after Kuwait gained independence in 1961. Indeed, until 1961 the Indian Rupee was the legal currency in Kuwait. There were visits both from Kuwait and India to each other from 1960s till 1980s. However, the relationship strained following the Iraqi invasion, occupation and annexation of Kuwait in 1990. The Indian stand was seen as less sympathetic towards Kuwait and a tacit acceptance of the Iraqi actions. India's decision to quickly close its embassy in Kuwait was not viewed kindly by the Kuwaiti leadership. Though India did not endorse the Iraqi actions, its position was viewed to be unsympathetic. Thus, in the aftermath of the reversal of the Iraqi occupation in February 1991, the bilateral relations remained strained and India had to invest considerable political and diplomatic capital to overcome the bitterness and disappointment in Kuwait.

Political Relations

The defining moment of reconciliation was the visit by Emir Sheikh Sabah al-Ahmed al-Jaber al-Sabah in June 2006.[29] Since then, there were periodic but less frequent political contacts. In 2009, Vice President of India Hamid Ansari visited Kuwait during which three agreements were signed covering education. Minister of External Affairs S. M. Krishna visited Kuwait in February 2010 and again in February 2011. Minister of State for External Affairs E. Ahamed and Minister of State for Petroleum & Natural Gas and Corporate Affairs R. P. N. Singh also visited Kuwait in 2011.[30] Minister of Oversees Indian Affairs Vayalar Ravi visited Kuwait in November 2012 to promote the 11th Pravasi Bhartiya Divas (PBD). T. K. A. Nair, advisor to the Prime Minister of India, visited Kuwait from 10 to 12 May 2012 to discuss bilateral issues.[31]

Economic Relations

There is traditionally a thread of friendly relations between India and Kuwait. Geographical proximity, historically created trade links which tend to continue till now, cultural connections and presence of a large number of Indian expatriates helped in maintaining that relationship till the present days. Until 1961, the Indian Rupee was legal tender in Kuwait.[32] India–Kuwait bilateral trade was US$17.55 billion in 2011–12 (Table 5.1 and Figure 5.1), of which non-oil trade accounted for approximately US$1.9 billion while petroleum exports from Kuwait to India were approximately US$15.67 billion. Indian exports to Kuwait during 2010–11 and 2011–12 were over US$1 billion. India's imports from Kuwait went up by 58.77 per cent from US$10.313 billion in 2010–11 to US$16.375 billion in 2011–12 (Table 5.2). India imported US$15.67 billion worth of petroleum, oil and lubricants (POL) from Kuwait in the year 2011–12. India's imports from Kuwait, excluding petroleum and its products, were US$708.26 million in 2011–12.[33]

Retail stores like Bikanervala Foods Pvt. Ltd., Café Coffee Day, Asha's and Nirula's have their outlets in Kuwait. In the food sector, Hart Foods, KRBL (exporter of basmati rice), Naturo Food and Fruit Products Pvt.

Table 5.1
India–Kuwait Bilateral Trade (in US$ Million)

	2009–10	*2010–11*	*2011–12*
Exports	782.45	1,856.01	1,181.41
Imports	8,249.49	10,313.64	16,375.37
Total trade	9,031.95	12,169.65	17,556.78
Share of Kuwait in total trade	1.93	1.98	2.13

Source: Director General of Foreign Trade, http://www.dgft.gov.in

Figure 5.1
India–Kuwait Bilateral Trade

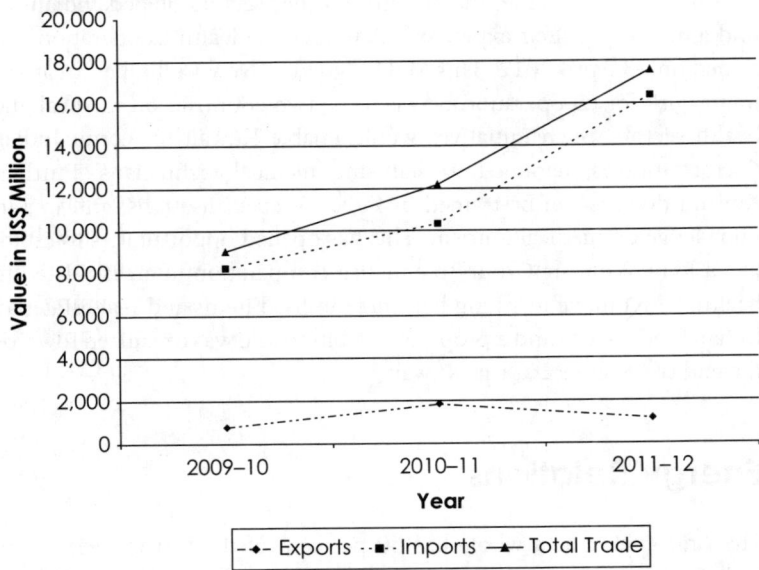

Source: Director General of Foreign Trade, http://www.dgft.gov.in

Ltd., Eastern Curry Powder of Eastern Group, Viraj Exim Pvt. Ltd., Namakkal poultry industry, etc., have their significant share of export to Kuwait. In the field of technology, both India and Kuwait have been working together in areas such as machine tools manufacture, telecom, cement production, banking, insurance and shipping.[34]

Table 5.2
Share of Oil in India's Imports from Kuwait (in US$ Million)

Year	Oil imports from Kuwait	Total oil imports	Kuwaiti share in total oil imports	Imports from Kuwait	Per cent of oil in imports from Kuwait
2009–10	7,909.80	96,321.16	8.21	8,249.49	95.88
2010–11	9,729.09	115,929.06	8.39	10,313.64	94.33
2011–12	15,667.11	172,753.97	9.07	16,375.37	95.67

Source: Adapted from Director General of Foreign Trade, http://www.dgft.gov.in

Along with the trade, the growth of other sectors helped Indians to find a market for their expertise.[35] An MoU on Health Cooperation was signed on 23 April 2012. This MoU, signed in New Delhi, has created a framework for co-operation between the two countries on medical and health sectors. Such initiatives would enable Kuwait to recruit Indian doctors, nurses, paramedical staff and medical technicians. Further, Kuwaiti doctors can be trained in India for specialisations, and impart knowledge on medical tourism. This has opened opportunities to establish a Joint Working Group to enhance co-operation in areas related to health.[36] In a move to strengthen trade in food items and real estate, an Indian food festival and a property exhibition sale was organized towards the end of October 2011 in Kuwait.[37]

Energy Relations

The Arab region as a whole has 60 per cent of the proven reserves of global oil, and Kuwait has nine per cent of world's oil deposit. During 2011–12, Kuwait was third major supplier of oil to India from the Gulf region after Saudi Arabia and Iraq (Table 5.3 and Figure 5.2). When India's Vice President Hamid Ansari visited Kuwait in 2009, he expressed the hope that the Kuwait Petroleum International (KPI) would be actively involved in the Indian petrochemical sector.[38] No progress, however, has been made. Following the increasing uncertainty over crude imports from Iran, India has increased imports from Kuwait.

Table 5.3
India's Energy Imports from Kuwait (in US$ Million)

	2009–10	*2010–11*	*2011–12*
Energy import from Kuwait	7,909.80	9,729.09	15,667.11
Total energy import	96,321.16	115,929.06	172,753.97
Total import from Persian Gulf	55,904.14	66,688.40	103,915.24
Share in total imports	8.21	8.39	9.07
Share in imports from Persian Gulf	14.15	14.59	15.08

Source: Adapted from Director General of Foreign Trade, http://www.dgft.gov.in

Figure 5.2
Share of Oil in India's Total Imports from Kuwait

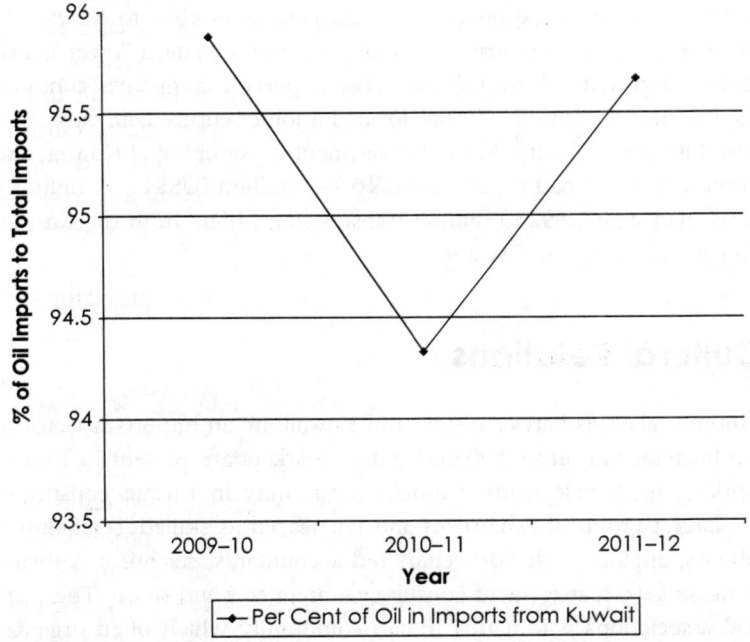

Source: Adapted from Director General of Foreign Trade, http://www.dgft.gov.in

A number of Indian companies are active in Kuwait. The state-owned Oil and Natural Gas Corporation (ONGC) has tied up with the Hinduja group for acquiring oilfields and sourcing liquefied natural gas (LNG) from Kuwait. Larsen & Toubro (L&T) has already established a joint venture in Kuwait for electromechanical construction in oil and gas, power and infrastructure projects. Its heavy engineering division has got an order from Kuwait National Petroleum Company (KNPC) for its 'Clean Fuel Project 2020'. The division has to manufacture and supply 22 hydrocracker and atmospheric residue desulphurisation reactors to KNPC. The ONGC and Bharat Petroleum Corporation Limited (BPCL) are also importing LNG from Gulf countries including Kuwait. India and Kuwait have jointly set up a US$110 million petrochemical plant on Jurong Island, in Singapore. Travancore Titanium Products Ltd., a producer of Titanium Oxide promoted by government of Kerala, is sourcing sulphur from the Kuwait Petroleum Corp. Government of Kerala is seeking a long term deal with this company for the purpose. Goa Carbons Manufacturer exports its calcined petroleum coke to Kuwait. In the power sector, Jyoti Structures Ltd. (JSL) and Kalpataru Power Transmission Ltd. (KPTL) are the two most important companies conducting business in Kuwait. JSL has formed a joint-venture company, Gulf Jyoti International with the Gulf Investment Corporation of Kuwait, and in the year 2010 had orders worth ₹6,740 million (US$123.5 million). KPTL had won US$250 million transmission orders from the Kuwaiti Ministry of Energy and Water.

Cultural Relations

Cultural relations between India and Kuwait are an important factor in the bilateral ties. Over 500,000 Indian workers are present in Kuwait working in diverse fields.[39] Indian community in Kuwait constitutes the largest group of expatriates and is engaged as skilled, semi-skilled labours, engineers, doctors, chartered accountants, scientists, software professionals, management consultants, architects and so on. There are 300 associations within this Indian community which often organize cultural events.[40] Owing to very high numbers of emigration from India to Kuwait, both the countries have increased the capacity of air services from 8,320 to 12,000 seats per week, and during 2012 carriers were granted three additional points of call in India, namely, Hyderabad, Kolkata and Bangalore.[41]

Despite the sizeable expat population, there were certain limitations. Trouble between India and Kuwait occurred on issues such as detention of visa violators by the Kuwaiti authorities of whom many were Indians.[42] Furthermore, semi-literate or illiterate unskilled or semi-skilled Indian labourers faced problems like underpayment, delayed payment, long working hours with insufficient or no welfare schemes, cheating, harassment and threats to their jobs on complaints.

Challenges

Despite such developments in their cordiality, Indo–Kuwaiti relations faced certain challenges and problems. In the economic sphere, there are several issues in bilateral relations between the two countries that need attention. There is lack of special attention in case of machine tools, hand tools, sophisticated appliances and goods produced in the small-scale sector, which accounts for more than 30 per cent of the total exports of the Indian manufacturing sector. Hence, better exploitation of India's competitive potentials in this respect is a necessity to increase the quality of the goods. In the absence of a continuous and regular publicity of Indian goods in the market, the Kuwaiti buyers are generally ignorant about the progress and achievements of India in the field of technological developments. For that matter publicity and marketing expertise are required.[43] Moreover, in spite of signing an Indo–Kuwaiti Trade Agreement on 13 February 1974, the level of trade and economic co-operation has not shown significant developments which may be due to the fact that no serious effort has been made to implement them effectively.[44]

The bilateral trade is highly skewed in favour of Kuwait. On one hand, India is facing the problem of growing adverse balance of payment and making massive efforts to explore oil and natural gas deposits and increase domestic production of petroleum products to meet its growing domestic consumption. On the other hand, Kuwait cannot afford to increase imports at the cost of its oil exports because petroleum products are the basic foundation of the Kuwaiti economy. These conflicting interests of the two countries are among the constraints in Indo–Kuwaiti trade.

The arid climatic condition impact on Kuwait's agriculture heavily. Almost 100 per cent of its foodgrains are imported. This provides an opportunity for India to explore the possibility of assisting Kuwait in food processing industries, providing quality seeds, technology and expertise. Both countries can also work together in solar and silicon industries. According to Khaldoon Tabaza, Chairman and CEO of Riyada, a venture capital firm based in Jordan, 'This part of the world, with an abundance of sunlight and silica, is a very appealing location for renewable energy, which can leverage the natural resources of the region in the same way we have done with oil and gas.'[45] India can work together with Kuwait in field of Islamic Banking as well which has a significant percentage of total bank deposits in Kuwait.

External Players

The US: The US is one of the most important players in the Persian Gulf region, and its relation with the countries here has impacts over others as well. After its independence, Kuwait was the first country in the Gulf region to establish relations with the Soviet Union, and this did not favour closer relations with the US until the Iran–Iraq War. From the time of Iraq's invasion and the US coming to its rescue, the Kuwait–US relations have been strong.[46] Kuwait has played a pivotal role in US-led invasion of Iraq in March 2003. Kuwait sends military cadets to US military institutions to study intelligence, pilot training and other disciplines.[47] Presently, the increasing influence of Iran in this region has made Kuwait suspicious of its intention and led Kuwait to form even stronger ties with the US. Following the Arab Spring, Kuwait was mildly stirred with protests. However, towards the end of 2012, when anti-government protests were taking place, the US criticized Kuwaiti authorities' ban on large public gatherings and suggested both sides to 'exercise restraint'.[48]

China: China is Kuwait's third largest oil importer after South Korea and India. During the Gulf Crisis in 1990, China resolutely opposed Iraq's invasion and occupation of Kuwait and demanded that Iraq should withdraw its troops from Kuwait and restore and respect the independence, sovereignty and territorial integrity of Kuwait. China and Kuwait began direct civil trade as early as in 1955 and both the countries have carried out friendly contacts in the fields of culture, education, sports and religion, with very frequent exchange of visits. China has dispatched many sports coaches to Kuwait and sent students to the Arab country annually.[49] Since the visit of Sheikh Sabah al-Ahmad al-Jaber al-Sabah to China in 2009, the two states have been seeking to further bolster their friendly ties and co-operation. From the energy perspective, China is one of Kuwait's most important importers with its huge market. The refiners in China have imported around 250,000 barrels of crude oil per day in 2012.[50] Such increasing relation is a potential challenge to India–Kuwait energy relations. In 2008, China had an overall trade surplus of US$296 billion.[51] Ideally, a Free Trade Agreement should be rewarding to both the parties and in 2012, in a conference organized by the Sharjah Chamber of Commerce and Industry, Chinese Premier Wen Jiabao again called for establishment of a Free Trade Agreement between China and GCC.[52]

Pakistan: Trade links between Pakistan and Kuwait can be traced prior to the discovery of oil. When Kuwait and the Indian subcontinent were involved in pre-oil trade, Karachi was the first port of call for Kuwaiti ships. After the oil boom in Kuwait, a large influx of Pakistani workers became part of development of Kuwait. Presently, around 120,000 Pakistanis live and work in Kuwait.[53] In Kuwaiti Universities, two seats are allocated for Pakistani nationals. There had been some troubles regarding giving visas to Pakistani nationals. In 2011, Kuwait banned issuing of visa to the Pakistani nationals fearing a spillover of the political turmoil of Pakistan. However, presently Kuwait is considering lifting the ban on Pakistani workers.[54]

Efforts are being made towards promoting investments between Pakistan and Kuwait. In 1979, the Pakistan Kuwait Investment Company, a development financial institution with the backing of the governments of Pakistan and Kuwait, was established. The Seventh Pakistan Expo 2012 had participation of 12 Kuwaiti companies. Pakistani diplomats pointed out that the trade between Pakistan and Kuwait had crossed US$3.5 billion, primarily in crude oil import from Kuwait. Total Pakistani marine-products export to Kuwait till now is approximately US$8 billion to US$10 billion.[55]

Pakistani Prime Minister Raja Pervez Ashraf visited Kuwait from 15 to 17 October 2012 to attend the First Summit of Asian Cooperation

Dialogue (ACD), which is aimed at promoting co-operation in all fields including expansion of the market among the Asian countries.[56] India is also part of this regional group but sent a lower representation. Such summits where all the Asian powers join together to discuss issues of mutual interests can help in clearing the strenuous relationship that countries like India and Pakistan are facing.

Conclusion

In the years of turmoil, Kuwait managed to remain calm and keep out of trouble as much as possible. India's economic, political relations with Kuwait have remained stable. The general trend is towards focusing on soft power along with the traditional usage of hard power. Therefore, with the emphasis on strategic relation, there has been development of exchanges of professionals, educationists, medical professionals and expertises. The Indian community in Kuwait, which is again the largest group of expatriates there, also helped in strengthening of the varied range of relations between the two countries.

Notes

1. 'Al Sabah and Kuwait', Al-Diwan Al-Amiri, State of Kuwait, http://www.da.gov.kw/eng/picsandevents/
2. 'Prospering Relations of Kuwait and India', *Hindustan Times,* 23 February 2012, http://www.hindustantimes.com/business-news/Features/Prospering-relations-of-Kuwait-and-India/Article1-816052.aspx
3. 'The Arab Spring Comes To Kuwait: Will Democracy Arrive and Liberty Thrive?' *Forbes,* 12 October 2012, http://www.forbes.com/sites/dougbandow/2012/12/10/the-arab-spring-comes-to-kuwait-will-democracy-arrive-and-liberty-thrive
4. Abdus-Sattar Ghazali, 'Fabricating a Fig Leaf of Democracy in Kuwait', *OpEdNews.Com,* 12 June 2012, http://www.opednews.com/articles/2/Fabricating-a-fig-leaf-of-by-Abdus-Sattar-Ghaza-121205-482.html
5. 'To Mark Key Milestones, Kuwaiti Emir Doles Out Cash', *The Indian Express,* 17 January 2011, http://www.indianexpress.com/news/to-mark-key-milestones-kuwaiti-emir-doles-out-cash/738598
6. Human Rights Watch, 'World Report 2013', http://www.hrw.org/world-report/2013/country-chapters/kuwait

7. Human Rights Watch, 'World Report 2012'.
8. 'Kuwait Profile', *BBC News*, 11 December 2012, http://www.bbc.co.uk/news/world-middle-east-14644252
9. 'Kuwait Introduces Death Penalty for "Cursing God and Prophets"', National Secular Society, 12 December 2012, http://www.secularism.org.uk/news/2012/12/kuwait-introduces-death-penalty-for-cursing-god-and-prophets
10. Human Rights Watch, 'World Report 2012'. However, Hamad al-Naqi claimed that someone had hacked his Twitter account and impersonated him.
11. 'Kuwaiti Protesters Blocked from Rallying outside Parliament', *The New York Times,* 16 December 2012, http://www.nytimes.com/2012/12/17/world/middleeast/kuwaiti-protesters-blocked-from-rallying-outside-parliament.html?_r=0
12. 'The Quiet Influence of Salafis', *Reuters,* 27 June 2012, http://www.reuters.com/article/2012/06/27/us-kuwait-salafi-idUSBRE85Q0Y220120627
13. 'Kuwait Elections: Islamist-led Opposition Makes Gains', *BBC News*, 3 February 2012, http://www.bbc.co.uk/news/world-middle-east-16869108
14. 'Kuwait: Court Nullifies Elections and Restores Previous Parliament', *The New York Times,* 20 June 2012, http://www.nytimes.com/2012/06/21/world/middleeast/kuwait-court-nullifies-elections-and-restores-previous-parliament.html?_r=0
15. Muhammad Badri Eid, 'Early Parliamentary Elections in Kuwait', *Al Jazeera Centre for Studies,* 25 November 2012, http://studies.aljazeera.net/en/reports/2012/11/2012112564831970746.htm
16. Sylvia Westall, 'Kuwait Elects New Parliament on Record Low Turnout', *Reuters,* 2 December 2012, http://www.reuters.com/article/2012/12/02/us-kuwait-election-idUSBRE8B102620121202
17. 'Kuwait Emir Denounces Protests', *Arab News*, 17 December 2012, http://www.arabnews.com/kuwait-emir-denounces-protests
18. 'Youth Group Fifth Fence Calls for Kuwait Government to Go', *The National*, 8 February 2011, http://www.thenational.ae/news/world/middle-east/youth-group-fifth-fence-calls-for-kuwait-government-to-go
19. Rajeev Agarwal, 'Is Arab Spring Part-2 Unravelling', *IDSA Comment*, Institute of Defence Studies Analyses, 12 October, 2012, http://idsa.in/idsacomments/IsArabApringPart2Unravelling_ragrawal_121012
20. Kenneth Katzman, 'Kuwait: Security, Reform and US Policy', *Congressional Research Service*, 6 December 2012.
21. 'Kuwaiti Ruler Grants $4b, Free Food to Citizens', *Gulf News,* 17 January 2011, http://gulfnews.com/news/gulf/kuwait/kuwaiti-ruler-grants-4b-free-food-to-citizens-1.747643
22. Human Rights Watch, 'World Report 2012'.
23. 'Kuwait MPs Pass Law to Naturalise 4,000 Stateless Bidun', *BBC News*, 20 March 2013, http://www.bbc.co.uk/news/world-middle-east-21857431

24. Jane Kinninmont, 'Kuwait: Testing the Limits', *Chatham House*, 1 November 2012, http://www.chathamhouse.org/media/comment/view/186925
25. Human Rights Watch, 'World Report 2012'.
26. Ibid.
27. 'Indonesia Slaps Worker Ban on Saudi, Kuwait', *ArabianBusinnes.com*, 4 November 2009, http://www.arabianbusiness.com/indonesia-slaps-worker-ban-on-saudi-kuwait-11249.html
28. 'Kuwait, Manila MoU Will Protect Rights of Domestics: Lanka Asks Salary Review for Workers', *Arab Times*, 31 March 2012, http://www.arabtimesonline.com/NewsDetails/tabid/96/smid/414/ArticleID/181444/reftab/56/Default.aspx
29. P. R. Kumaraswamy, 'Re-energizing the Gulf Bilateral', *The Indian Express*, 13 June 2006, http://www.indianexpress.com/news/reenergising-the-gulf-bilaterals/6327/
30. 'Kuwait, Manila MoU Will Protect Rights of Domestics: Lanka Asks Salary Review for Workers', *Arab Times*, 31 March 2012, http://www.arabtimesonline.com/NewsDetails/tabid/96/smid/414/ArticleID/181444/reftab/56/Default.aspx
31. 'Visit of Mr. T.K.A. Nair to Kuwait', Embassy of India, Kuwait, 12 May 2012, http://www.indembkwt.org/press/24feb11.htm
32. Yaser Arafat Ilahi and Anisur Rehman, 'India's Trade Potential to Kuwait: Problems and Opportunities', *International Journal of Computing and Corporate*, November 2012, http://www.ijccr.com/November2012/6.pdf
33. Ibid.
34. Yaser Arafat Ilahi and Anisur Rehman.
35. *Ministry of External Affairs Annual Report 2011–2012*, India, 43. As a precursor, a Medical Tourism Destination Exhibition and Conference was organised in Kuwait in November 2011, attended by more than 28 leading hospitals from India.
36. '"Indian Community Is Well Respected in Kuwait for Their Endearing Traits"—Indian Ambassador HE Satish C Mehta', IndiansinKuwait.Com, 13 August 2012, http://www.indiansinkuwait.com/ShowArticle.aspx?ID=1 9152&SECTION=12#ixzz2LCXqRFSP
37. *Ministry of External Affairs Annual Report 2011–2012*, India, 43.
38. Zakir Hussain, 'India and Kuwait: New Hopes and Aspirations', *IDSA Comment*, Institute for Defence Studies and Analysis, 22 April 2009, file:///E:/study%20materials/MEI/persian%20gulf%202013/India%20and%20Kuwait%20%20New%20Hopes%20and%20Aspirations%20_%20Institute%20for%20Defence%20Studies%20and%20Analyses.htm
39. '"Indian Community Is Well Respected in Kuwait for Their Endearing Traits"—Indian Ambassador HE Satish C Mehta', IndiansinKuwait.Com
40. 'Indian Classical Music Concert Held at Embassy of India', Embassy of India, Kuwait, http://www.indembkwt.org/press/24feb11.htm
41. Hussain, 'India and Kuwait: New Hopes and Aspirations'.

42. 'Hundreds of Indians Held in Kuwait', *The Hindu*, 22 September 2012, http://www.thehindu.com/news/national/hundreds-of-indians-held-in-kuwait/article3927113.ece. Indeed, in 2007 both countries signed an agreement concerning labour, employment and manpower development.

43. Yasir Arafat Elahi and Anisur Rahman, 'India's Trade Potential to Kuwait: Problems and Opportunities'.

44. Ibid.

45. Hussain, 'India and Kuwait: New Hopes and Aspirations'.

46. Kenneth Katzman, 'Kuwait: Post Saddam Issues and US Policies', *Congressional Research Service*, 29 June 2005.

47. Katzman, 'Kuwait: Security, Reform and US Policy'.

48. Ibid.

49. 'China and Kuwait', Embassy of the People's Republic of China, Kuwait, file:///E:/study%20materials/MEI/persian%20gulf%202013/China%20and%20Kuwait.htm

50. Chen Aizu, 'China to Keep Kuwait Crude Imports Steady in 2013–Traders', *Reuters*, 15 November 2012, http://www.reuters.com/article/2012/11/15/china-oil-sinopec-idUSL3E8MF0Y220121115

51. Jasim Ali, 'GCC Focus GCC FTA with China No Easy Task', *Gulf News*, 28 March 2010, http://gulfnews.com/business/opinion/gcc-focus-gcc-fta-with-china-no-easy-task-1.603754

52. 'Chinese Premier Calls for GCC Free Trade Agreement', *Khaleej Times*, 19 January 2012, http://www.khaleejtimes.com/DisplayArticle.asp?xfile=data/business/2012/January/business_January334.xml&section=business&col

53. 'Kuwait, Pakistan Leaders Discuss Visa Facilitations', *Kuwait Times*, 18 February 2013, file:///E:/study%20materials/MEI/persian%20gulf%202013/Kuwait,%20Pakistan%20leaders%20discuss%20visa%20facilitations%20_%20Kuwait%20Times.htm

54. Andy Sambridge, 'Kuwait Mulls Lifting Ban on Pakistani Visas', *ArabianBusiness.com*, 12 January 2013, http://www.arabianbusiness.com/kuwait-mulls-lifting-ban-on-pakistani-visas-485352.html

55. Muhammad Al-Mumen, 'Pakistani Ambassador Lauds Bilateral Economic Relations with Kuwait', *Kuwait News Agency*, 1 October 2012, http://www.kuna.net.kw/ArticleDetails.aspx?id=2265592&language=en

56. 'ACD Meet: PM Reaches Kuwait to Attend Asian Summit', *The Express Tribune*, 16 October 2012, http://tribune.com.pk/story/452187/acd-meet-pm-reaches-kuwait-to-attend-asian-summit/

6

Oman

Marimuthu Ulaganathan

Key Indicators

Area: 309,500 sq km; **Population:** 3.15 million; **Youth population:** 20.2 per cent; **Population growth rate:** 2.043 per cent; **Life expectancy at birth:** 73.2 years; **GDP:** US$90.66 billion; **Per capita income:** US$28,500; **Foreign trade:** US$78.80 billion; **Oil reserves:** 4.902 billion bbl; **Gas reserves:** 849.5 billion m³; **Ruling family:** Al-Said; **Ruler:** Sultan Qaboos bin Said al-Said (since 23 July 1970); **National Day:** 18 November; **Defence budget:** 11.4 per cent of GDP; **HDI rank:** 84; **Literacy rate:** 81.4 per cent; **UN education index:** 0.576; **Gender inequality index:** 0.340.

Source: CIA, *The World Factbook*, https://www.cia.gov/library/publications/the-world-factbook/index.html UN Human Development Report, Statistics, http://hdr.undp.org/en/statistics/
Note: All data for 2012.

The relations between the Sultanate of Oman and India are important to each other: from the Oman perspective, India is an important and reliable trade partner, and for India, Oman is a trading partner which has a potential to be a strategic ally. After the 2008 visit of Prime Minister of India Manmohan Singh, the bilateral relations shifted from trade to strategic partnership. Officials of both the states have periodically visited one another and signed bilateral agreements in various sectors ranging from oil and gas to information technology and defence coordination. Currently, India and Oman are conducting joint military and navy exercise against piracy along the Somalian coast.

Domestic Developments

Since the mid-eighteenth century the ruling Said dynasty has played a crucial role in political history of Oman. When the Arab world was witnessing a wave of colonial influence, particularly from the French and the British, Oman was among the few countries that escaped from the colonial domination.[1] The Sultanate of Muscat and Oman dates back to 1744 when the current dynasty came to the throne. In 1898, the Sultanate became a protectorate of the British and when this agreement was annulled in 1954, Oman continued to retain its strong ties with Great Britain.

The country continued to be secluded and backward until 1970, when Sultan Qaboos grabbed power from his father, renamed the country as Sultanate of Oman and started a drive for modernization. While he created the institutions including an elected legislature and a constitution which promises human rights, the Sultan has all powers. His traditional authority as head of the Ibadhi sect has prevented the emergence of a serious political opposition. The large populations of migrant workers in Oman have no political rights.[2]

Starting January 2011, Oman started witnessing the turmoil of Arab Spring when hundreds of people gathered in Muscat and raised slogans against the cabinet ministers. However, the protesters did not target the Sultan. In the following months, hundreds of people obstructed roads and burnt a supermarket and other state properties in Sohar, Oman's second largest economic and port city. The protesters raised slogan like 'the trial of all minister' and the 'abolition of taxes'.[3] Protest organizers set up a Facebook page called '2 March Uprising for Dignity and Freedom' to urge demonstrations across the country.[4]

Further, they demanded changes in job creation, controlling food inflation, more power for Majlis al-Shoura (Lower house of parliament), and to stop corruption among ministers and officers of the government. However, Oman's Arab Spring never asked for regime change because there is no sectarian conflict and dictatorship engaging in violent acts. The protesters never criticized the Sultan of Oman, who recently celebrated 40th anniversary in power. Nonetheless, to stem the tide sweeping across the Middle East from seriously affecting Oman, Sultan Qaboos took a number of conciliatory steps. He dismissed 12 ministers including the Finance Minister Ahmed Makki[5] and announced a slew of economic measures and dole-outs. In April 2011, the Sultan announced a package of US$2.6 billion to 'satisfy the demands' of the protesters.[6] He ordered monthly allowance of US$390 (150 Omani Riyal) for each registered jobseeker and the creation of 50,000 new jobs.[7] Earlier in March 2011, the GCC had announced an aid of US$10 billion to Oman to help generate employment through upgrading housing and infrastructure over 10 years.[8]

Towards mitigating the situation, in August 2012, Sultan Qaboos announced a plan for the creation of 56,000 job opportunities, out of which 36,000 would be in public sector (civilian and military) and 20,000 in the private sector. Vital jobs would be given to those with the educational qualifications, skills and training wanted by the diverse sectors.[9] On 14 August 2012, Qaboos ordered that all beneficiaries of loans from the Oman Housing Bank listed up to that date should be exempted from all banking and administrative service charges until final settlement of their outstanding loans. The fees for those seeking fresh home loans would be reduced by 75 per cent. Thus, about 11,700 citizens across the country benefitted from these exemptions.[10]

The Basic Law of Oman was amended in 2011 as a response to the protests and was designed to grant the Council of Oman legislative and regulatory powers.[11] Accordingly, the seventh parliamentary elections were held in Oman on 15 October 2011, to elect 84 members of the Consultative assembly.[12] Many women turned out to cast ballots in the 105 polling stations across Oman, raising the prospect that women would win parliamentary seats they failed to capture four years ago. According to one Omani resident, 'We are now more confident and we are not letting our husbands decide who to vote for this time'.[13] However, only one woman was elected to the assembly in 2011.[14] Continuing the modest reforms, Oman held its first municipal elections in December 2012 for 192 local councils.[15] The Sultan's Royal Decree in 2008 gave women the equal right to own lands as held by their male counterparts. Sultan Qaboos also signed the Decent Work Country Programme, a service dedicated to increase job opportunities for women as well as stand for justice, equality and freedom. The programme is being implemented from 2010 to 2013.[16]

Despite the economic and legislative measure taken to appease the protesters, a few challenges remain for the Omani regime, most important being the accusations of lack of civil liberties. A Report by *Bertelsmann Stiftung* declared that Oman's legal code theoretically protects civil liberties and personal freedoms but both are regularly ignored by the regime.[17] On 9 September 2012, trials of activists, accused of posting 'abusive and provocative' criticism of the government online, began amid reports of a crackdown on protest over unemployment and lack of democracy. Six were given jail terms of 12–18 months and fines of about US$2,500 were imposed on each to the convicts.[18] Continued persecution of dissidents and lack of freedom of speech pose a threat to the fragile stability of Oman. A string of recent court rulings in the Omani capital Muscat have been criticized as detrimental to free speech in the Gulf State, with the Amnesty International and other international and national organizations demanding the release of jailed dissidents.[19]

Economy

Though exploration activities began in 1920, it was not until 1962 that the first successful oil discovery was made in Yibal and was followed by other wells at Naith and Fahud. Oil production on a commercial scale began in 1967. When Qaboos came to power in 1970, he used the oil wealth for development of Omani economy on par with other Gulf States. The 2012 Budget was the largest in Oman's history, with estimated expenditure topping US$25.97 billion, an increase of nine per cent compared to 2011.[20] A huge amount of the budget's financial distributions went to the education sector, confirming that the emphasis remains upon the progress of the human element in ongoing and future development plans. Meanwhile, the ongoing economic planning has increased the number of nationwide transport and road projects that will improve the country's infrastructure.[21]

Oil and gas provide a majority share of the General State Budget's revenues. In the 2012 Budget, they represented 81.8 per cent of the total, with oil accounting for an estimated US$15.84 billion based on an average daily production figure of 915,000 barrels per day (bpd) and a price of US$75 per barrel. The year 2012 was the start of a new era which saw Islamic banks working alongside the traditional banks.[22] The Eighth Five-year Plan for the agricultural sector (2011–15) includes several agricultural programmes and projects aimed at boosting agriculture and livestock production.[23]

The strength of the Omani economy is built on developing trade, benefiting from a large merchant fleet and the support of a distinguished naval force. Oman continues to develop itself into a regional powerhouse for the shipping and transhipment of dry bulk goods such as iron ore. To this end a new port is being constructed at Duqm and new cargo terminals at Salalah and Sohar. The new Duqm port would also have a refinery. Further port developments include the announcement that all cargo operations are to be moved from the Muscat port of Sultan Qaboos to Sohar by the end of 2012. All of this is aided by Oman's position on the Arabian Sea, outside the Persian Gulf, enabling it to offer shorter shipping lines than ports within the congested body of water.[24]

In mid-2012, the Ministry of Transport and Communications was engaged in 65 road projects in various parts of the country with an overall length of around 2,065 kilometres, at an estimated cost of US$3.89 billion.[25] In late 2011, the Sultanate began opening technical bids from companies eligible to tender for planning and supervisory consultancy services for its railway project. The Omani railway system will be around 1,061 kilometres long and will extend from the border towns of al-Ain in the United Arab Emirates (UAE) and Buraymi (in Oman) to the wilayat of Sohar (136 kilometres), then from Sohar to the governorate of Muscat (242 kilometres) and from Muscat to the wilayat of al-Duqm (486 kilometres).[26]

Bilateral Relations

The Indo–Omani relationship goes way back into history, and has been historically maintained through maritime trade. During the colonial period, both countries were under the British domination. The earliest evidence of the trade between these two states can be traced to the Harappa Civilization. At that time, Oman was called as *Magan* or *Makkan* where many Harappan zeal copper coin remnants have been found. Recently, a Tamil–Brahmi script inscribed on a potsherd was found at the Khor Rori area in Oman. Archaeologists feel that 'Pattam' could be from Muziris/Muciri, which was a flourishing port on the west coast during the Tamil Sangam age (BC 300–AD 300), which coincided with the classical period of the West.[27] This discovery shows the prehistoric maritime trades between ancient city Sumhuram and Tamil Kingdoms. Due to the geographical proximity between Oman and India, a close co-operation in trade existed throughout history. During the Medieval period, India exported mainly cotton, spices, rice, etc., to Oman. On the other hand, Oman exported dates, copper, horses, etc. Middlemen in maritime trade became very prominent, particularly Gujarat Bhattias, some of whom even settled in Oman. The Bhattia communities even competed with the Portuguese in their trade with India and the West.[28]

In the eighteenth century, India and Oman enjoyed close relationship in the spheres of trade, diplomacy and politics. Tipu Sultan, ruler of the south Indian state of Mysore, had extensive relationship with Gulf States, particularly with the Imam of Oman. He established a diplomatic relation with the Imam of Oman to contain the British preeminence in the maritime trade and made allies against the British. Tipu Sultan's emissaries were posted at Muscat to supervise their trade and implement their interest in the region; on the other hand, Oman also posted its representative in Mangalore.[29]

After independence, an Indian consulate was established in Oman in 1955, and both countries signed the Treaty of Friendship, Commerce and Navigation when the pre-independence 1939 Treaty was terminated by Britain. The new agreement extended '[p]olitical recognition and the establishment of consulates and most favoured nation treatment in trade'.[30] Presently, Indian expatriates number more than 500,000, and they are considered one of the largest groups of expatriates in Oman.[31] They are working as skilled and un-skilled workers in various sectors such as health, education, oil-refineries, etc., without disturbing the internal harmony.

Political Relations

At present, India and Oman relations continue to progress in the right direction, particularly after the visit of the Indian Prime Minister Manmohan Singh to Oman in November 2008. During that visit, Indo–Omani relations transformed from bilateral relation to strategic partnership. There were several high-level visits to Oman from India since then, including visits by External Affairs Minister Pranab Mukherjee (January 2008), National Security Advisor M. K. Narayanan (November 2008), Minister of Overseas Indian Affairs Vayalar Ravi (June 2009), President A. P. J. Abdul Kalam (November 2009), Defence Minister A. K. Antony (May 2010), Commerce Minister Anand Sharma (September 2010), Deputy Chairperson of the Planning Commission Montek Singh Ahluwalia (December 2010) and Minister of State for External Affairs E. Ahamed (October 2007, January 2012).[32]

During 3–5 March 2012, India's National Security Advisor (NSA) Shiv Shankar Menon led a delegation to the Sultanate and had a number of meetings.[33] India's Minister of State for External Affairs E. Ahamed visited Oman in January 2012 and 7–8 November 2012. Minster of Overseas Indian Affairs also visited Oman twice, during 6–8 March 2012 and on 13 November 2012. These visits also showed that relation between India and Oman is not merely concentrated on economic relations but also on the importance both the countries attach to one another.

From Oman, dignitaries who visited India were Deputy Prime Minister Sayyid Fahd bin Mehmoud al-Said (December 2007), Minister of Tourism Rajiha bint Abdul Ameer bin Ali (April 2008), Oil and Gas Minister Mohammed bin Hamad al-Rumhi (May 2009), Junior Minister of Foreign Affairs Yousuf bin Alawi bin Abdullah (October 2010), Minster of Commerce & Industries Bin Ali Sultan (February 2011) and Minister of Armed forces Sayyid Badr bin Saud al-Busaidy (December 2011).[34] However, the long-awaited visit of Sultan Qaboos has been delayed because of several reasons. He is yet to be bestowed the Jawaharlal Nehru Award for International Understanding that was awarded for 2004. In 2011, his plan to visit India was postponed due to Arab Spring in Oman. Then once again in 2013, due to his pre-scheduled events, he politely declined the invitation to attend the 64th Republic Day celebrations as the chief guest.[35]

The first visit from Oman in 2012 was by Minister of Agriculture and Fisheries Fuad bin Ja'afar bin Mohammed al-Sajwani in March 2012. During his visit, India and Oman signed various treaties for co-operation in agriculture. Then, Chairman of Tender Board of Oman Rasheed bin al Safi bin Khamis visited India in February 2012. Chairman of the State Financial and Administrative Audit Institution (SFAAI) Sheikh Nasser bin Hilal al-Mawali also visited India in May 2012. During this visit, an agreement for co-operation between the State Audit Institution of Oman and the Office of the Comptroller and Auditor General of India was signed. Both sides also signed agreements on Avoidance of Double Taxation, bilateral investment promotion and protection in financial sectors. Omani Foreign Minister Yusuf bin Alawi bin Abdullah attended the Indian Ocean Rim Association for Regional Cooperation (IOR-ARC) meeting in Gurgaon on 2 November 2012.[36]

The visits by the Indian Prime Minister in 2008, along with those of National Security Advisors M. K. Narayanan (November 2008) and Shivshankar Menon (March 2012) and Defence Secretary Vijay Singh (November 2008) indicate the growing security contacts between the two. India and Oman decided to speed up their co-operation in maritime security and regional security issues, especially in the wake of the 26 November terror attacks in Mumbai in 2008. Maritime security has also become a global anxiety due to the outbreak of international piracy in the Gulf of Aden.[37] The first Oman and India joint air exercises were held at the Royal Air Force base of Thumrait in Oman in October 2009. The second India and Oman joint air exercises, named 'Exercise Eastern Bridge-2011', were held at Jamnagar, Gujarat in October 2011.[38]

India's mechanisms to build strategic ties with Oman assume significance in light of the fact that Omani ports have been utilized by Indian Navy frigates on anti-piracy duty off the Gulf of Aden. For this purpose, the navies of both the countries conducted a joint exercise called as 'Naseem al-Bahr' off the coast of Mumbai from 26 to 31 December 2011. The bilateral defence relationships was extended for another five years by Indian Defence Minister A. K. Antony and his counterpart Omani Defence Minister Badar bin Saud bin Harib al-Busaidi when the latter visited New Delhi in December 2011.[39]

Economic Relations

India and Oman have been sharing a historical economic relationship and have never been affected by the political system which is ruling the country. Presently, the bilateral trade between India and Oman stands at US$4.6 billion (Table 6.1 and Figure 6.1), and the bilateral investment is

Table 6.1
India–Oman Bilateral Trade (in US$ Million)

	2009–10	2010–11	2011–12
Exports	1,032.93	1,086.48	1,322.13
Imports	3,499.89	4,002.07	3,329.31
Total trade	4,532.82	5,088.55	4,651.45
Share of Oman in total trade	0.97	0.82	0.58

Source: Adapted from Director General of Foreign Trade, New Delhi, http://www.dgft.gov.in

Figure 6.1
India–Oman Bilateral Trade

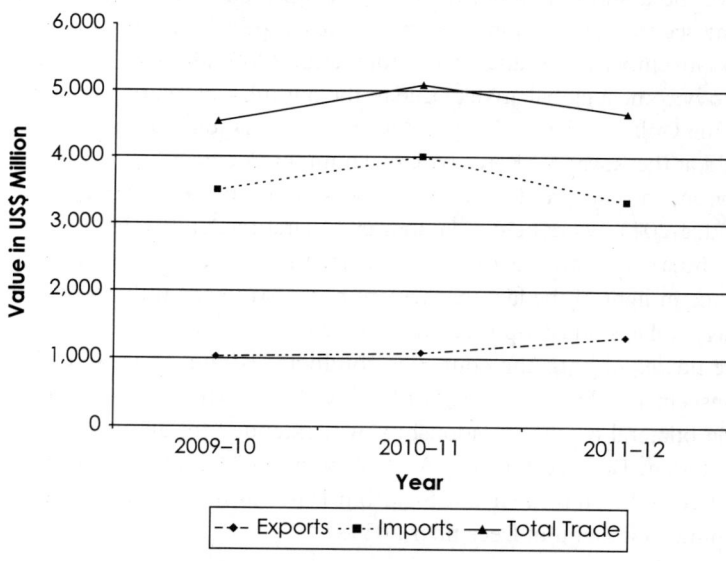

Source: Adapted from Director General of Foreign Trade, New Delhi, http://www.dgft.gov.in

worth around US$7.53 billion.[40] The main items exported to Oman from India are textiles and garments, machinery and equipment, electrical and electronic items, chemicals, iron and steel products in addition to traditional export items such as tea, coffee, spices, rice and meat products, eggs and seafood.[41]

Oman banned the import of eggs from India on 27 March 2012 following an outbreak of bird flu in Odisha and the issuance of a notice by the World Health Organization (WHO). Oman accounts for 33 per cent of the total egg export from India. Egg exports, which stood at 5.5 million eggs in March, dropped to 4.15 million in April, a month after the ban was imposed by Oman. It dropped to 2.40 million in May and touched a 10-year-low monthly export of 897,000 eggs in June. But the ban was lifted on 22 November 2012 after the WHO cleared India's name from the swine flu-affected list.[42]

Oman's cumulative Foreign Direct Investment (FDI) into India has grown from US$24 million in 2005, when it was the third-biggest Gulf investor behind Bahrain and the UAE, to currently being the second largest behind the UAE, with an investment of US$2.2 billion as of January 2012. As a result, *Alpen Research* ranks Oman as the 26th-largest investor in India, with Omani companies in India spread across a range of sectors including oil and gas, healthcare, manufacturing, IT and telecom, hospitality and financial services.[43]

Oman Container Lines Inc. (OCL) announced the most recent addition to their growing network of independent container feeder connections. The India Express (IEX) common feeder service will create a unique direct link between Nhava Sheva, India and Salalah. Starting in July 2012, the fixed-day weekly service will connect port Terminals Mumbai, the leading port facility in one of the most attractive growth markets, and the Port of Salalah, the region's second largest port.[44]

During the visit of the Prime Minister of India to Oman in November 2008, a Memorandum of Understanding was signed for Joint Venture Agreement. Presently, there are some 140 large Indian companies operating in Oman. By July 2010, there were 1,537 joint ventures between both countries in Oman and investments from both sides totalled at US$7.5 billion.[45] In 2010, the State Bank of India and the State General Reserve Fund of Oman signed a Joint Venture Agreement to form a Joint Investment Fund. This fund has a corpus of US$100 million to be contributed equally by both the parties and would explore opportunity in all sectors without any specific preference. The purpose of the collaboration is to attract capital into India from that region.[46] In 2011, this Joint Investment Fund was increased to US$1.50 billion, and it funded three main areas of investment, namely, pharmaceuticals and petrochemical, infrastructure in aviation service and financial service.

The Oman–India Fertilizer Company (OMIFCO), a US$969 million joint venture between the two countries that feeds the Indian agricultural market, was officially inaugurated in August 2002 at Sur Oman and started production in 2006.[47] Bharat Oman Refineries Ltd. (BORL), a Joint Venture of Bharat Petroleum Corporation Limited and Oman Oil Company Limited, is setting up a state-of-the-art grass-roots refinery with a capacity of 6 million metric tonnes per annum (MMTPA) at Bina in the state of Madhya Pradesh. The total cost of the project was around US$1.6 billion and it was expected to start operations from 2011, but has been delayed. The project includes a 935-km-long cross-country crude pipeline from Vadinar (Gujarat) to Bina.[48] India-based private multinational company Jindal Steel acquired Shadeed Iron and Steel Company, situated in Sohar district of Oman, in May 2010, from Abu-Dhabi's Al Ghaith Holdings for US$464 million. The integrated steel complex of Jindal Shadeed was dedicated to the nation at the Port of Sohar in May 2010.[49] In another example of close Indo–Omani business relations, Larsen & Toubro Modular Fabrication Yard LLC (L&T MFY), a joint venture between Indian engineering conglomerate Larsen & Toubro (L&T) and the Zubair Corporation of the Sultanate dedicated its state-of-the-art fabrication facility at the Port of Sohar to the Omani nation.[50]

The Indian information technology giant Infosys signed a treaty with Oman's International Information Technology Company (IITC), part of OHI (Oman Holdings International) group, for its popular universal banking solution product 'Finacle' on 5 February 2012.[51] On 30 March 2012, Balaji Shipping Lines from India declared their direct service to Sohar Port from Mundra port Gujarat, further connecting Dammam, Jebel Ali, Karachi and the North Indian ICD via Mundra port.[52]

A high-level business delegation coordinated by Confederation of Indian Industries (CII) visited Oman in June 2012 to explore new opportunities in the Omani composite industrial segment. The delegation had meetings in Ministry of Oil & Gas, Tender Board of Oman, Ministry of Agriculture and Fisheries, Ministry of Transport and Communication, Salalah Free Zone Muscat Office. The delegation also visited Sohar Port, Sohar Industry and Port Company.[53]

In August, the Oman–India Joint Investment Fund invested US$13 million in Solar Industries India Ltd, a Bombay Stock Exchange (BSE) listed company involved in the manufacturing of industrial explosives. Earlier in July, the Oman–India Joint Investment Fund picked up a nearly 20 per cent stake in Chennai based Indus Teqsite Pvt. Ltd. for US$9.8 million.[54] Larsen & Toubro (Oman) LLC has secured an engineering, procurement and construction contract valued around US$235 million from Petroleum Development Oman (PDO). Earlier this year, L&T had also won a US$150 million contract for the Lekhwair gas field development project from PDO.[55]

During 4–6 September 2012, 70 companies from India, including from Federation of Indian Export Organisations, participated in the Fifth Indexpo Muscat. They exhibited sample goods in various sectors, particularly, health care, engineering, property, plastics, herbal medicines, etc. This event was supported by the Ministry of Commerce and Industry India.[56] In the same month, another industrial delegation from Federation of Chambers of Commerce of India (FICCI) visited Oman and held meetings with Oman Chamber of Commerce & Industry and the Public Authority for Investment & Promotion of Export Development. A large number of Indian companies are investing in this free zone, including a New Delhi–based company which is investing US$30 million to set up a chemical plant.[57]

On 27 November 2012, Oman Engineering and Contracting Company Galfar bagged two road construction contracts worth US$41.56 from the National Highway Authority of India (NHAI) in the states of Uttarakhand, Uttar Pradesh and Rajasthan.[58] Another Omani company, Muttawar Omani Co. SAOC, has bagged the tender from L&T (Oman).[59]

In Oman, many Indian financial institutions are working to facilitate Indian interests and Bank of Baroda, the first Indian Bank to open a branch in Oman, is operating since 1975. The State Bank of India is operating since 2004 and is followed by New India Assurance Company, LIC, ICICI Bank and HDFC Bank.[60] Presently, Indian companies have reinforced their presence in Oman securing valuable contracts. India and Oman Strategic Consultative Group Meetings (IOSCG) were started at the secretary level in 2003, to provide a forum for open and frank exchange of views on bilateral regional and international issues. The ninth meeting of the IOSCG was held in Muscat on 2 December 2012.[61]

Energy Relations

Energy supplies play a crucial part in the India–Oman bilateral relations. India imports just over one per cent of its total oil supplies from Oman (Tables 6.2 and 6.3 and Figure 6.2). Petroleum imports have amounted to over 80 per cent of total imports from Oman for the last few years. In the first quarter of 2012, India's imports of crude oil from Oman fell by over 88 per cent, from 15.1 million barrels in January–March 2011 to merely 1.8 million barrels in the corresponding period in 2012.[62]

India has shown foresight in trying to build a 1,100-km-long deep-sea gas pipeline from Oman. The Indian Oil Corporation (IOC) and South Asian Gas Enterprises (SAGE) inked an agreement to pursue deep

Table 6.2
Share of Oil in India's Imports from Oman (in US$ Million)

Year	Oil imports from Oman	Total oil imports	Omani share in total oil imports	Imports from Oman	Per cent of oil in imports from Oman
2009–10	2,904.41	96,321.16	3.02	3,499.89	82.99
2010–11	3,293.14	115,929.06	2.84	4,002.07	82.29
2011–12	2,081.05	172,753.97	1.20	3,329.31	62.51

Source: Adapted from Director General of Foreign Trade, New Delhi, http://www.dgft.gov.in

Table 6.3
India's Energy Imports from Oman (in US$ Million)

	2009–10	2010–11	2011–12
Energy imports from Oman	2,904.41	3,293.14	2,081.05
Total energy imports	96,321.16	115,929.06	172,753.97
Total imports from the Persian Gulf	55,904.14	66,688.40	103,915.24
Share in total imports (in per cent)	3.02	2.84	1.20
Share in imports from Persian Gulf (in per cent)	5.20	4.94	2.00

Source: Adapted from Director General of Foreign Trade, New Delhi, http://www.dgft.gov.in

Figure 6.2
Share of Oil in India's Total Imports from Oman

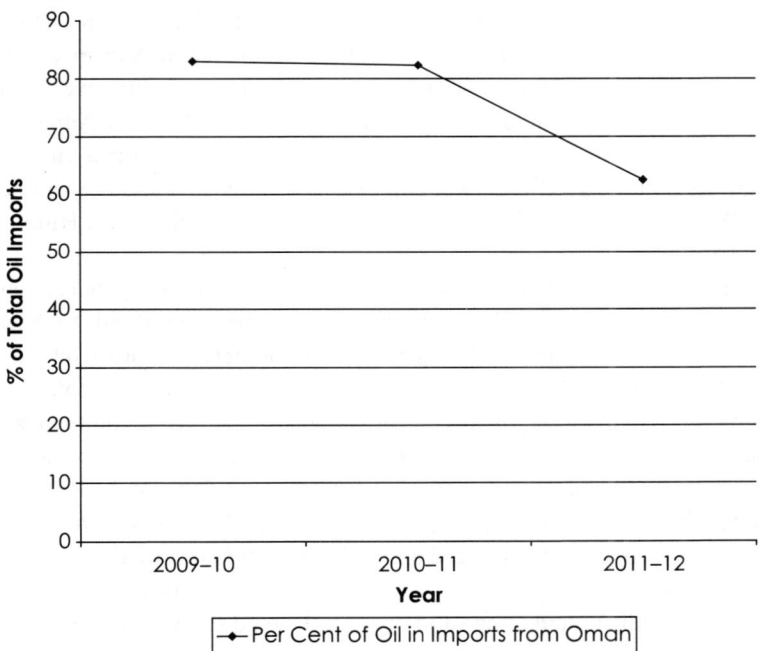

Source: Adapted from Director General of Foreign Trade, New Delhi, http://www.dgft.gov.in

sea natural gas pipeline project, in co-operation with other international companies. SAGE is a project development vehicle to set up for the proposed deep sea natural gas pipeline from the Gulf States to India. SAGE pipeline is anticipated to transport 30 million metric cubic metres of gas per day, and charge a fee of only around US$1 per million metric British thermal unit (mmBtu) of gas transported.[63] The project is expected to cost US$3 billion and is slated for completion in 2014.[64]

Cultural Relations

The 500,000 strong Indian community is keeping its cultural linkage and traditions alive in Oman. Visits of popular Indian artistes from the fields of films and music have strengthened the cultural bondage with Omanis, who cherish their cultural links with India. Indian Council for Cultural Research (ICCR) regularly sponsors visits of artistes to Oman. On 22 November 2010, India's Minister for State for Minority and Corporate Affairs Salman Khurshid visited Oman's during the 40th anniversary of the Sultan's reign. During that visit Oman's Religious Affairs Minister informed him that Oman decided in principle to give permission for a gurdwara (worship place for Sikhs) and another temple in Oman. Muscat already has two temples and one gurdwara for Hindus and Sikhs, respectively.[65]

In April 2011, a National Records and Archives Authority delegation from Oman visited the National Archives of India, New Delhi, to view and reproduce documents dating back to the eighteenth century relating to Oman. The research would endure for several months to comprehensively assemble the history of India–Oman relations in commercial, political and cultural fields from the archives. The head of the National Records and Archives Authority of Oman lead a delegation to India in September 2012 for the meeting of the Heads of the IOR-ARC member countries. Oman also organized a mobile exhibition during the meeting showcasing bilateral relations.[66] On 14 October 2012, a cultural delegation from India visited Oman and organized a road show under theme of 'Incredible India' to promote tourism.[67]

External Players

The US: Oman plays a significant role in aiding the US carry out its regional stability objectives. Oman is strategically located on a key naval chokepoint, Strait of Hormuz, through which almost 40 per cent of the world's oil supply is transported. The Sultan of Oman relies heavily on foreign assistance for capacity-building that allows it to keep this critical sea lane open to naval vessels and commercial traffic. Oman too faces its security challenges, which include combating piracy, weapons smuggling, narcotics trafficking, human trafficking, particularly trafficking of women, and monitoring and controlling Oman's borders. The Omani security forces have had to deploy assets to address increased insecurity along Oman's land and sea border with Yemen, due to instability in

Yemen and the activities of al-Qaeda in the Arabian Peninsula. US assistance helps fund anti-piracy efforts and strengthens Oman's capability to monitor and control its borders against cross-border terrorism and improve interoperability of the Oman military with the US forces.[68] Currently, the Omani Air Force operates the Lockheed Martin F-16. Oman maintains 12 F-16s in operation, and has further ordered another 12 jets from Lockheed Martin.

In September 2012, a small group of Omani citizens peacefully demonstrated near the US Embassy in Muscat over the anti-Islam film that sparked protests across Arab nations.[69] In November 2012, the US State Department had noted religious tolerance shown in Oman in its annual International Religious Freedom Report.[70] Oman has long been a useful Arab ally to the US, not least because of its steady relations with the increasingly isolated Iran. It was Oman's participation that helped secure the release of US hitch-hiker Sarah Shourd from Tehran prison in September 2011.[71]

China: Oman and China established diplomatic relations in May 1978 and, during the Cold War period, both attached little importance to the other. The friendly relations and co-operation between the two grew steadily since 2009. The collaboration between the two countries in the arenas of politics, economy, culture and military has increased into a productive relationship.[72] China is Oman's biggest trading partner, with bilateral trade amounting to US$10.7 billion in 2010.[73] In 2011, total trade between the two countries reached US$15.3 billion.[74] China is the biggest importer of Oman's crude oil, accounting for 41 per cent of total Omani crude exports.[75] Enterprises from the two countries are engaged in a number of new co-operation treaties on power plants, roads, water management, port development and shipbuilding.[76] After the devastating Wenchuan earthquake, the government of Oman decided to help build 350 units of residential housing and subsidiary services such as education and health care in Guangyuan of Sichuan Province.[77] While there were no high-level political visits during 2012, there were considerable political exchanges between the two.

Pakistan: Oman and Pakistan have had long historical proximity in the littoral of Persian Gulf. People belonging to the ethnic Baloch have been in Oman since the late-Medieval period, and now constitute a majority in the South-Eastern part of Oman. These people mainly migrated from Gwader area of British India which was administered by Oman. After its independence, Oman exercised minimal control over the Gwader area. Under mutual agreement, Gwader was transferred to Pakistan on 8 September 1958 and was united within Baluchistan on 1 July 1977.[78]

Presently, Oman is home to over 175,000 Pakistanis, majority of whom are unskilled labourers, although a significant number of Pakistani doctors and engineers are also working in Oman. The remittance sent by Pakistani workforce increased two-fold during 2006–10.[79] The Omani–Pakistani relations have enjoyed deep camaraderie as both share historic and cultural ties and also face volatile situation in their neighbourhood.[80] The political bonhomie between the two countries has not been reflected in the trade relations, with trend being inconsistent in the last decade. From 2008 to 2009 bilateral trade increased from US$393 million to US$417 million. However, in 2010, total trade registered a sharp decrease to US$297 million. Pakistan's imports from Oman have registered a constantly decreasing trend over the corresponding years, from US$293 million in 2008 to US$141 million in 2010.[81]

Oman has security and defence needs and has to build alliance with its neighbours. There is a sizable number of Pakistanis working in Oman. Those bonds are now becoming more crucial to Oman. The January 2011 visit of Prime Minister Yusuf Raza Gilani is part of the growing alliance which will benefit the entire region.[82] The military relations between Pakistan and Oman are broad and continue to grow in various dimensions including joint exercises by both countries' navies under the title of 'Join hands to fight human and drug trafficking'. India views these collaborations with some concern, but has to accept the fact that Oman has to maintain a balance in its relations in the region, especially in view of its dependence on the countries of the Indian Ocean littoral for its trade, economic and maritime security.[83]

Great Britain: Even after ending the protectorate status of Oman in 1954, Great Britain maintains close political and diplomatic ties with the Sultanate. Queen Elizabeth, for example, visited Oman in 2010 for the 40th anniversary of Sultan in power. Defence relations between Oman and Britain have been steady and reliable. Nearly 100 British army personnel are on loan to Oman to train Omani security forces. The Royal College of Defence Studies regularly sends groups of students to Oman as part of their learning experience. Oman also provides location and expertise training to UK forces. In 2011, a group of UK paratroopers were trained by Omani trainers in Oman. A UK naval vessel helped update the underwater survey of Port Sultan Qaboos in Muscat in order to improve access and safety for all shipping in the port.[84]

In 2012, BAE (British Aerospace) has secured a US$3.76 billion deal with Oman to supply Typhoon fighters and Hawk jet trainers.[85] The British Council in Oman maintains a high reputation and conducts several socio-educational and cultural programmes which promote bilateral ties. Education plays vital role in Omani–British relationship and over 20 UK universities and higher education institutions have either affiliates or programmes in Oman.[86]

Conclusion

India's relations with Oman continued to grow in 2012, aided by the robust economic relations and exchange of diplomatic and business visits. Presence of a vibrant and active Indian community has helped bring the two countries closer. Although, political instability in Oman was brought under control by means of an economic package and modest political reforms, the protests have succeeded in making the need for economic diversification urgent. With employment generation being the most crucial demand of protesters, Oman is bound to accelerate its drive for diversification, which presents India with an opportunity to further strengthen its ties with Oman. India can share its expertise with Oman in creating skilled human resources and a diversified economy. A deeper engagement would also enable India to safeguard its historic ties and strategic interests in Oman and the wider region.

Notes

1. Ministry of Foreign Affairs Oman, 'Oman in History (Albusaidi State)', http://www.mofa.gov.om/mofanew/index.asp?id=43

2. 'Oman Introduction Page', Adam Carr Home Page, http://psephos.adam-carr.net/countries/o/oman/statsoman.shtml
3. 'Oman Protests: More Unrest despite Sultan's Reform Vow', BBC News, 28 February 2011, http://www.bbc.co.uk/news/world-middle-east-12600098
4. 'Oman', The New York Times, 1 March 2011, http://topics.nytimes.com/top/news/international/countriesandterritories/oman/index.html
5. 'Sultan Fires Ministers amid Oman Protests', The Financial Times, 7 March 2011, http://www.ft.com/intl/cms/s/0/95626aec-48ea-11e0-af8c-00144fea-b49a.html#axzz2QngVBNjs
6. 'Oman to Spend $2.6 Billion to Satisfy Protest Demands', Daily Times, 18 April 2011, http://www.dailytimes.com.pk/default.asp?page=2011%5C04%5C18%5Cstory_18-4-2011_pg7_23
7. Jacques Charmelot, 'Oil-rich Arab States Open Their Coffers', Agence France Presse, 27 February 2011, http://www.google.com/hostednews/afp/article/ALeqM5iEbFoiaf3y5011Vp3yrALFAa0kjQ?docId=CNG.3bcc0040b48d45bb31070d5319019b17.121
8. 'GCC to Set Up $20bn Bailout Fund for Bahrain and Oman', The National, 11 March 2011, http://www.thenational.ae/news/world/middle-east/gcc-to-set-up-20bn-bailout-fund-for-bahrain-and-oman
9. 'Qaboos the Leader', Oman 2012–2013, http://www.omanet.om/english/oman2012-2013/p42-50.pdf
10. Ibid.
11. Ibid.
12. Oman's first general elections for the legislature were held in 1990. In 2002, elections to the legislative body were opened to all Omani citizens. Prior to 2002, only 25 per cent of citizens, selected by community and tribal leaders, were eligible to vote. Last elections to the Majlis were held in 2007. See 'Oman: Majles A'Shura (Consultative Council)', Inter-Parliamentary Union, http://www.ipu.org/parline/reports/2378.htm. On 4 October 2003, Oman conducted parliamentary elections for its Consultative Assembly, and in 2007, another election for Consultative Assembly.
13. 'Omanis Vote in Shura Council Elections', Al Jazeera, 15 October 2011, http://www.aljazeera.com/news/middleeast/2011/10/2011101512500300244.html
14. 'One Woman, Three Activists Get Elected in Oman's Shura Council', Gulf News, 16 October 2011, http://gulfnews.com/news/gulf/oman/one-woman-three-activists-get-elected-in-oman-s-shura-council-1.893059
15. 'Omanis Vote in Municipal Elections', Al Jazeera, 23 December 2012, http://www.aljazeera.com/news/middleeast/2012/12/2012122316570710943.html
16. 'Sultanate of Oman Signs Decent Work Country Programme, the Second Gulf County after the Kingdom of Bahrain', International Labour Organization,

15 June 2010, http://www.ilo.org/global/about-the-ilo/newsroom/news/WCMS_141756/lang—en/index.htm

17. This report is part of Bertelsmann Stifung's transformation Index (BIT) 2012.

18. 'Oman: Convictions Continue to Crush Free Speech', *Amnesty International*, 9 September 2012, http://www.amnesty.org/en/news/oman-convictions-continue-crush-free-speech-2012-09-11

19. Ibid.

20. 'Qaboos the Leader', *Oman 2012–2013*, http://www.omanet.om/english/oman2012-2013/p51-59.pdf

21. Ibid.

22. 'Economic Development', Oman 2012–2013, http://www.omanet.om/english/oman2012-2013/P230-240.pdf

23. Ibid.

24. Port of Sohar and Port of Rotterdam signed a joint venture to develop Sohar port to handle more goods and modernization. Ministry of Economic Affairs Netherlands, 'Oman Maritime kwartal IV—2012', http://www.agentschapnl.nl/onderwerp/oman-maritiem-kwartaal-iv-2012

25. 'Environment and Modern Utilities', *Oman 2012–2013*, http://www.omanet.om/english/oman2012-2013/P310-320.pdf

26. Ibid.

27. P. J. Cherian, Director of Kerala Council of Historical Studies, has commented on these archaeological remnants. 'Potsherd with Tamil-Brahmi Script Found in Oman', *The Hindu*, 28 October 2012, http://www.thehindu.com/news/national/potsherd-with-tamilbrahmi-script-found-in-oman/article4038866.ece

28. Bansidhar Pradhan, 'Indo–Oman Relations: Political, Security and Sociocultural Dimensions', in A. K. Pasha (ed.), *India and Oman: History, State, Economy and Foreign Policy* (Delhi: Gyan Sagar Publications , 1999), 73–76.

29. A. K. Pasha, 'Tipu Sultan's Relation with Oman,' in A. K. Pasha (ed.), *India and Oman: History, State, Economy and Foreign Policy* (Delhi: Gyan Sagar Publications, 1999).

30. Pradhan, 'Indo–Oman Relations'.

31. 'Country-specific Indian Diaspora: Oman', Ministry of Overseas Indian Affairs (MOIA), New Delhi, http://moia.gov.in/pdf/Oman.pdf

32. Ministry of External Affairs, Government of India, "Annual Report 2012–13", http://www.mea.gov.in/Uploads/PublicationDocs/21385_Annual_Report_2012-2013_English.pdf

33. 'Royal Office Minister/Meeting', *Oman News Agency*, 4 March 2012, http://www.omannews.gov.om/ona/english/newsDetails.jsp?newsID=69807

34. 'Visit from Oman to India', Embassy of Oman in India, http://www.omanembassy.in/visits_from_oman.asp

35. 'Republic Day: Bhutan King in after Oman Sultan Says No', *The Indian Express*, 29 December 2012, http://www.indianexpress.com/news/rday-bhutan-king-steps-in-after-oman-sultan-says-no/1051706/0

36. 'The Sultan of Oman Guest of Republic Day Parade', *The Indian Express*, 1 November 2012, http://www.indianexpress.com/news/sultan-of-oman-to-be-rday-chief-guest/1024787

37. 'India and Oman to Step Up Cooperation in Maritime Security', Press Release, Press Information Bureau, India, 18 May 2011 (New Delhi), http://www.pib.nic.in/newsite/erelease.aspx?relid=61916

38. 'Second India–Oman Joint Air Exercises End', *The Hindu*, 22 October 2011, http://www.thehindu.com/news/national/second-indiaoman-joint-air-exercises-end/article2562726.ece

39. 'India, Oman Ink Pact on Extending Military Co-Operation', *Firstpost*, 28 December 2011, http://www.firstpost.com/fwire/india-oman-ink-pact-on-extending-military-co-operation-167802.html

40. 'India and Oman Bilateral Relations', Ministry of External Affairs, Government of India, http://www.mea.gov.in/Portal/ForeignRelation/Oman-January-2012.pdf

41. 'India and Oman Bilateral Relations', Embassy of India, Oman, Muscat, February 2012, http://www.indemb-oman.org/India_Oman_relations.asp

42. 'Oman Lifts Ban on Eggs from India', *The Hindu*, 22 September 2012, http://www.thehindu.com/news/national/tamil-nadu/oman-lifts-ban-on-eggs-from-india/article3923463.ece

43. 'Oman Second Biggest GCC Investor in India: Report', *Muscat Daily*, 20 May 2012, http://www.muscatdaily.com/Archive/Business/Oman-second-biggest-GCC-investor-in-India-Report

44. 'OCL Launches Indian Express Service', *Marine Insight News*, 28 June 2012, http://marineinsight.com/news/ocl-launches-india-express-service/

45. 'Report on India–Oman Economic Relations 2012', Report of the Federation of Indian Chamber of Commerce and Industry (FICCI), New Delhi.

46. 'India Oman Joint Investment Fund', Press Release, Press Information Bureau, India, 14 July 2010 (New Delhi), http://www.pib.nic.in/newsite/erelease.aspx?relid=63237

47. 'The India–Oman Fertilizer Project Starts', *The Economic Times*, 29 January 2006, http://economictimes.indiatimes.com/oman-india-fertiliser-project-starts/articleshow/1391415.cms

48. 'Refinery', Bharat Oman Oil Limited, http://www.borl.in/binarefinery/overview.aspx

49. 'Jindal Steel Raises US$475m for Oman Expansion', *Business Line*, 24 August 2010, http://www.thehindubusinessline.com/companies/jindal-steel-raises-475-m-for-oman-expansion/article2391835.ece

50. 'High-Tech Fabrication Yard at Sohar Dedicated to Nation', *Oman Daily Observer*, 8 November 2010, http://main.omanobserver.om/node/29332

51. 'Report on India–Oman Economic Relations 2012', FICCI, New Delhi.
52. 'Balaji Shipping Starts Direct Service in India–Sohar Sea Route', *The Economic Times,* 16 March 2012, http://articles.economictimes.indiatimes.com/2012-05-16/news/31726780_1_deep-sea-port-mundra-port-sea-route
53. 'Indian Industrial Delegation Visits Oman', Press Release, Embassy of India, Oman, Muscat, 25 June 2012, http://www.indemb-oman.org/What's-new-prCII.asp
54. 'Oman–India Fund to Invest $13MN in Explosive Firm', *Muscat Daily,* 3 August 2012, http://www.muscatdaily.com/Archive/Business/Oman-India-fund-to-invest-13mn-in-explosives-firm-1lsh
55. 'L&T Secures RO90mn PDO Contract', *Muscat Daily,* 27 August 2012, http://www.muscatdaily.com/Archive/Business/L-T-secures-RO90mn-PDO-contract-1nl6
56. 'Al Maimani Inaugurates Indexpo Muscat 2012', *Oman Tribune,* 6 September 2012, http://www.omantribune.com/index.php?page=news&id=12688 3&heading=Oman
57. 'Indian Firms Plan Operations in Freezone Sohar', *Muscat Daily,* 7 September 2012, http://www.muscatdaily.com/Archive/Business/Indian-firms-plan-operations-in-Freezone-Sohar-1ofp
58. 'Galfar Bags India Road Projects', *Muscat Daily,* 7 November 2012, http://www.muscatdaily.com/Archive/Business/Galfar-bags-India-road-projects-1v4d
59. 'Muttawar Signs Pact with L&T for New Development', *Oman Daily Observer,* 8 December 2012, http://main.omanobserver.om/node/132302
60. 'India and Oman Bilateral Relations', Embassy of India.
61. 'MEA, GoI, "Annual Report 2012–13".
62. 'Oman's Oil Exports to India Drop 88% in Q1', *Business Standard,* 29 May 2012, http://www.business-standard.com/article/economy-policy/oman-s-oil-exports-to-india-drop-88-in-q1-112052903001_1.html
63. 'IOC Seeks Nod to Join Deep Sea Gas Pipeline Project of SAGE', *The Hindu,* 19 June 2012, http://www.thehindu.com/business/companies/article3547257.ece
64. 'India Mulls Deepwater Natural Gas Pipeline System', *Pipeline and Gas Journal* 236, no. 7 (July 2009), http://www.pipelineandgasjournal.com/india-mulls-deepwater-natural-gas-pipeline-system
65. 'Oman to Have More Places of Worship for Indians', *Gulf News,* 23 November 2010, http://gulfnews.com/news/gulf/oman/oman-to-have-more-places-of-worship-for-indians-1.717299
66. 'India and Oman Bilateral Relations, February 2013', Ministry of External Affairs.
67. Ibid.
68. 'US Relations with Oman', US Department of State, 18 October 2012, http://www.state.gov/r/pa/ei/bgn/35834.htm

69. 'Stay Off Embassy Area, Americans in Oman Told', *Muscat Daily*, 14 September 2012, http://gulfnews.com/news/gulf/oman/stay-off-embassy-area-americans-in-oman-told-1.1075252

70. 'International Religious Freedom Report for 2011', US Department of State, Diplomacy In Action, http://www.state.gov/j/drl/rls/irf/religiousfreedom/index.htm#wrapper

71. 'Muslim and Christian Envoys Urge Iran to Free US Hitchhikers Jailed for Spying', *The National*, 20 September 2011, http://www.thenational.ae/news/world/middle-east/muslim-and-christian-envoys-urge-iran-to-free-us-hitchhikers-jailed-for-spying

72. 'Bilateral Relations', Embassy of the People Republic of China, Oman, Muscat, 15 January 2011, http://om.chineseembassy.org/eng/sbgx_1_1_1/t786092.htm

73. 'Oman–China Trade Touches $6bn in First Half of 2011', *Oman Tribune,* http://www.omantribune.com/index.php?page=news&id=100553&heading=Oman

74. 'Trade Exchange between Sultanate of Oman and China', Ministry of National Economy, Sultanate of Oman, http://www.moneoman.gov.om/PublicationAttachment/Sultanate%20of%20Oman&%20china.pdf

75. 'China Tops Oman Crude Export List', *OneOman.com*, 7 August 2012, http://oneoman.com/2012/08/07/china-tops-oman-crude-export-list-3/

76. 'Bilateral Relations', Embassy of the People Republic of China in Oman.

77. Ibid.

78. 'History of Pakistan', Embassy of Pakistan, Oman, Muscat, http://www.mofa.gov.pk/oman/contents.aspx?type=contents&id=7

79. 'Pak Community in Oman Bringing Dividends to Economy', *The Nation,* 27 December 2010, http://www.nation.com.pk/pakistan-news-newspaper-daily-english-online/Business/27-Dec-2010/Pak-community-in-Oman-bringing-dividends-to-economy

80. 'Visit of Excellency Syed Yusuf Raza Gilani, Prime Minister of Pakistan to Oman from 27–28 December 2010', Embassy of Pakistan, Oman, Muscat, http://www.mofa.gov.pk/oman/contents.aspx?type=statements&id=6

81. 'Ambassador of Oman at LCCI', *Pakistan Today*, 11 March 2012, http://www.pakistantoday.com.pk/2012/03/11/news/profit/ambassador-of-oman-at-lcci/

82. 'Strategic Pakistan Oman Relations: Revitalizing 5000 Year Old Indus Gulf Trade', *Rupee News,* 1 January 2011, http://rupeenews.com/2011/01/strategic-pakistan-oman-relations-revitalizing-5000-year-old-indus-gulf-trade/

83. 'Oman, Pakistan Join Hands to Fight Human and Drug Trafficking', *Muscat Daily*, 15 January 2011, http://www.muscatdaily.com/Archive/Stories-Files/Oman-Pakistan-join-hands-to-fight-human-and-drug-trafficking

84. 'The UK and Oman: Our Relationship', British Embassy, Oman, Muscat, http://ukinoman.fco.gov.uk/en/about-us/working-with-oman/uk-in-oman/uk-oman/

85. 'Oman, BAE Reach Agreement on Typhoon and Hawk Deal', *Defence News*, 21 December 2012, http://www.defensenews.com/article/20121221/DE-FREG04/312210001/Oman-BAE-Reach-Agreement-Typhoon-Hawk-Deal?odyssey=tab%7Ctopnews%7Ctext%7CFRONTPAGE

86. 'The UK and Oman: Our Relationship', British Embassy.

7

Qatar

Manjari Singh

Key Indicators

Area: 11,586 sq km; **Population:** 2.04 million; **Native:** 40 per cent; **Expats:** 60 per cent; **Youth:** 13.9 per cent; **Population growth rate:** 4.93 per cent; **Life expectancy at birth:** 78.5 years; **GDP:** US$189.00 billion; **Per capita income:** US$102,800; **Foreign trade**: US$141.19 billion; **Oil reserves:** 15.57 billion bbl; **Gas reserves:** 25.2 trillion m3; **Ruling family:** Al-Thani; **Ruler:** Emir Hamd bin Khalifa al-Thani (since 27 June 1995); **National Day:** 18 December; **Defence budget:** 10 per cent of GDP; **HDI rank:** 36; **Literacy rate:** 96.3 per cent; **UN education index:** 0.629; **Gender inequality index:** 0.546.

Source: CIA, *The World Factbook*, https://www.cia.gov/library/publications/the-world-factbook/index.html; UN Human Development Report, Statistics, http://hdr.undp.org/en/statistics/
Note: All data for 2012.

India has a long history of friendly relations with Qatar marked by commercial ties and people-to-people contacts. The large Indian community acts as a catalyst for enhanced ties across the spectrum of bilateral relations. There is a growing synergy in the hydrocarbon and other sectors. More recently, a number of steps have been taken to further strengthen and expand bilateral relations. These include exchanges of high-level visits, co-operation in multilateral institutions, political consultations, etc.

Domestic Developments

Rich in oil and gas reserves, Qatar's sole land border is with Saudi Arabia to the south, while the rest of its territory is surrounded by the Persian Gulf. Ruled by the al-Thani family since the mid 1800s, Qatar transformed itself from a poor British protectorate noted mainly for pearling into an independent state with significant oil and natural gas revenues. During the late 1980s and early 1990s, the Qatari economy was crippled by the petroleum revenues being continuously siphoned off by the then Emir Khalifa bin Hamad al-Thani, who had ruled the country since its independence in February 1972 from the British. His son, Hamad bin Khalifa al-Thani, overthrew him in a bloodless coup in June 1995 and has been ruling the country since then.

In 2001, Qatar resolved its longstanding border disputes with both Bahrain and Saudi Arabia. As of 2007, oil and natural gas revenues had enabled Qatar to attain the highest per capita income in the world and in 2012 its per capita income is estimated at US$102,943.[1] This financial situation is reflected in Qatar not being affected by the widespread popular protests that dominated the Arab world since early 2011.[2] Due in part to its immense wealth and the high standard of living of its citizens, the country has managed to provide a welfare system that enjoys near universal endorsement.

On the economic front, the situation is extremely favourable. The country has the world's highest GDP per capita income. Less than 20 per cent of the total population of 1,699,435 (2010 estimate) is Qatari citizens, and the rest are foreigners on temporary work permits. During 2009–11, when most of the world's economies have struggled to recover from the global financial meltdown, Qatar reached another high point of having a GDP of US$182 billion at Purchasing Power Parity.[3]

In February 2012 *Forbes* declared Qatar as the world's richest country and observed:

> If wealth is power, then Qataris have some serious muscle to flex. The Persian Gulf emirate of 1.7 million people ranks as the world's richest country per capita thanks to a rebound in oil prices and its massive natural gas reserves. Adjusted for purchasing power, Qatar booked an estimated gross domestic product per capita of more than US$88,000 for 2010. Qatar has

the third-largest reserves of natural gas in the world, and it has invested heavily in infrastructure to liquefy and export it, as well as to diversify its economy, without overreaching as much as nearby Dubai. Qatar has lured multinational financial firms to the country, as well as satellite campuses of US universities. The government is pouring money into infrastructure, including a deepwater seaport, an airport and a railway network—all with an eye to making the country a better host for businesses and the 2022 World Cup.[4]

Talking of politics within the region, Qatar emerges as an important player. According to Paul Alster,

> With the dangerous and ever-changing political dynamic in the Middle East and North Africa replacing the previous status quo with new governments with very different agendas, the tiny Gulf state of Qatar has emerged as an increasingly significant player in the power-politics of the region.[5]

In addition, Qatar played a significant role in the Libyan revolution by pressing the Gulf Cooperation Council and the Arab League to assist the Libyan rebels.[6] The same can be said about the ongoing unrest in Syria where Qatar has emerged as the principal support behind the Syrian opposition that seeks to overthrow the Assad regime.[7] Since its founding on 1 November 1996, the al-Jazeera satellite channel has emerged as the principal vehicle through which Qatar seeks to influence the regional discourse in the Middle East and in the process carve out a niche for the al-Thani regime.[8] With an effective use of its financial resources, Qatar has been seeking a greater role for itself in a number of crises and tensions in the region. Its mediatory role was apparent in Lebanon, Sudan and in the inter-Palestinian dialogue.[9]

In October 2012, the Qatari Emir visited the Gaza Strip, first such visit by any foreign leader, during which he made a massive US$400 million donation for 'infrastructure projects'. Pro-Western Qatar could undermine Iran's often-nefarious influence in the region, David B. Roberts argued:

> While Israel and the Palestinian Authority may view Qatar's embrace of Hamas with chagrin, it is Iran that is the central loser in this drama. The Emir's visit is part of a larger Qatari policy to unseat and reorient crucial Iranian allies around the Middle East—and by extension, amputate a long-used, effective limb of Iranian foreign policy.

This is surprising, since Qatar has long maintained friendly relations with Iran, its much more powerful northern neighbour. He added,

> The fact that Qatar is overturning one of the key tenets of its foreign policy by antagonising Iran is a surprising and forthright move by the Qatari elite, which clearly does not accept conventional limits on what is and what is not possible in the Middle East.[10]

Along with the impressive performance of its economy, Qatar also faces some problems. It relies heavily on foreign labour to grow its economy, to the extent that migrant workers comprise 94 per cent of the workforce. According to the International Trade Union Confederation (ITUC), the visa sponsorship system, currently in vogue in Qatar, leads to forced labour by making it difficult for a migrant worker to leave an abusive employer or travel overseas without permission.[11] In June 2012, further problems faced by workers came to light, when Human Rights Watch reported that hundreds of thousands of construction workers, mostly from South Asia, risk serious exploitation and abuse, sometimes amounting to forced labour. According to the Human Rights Watch,

> Both the government and the *Fédération Internationale de Football Association* (FIFA) need to make sure that their commitments to respect workers' rights in preparation for the 2022 World Cup are carried out. Construction contractors should also make specific, public commitments to uphold international labour standards.[12]

Exploitation and abuse of migrant workers is one of the biggest challenge faced by Qatar in its quest to emerge as a favourite destination for international events. The 146-page report on *Building a Better World Cup: Protecting Migrant Workers in Qatar Ahead of FIFA 2022* examines a recruitment and employment system that effectively traps many migrant workers in their jobs. The problems they face include exorbitant recruitment fees, which can take years to pay off, employers' routine confiscation of worker passports and Qatar's restrictive sponsorship system that gives employers inordinate control over their employees. Workers' high debts and the restrictions they face if they want to change employers often effectively force them to accept jobs or working conditions they did not agree to in their home countries, or to continue working under conditions of abuse.[13]

Bilateral Relations

The bilateral relationship between India and Qatar dates back in history when trade was merely targeted through maritime contacts with Arab sailors who exchanged goods, ideas, beliefs and thoughts. After India's independence and during and after the Cold War, traditional trade ties emerged with clear ideas to engage in a globalized world of today.[14] Trade interactions in the modern era began at a time when several Gulf-origin business activities were carried out from the city of Bombay (now Mumbai) during the British Raj. Over the period of time, both the countries forged multidimensional relationships, though economic relations remain the most important factor of their bilateral ties. Along the course of their co-operation, India has begun to see Qatar as a reliable partner in the field of energy as well as the security sector. Remarkable improvements have been made in people-to-people interactions and cultural exchanges between the two countries. As of today, the relationship is described as 'rich, close and multidimensional'.[15]

Political Relations

Since assuming the throne in June 1995, Emir Sheikh Hamad bin Khalifa al-Thani of Qatar visited India thrice, in April 1999, May 2005 and April 2012.[16] Prime Minister Manmohan Singh made a state visit to Qatar in November 2008.[17] In addition, there have been innumerable ministerial level visits between the two countries. The most prominent ones are those by Minister of Petroleum Mani Shankar Iyer (November 2005), Minister of Overseas Indian Affairs Vayalar Ravi (March 2006 and April 2007), Minister of Petroleum Murli Deora (December 2009) and Minister of New and Renewable Resources Farooq Abdullah (March 2010); and National Security Adviser Shivshankar Menon (December 2011). Indeed, Minister of State for External Affairs E. Ahamed has made numerous annual trips to Qatar since 2005: in June 2005; March, May, October–November and December 2006; April 2007; January, May, September and December 2008; March 2009; December 2011; and March 2012. Prominent visits from Qatar include those of Prime Minister and Foreign Minister Sheikh Hamad bin Jassim al-Thani (April 2006),

Chief of Staff General Hama bin Ali al-Attiyah (August 2006), and Minister of Finance Yousuf Hussain Kamal (October 2006); Minister of State for International Cooperation Khalid bin Mohamed al-Atiyah (January 2011), for the India–Qatar High Level Monitoring Mechanism (HLMM),[18] and Minister of Energy and Industry Mohammed bin Saleh Al-Sada (October 2011).[19]

In a marked departure from the prevailing practices in the Arab world, Queen Sheikha Mozah bint Nasser al-Missned, who had accompanied the Emir during his state visits in May 2005 and April 2012, also made a separate visit to India in February 2006. Recognizing the modern view prevalent in Qatar, in March 2008, India appointed Deepa Gopalan Wadhwa as the ambassador in Qatar's capital Doha, the first Indian woman ambassador to any Gulf country.[20]

The high point of the bilateral relations during 2012 was the visit by Emir Hamad bin Khalifa al-Thani to India from 8 to 10 April. This was his third visit since he assumed office. Al-Thani and Prime Minister Manmohan Singh took forward the initiatives on mutual investments agreed upon during their previous interaction in Doha in November 2008. During the discussions between various ministries, a total of six agreements were signed between the two countries.[21] An agreement was signed for establishing a co-operative framework to increase bilateral co-operation in oil and gas. It is likely to encourage and promote investment and co-operation between the two ministries of oil and gas and through affiliated companies. A Memorandum of Understanding (MoU) was signed between the Reserve Bank of India and Qatar Central Bank for sharing of supervisory information and enhancing co-operation in the area of banking supervision.[22] Three agreements were signed in the fields of educational exchanges, cultural contacts and promoting tourism. The two sides also signed an agreement on establishing a joint business council between Qatar Chamber of Commerce and Industry and the Federation of Indian Chambers of Commerce and Industry.[23]

Qatar is among the few countries in the region with which India has a structure for joint maritime security and training. Qatar is home to a US naval base and with signing a defence pact with this Gulf State, India is signalling its readiness to play a larger-than-before role as it polices the Indian Ocean and the waters up to the Gulf of Aden. The pact allows India to take care of the defence requirements of Qatar, including intelligence sharing and manpower training.[24] India and Qatar, in March 2012, eschewed discussions of a political nature such as Taliban's opening of an office in Doha and the situation in Syria and Bahrain.[25]

Indicating its desire to work with India in the field infrastructure development, Qatar had agreed to invest US$100 million in the sector. However, some reports are now suggesting that Qatari investment can be expected to go up to a massive US$5.5 billion. Qatar in turn welcomed Indian companies to bid for projects and requested support for facilitating its investments in the Indian infrastructure projects. There have been three meetings, in the month of April 2012, which focused this issue. The visit of the Emir was followed by that of Dr Mohammed al-Sada, Minister of State for Energy and Industry. Further, Anand Sharma, Minister of Commerce, Industry and Textile, visited Qatar in the same month.

At strategic and security levels, both the nations face similar threats to the sea line of communication. During the state visit of Prime Minister Manmohan Singh in 2008, India and Qatar signed a Defence Cooperation Pact, which incorporated joint training exercises, training of personnel and maritime co-operation. There have been many visits by both the countries in recent years. For instance the al-Thani visited India in 1999, 2005 and 2012. Key ministers and delegates have also continued to visit.[26]

Economic Relations

India is one of the major export destinations for Qatar, ranking third (3.1 per cent of total Qatari exports) after Japan (26.5 per cent) and Korea (18.3 per cent).[27] India's bilateral trade with Qatar increased from US$5.1 billion in 2009–10 to US$13.7 billion in 2011–12 (Table 7.1 and Figure 7.1). Major items of Indian exports are machinery and equipment, transport equipment, textiles, food products, ores and minerals, etc., while oil and gas constitute the major item of import. India has signed a long-term agreement to purchase 7.5 million tonnes of Liquefied Natural Gas (LNG) every year from Qatar; the first shipment reached India in 2004. In addition, India has been buying its energy needs from Qatar on spot purchases. India also bought 4 million tonnes of crude oil from Qatar in 2011.

Table 7.1

India–Qatar Bilateral Trade (in US$ Million)

	2009–10	2010–11	2011–12
Exports	536.97	375.39	807.95
Imports	4,648.52	6,819.87	12,923.82
Total trade	5,185.49	7,195.27	13,731.77
Share of Qatar in total trade	1.11	1.16	1.73

Source: Adapted from Director General of Foreign Trade, New Delhi, http://www.dgft.gov.in

Figure 7.1

India–Qatar Bilateral Trade

Source: Adapted from Director General of Foreign Trade, New Delhi, http://www.dgft.gov.in

A large number of Indian companies such as Larsen & Toubro, Punj Lloyd, Voltas, Simplex, TCS, Tech Mahindra, Satyam Mahindra, Wipro, NIIT, etc., have set up their offices in Qatar and have secured major contracts or businesses. India is showing interest in extending relations and economic tie-ups with Qatar. Recently India has sought additional 2 to 5 million tonnes of LNG from Qatar, in addition to the existing 7.5 million tonnes which India imports from it.[28] Apart from this, quite a few Indian companies are planning to venture into Qatar. Qatar is the largest producer of fertilizers, and India has a large and potent agricultural sector which needs high amount of fertilizers.

The data in Table 7.1 highlights the export, import and total trade between India and Qatar over the years. The data (Figure 7.1) shows that there is less of export than import which means that India has a negative trade balance. India's import from, export to and total trade with Qatar have increased during 2011–12. India's exports to Qatar jumped from US$375.39 million in 2010–11 to US$807.95 million in 2011–12, and similarly its imports from Qatar rose from US$6,819.87 million to US$12,923.82 million during the same period (Table 7.2 and Figure 7.2). This significant rise could be attributed to the visit of the Emir to India in April 2012, when both the countries pledged to enhance their bilateral trade relations.

Energy Relations

Energy relations between India and Qatar are the most talked-about aspect of their bilateral ties. Energy is clearly the driving force in India–Gulf relations and Qatar remains the exclusive supplier of natural gas to India.[29] Qatar is also the world's largest LNG supplier. With the Iran–Pakistan–India natural gas pipeline project[30] becoming a casualty to the United

Table 7.2
Share of Oil in India's Imports from Qatar (in US$ Million)

Year	Oil imports from Qatar	Total oil imports	Qatar's share in total oil imports	Imports from Qatar	Per cent of oil in imports from Qatar
2009–10	4,101.68	96,321.16	4.26	4,648.52	88.24
2010–11	6,060.95	115,929.06	5.23	6,819.87	88.87
2011–12	11,702.89	172,753.97	6.77	12,923.82	90.55

Source: Adapted from Director General of Foreign Trade, New Delhi, http://www.dgft.gov.in

Figure 7.2
Share of Oil in India's Total Imports from Qatar

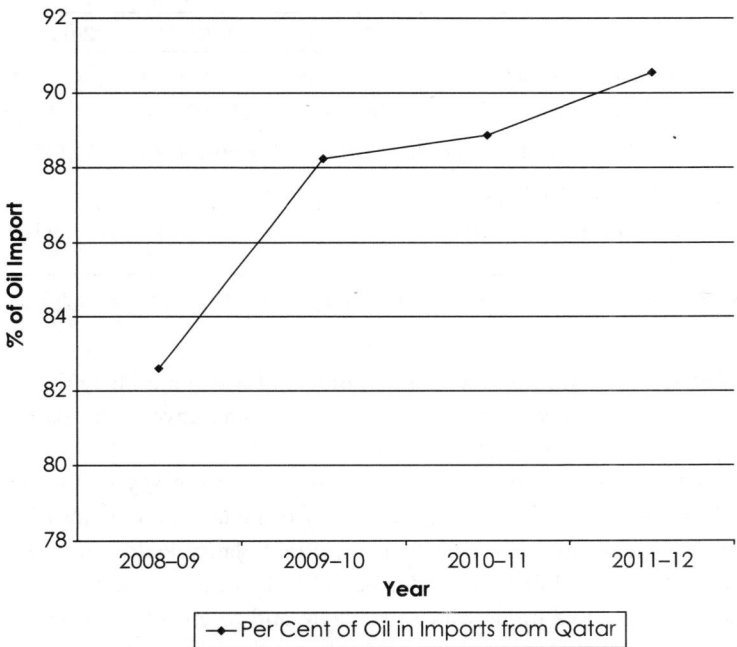

Source: Adapted from Director General of Foreign Trade, New Delhi, http://www.dgft.gov.in

States (US) opposition[31] and persistent mistrust between New Delhi and Islamabad, India has increasingly turned to Qatar to meet its growing natural gas requirements. Holding the world's third-largest gas reserves after Russia and Iran, Qatar is a natural choice for such a role.[32] After the visit of Qatari Emir to India in April 2012, the two states are looking to broaden their economic ties beyond trade in energy,[33] which is well reflected in the data (Table 7.3).

India is fully aware about the risk involved in depending solely upon Qatari LNG supply, and since 2008 it has started signing contracts for LNG imports with other countries. These countries include Australia, France, Russia and the US.[34] Qatar's LNG export to India was high on agenda during the visit of Emir al-Thani. The Emir made commitments to increase Qatar's gas supplies to India. Eventually, this gas relationship

Table 7.3
India's Energy Imports from Qatar (in US$ Million)

	2009–10	2010–11	2011–12
Energy imports from Qatar	4,101.68	6,060.95	11,702.89
Total energy imports	96,321.16	115,929.06	172,753.97
Total imports from the Persian Gulf	55,904.14	66,688.40	103,915.24
Share in total imports (in per cent)	4.26	5.23	6.77
Share in imports from Persian Gulf (in per cent)	7.33	9.09	11.26

Source: Adapted from Director General of Foreign Trade, New Delhi, http://www.dgft.gov.in

between Qatar and India would continue and it is quite likely that this relationship could be expanded to other economic investment partnerships in addition to the oil and gas.

Furthermore, enhancement of co-operation in the key sector of oil and gas exploration was among the six agreements inked in April 2012 between India and Qatar. Petroleum Minister S. Jaipal Reddy and Qatar's Energy Minister Mohammed Bin Saleh al-Sada signed an MoU to establish a co-operative framework to facilitate and to enhance bilateral co-operation in the oil and gas sector. Such an initiative has been expected to encourage and promote investment and co-operation between two ministries of oil and gas and through affiliated firms.[35] Qatar is set to emerge as a strategic investor in India's infrastructure plans, while India is holding steady on its support to the Persian Gulf emirate.[36]

Cultural Relations

In terms of ethnic composition, Arabs make up 40 per cent of residents of Qatar while Indians make up 18 per cent, Pakistanis 18 per cent, Iranians 10 per cent, and others 14 per cent.[37] Indian professionals constitute an important component. There are eight Indian schools following the CBSE syllabus. The annual remittance from Qatar is estimated to be over US$1 billion.[38] An important dimension of the Indo-Qatari relations is the presence of a large Indian community in Qatar estimated at over 500,000. By virtue of its professionalism, dedication and hard work, the Indian community has acquired a positive reputation in Qatar. The community constitutes a very important asset for India.

Air India, Jet Airways and Qatar Airways operate direct flights between the two countries. By its day-to-day interaction with Qatari citizens at every level and in every walk of life, the Indian community provides strong cultural and economic links between India and Qatar and contributes in a very meaningful way to the development of friendship and understanding between the two countries.

A majority of the Indian population in Qatar are engaged in unskilled and semi-skilled work, which means that it may be considered as belonging to the low- or middle-income group. Indian professionals and businessmen constitute a small but important component of the Indian community in Qatar.[39] The Indian Business and Professionals Network (IBPN), the Institution of Engineers India (IEI), Indian Medical Association (IMA) and the Institute of Chartered Accountants of India (ICAI) maintain active chapters in Qatar with an expanding membership and ongoing activities. In addition, there are a number of specialists working in other fields like management, education, pharmaceuticals, software, etc. As Qatar's economic development accelerates, the numbers and involvement of Indians at all levels in Qatar is expected to grow despite a reduction in visas issued for labourers, etc.[40]

Moreover, giving importance to India–Qatar cultural ties, the decision to establish an Indian Cultural Centre (ICC) was taken during a meeting of prominent Indian community members held in September 1991, and the Centre was formally inaugurated on 26 October 1992 in Doha. The ICC is the official body of Indian expatriate community functioning under the patronage of Embassy of India for the purpose of advancement of sports, social and cultural activities of the Indian community in Qatar. The ICC is also the platform to serve the interest of almost 500,000 Indians residing in Qatar. This body is also committed to promote the rich Indian culture among Qatari nationals and expatriate communities of all other nationalities living in Qatar. It also functions as a body of Indian Embassy to strengthen the deep-rooted Indo–Qatar friendship and cultural relationship.[41]

External Players

The US: While Qatar is seen in some quarters as a progressive Arab state and enjoys generally good relations with the US and other western democracies, concerns have been growing over the apparent ambitions of the Crown Prince, specifically in terms of the desire to step into the vacuum left by the recent travails of both Syria and Iran, the long-time sponsors of both Hamas and Islamic Jihad in Gaza. The official visit of the Qatari leader to the Gaza Strip in November 2012 has increased a sense of unease in some quarters that al-Thani's huge wealth was being used to insert him as a major figure in the Israel/Palestinian conflict and complicate the already near-impossible impasse in the peace process. Noel Clay, spokesman for the US State Department, said,

> We share the international community's deep concern for the welfare of the Palestinian people, including those Palestinian civilians residing in Gaza. We urge all those wishing to provide international humanitarian support to Gaza to do so through established channels to ensure that the Palestinians' humanitarian needs and Israel's legitimate security needs are both met.[42]

Moreover, on 30 November 2012, the US Defence Security Cooperation Agency approved the sale of US$6 billion in missile defence systems to Qatar and the United Arab Emirates (UAE). Days later Qatar submitted a new US$10 billion request for interceptor missiles to fill those launchers. This shows that both the countries share good military and strategic relations.[43]

China: When judged against its ties with major players in the Middle East such as Saudi Arabia or Iran, China's relationship with the tiny Persian Gulf emirate of Qatar tends to be overshadowed. China's pursuit of energy resources, particularly natural gas, underpins Sino–Qatari relations. Qatar is the world's largest producer and exporter of LNG, third largest holder of natural gas reserves, and is also a major producer and exporter of crude oil. Qatar is an important source of China's LNG needs, satisfying around 20 per cent of Chinese demand for LNG. Chinese imports of Qatari crude, in comparison, are negligible.[44] As Qatar places a heavy premium on satisfying the rapidly growing demand for LNG across Asia, Doha and Beijing continue to look for ways to further develop energy ties. The centrality of energy to Sino–Qatari relations was not lost during Chinese Premier

Wen Jiabao's two-day state visit to Doha on 18–19 January 2012.[45] During a press conference, Wen stressed the strategic significance of Qatar to China's energy security paradigm: 'Establishing a long-term, stable and comprehensive cooperative partnership with Qatar on natural gas is an important topic between us.' Wen's meetings with Qatari Emir Sheikh Hamad bin Khalifa al-Thani and other political, diplomatic and business leaders also touched on other economic matters, including a proposal by China to manufacture downstream oil products in Qatar. This way China can also emerge as a competing energy partner for India.[46]

Pakistan: Pakistan and Qatar have been expressing their desires to enhance their relations, both politically and economically. This was reflected when Qatar's Prime Minister Sheikh Hamad bin Jassim bin Jaber al-Thani, on 6 February 2012, termed the visit of Pakistani Prime Minister Syed Yusuf Raza Gilani to Qatar as 'another heartening moment'.[47] Both the countries promised to further strengthen the bilateral ties, particularly in areas such as defence, defence production, energy and construction.[48] Both President of Pakistan Asif Ali Zardari and Emir of Qatar Sheikh Hamad bin Khalifa al-Thani visited India in the beginning of April 2012.[49] Pakistan signed an MoU with Qatar to increase the import of LNG to 500 million cubic feet per day as part of its efforts to cement ties. The Trade Development Authority of Pakistan (TDAP) organized an exhibition in Doha to showcase products for which the government of Qatar had extended full co-operation.[50] Interestingly, as of now, Pakistan does not appear to be a major factor in Indo–Qatari relations. However, it has the potential to emerge as an active competitor if India fails to strengthen its bilateral relations with Qatar, especially in energy and defence sectors.

Challenges

The India–Qatar bilateral relations during the year 2012 were not engulfed by any major controversies. However, there were few issues that undermined the relations. Firstly, flowing allegations of foul play, in February 2012, Petroleum Minister S. Jaipal Reddy ordered probe into changes made in a multi-billion dollar contract for import of LNG from Qatar. In this regard, Reddy asked Oil Secretary G. C. Chaturvedi, who was also the chairman of Petronet LNG, to probe allegations that the company quietly switched to buying lean gas, which can only be used as fuel, instead of rich gas that can also produce petrochemicals and cooking gas.[51] Secondly, in April 2012, an issue in which India rejected the price sought by Qatar for supplying an additional 5 million tonnes a year of gas in ships made headlines. India's rejection was based on the reason that the price was too stiff for domestic consumers.[52]

Otherwise, the bilateral relations between India and Qatar were quite smooth in 2012 as both focused more on trade, economics and energy sector. Yet, there are a few more challenges which need to be discussed between the two countries which would help in strengthening ties. First, the living standard of Indian workers in Qatar needs an adequate attention. The Indian expatriate community in Qatar constitutes almost one-third of the population in the Gulf emirate. Therefore, both the countries should bring out a mechanism to safeguard the interests of low-paid workers, and this can be done through the liberalization of visa and other labour-related norms. In most of the cases, workers are barred from leaving the country without any exit permit as the employers often keep their passport. Such a practice results in the exploitation of the workers. This remains one of the major challenges, particularly because the Indian workers have been playing a significant role in the development and growth of the country.[53]

Second, India cannot completely rely on Qatar for its energy needs because much of the oil and gas which come from Qatar passes through the Hormuz Strait. There are concerns that Iran could try and block the waterway because of the recent sanctions by the West. In such a situation, India would require reliable and alternative supplier for its huge domestic demand for oil and gas. This is the reason why India, since 2008, started signing LNG importing contracts with countries other than Qatar, such as Australia, France, Russia and the US.[54]

Conclusion

The relationship between India and Qatar looks very promising, particularly considering the developments witnessed during the last few years. Not only the energy and trade relations seem to get better but the betterment of the expatriates in Qatar has been promised by the Emir during his visit. One can say that the relationship which was once based primarily on oil and gas is expanding to other realms as well. Military and security co-operation, trade in other commodities and cultural relations can be mentioned here. To further strengthen the ties, leaders of both the countries should meet on a regular basis and to resolve differences.

Notes

1. 'World Economic Outlook Database', International Monetary Fund, April 2012, http://www.imf.org/external/pubs/ft/weo/2012/01/weodata/weorept. aspx?pr.x=27&pr.y=8&sy=2009&ey=2012&scsm=1&ssd=1&sort=countr y&ds=.&br=1&c=453&s=NGDPD%2CNGDPDPC%2CPPPGDP%2CPPPP C%2CLP&grp=0&a=#download

2. Although Qatar did not face mass protests, there have been a few instances of official purge and high-handedness. Most high profile was the incarceration of the blogger and founder of a rights group, Sultan al-Khalaifi, in March 2011 for writing against censorship. See 'Amnesty: Qatari Blogger Detained', Al Jazeera, 5 March 2011, http://www.aljazeera.com/news/middleeast/2011/03/20113511455929372.html

3. Bertelsmann Stiftung, BTI, Qatar Country Report (Gutersloh: Bertelsmann, 2012), http://www.bti-project.de/fileadmin/Inhalte/reports/2012/pdf/BTI%202012%20Qatar.pdf

4. 'The World's Richest Countries', Forbes, 22 February 2012, http://www.forbes.com/sites/bethgreenfield/2012/02/22/the-worlds-richest-countries/

5. Paul Aster, 'Time for US to Review Links with Hamas Sponsor Qatar', Fox News, 23 November 2012, http://www.foxnews.com/world/2012/11/23/time-for-us-to-review-links-with-hamas-sponsor-qatar/#ixzz2LDSsFLHg

6. Central Intelligence Agency (CIA), The World Factbook, https://www.cia.gov/library/publications/the-world-factbook/geos/qa.html

7. 'Arab League Threatens to Turn to UN over Syrian Crisis', Xinhua, 18 December 2012, http://news.xinhuanet.com/english/world/2011-12/18/c_131313498.htm

8. Hugh Miles, Al-Jazeera: The Inside Story of the Arab News Channel That is Challenging the West (New York: Grove Press, 2005), 346.

9. Bertelsmann Stiftung, BTI, Qatar Country Report.

10. Max Fisher, 'Qatar's Foray into Gaza Politics: Bad for Iran, Good for Israel?', The Washington Post, 26 October 2012, http://www.washingtonpost.com/blogs/worldviews/wp/2012/10/26/qatars-foray-into-gaza-politics-bad-for-iran-good-for-israel/

11. 'International Unions Warn Qatar's Work Visa System Allows Employers to Use Forced Labour', International Trade Union Confederation, 18 January 2013, http://www.ituc-csi.org/international-unions-warn-qatar-s?lang=en

12. Human Rights Watch, 'Qatar: Migrant Construction Workers Face Abuse', 12 June 2012, 14, http://www.hrw.org/news/2012/06/12/qatar-migrant-construction-workers-face-abuse

13. Ibid.

14. Ibid.

15. 'India–Qatar Bilateral Economic Relations', Embassy of India, Qatar, Doha, http://www.indianembassyqatar.org/bilateraleconomic.html

16. 'Visit of Emir of the State of Qatar', Press Release, 12 April 2005, Ministry of External Affairs, New Delhi, http://meaindia.nic.in/mystart.php?id=10059339

17. 'Briefing by Secretary (East) on Prime Minister's Visit to Oman and Qatar and the Forthcoming BIMSTEC Summit', Media Briefings, 7 November 2008, Ministry of External Affairs, New Delhi, http://meaindia.nic.in/mystart.php?id=530314390

18. 'Ready to Meet India's LNG Needs: Qatar', *The Economic Times,* 14 January 2011. HLMM was set up by India and Qatar during the Indian PM's visit to Qatar in 2008. This mechanism has been mandated to monitor the progress made by both the countries in the implementation of the areas of co-operation agreed to by the leaders of India and Qatar for the further enhancement of the bilateral co-operation.

19. 'India Seeks Additional Oil and Gas from Qatar', *Business Line,* 28 October 2011, http://www.thehindubusinessline.com/industry-and-economy/india-seeks-more-oil-gas-from-qatar/article3273541.ece

20. 'Smt. Deepa Gopalan Wadhwa to Be Ambassador to Qatar', Press Release, Ministry of External Affairs, New Delhi, 5 March 2008, http://meaindia.nic.in/mystart.php?id=100513660

21. 'Emir of Qatar to Visit India; LNG, Crude Oil Supply on Agenda', *The Economic Times,* 4 April 2012, http://articles.economictimes.indiatimes.com/2012-04-04/news/31287879_1_khalifa-al-thanisheikh-hamad-lng

22. 'India and Qatar Signed Six Agreements including a Pact on Cooperation in Oil and Gas Exploration', Jagran Josh, 10 April 2012, http://www.jagranjosh.com/current-affairs/india-and-qatar-signed-six-agreements-including-a-pact-on-cooperation-in-oil-and-gas-exploration-1334062044-1

23. 'Qatar, India Sign Six Agreements', *The Peninsula,* 10 April 2012, http://www.thepeninsulaqatar.com/qatar/190249-qatar-india-sign-six-agreements.html

24. 'PM Gulf Mission—Defence Pact with Qatar Inked', *Asia News Agency,* 17 November 2008, http://teleradproviders.com/nbn/story.php?id=MjAzNzM=

25. Ibid

26. 'India-Qatar, 2012', *Diplomatist Plus,* Special Report, http://www.lbassociates.com/supplements/Qatar2012.pdf

27. Compiled by the market information and research section, Australian Department of Foreign Affairs and Trade (DFAT), using the latest data from American Bureau of Shipping (ABS), the IMF and various other international sources.

28. 'India Petronet Eyes Extra 2–3 mln t/yr Qatar LNG', *Reuters*, 24 March 2012, http://www.reuters.com/article/2012/03/24/india-qatar-gas-idUSL3E8 EO05T20120324

29. Alessandro Bacci, 'Qatar and India: A Gas Relationship Due to Continue', DAO's Board of Directors, 23 March 2012, http://www.daoonline.info/public/foto/BACCI%20-%20IKA%20-%20Qatar%20And%20IndiaMar%20 2012.pdf

30. 'Iran-Pakistan-India Pipeline: Is It a Peace Pipeline?', *MIT Center for International Studies Audit of the Conventional Wisdom* 7, no. 16 (September 2007), http://belfercenter.ksg.harvard.edu/publication/17518/iranpakistanindia_ pipeline.html. Also see 'The Iran-Pakistan-India Pipeline Project: Cross-Border Gas Pipeline Challenges', A Case Study Prepared for International Gas Union's Gas Market Integration Task Force, Instituto Argentino Del Petroleo Y Del Gas, http://www.iapg.org.ar/WGC09/admin/archivosNew/ Special%20Projects/3.%20IGU%20GMI%20Guidelines/3.%20IGU%20 GMI%20Guidelines%20FINAL%20-%20CD%20contents/Iran%20Pakistan%20India.pdf

31. 'IPI Gas Pipeline: India Shows Renewed Interest despite "US Pressure"', *The Express Tribune*, 24 August 2011, http://tribune.com.pk/story/238114/ india-renews-interest-in-ipi-project-keeps-eye-on-tapi/

32. Ibid.

33. 'Emir of Qatar to Visit India; LNG, Crude Oil Supply on Agenda', *The Economic Times*, 4 April 2012, http://articles.economictimes.indiatimes. com/2012-04-04/news/31287879_1_khalifa-al-thanisheikh-hamad-lng

34. Bacci, 'Qatar and India: A Gas Relationship Due to Continue'.

35. 'India, Qatar Sign Pact to Boost Oil & Gas Cooperation', *The Indian Express*, 10 April 2012, http://www.indianexpress.com/news/india-qatar-sign-pact-to-boost-oil-&-gascooperation/934631

36. 'India Qatar Broaden Ties beyond Energy Trade', *World Politics Review*, 27 April 2012, http://www.worldpoliticsreview.com/articles/11896/india-qatar-broaden-ties-beyond-energy-trade

37. CIA, *The World Factbook*, https://www.cia.gov/library/publications/the-world-factbook/index.html

38. 'India-Qatar Relations', Ministry of External Affairs, New Delhi, January 2012, http://mea.gov.in/Portal/ForeignRelation/Qatar-January-2012.pdf

39. 'Qatar', Ministry of Overseas Indian Affairs (hereafter MOIA), New Delhi, http://moia.gov.in/pdf/qatar.pdf

40. 'India–Qatar Bilateral Economic Relations', Embassy of India, Doha.

41. Indian Cultural Centre (IIC), Doha–Qatar, http://iccqatar.com/index.php

42. Aster, 'Time for US to Review Links with Hamas Sponsor Qatar'.
43. Ibid.
44. U.S. Energy Information Administration, *China Country Data*, 4 September 2012, http://www.eia.gov/countries/cab.cfm?fips=CH
45. Chris Zambellis, 'China and Qatar Forge a New Era of Relations around High Finance', *China Brief* 12, no. 20 (19 October 2012): 11, http://www.jamestown.org/single/?no_cache=1&tx_ttnews[tt_news]=39994
46. 'Chinese Premier Starts Official Visit to Qatar', *Xinhua*, 18 January 2012, http://news.xinhuanet.com/english/china/2012-01/18/c_131367343.htm
47. 'Qatar's PM term Gilani's visit an addition to heartening moments for Arab world', Associated Press of Pakistan, 6 February 2012, http://app.com.pk/en_/index.php?option=com_content&task=view&id=178441&Itemid=1
48. 'Pakistan, Qatar to Further Foster Ties in Multiple Fields: Gilani', Associated Press of Pakistan, 8 February 2012, http://app.com.pk/en_/index.php?option=com_content&task=view&id=178807&Itemid=1
49. Ed Husain, 'What Qatar Can Learn from Pakistan', *The Arab Street*, 11 April 2012, http://blogs.cfr.org/husain/2012/04/11/what-qatar-can-learn-from-pakistan/
50. 'Pakistan, Qatar Agree on Cooperation in Energy, Trade', Associated Press of Pakistan, 7 November 2012, http://app.com.pk/en_/index.php?option=com_content&task=view&id=213869&Itemid=1
51. 'Oil Minister Orders Probe into Petronet LNG's Qatar Contract', *The Economic Times*, 20 February 2012, http://articles.economictimes.indiatimes.com/2012-02-20/news/31079486_1_petronet-lng-sqatar-rich-gas-kochi-terminal
52. 'India Rejects Qatar's Offer for LNG Supply', *The Times of India*, 3 April 2012, http://timesofindia.indiatimes.com/business/india-business/India-rejects-Qatars-offer-for-LNG-supply/articleshow/12512235.cms?
53. 'Qatar', MOIA.
54. Bacci, 'Qatar and India: A Gas Relationship Due to Continue'.

8

Saudi Arabia

Md. Muddassir Quamar

Key Indicators

Area: 2,149,690 sq km; **Population:** 26.93 million; **Youth population:** 19.6 per cent; **Population growth rate:** 1.523 per cent; **Life expectancy at birth:** 74.1 years; **GDP:** US$740.5 billion; **Per capita income:** US$25,700; **Foreign trade:** US$518.3 billion; **Oil reserves:** 264.6 billion bbl; **Gas reserves:** 8.018 trillion m³; **Ruling family:** Al-Saud; **Ruler:** King Abdullah bin Abdulaziz al-Saud (since 1 August 2005); **National Day:** 23 September; **Defence budget:** 10 per cent of GDP; **HDI rank:** 57; **Literacy rate:** 86.6 per cent; **UN education index:** 0.703; **Gender inequality index:** 0.682.

Source: CIA, *The World Factbook*, https://www.cia.gov/library/publications/the-world-factbook/index.html; UN Human Development Report, Statistics, http://hdr.undp.org/en/statistics/
Note: All data for 2012.

India and Saudi Arabia have maintained friendly relations encompassing trade, economic and sociocultural ties built over millennia of historical linkages between the Indian subcontinent and the Arabian Peninsula. The modern era of bilateral relations started with the establishment of diplomatic ties after India's independence in 1947. However, relations came under a lull due to international and regional events and a period of lesser interactions and engagements followed the initial exchange of high-level visits. With the change in global order and resultant realignment of their foreign policies, the two sides cultivated bilateral relations envisaging closer economic ties. The January 2006 visit of King Abdullah bin Abdulaziz al-Saud to India and signing of the 'Delhi Declaration'[1] provided a fresh impetus to the bilateral relations. Prime Minister Manmohan Singh reciprocated the visit in 2010 and signed the 'Riyadh Declaration'[2] that provides a framework for enhanced co-operation in security, defence, economic and political engagements raising the bilateral relations to 'strategic partnership'.[3]

If 2011 was a year of trade and energy ties then 2012 proved to be a year of defence and security relations. Indian Defence Minister visited Saudi Arabia for the first time, signed a Memorandum of Understanding (MoU) on defence co-operation and returned with promises of enhanced strategic relations. The extradition of three terror suspects despite pressures and protests from Pakistan was proof of a forward movement in this direction. If high-level political visits from both sides underlined the improved level of official engagements then huge rise in import and export bills signified the growth and potential in trade between the two countries. The year also witnessed remarkable increase in cultural activities with continued flow of labour to the Saudi market. A large number of Indians performed Hajj, marking better arrangement with mutual co-operation. India, however, needs to cultivate the 'strategic partnership' to tap the goodwill created through its expatriate community, its growing economic profile and its stable, inclusive and participatory polity to pursue its interest in the region.

Domestic Developments

Saudi Arabia is one of the prominent countries in the world because it is the largest producer and exporter of petroleum and is the birth place of Islam. Its pre-eminence in the region emanates from its geographical enormity, financial leverage and closer ties with the United States (US). It has a population of nearly 26 million including an estimated 6 million expatriates and a land mass of 2,149,690 sq km. A coastline of nearly 2,640 km opening mainly in the Red Sea and the Persian Gulf serves as its opening to international maritime trade. Almost 50 per cent of the

Saudi population is below the age of 25. The country has a robust oil-based economy, but unemployment among Saudi youth is high due to lack of skilled manpower. The kingdom is trying to diversify the economy by encouraging private investments in various fields.

The population comprises mainly of Sunni Muslims and a minority Shia population. Shias are estimated between 10 per cent and 12 per cent and live mainly in the Eastern Province and southern province of Najran. The country was united under the rule of al-Saud family of central Najd region in an expedition beginning 1902 that finally ended with the establishment of the Kingdom of Saudi Arabia in 1932 under the leadership of the founder king, Abdulaziz bin Abdulrahman al-Saud. The Shia minority and other ethnic and tribal groups have often complained of discrimination and exclusion at the hands of the ruling family since the foundation of the kingdom. The main complaint has been lack of equal allocation and distribution of wealth. However, for the past eight decades the al-Saud maintained a strong hold on power, gaining legitimacy through a mixture of Islam, tribal affiliations, financial leverage and coercion.[4]

The kingdom has avoided significant external threat by aligning with great powers, initially with the British and later with the US. But it faced some major internal threats in the form of Kaaba siege in 1979,[5] periodic Shia unrests in Najran and Eastern Provinces[6] and the rise of radical Islam in the form of al-Qaeda.[7] The rulers have dealt with dissents with an iron hand. Since the early 1990s, the monarchy also faces challenge in the form of internal demands for reform, political participation, educational reforms, freedom of the press, women's rights and judicial reforms. The monarchy skilfully responded to these demands, particularly under the leadership of King Abdullah, but the response has been slow and limited because of the opposition of the conservative ulema and the rise of radical Islam.

Another major challenge faced by the monarchy is the succession problem.[8] The kingdom has witnessed five successions among the sons of the founder king. With the death of Crown Princes Sultan (October 2011) and Nayef (June 2012) and the appointment of the youngest surviving son of the founder, Prince Muqrin, as the Second Deputy Prime Minister in January 2013, it has become clear that the third generation of al-Saud, the grandsons of Ibn Saud would now stake claim to head the monarchy. This was envisaged by the family, and King Abdullah has established an Allegiance Council in 2007 comprising representation from all the sons of the founder king. The council has been established to develop consensus in choosing the heir from among the third generation Princes through *baya't* (allegiance). However, it is not very clear as to what extent the Allegiance Council played a role, if any, in the recent appointments of Prince Salman as the Crown Prince (upon the death of Crown Prince Nayef in June 2012) and Prince Muqrin as the Second Deputy Prime Minister.

Political Developments

Since the outbreak of Arab Spring in Tunisia in December 2010, Saudi Arabia has faced numerous challenges both at home and on the regional front. The possible spread of protests inside the kingdom was taken seriously by the ruler and efforts were made to keep the situation under control. The King announced economic packages in February–March 2011 which included building new housing complex for the poor, unemployment allowance, bonuses for public servants and enhanced scholarships for students.[9] A few calls for protest were given by some elements that brought the monarchy into action and security was enhanced mainly in the capital Riyadh and Shia-dominated areas in Eastern province and Najran. In order to keep the youth away from protesting, religion was also used. Senior ulema, like the Grand Mufti Sheikh Abdulaziz bin Abdullah al-Shaikh and Imam of Kaaba Abdul Rahman al-Sudais issued statements terming protests as 'acts of chaos' and fitna (strife).[10]

However, things are not completely peaceful and tranquil; news about protests, particularly in Shia-populated areas, has filtered out in the international media. During 2012, Shia protests in various cities have increased and violent clashes between security forces and protestors have been reported from many places. There have been instances of peaceful protests by the Sunni population in a number of cities, particularly in old quarters of Jeddah as torrential rains flooded the city. In a major incident in July 2012, Saudi security forces detained a number of protestors in the city of Qatif, who were demanding the release of detained Shia cleric Sheikh Nimr al-Nimr and other political detainees. Earlier in

April, trial began against 50 men suspected to be members of al-Qaeda and allegedly involved in the 2003 Riyadh bombings.[11] In September, the international media reported that two reformist political activists, Mohammad al-Qahtani and Abdullah al-Hamid, have been charged with setting up an unauthorized organization and trial began against them.[12] In December, a protestor was killed in Qatif as security forces resorted to firing to control the crowd.[13] With the question of security looming large and trouble in the neighbourhood, Saudi Arabia entered into a US$2.5 billion deal with British firm BAE to supply Hawk trainer jets in May 2012.[14] This was preceded by another US$30 billion arms deal with the US concluded in December 2011.[15]

As a part of political developments, a number of decisions were taken by the monarchy during 2012 indicating its commitment to continue with the reform process, particularly regarding the rights of women and their political participation. A major area that witnessed some changes has been the issue of religious police, the *mutawwayin* as they are known in the country. In January, King Abdullah replaced Abdulaziz al-Humayn, the head of Commission for the Promotion of Virtue and Prevention of Vice (known in short as *hai'a* commission) with Abdul Latif al-Shaikh. Later in October, he announced that the powers of the religious police would be restricted and they would be barred from making arrests, conducting interrogations and carrying out searches without a warrant from the local governor.[16]

After numerous flip-flops, the Saudi authorities finally allowed women to be part of the official team for the London Olympic Games in 2012, which was a first since the founding of the Kingdom in 1932.[17] Earlier in September 2011, King Abdullah had announced that women would be nominated for the Shoura Council (consultative legislative body) and would be allowed to vote and participate in municipal elections from 2015. In tune with this commitment, 30 women were appointed when a new 150-member Shoura council was announced in January 2013. The move was seen as a measure to satisfy the youth which is becoming more and more restless with the stifling of their political and economic aspirations. King Abdullah intervened and pardoned when two women were arrested and punished for driving. By doing this, he exhibited an indication to the population that the rulers are aware of the problems faced by the society.

The year 2012 witnessed a number of changes in the government. In June 2012, Prince Salman, a long-term ally of King Abdullah, was appointed the Crown Prince following the death of Crown Prince Nayef. Nayef's son Muhammad, who had long served as the Assistant Deputy Minister in charge of internal security, was appointed as the Interior Minister replacing his uncle Ahmed who fell out of favour due to differences with the King and the Crown Prince.[18] Another important decision that came in 2012 was the appointment of Prince Bandar bin Sultan (son of Prince Sultan bin Abdulaziz) as the intelligence chief. The move was largely seen as an indication to deal with security concerns with stern action.

Economy

As far as the Saudi economy is concerned, the country remains a leading producer of oil and natural gas and holds about a fifth of world's proven oil reserves. The government continues to pursue economic reform and diversification, and has been trying to promote foreign investment in the Kingdom. However, what remains a primary concern is the burgeoning population and an economy largely dependent on petroleum output and their prices.

A major economic concern of the country is its near total dependence on the petroleum sector, which accounts for roughly 80 per cent of the budget revenue, nearly 45 per cent of the GDP and as much as 90 per cent of the export earnings. Saudi Arabia is trying to diversify its economy, particularly in the areas of power generation, telecommunications, natural gas exploration and petrochemical sector. According to an IMF survey, the non-oil sector recorded an eight per cent growth in Saudi Arabia in 2012.[19] The government has been encouraging private investments in many sectors including manufacturing and construction, and this led to their substantial growth in 2012. The role of private sector in the economy has grown. The survey estimated that the GDP will grow by six per cent in 2012, with particularly good growth rate in the private sector.[20]

Another important area of concern has been the large-scale unemployment among the youth that is estimated to be as high as 30 per cent. In 2011, the authorities launched a new Saudization plan known as *Nitaqat* that envisaged increasing employment of Saudi nationals in the private sector. The government launched a new programme of unemployment allowance, *Hafiz*, in 2011. The government is trying to tackle the problem by increasing spending in training and education. In 2012, Saudi Arabia allocated a massive 24 per cent of its total 2012 budgetary allocation for human resource development including education and training, which is expected to create more employment opportunities.[21] This includes plans to build new schools and refurbish existing ones. The funds will also be used to establish 40 new colleges in various areas and for the development of the existing universities, and in increasing the number of scholarship programmes that allow Saudi students to study abroad.[22]

Overall, the Saudi economy had a good year in 2012, particularly with a buoyant oil sector growth due to international oil price rise. The prospects for the economy are excellent with the world oil market remaining strong and growing efforts for diversification of the economy. Reforms that have been enacted both as part of the Kingdom's accession to the World Trade Organization in 2005 and under King Abdullah's modernization programme have stabilized the economy and are likely to expedite economic growth. The steps are expected to bring more Saudi nationals into employment within the country, especially as the reforms have focused on promoting entrepreneurial activity and small businesses.

On the domestic front, during 2012, Saudi Arabia witnessed major events at the political, economic and societal level, which are an indication that the country is going through a phase of evolutionary change. Though slow, it is backed by the rulers and is endorsed by the populace.

Bilateral Relations

India shared good relations with the Arabian Peninsula through trade and commerce since times immemorial. The cultural and civilizational linkages go back to third millennium before Christ and Indian and Arab traders have travelled through land and sea paving way for continued exchange of goods and ideas. Maritime trade between India and Arabia flourished during medieval times but the advent of European powers reduced the leadership position of Indian and Arab traders in the region. However, the presence of Indian merchants in various trading centres in the Arabian Peninsula continued during the British period. Indian merchants, particularly the Gujaratis, Parsis, Sindhis and Khojas, played a crucial role in trade and commerce of Jeddah, Muscat, Kuwait and Dubai during the early twentieth century.

Based on the heritage of Indo–Arab relations, India and Saudi Arabia established formal diplomatic relations immediately after India's independence. After initial bonhomie the ties between the two strained due to differences over the global political order. India's friendly relations with Gamal Abdul Nasser's Egypt during the 1950s and 1960s further complicated Indo–Saudi relations. Saudi Arabia's stand on Kashmir and support for Pakistan during the 1971 Indo–Pak War did not help the matter either. Major regional events such as the Islamic Revolution in Iran in 1979, the Soviet invasion of Afghanistan later that year and the 1980–88 Iran–Iraq war did not change the situation. The lack of any high-level political exchanges between 1955 and 1982 demonstrated the lull in bilateral relations. The visit by Indira Gandhi in 1982, however, helped in reinforcing the fact that the two countries cannot ignore each other for long, though it did not drastically alter the ties.[23] The inflow of Indian labour, professionals and businessmen following the oil boom played an important part in changing the dynamics of bilateral relations.

It was in the 1990s that Indo–Saudi ties started to take new shape. With the change in global order, India started to realign its foreign policy and liberalized its economy and these in turn made it imperative for India to improve its bilateral relations with Saudi Arabia. On the Saudi part, the importance of Indian skilled and professional manpower, as well as the economic possibilities of its market, made it impossible to ignore India anymore.

Political Relations

The first high-level political visit occurred a few years after the establishment of diplomatic relations when King Saud bin Abdulaziz al-Saud visited India in November–December 1955 and this was followed by a reciprocal visit of Prime Minister Jawaharlal Nehru in September 1956. However, it took another 26 years for the next political visits when Prime Minister Indira Gandhi visited the kingdom in April 1982. Following on the trend, a lull in political contacts continued for the next two decades. The frost could be broken only in January 2006 when King Abdullah visited India as the chief guest for the Republic Day celebrations. Four years later, Prime Minister Manmohan Singh visited Saudi Arabia from 27 February to 1 March 2010.[24] This exchange of political visits at the highest level and the signing of the Delhi and Riyadh Declarations set the tone for thriving bilateral relations in various areas of mutual interest and concern.

There have been a number of high-level political contacts between the two countries since 2006. These include visits by Saudi Minister of Foreign Affairs Prince Saud al-Faisal (February 2006, February 2008 and December 2008); Minister of Justice Abdullah bin Mohammad al-Shaikh (April 2006); Minister of Health Hamad bin Abdullah al-Manea (November 2006), Intelligence Chief and now Second Deputy Prime Minister Prince Muqrin (January 2009); Governor of Riyadh and now Crown Prince Salman (April 2010); Commerce Minister Abdullah Zainal Alireza (August 2009 and November 2010) and Minister for Economy and Planning Khalid bin Muhammad al-Qusaibi (February 2011). Prince Bandar bin Sultan, Secretary General of Saudi National Security Council, visited India in March 2011 as the special emissary of King Abdullah close on the heels of Saudi military intervention in Bahrain and turbulent political atmosphere in the Middle East.[25]

From the Indian side, External Affairs Minister Pranab Mukherjee (now President) paid a visit to Riyadh in April 2008. Other visits include Minister of Human Resources Development Arjun Singh (May 2006); Ministers of State for External Affairs E. Ahamed (April 2009) and Shashi Tharoor (March 2010) and Minister of Overseas Indian Affairs Vayalar Ravi (September 2010). In 2011, External Affairs Minister S. M. Krishna (March 2011); Chairperson of Hajj Committee of India Mohsina Kidwai (March 2011); Petroleum Minister S. Jaipal Reddy (February 2011); Minister of State for External Affairs E. Ahamed (April 2011) and National Security Advisor Shivshankar Menon (December 2011) visited Saudi Arabia. On 25 October 2011, Minister of Health and Family Welfare Ghulam Nabi Azad represented India at the funeral of Crown Prince Sultan.[26]

The year 2012 started on a positive note for Indo–Saudi bilateral relations when India dropped dumping cases against a number of Saudi propylene products and lifted the 6.5 per cent anti-dumping duty.[27] Tawfiq Bin Fawzan al-Rabiah, Minister of Commerce and Industry of Saudi Arabia, thanked India for this gesture during his meeting with Indian counterpart, Anand Sharma in New Delhi. Al-Rabiah, accompanied by a 76-member delegation, was in India to co-chair the ninth India–Saudi Arabia Joint Commission Meeting on 4–5 January 2012 with the then Finance Minister Pranab Mukherjee, where India proposed a US$750 million India–Saudi investment fund.[28] During the visit, the Minister also met the Prime Minister, the External Affairs Minister and the Minister of Petroleum and Natural Gas.

Later, Minister of Defence A. K. Antony visited Saudi Arabia during 13–15 February 2012, which was the first ever visit by an Indian Defence Minister to the kingdom. The visit was aimed at strengthening the strategic ties and to explore possibilities for defence co-operation. During the visit Antony met King Abdullah and Defence Minister Prince Salman.[29] On 24 February 2012, Saudi Deputy Minister of Petroleum and Mineral Resources Abdulaziz bin Salman al-Saud visited India and held meeting with Indian Petroleum and Natural Gas Minister S. Jaipal Reddy. Deputy Chairman of Rajya Sabha K. Rahman Khan visited Saudi Arabia to attend the G-20 Parliament Speaker's Consultative Meeting in Riyadh during 25–26 February 2012 and held meetings with various Saudi leaders. In May, 11-memeber Saudi parliamentary delegation led by Shoura Council Chairman Dr Abdullah bin Mohammad bin Ibrahim al-Shaikh visited India and held meetings with the Vice President, the Prime Minister, the Lok Sabha Speaker and the External Affairs Minister to enhance co-operation in parliamentary affairs.[30] The visit highlighted improved level of political interactions between the two countries. Minister of State for External Affairs E. Ahamed visited Saudi Arabia during 23–26 May 2012 to attend the Friends of Yemen meeting in Riyadh and again during 17–20 September to meet Saudi Hajj Minister Bandar bin Mohammad al-Hajjar and discuss Hajj-related issues. Minister of Law and Justice Salman Khurshid led a three-member delegation to the kingdom during 17–18 June 2012 to offer condolences on the death of Crown Prince Naif bin Abdulaziz al-Saud.

In September 2012, an 11-member Saudi delegation led by Chief of the Armed Forces Operations Major General Suleiman Saleh al-Khalifa visited India to hold the first meeting of India–Saudi Arabia Joint Committee on Defence Cooperation to enhance military ties. The year also marked India's diplomatic and political achievement in its relations with Saudi Arabia in the context of Pakistan. The kingdom extradited Zabiuddin Ansari and two others accused for terrorist offenses to India after sustained effort by the Indian security agencies, and this was the first concrete measure since both countries signed an extradition treaty in 2010.

Economic Relations

India and Saudi Arabia share a thriving economic relation. Bilateral trade has witnessed tremendous growth during the past five years. In 2005–06, India's total trade with Saudi Arabia was US$3,442.11 million; it grew nearly five times to reach US$15,946.10 million in 2006–07 and marked an increase of 60 per cent in the next two years to reach US$25,083.12 million in 2008–09. It witnessed a minor decline the following year but again gained momentum and has crossed US$36 billion in 2011–12 (Table 8.1 and Figure 8.1). Saudi Arabia is the fourth largest trading partner of India and is second only to the UAE among the Persian Gulf states. Trade balance, however, is highly skewed in favour of Saudi Arabia owning mainly to India's oil imports, which forms a major component of the bilateral trade. Saudi Arabia is India's largest supplier of crude oil, accounting for almost one-fifth of its needs and comprising nearly 90 per cent of its total imports from Saudi Arabia (Table 8.2 and Figure 8.2). Saudi Arabia is the 14th largest market in the world for Indian exports and accounts for 1.86 per cent of India's global exports. Saudi Arabia is also the source of 6.35 per cent of India's global imports.

In 2011–12, India's total import from Saudi Arabia stood at US$31.06 billion while India exported goods and commodities to the tune of US$5.68 billion. Major Indian imports from Saudi Arabia comprise crude oil, chemicals and fertilizers, plastic and rubber and products, paper and wood products, animal products, dry fruits and nuts, pearls, metals and metal articles, etc., while major export commodities include

Table 8.1
India–Saudi Arabia Bilateral Trade (in US$ Million)

	2008–09	2009–10	2010–11	2011–12
Exports	5,110.38	3,907.00	4,684.40	5,683.29
Imports	19,972.74	17,097.57	20,385.28	31,060.10
Total trade	25,083.12	21,004.57	25,069.68	36,743.40
Per cent of total trade	5.13	4.50	4.04	4.62

Source: Adapted from Director General of Foreign Trade, New Delhi, http://www.dgft.gov.in

Figure 8.1
India–Saudi Arabia Bilateral Trade

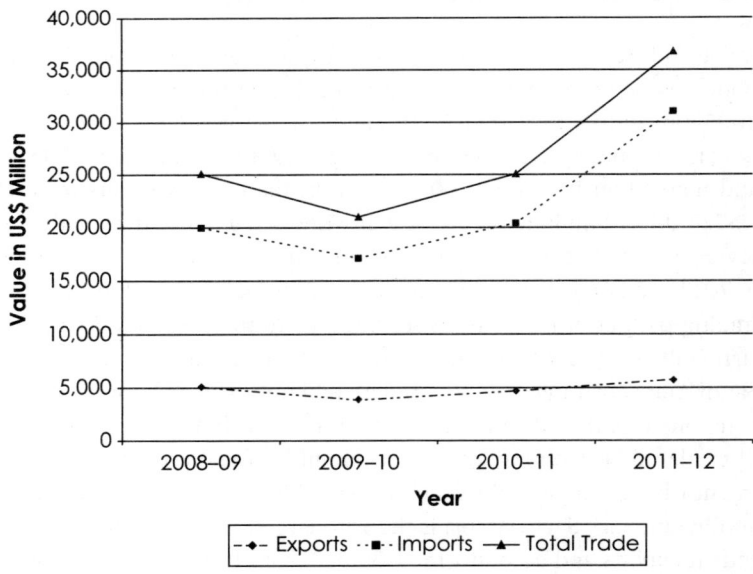

Source: Adapted from Director General of Foreign Trade, New Delhi, http://www.dgft.gov.in

animal and dairy products, cereals, oil products, cotton and textile, machinery, etc. In comparison to the previous financial year, 2011–12 witnessed an increase of 52.37 per cent in India's total imports from Saudi Arabia while India's exports also saw a rise of 21.32 per cent.[31] For

Table 8.2
India's Oil Imports from Saudi Arabia (in US$ Million)

Year	Oil imports from Saudi Arabia	Total oil imports	Saudi share in total oil imports	Imports from Saudi Arabia	Per cent of oil in imports from Saudi Arabia
2008–09	18,386.52	103,933.81	17.69	19,972.74	92.06
2009–10	15,390.04	96,321.16	15.98	17,097.57	90.01
2010–11	17,932.31	115,929.06	15.47	20,385.28	87.97
2011–12	27,940.11	172,753.97	16.17	31,060.10	89.95

Source: Adapted from Director General of Foreign Trade, New Delhi, http://www.dgft.gov.in

Figure 8.2
Share of Oil in India's Total Imports from Saudi Arabia

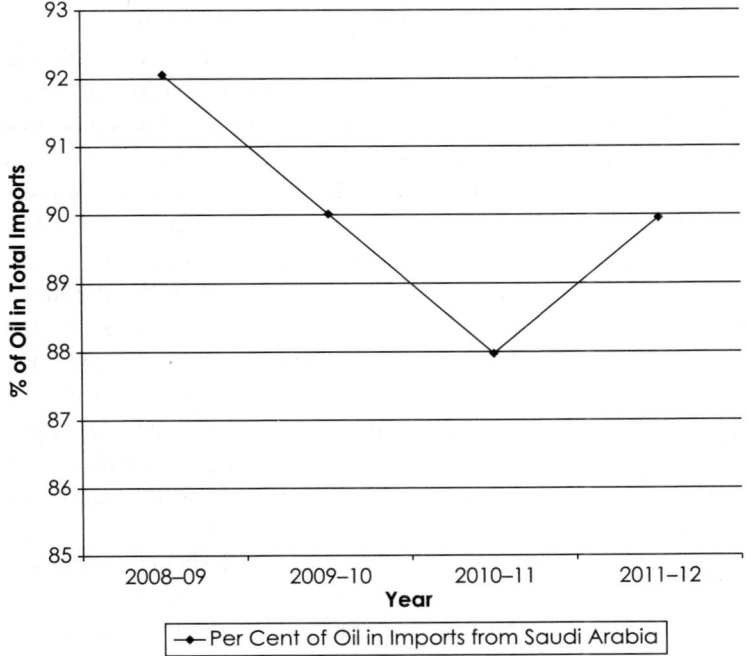

Source: Adapted from Director General of Foreign Trade, New Delhi, http://www.dgft.gov.in

Saudi Arabia, India is the fifth largest export market, accounting for 7.55 per cent of its global exports. In terms of imports by Saudi Arabia, India ranks ninth and is the source of around 3.77 per cent of the former's total imports.[32]

The two-way flow of investments between India and Saudi Arabia has played a small but significant role in shaping the bilateral relations and growth and development of various sectors in respective countries. After India adopted a policy of liberalization in 1991 and started to open its economy for Foreign Direct Investments (FDI), between April 2000 and October 2012 Saudi companies have invested US$40.82 million in Indian ventures.[33] Saudi Arabia is 45th-biggest investor in India and accounted for 0.02 per cent of total FDI flow.[34] During the financial year 2011–12, India received US$0.7 million worth of FDI from Saudi Arabia in fields as varied as paper manufacturing, chemicals, computer software, granite processing, industrial products and machinery, cement, metallurgical industries, etc.[35] Moreover, among the Persian Gulf countries, Saudi Arabia is the third-largest source of FDI into India.

On the other hand, Indian investments in Saudi Arabia are much larger and varied. The official figures show that Indian companies invested US$2.07 billion in Saudi Arabia between 2000 and 2009. According to one observer, Indian firms have shown remarkable interest in Saudi market after implementation of new Saudi laws and have established joint venture projects or wholly owned subsidiaries in the kingdom.[36] The data available with Saudi Arabian General Investment Authority (SAGIA) confirm that as many as 426 licences have been issued to Indian companies for joint ventures or fully owned subsidiaries till 2010, which are expected to bring total investments worth of US$1.62 billion in Saudi Arabia.[37] These licences were issued for projects in diverse sectors such as management and consultancy services, construction projects, telecommunications, information technology, pharmaceuticals, etc. Moreover, several Indian companies have established collaborations with Saudi companies and are working in the Kingdom in the areas of designing, consultancy, financial services and software development.[38]

The rise in volume of trade and commerce and enhanced two-way investments have also resulted in a spur in interactions at government as well as private levels. In the last couple of years, a large number of Indian business delegations have visited Saudi Arabia 'to explore the opportunities for long-term partnerships and cooperation'.[39] In January 2012, a tourism delegation comprising representatives from state tourism departments, including from Jammu and Kashmir, visited Saudi Arabia.[40] A three-member delegation from the Gems & Jewellery Export Promotion Council (GJEPC) of India visited Riyadh and Jeddah during 27–29 May 2012 and organized road shows in the cities of Jeddah and Riyadh.[41] Likewise, a seven-member business delegation consisting of growers and exporters of cardamom, headed by a senior official of the Spices Board of India, visited Riyadh and Jeddah in June 2012 and held Buyer-Seller Meetings.[42] In the same month, a five-member high-level official delegation comprising officials from Ministries of Finance and Commerce, and Reserve Bank of India and the Securities and Exchange Board of India visited Riyadh and organized a road show on 'Investment Opportunities in India'. The delegation also had interactive meetings with senior officials of Saudi Arabian Monetary Agency (SAMA) and SAGIA.[43] Moreover, official-level delegations from Ministry of Commerce and Industry visited Saudi Arabia to hold meetings with officials from Saudi Basic Industries Corporation and Saudi Petrochemical Company to explore business opportunities during June–July 2012.[44] In September 2012, another official-level delegation from Ministry of Heavy Industries and Public Enterprises visited Saudi Arabia.[45] Thirty-eight Indian companies under the umbrella of the India Trade Promotion Organisation (ITPO) participated in the international trade fair for food and food products, *Saudi Agro Food 2012*, organized by Riyadh Exhibitions Company at Riyadh from 24 to 27 September 2012.[46]

Business delegation visits have been reciprocated with equal enthusiasm from the Saudi side demonstrating the eagerness on both sides to augment trade and commerce. The Saudi-India Business Council (SIBC) set up by Council of Saudi Chambers of Commerce and Industry regularly holds joint meetings since its formation in 2009. The third meeting of the Council was held in New Delhi on 23 February 2011 where host of issues came under discussion to help enhance business between the two countries. The year 2012 began with the ninth India–Saudi Joint Commission Meeting which was held in New Delhi on 4–5 January.[47] A Saudi delegation led by the Commerce and

Industry Minister, Tawfiq Bin Fawzan al-Rabiah, comprising 76 officials and businessmen visited India to take part in the meeting. The then Finance Minister Pranab Mukherjee chaired the Indian delegation and a whole range of issues were deliberated upon at great length. Mukherjee emphasized on the need to give 'high priority' to India–Saudi investment fund for development of infrastructure, promotion of joint exploration and production of hydrocarbons. The meeting issued a call for expansion of bilateral trade basket. The Finance Minister said that 'there is a great scope to expand our bilateral trade basket to include non-oil products and we need to mount a concerted effort to enlarge and widen our trade basket'.[48] A 40-member Saudi business delegation led by Abdulrahman Alrabiah, Chairman of the SIBC, visited India during January 2012 to attend the fourth India–Saudi Joint Business Council Meeting held on the sidelines of the ninth Joint Commission Meeting.[49] The delegation also held a meeting with members of the Confederation of Indian Industry during their visit. The enhanced level of business visits from both sides during 2012 is yet 'another testimony to the growing business interaction' between India and Saudi Arabia. In November 2012, a 15-member business delegation of Saudi India Business Network (SIBN) headed by its president Ghazi Binzagr visited New Delhi, Bangalore and Mumbai to explore opportunities for business in India.[50]

The large volume of trade notwithstanding, there is still scope for further strengthening of trade ties. There are untapped opportunities for Indian businessmen to invest in Saudi Arabia in sectors like construction industry, petrochemicals, health and pharmaceuticals. On the other hand, Saudi companies and businessmen can benefit from growing Indian market by investing in infrastructure, real estate and other sectors as India provides a conducive financial environment for investments. During the visit of Saudi Minister of Commerce and Industry in January 2012, India had 'expressed interest in participating in the petroleum and gas sectors in Saudi Arabia, including upstream and downstream', reflecting the untapped economic opportunities between the two sides.[51] In return, India invited Saudi Arabia 'to invest in the Indian petroleum and gas-based mega industrial estates, fertilisers, petrochemical plants and refineries'.[52] In December 2012, Tata Motors signed a letter of intent with Saudi Arabia to set up Land Rover plant in the country with an initial investment of US$1.2 billion.[53]

Energy Relations

The story of India's economic growth cannot be divorced from energy security concerns. India imports nearly 75 per cent of its energy requirements. At present, India is the sixth-largest energy consumer but may soon overtake others to emerge as the fourth-largest after the US, China and Japan. Saudi Arabia, on the other hand, is the largest producer and exporter of oil and has the largest known oil reserves in the world accounting for one-fifth of the proven oil reserves. It is the largest source of energy for India and fulfils nearly 20 per cent of India's energy requirements. Energy has been one of the driving forces behind India's relations with Saudi Arabia and it will continue to dominate the Indo–Saudi ties. As Table 8.3 and Figure 8.3 show, the Saudi share in total oil imports by India continues to range between 15 and 17 per cent during the past three years.

In 2011, Saudi Arabia had agreed to double its crude exports to India and annual imports of Saudi oil were expected to reach more than 800,000 barrels per day.[54] The year 2012 witnessed an increase of US$10 billion in India's energy import bills from Saudi Arabia mainly due to increased volume. Saudi Deputy Minister of Petroleum and Mineral Resources Abdul Aziz bin Salman al-Saud visited India and held meeting with Indian Petroleum and Natural Gas Minister S. Jaipal Reddy

Table 8.3

India's Energy Imports from Saudi Arabia (in US$ Million)

	2008–09	2009–10	2010–11	2011–12
Energy import from Saudi Arabia	18,386.52	15,390.04	17,932.31	27,940.11
Total energy import	103,933.81	96,321.16	115,929.06	172,753.97
Total import from Persian Gulf	62,282.89	55,904.14	66,688.40	95,915.24
Share in total imports	17.69	15.98	15.47	16.17
Share in imports from Persian Gulf	29.52	27.53	26.89	29.13

Source: Adapted from Director General of Foreign Trade, New Delhi, http://www.dgft.gov.in

Figure 8.3
Share of Saudi Arabia in India's Total Oil Imports

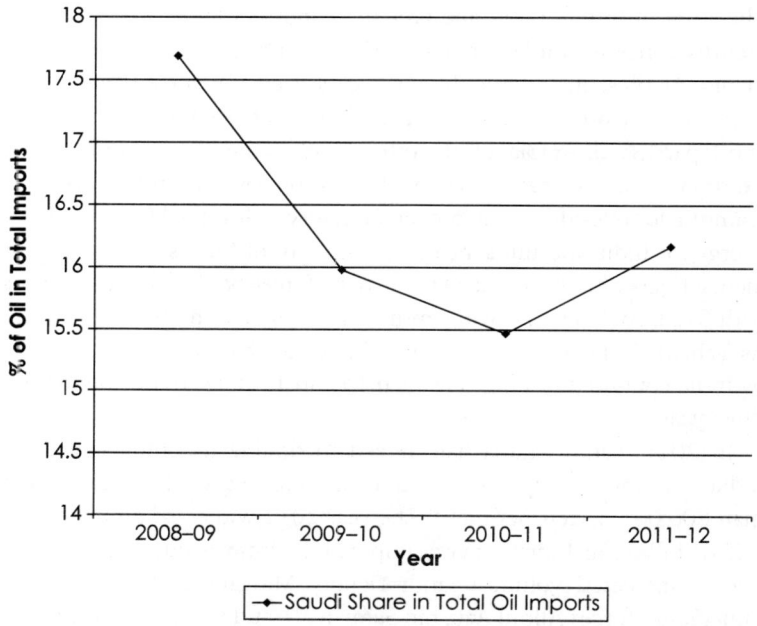

Source: Adapted from Director General of Foreign Trade, New Delhi, http://www.dgft.gov.in

in February 2012. During the visit, India sought additional supply of crude oil and LPG from Saudi Arabia. The host also made an offer to the visiting minister to consider equity participation in ONGC Petro Additions Limited's (OPaL) Petrochemical project at Dahej and ONGC Mangalore Petrochemicals Limited's (OMPL) plant in Mangalore.[55] A positive response that was received from the Saudi side has not resulted into concrete results during the financial year and 2012 did not witness much in terms of Indo–Saudi energy ties.

The Indo–Saudi energy ties acquire more importance against the backdrop of India's need to decrease its hydrocarbon imports from Iran due to international sanctions. India has tried to shift towards Iraq, and thus the Indian hydrocarbon imports from Iraq have witnessed an increase. The availability of hydrocarbons from Iraq and other sources notwithstanding, India needs to keenly watch the regional geopolitical climate.

As far as energy is concerned and looking at Saudi Arabia's leadership role in the OPEC, India's need for energy security and Saudi apprehensions over Iranian nuclear programme, India needs to closely monitor its interests, policies and options in the Persian Gulf.

Defence Relations

In recent years, Indo–Saudi defence and security ties have shown signs of improvement. In March 2011, Prince Bandar bin Sultan al-Saud, the Secretary General of the National Security Council of Saudi Arabia, had visited India in the wake of Arab Spring and upheaval in Bahrain and had met Prime Minister Manmohan Singh. The strategic and security co-operation was taken a step further when three Indian navy ships from the Southern Naval Command, namely, INS Teer, INS Krishna and ICGS Veer, made a port call at Jubail Port on 24 March 2011 as part of the efforts to enhance relations with Saudi Arabia. Commenting on the development, the then Indian ambassador to the Kingdom Talmiz Ahmed, said that the bilateral relations between the two countries were improving 'with strategic partnerships in defence, culture, politics, energy and economics'.[56] The ships also participated in joint maritime exercises. Moreover, National Security Advisor Shivshankar Menon participated in the Gulf Forum 2011, organized in Riyadh on 4–5 December 2011 that aimed to look at the ensuing political changes and its implications, regional security dynamics, global power shifts and future prospects in the field of energy, as well as into maintaining growth in economically volatile situations.[57] Discussions related to the Gulf dynamics were also taken into account, and the importance of the wider neighbourhood, including India, was addressed.

During the visit of Defence Minister A. K. Antony in February 2012, both countries agreed to sign an MoU on defence co-operation for which a joint committee was formed to explore further areas for defence co-operation including high-level visits from defence establishments, joint training programmes and co-operation in defence industries.[58] The issue of terrorism came under discussion during Antony's meeting with his Saudi counterpart Crown Prince Salman bin Abdulaziz and the two countries agreed to fight terrorism together. It was agreed to sign an MoU on co-operation in hydrography while joint exercise against piracy in Indian Ocean was also discussed.[59] The visit underlined the willingness on both sides to take Indo–Saudi 'strategic partnership' envisaged in the Riyadh Declaration to a new level and enhance co-operation in the areas of defence, security and terrorism. It is important for the two countries to enhance their defence interactions and co-operation to deal with joint security concerns. It is also, however, important that the issue of terror financing and spread of religious fundamentalism be brought under deliberations. Later, in September 2012, an 11-member Saudi delegation headed by Major General Suleiman Saleh al-Khalifa, Chief of Saudi Armed Forces Operations, visited India to participate in the first joint committee meeting. The two sides expressed their interest in further enhancing defence exchanges and interactions between their armed forces. Proposals for exchange of high-level visits, training exchanges and functional exchanges in various areas were discussed.[60]

In between Antony's visit and the joint committee meeting, India achieved a major success as far as Indo–Saudi security co-operation is concerned. On 25 June 2012, Saudi Arabia deported Zabiuddin Ansari (Abu Jundal), a terror accused wanted for his involvement in the 26 November 2008 Mumbai terror attacks. The most important aspect of this deportation was that the person held a Pakistani passport. Pakistan pressurized Saudi Arabia to prevent the deportation but heightened Saudi anxieties over Pakistani involvement worked in favour of India.[61] Later, in October two more terror accused A. Rayees, wanted by the Kerela Police, and Fasih Mohammad were deported to India from Saudi Arabia. The development evoked numerous reactions in the media and intelligentsia at the national and international level. It was argued that Saudi Arabia seems to have decided to move away from a 'brother' to a 'friend', while some dubbed it as 'good but peculiar' relations.[62] Chairman of India's National Security Advisory Board Naresh Chandra said that 'there's a genuine concern in the Saudi establishment that things may get out of hand' in Pakistan while a former Pakistani general, Talat Masood, observed that 'the Saudi relationship is no longer a monopoly of Pakistan'.[63] It was also argued that the Saudi tilt towards India is a result of power tussle between Iran and Saudi Arabia in the Persian Gulf.[64] From India's strategic and security viewpoint, this was an achievement and an indication of Saudi willingness to take the bilateral defence co-operation to another level. India needs to work towards consolidating this lead and develop a strong defence co-operation agreement with Saudi Arabia that can go a long way in combating terrorism and improving security at national, regional and global levels. On the other hand, India needs to be cautious as far as Saudi moves in the Persian Gulf are concerned and watch out for its options before putting its weight behind any country in regional geopolitics.

Cultural Relations

The Indo–Arab cultural relations date back several millennia; trade and exchange of people and goods through Arabian Sea have continued since antiquity. If Arabian horses were popular among Indian princely states for their strength, then Indian swords were famous among Arabs for its sharpness. Trading of spices and textile from India and dates and dried fruits from Arabia has continued to modern times. People-to-people contacts for trade spurred cultural and linguistic influences and flow of ideas from both sides. Many Indian stories and literary texts reached Arabia through translations and became popular. For example, the Indian stories of *Panchatantra* were translated into Arabic as *Kalila wa Dimna* and became part of Arabian folklores. India's advancement in science and astronomy were well respected among Arabs during ancient times.

These people-to-people contacts did not vanish with the advent of Islam and early Islam reached western coasts of India through Muslim traders. During the latter period of Umayyad rule (661–750 AD/41–132 AH), Muslim rulers reached Sind. It has been argued that the name *Hind* that later acquired new forms to become India was given by Arabs. As Muslim rulers established their rule in India and with the coming of Sufi preachers, Islam spread in various parts of India. India now houses second-largest population of Muslims in the world, after Indonesia.[65] The cultural exchanges since the formation of Kingdom of Saudi Arabia in 1932 and India's independence in 1947 have continued. India has an MoU on Cultural Cooperation with Saudi Arabia, an Agreement in the field of youth and sports and another MoU of Scientific and Educational Cooperation. Both the countries wish to increase co-operation in the field of education and research. It is in this regard that an MoU for joint research programmes was signed between the two countries. Moreover, an agreement has been signed between King Abdulaziz Foundation for Research and Archives and India-Arab Cultural Centre at Jamia Millia Islamia, New Delhi to translate important Arabic books on history and culture of the Kingdom into Indian languages.[66]

In 2011, the Imam of Masjid-al-Haram in Mecca, Sheikh Abdul Rahman al-Sudais, became the first Imam of Kabaa to visit India.[67] The increased level of cultural exchanges and people-to-people interactions continued in 2012. A parliamentary delegation from Saudi Arabia visited India in May. Earlier in January, the Indian Embassy at Riyadh, in association with Ministry of Tourism, organized road shows at various places in the kingdom to promote Indian tourism in Saudi Arabia. The Indian Ambassador to Saudi Arabia, Hamid Ali Rao, said that India would sign an MoU with Saudi Arabia to boost tourism.[68] During 3–7 November 2012, the Indian embassy and the Indian Council for Cultural Research, in association with Saudi Ministry of Culture and Information, organized Indian Cultural Week in Riyadh.[69] Speaking on the occasion, Saudi Deputy Minister of Culture and Information, Abdullah Bin Saleh al-Jasser said that 'this cultural festival in Riyadh has brought to people of Saudi Arabia a comprehensive package of Indian culture including dance, music, literature, paintings, poetry and Indian delicacies' that should go a long way in improving people–to-people contact and strengthening bilateral ties.[70] As part of the week, an exhibition of Monuments of India by Kashinath Das was put on display.[71] Earlier during 22–30 March 2012, a 40-member youth delegation from Saudi Arabia visited Indian cities of Hyderabad, Bengaluru and Delhi and visited various young business leaders, educational institutions as well as met leaders including former president A. P. J. Abdul Kalam.[72]

In addition to increased cultural exchanges during the past few years with focus on improving bilateral relations, the presence of a large number of Indian expatriate community and Hajj pilgrimage are two other important aspects of India's cultural relations with Saudi Arabia.

Indians comprise the largest expatriate community in Saudi Arabia accounting for nearly one-third of the total expatriate population. Currently, the total population of Indians engaged in various works has been estimated at 2 million.[73] In fact, Indian engagement with the economic and social life of Saudi Arabia was high even before the oil boom in 1970s and Hajj vessels that brought food and affluent Indian pilgrims were sought-after among the Saudis, while a number of Indian spices and cereal merchants had established flourishing business in the Kingdom.[74] Large majority of Indians, nearly 80 per cent, are engaged in industrial and construction sectors while nearly 10 per cent of Indian workers are engaged in white collar jobs. Another 10 per cent comprise skilled professionals like doctors, engineers, scientists, managers and educationists. That apart, some illegal Indian migrants can be found working in Saudi Arabia. Owing to the presence of such a large number of Indians and due to historical cultural relations, there is immense goodwill and interest for India in Saudi Arabia. Indian workers are preferred because of their hard-working and law-abiding nature and high quality of technical and professional expertise. That apart, India receives a large some of foreign exchange from expatriates in Saudi Arabia in the form of remittances, amounting to US$3.5 billion annually, which is the largest inward flow of foreign exchange from a single country.[75]

Indians continue to go to Saudi Arabia and other Persian Gulf countries to find work. Continuing with the trend, majority of Indian migrant workers went to Persian Gulf countries to find work during 2011–12. Of the total 626,565 workers who sought emigration clearance during 2011, 289,297 went to Saudi Arabia which is largest to any country.[76] However, the experiences of workers immigrating to the Persian Gulf countries are not always pleasant. Harsh working conditions and uneven labour laws lead to difficult situations. A recurring problem has been labour exploitation. In the case of Saudi Arabia, the *Kifala* (sponsorship) system adds to the problem.

The Indian Government tries to raise the issue of labour exploitation with the Gulf Cooperation Council (GCC) states in various forums. It has signed MoUs on labour issues with some of the GCC countries. In order to streamline the issue of labour exploitation and to secure the interest of its labours, India seeks an MoU on labour with Saudi Arabia. A breakthrough in this direction came during the visit of Saudi Labour Minister Adel bin Muhammad Fakieh during November 2012 when he met with Indian Minister of Overseas Affairs Vyalar Ravi. The two leaders agreed to take forward the discussion on labour issues and consented to sign an agreement in the near future.[77]

The Ministry of Overseas Indian Affairs (MOIA) has tried to do its bit to help the Indians workers going abroad. In 2012, it issued advisories for workers in English, Hindi, Malayalam, Tamil and Telugu for seeking employment in various countries including Saudi Arabia. This can be termed as a step in right direction to deal with the problem of exploitation of Indian workers in the kingdom.[78] During 2011, the MOIA also compiled a country manual on Saudi Arabia, among other countries, to help Indian workers make an informed choice in seeking work in the kingdom.[79]

Hajj

Since the advent of Islam and its spread in the subcontinent, Muslim faithfuls have travelled to Mecca and Medina for pilgrimage during the Hajj season. In the earlier times, Hajj not just provided a season of pilgrimage but opportunities for trade, exchange of ideas and people-to-people contacts. The religious event, thus, provided a platform for trade and commerce, making Hejaz a prominent trading centre in Arabia. It served as a meeting point for traders and merchants from various parts of the world. As has been noted above, Indian merchants and commodities, specially spices and cereals, were sought after among Saudi and other Arab merchants who travelled to the Holy cities during Hajj period. Moreover, rich Indian nawabs (members of aristocratic class similar to the peerage system) and princes donated large sums of money for the upkeep of Kaaba, which in turn earned them respect.

While the changes in global economy changed the nature of Hajj, it still spurs local trade. Though revenue generated through Hajj does not have the same significance as in the earlier times, it still is huge in terms of numbers. India has continued to send one of the largest groups of pilgrims for Hajj in modern times. In 2010, a record number of 171,671 Indian pilgrims visited Saudi Arabia for Hajj, while in 2011 the number was 170,362. Despite a request by India for increase in Hajj quota, the number for 2012 remained the same and a total of 169,971 Indian pilgrims visited Saudi Arabia to perform Hajj. In spite of all the precautions taken, 109 pilgrims were reported to have died during the course of the pilgrimage, according to the Indian consulate. Minister of State for External Affairs E. Ahamed led the Indian Hajj contingent and praised Saudi authorities for organizing a smooth and successful Hajj.[80]

In recent times, there have been a number of controversies around the Hajj in India. The Supreme Court in October 2011 issued an order to limit the number of VIPs going for Hajj on government quota which was seen as wasteful expense on the exchequer and 'bad religious practice'.[81] In another such order, which would have a long-term effect on the Indian Hajj consignment, the Supreme Court asked the government to gradually eliminate subsidy provided for Hajj.[82] In a related development, the Hajj Committee of India decided to tie up with the Saudi Airlines as the official carrier for Hajj pilgrims from India, thereby undercutting the long-standing monopoly enjoyed by Indian Airlines.

External Players

Saudi Arabia is an ally of the US, shares 'brotherly' relations with Pakistan and seeks to enhance its good relations with China—three countries that can be major external factors impacting, directly or indirectly, India's bilateral relations with the kingdom.

The US: Saudi Arabia is a strategic ally of the US and the two share close political, economic and, most importantly, military relations. The monarchy depends on American military supplies, training and guidance for external as well as internal security. In return, it helps further the US interest in the oil-rich Persian Gulf as well as outside. For example, in the 1980s Saudi Arabia sent mujahideen (religious fighters) to Afghanistan to counter Soviet moves. Later, it provided military base for the US military during the 1990–91 Kuwait crisis. In the recent times, with the Iranian nuclear issue on the forefront, the US has tried to bring India and Saudi Arabia closer against Iran. The US has particularly been using its leverage in coaxing India and Saudi Arabia into closer co-operation on terror and defence.[83] However, as far as the geopolitics in the Persian Gulf is concerned, India needs to weigh its options before jumping into one camp. The Saudi–Iranian rivalry has several contours and with changing global political climate, rising Saudi–Chinese relations, the Pakistan angle and strategic importance of the Persian Gulf, India needs to be careful in completely aligning with the US on the Iranian nuclear issue. It has to be mindful of the importance of political stability and security in the Gulf as far as India's interest in the regions is concerned.

China: Saudi relations with China have taken off to higher strides since the establishment of formal ties in 1990. Saudi Arabia looks at China not just as a market for oil, but also seeks closer ties for maintaining peace and security in the Persian Gulf region. On the other hand, China views the whole Gulf region as 'a natural and certain extension of China's neighbouring areas'. That apart, China depends on the oil-rich kingdom for its energy security. Its dependency on import of energy supplies is expected to rise to 77 per cent of its total consumption by 2020. Saudi Arabia is the biggest source of Chinese oil imports.[84] Other than energy, China has huge trade and economic interests in Saudi Arabia. When it comes to oil, trade and economy, Saudi Arabia looks at both China and India favourably and is building stronger ties with both economies. However, the most important aspect for India when it comes to Chinese–Saudi relations is not energy and economy; rather it is the strategic alliance which Saudi Arabia seeks to build with China looking beyond the US, and this could pose a challenge to India.[85]

Pakistan: While Saudi Arabia is increasingly seeking to further its bilateral ties with India, Saudi–Pakistan relations are going through a rough patch.[86] On the one hand, relations with India are growing significantly in all sectors: economic, energy and political. On the contrary, the relations with Pakistan have faced several stumbling blocks in the past two years. The situation came to a head with the killing of Osama bin Laden in Pakistan by American Navy Seals on 2 May 2011. Days after Laden's killing, Pakistan dispatched Interior Minister Rehman Malik to Riyadh to explain the situation. Malik reportedly delivered a message from Pakistani President Asif Ali Zardari to King Abdullah.[87] He gave an exhaustive briefing to top Saudi diplomatic, military and intelligence officials, including Saudi intelligence chief Prince Muqrin and Saudi Foreign Minister Prince Saud al-Faisal on the bin Laden episode, informing them that Pakistani military and intelligence officials were completely unaware of bin Laden's presence in the country.[88] However, Saudi–Pakistan relations remain constrained. This is also because of the recent spate of attacks on Saudi interests and personnel in Pakistan. In May 2011, within a month after a grenade attack at the Saudi Consulate in Karachi,[89] a Saudi diplomat was shot dead in the city.[90] Adding fuel to fire, Saudi Arabia extradited Zabiuddin Ansari, who was holding a Pakistani passport, in June 2012, to India despite Pakistani opposition. This caused heartburn in the Pakistani security establishment which was trying to prevent extradition of the alleged Lashkar-e-Taiba militant accused of masterminding the 2008 terror attacks in Mumbai. The June extradition was followed by two more terror accused being extradited to India later in the year. It has been argued that Saudi Arabia wants to balance its relation with Pakistan by tilting towards India because it is concerned about Pakistan's ability to control the religious militants once financed by Saudi Arabia.[91] On the other hand, it has been argued that Saudi Arabia wants to gain Indian confidence through these moves to enhance its bilateral relations, keeping the Iranian angle in mind, as Saudi Arabia has only extradited Indian nationals, not Pakistani nationals who are wanted in India for terror activities.[92] Another aspect has been the US involvement in bringing Saudi Arabia and India closer.

In addition to these three countries, Iran and Israel are two other countries that pose challenge to India's bilateral relations with Saudi Arabia. The relationship has come a long way from the days when the Saudis doubted India with regard to its relationship with Israel and the Saudi media described the launch by India of the Israeli communications satellite as 'a spy satellite that would watch Arabs'.[93] However, given the delicate nature of regional politics in the Middle East and the complexities and difference between Saudi Arabia, Iran and Israel, India has done well to maintain a fine balance in pursuing relations with them.

Challenges

The 'sore points' in India–Saudi relations, as stated by Richard Erdman, the US ambassador to Saudi Arabia, include India's concern about the Saudi funding of schools that contribute to extremism in South Asia.[94] Saudi Arabia seeks a leadership position in the Muslim world. It uses soft power and financial might to promote its leadership role and secure its position in countries in South East Asia, Central Asia, the Middle East as well as the Indian subcontinent. Saudi funding of religious education to promote Saudi–Wahhabi Islam has created major problems in Pakistan.

India has bore the brunt of religious zealots waging jihad against it, particularly using the troubled situation in Kashmir to propagate their cause. Moreover, funding of religious seminaries inside India, which arguably have perpetuated educational backwardness among Indian Muslims, is a concern. The situation has been believed to have led to radicalization of disgruntled elements among the Indian Muslims, which needs to be raised at some level with Saudi Arabia.

Another important challenge for India has been to secure rights of migrant labourers in the Kingdom. The treatment of Indian nationals living in the Kingdom has remained a contentious issue. The unskilled labourers especially bear the brunt of the restrictive Saudi foreign-labour practices.[95] The government of India has been raising these issues with their Saudi counterpart on different forums and has decided to sign an MoU on labour with the Kingdom to prevent exploitation of Indian nationals.

There are other aspects of challenges that need to be met by India and Saudi Arabia to further strengthen the bilateral relations. Foremost is to convert the robust economic ties into deeper political engagements, and finally into a 'strategic partnership' as envisaged in the 2010 Riyadh declaration. Indian and Saudi naval forces have been holding joint exercises for some years now, but India did not have a defence agreement with Saudi Arabia till very recently. India finally signed an MoU on defence co-operation with Saudi Arabia in January 2012 that will explore the ways to enhance defence relations between the two countries. Saudi role in Afghanistan is also a factor that figures in Indian foreign policy calculations in the immediate neighbourhood.

Conclusion

The year 2012 proved to be a fruitful year for India–Saudi Arabia bilateral relations. The highlights being the first-ever visit of an Indian Defence Minister to Saudi Arabia, the signing of an MoU on defence co-operation and the extradition of terror accused despite Pakistani reservations. It can be termed as a year of enhanced strategic and security relations between India and Saudi Arabia. On the political front, a number of high-level visits marked the importance the two countries attach to cultivating the bilateral ties. Economic relations between the two also witnessed growth and total trade increased by as much as 50 per cent. India also imported an increased quantity of crude oil from Saudi Arabia to compensate the lack of Iranian oil supply due to sanctions. Moreover, spur in cultural interactions during 2012 underlined the growing interests among the authorities to take forward the relationship. Nearly 170,000 Indians travelled to Saudi Arabia to perform Hajj while another 289,000 travelled to seek blue-collar jobs. In another important step forward, India and Saudi Arabia agreed to work towards signing an MoU on labour. On the flip side, a sense of lack of urgency can be located in the overall pursuance of the bilateral relations on the Indian side, particularly when it comes to responding to matters of immediate attention. Though India's options are limited, it can show some spark in responding to chances of pursuing its interest with Saudi Arabia.

Notes

1. 'Delhi Declaration, Signed by King Abdullah bin Abdulaziz Al Saud of the Kingdom of Saudi Arabia and Prime Minister Dr Manmohan Singh of India', *Speeches & Statements*, Ministry of External Affairs, New Delhi, 27 January 2006, http://www.mea.gov.in/Speeches-Statements.htm?dtl/2071/Delhi+D eclaration+Signed+by+King+Abdullah+bin+Abdulaziz+Al+Saud+of+the+Ki ngdom+of+Saudi+Arabia+and+Prime+Minister+Dr+Manmohan+Singh+of+ India
2. Sonia Roy, 'Prime Minister Manmohan Singh in Saudi Arabia, 27 February–1 March 2010', special issue, *India Speaks*, no. 4–S (8 March 2010), http://mei.org.in/front/cms/resourcesDetail.php?id=MTcz&cid=MTM=
3. 'Press Conference by External Affairs Minister Shri S M Krishna', Press Release, Press Information Bureau, New Delhi India, 7 January 2011, http://pib.nic.in/newsite/erelease.aspx?relid=68945
4. For a detailed analysis, please refer Tim Niblock, *Saudi Arabia: Power, Legitimacy and Survival* (New York: Routledge, 2006); Madawi Al-Rasheed, *Contesting the Saudi State: Islamic Voices from a New Generation* (Cambridge: University Press, 2007).
5. For full details, see Thomas Hegghammer and Stephanie Lacroix, *The Mecca Rebellion: The Story of Juhayman Al-Utaybi Revisited* (Bristol: Amal Press, 2011).

6. For a detailed study, please see Madawi al-Rasheed, 'The Shia of Saudi Arabia: A Minority in Search of Cultural Authenticity', *British Journal of Middle Eastern Studies*, 25, no. 1 (1998): 121–38; Human Rights Watch, *Denied Dignity: Systematic Discrimination and Hostility towards Saudi Shia Citizens* (New York, 2009).

7. For a detailed study, please see Natana J. Delong-Bas, *Wahhabi Islam: From Revival and Reform to Global Jihad* (Oxford: Oxford University Press, 2004); Anthony H. Cordesman, *Saudi Arabia Enters the Twenty-first Century: The Political, Foreign Policy, Economic and Energy Dimension* (Boulder, Colorado: Westview, 2003).

8. For details, please refer Joseph A. Kechichian, *Succession in Saudi Arabia* (New York: Palgrave Macmillan, 2001).

9. 'Saudi King Warns against Unrest while Boosting Benefits', *BBC News*, 18 March 2011, http://www.bbc.co.uk/news/world-middle-east-12781068

10. 'Religious Decree on Prohibition of Protests', *Al-Masri al-Youm*, 11 September 2011, http://www.almasryalyoum.com/node/494350

11. 'Saudi Arabia Puts al-Qaeda Suspects on Trial', *Al Jazeera*, 8 April 2012, http://www.aljazeera.com/news/middleeast/2012/04/201248155614703121.html

12. 'Two prominent Saudi Human Rights Activists on Trial in Riyadh', *Al Arabiya*, 3 September 2012, http://english.alarabiya.net/articles/2012/09/03/235859.html

13. 'Man Shot Dead as Police Clash with Shi'ites in Saudi Arabia', *Reuters*, 28 December 2012, http://www.reuters.com/article/2012/12/28/saudi-shiite-shooting-idUSL5E8NS3LP20121228

14. Rhy Jones and Rania El Gamal, 'BAE Secures $2.5 Billion Saudi Jet Deal', *Reuters*, 23 May 2012, http://www.reuters.com/article/2012/05/23/us-saudi-britain-defence-idUSBRE84M0JL20120523

15. Mark Lander and Steven Lee Myers, 'With $30 Billion Arms Deal, U.S. Bolsters Saudi Ties', *The New York Times,* 29 December 2011, http://www.nytimes.com/2011/12/30/world/middleeast/with-30-billion-arms-deal-united-states-bolsters-ties-to-saudi-arabia.html

16. 'Saudi Arabia Religious Police Chief Announces New Curbs', *BBC News*, 3 October 2012, http://www.bbc.co.uk/news/world-middle-east-19819791

17. Frank Gardner, 'London Olympics 2012: Saudis Allow Women to Compete', *BBC News*, 24 June 2012, http://www.bbc.co.uk/news/world-middle-east-18571193

18. Bill Law, 'New Saudi Interior Minister Moves Up Succession Ladder', *BBC News*, 6 November 2012, http://www.bbc.co.uk/news/world-middle-east-20220900

19. 'Strong Saudi Economy Gives Fillip to Region, Advances Social Agenda', IMF, 18 September 2012, http://www.imf.org/external/pubs/ft/survey/so/2012/car091812a.htm

20. Ibid.

21. 'Recent Economic Developments and Highlights of Fiscal Years 1432/33 (2011) and 1433/34 (2012)', Ministry of Finance, KSA, 26 December 2011, http://www.mof.gov.sa/English/DownloadsCenter/Budget/Statement%20 by%20the%20Ministry%20of%20Finance%202012%20Final.pdf
22. Ibid.
23. For details, please refer Prithvi Ram Mudiam, *India and the Middle East* (London: British Academy Press, 1994).
24. For the details of official Indian statements during the visit, including the Riyadh Declaration, see Roy, 'Prime Minister Manmohan Singh in Saudi Arabia, 27 February–1 March 2010'.
25. 'Manmohan: India for Deepening Ties with Saudi Arabia', *The Hindu*, 30 March 2011, http://www.hindu.com/2011/03/30/stories/2011033066401600.htm
26. 'King Receives Sultan's Body', *Arab News*, 24 October 2011, http://arabnews.com/saudiarabia/article523839.ece
27. 'Saudi Arabia Welcomes Lifting of Anti-dumping Duty by India', *The Economic Times*, 4 January 2012, http://articles.economictimes.indiatimes.com/2012-01-04/news/30589053_1_anti-dumping-duty-saudi-arabia-arab-news. They were imposed in 2009.
28. 'Pranab Calls for Top Priority to India–Saudi Investment Fund', *The Hindu*, 6 January 2012, http://www.thehindu.com/news/national/article2778359.ece
29. 'A K Antony Meets Saudi Arabia King to Boost Defence Co-operation', *The Times of India*, 13 February 2012, http://articles.timesofindia.indiatimes.com/2012-02-13/middle-east-news/31054552_1_m-r-pawar-defence-co-operation-salman-bin-abdul-aziz
30. Ghazanfar Ali Khan, 'Shoura Team in India Exploring Ways to Boost Ties', *Arab News*, 7 May 2012, http://www.arabnews.com/%5Btermaliasraw%5D/shoura-team-india-exploring-ways-boost-ties
31. Directorate General of Foreign Trade, New Delhi, http://www.dgft.gov.in
32. 'India–Saudi Bilateral Relations', Embassy of India, Kingdom of Saudi Arabia, Riyadh, 27 October 2012, http://www.indianembassy.org.sa/Content.aspx?ID=849&PID=690
33. 'Factsheet on FDI', Department of Industrial Policy & Promotion, New Delhi, www.dipp.nic.in
34. Ibid.
35. Farah Naaz Gauri, 'Indo–Saudi Trade Relations', *Arabian Journal of Business and Management Review* 1, no. 2 (2013): 45–57.
36. Ibid.
37. 'India–Saudi Bilateral Relations', Embassy of India, Riyadh.
38. Ibid.
39. 'India–Saudi Arabia Business Relations', Embassy of India, Kingdom of Saudi Arabia, Riyadh, 16 January 2013, http://www.indianembassy.org.sa/Content.aspx?ID=867&PID=686

40. 'Promotional Tour by Indian Tourism Delegation in the Kingdom', *Al-Jazi-rah*, 14 January 2012, Riyadh, http://www.al-jazirah.com/2012/20120114/fe4.htm
41. *Ideal Cut*, The newsletter of the Gem and Jewellery Export Promotion Council, 3, no. 6 (June 2012).
42. 'India–Saudi Arabia Business Relations', Embassy of India, Riyadh.
43. 'India Plans Road Show in KSA to Drum Up Investment', *Arab News*, 7 June 2012, http://www.arabnews.com/india-plans-road-show-ksa-drum-investment
44. 'India–Saudi Arabia Business Relations', Embassy of India, Riyadh.
45. Ibid.
45. 'Indian Firms Partake in Saudi Agri Exhibition', *The Saudi Gazette*, 24 September 2012, http://www.saudigazette.com.sa/index.cfm?method=home. regcon&contentid=20120924137252
47. 'Pranab Calls for Top Priority to India–Saudi Investment Fund'.
48. 'Union Finance Minister, Shri Pranab Mukherjee's Opening Remarks at the 9th India–Saudi Arabia Joint Commission Meeting', Press Release, Press Information Bureau, India, 5 January 2012 (New Delhi), http://pib.nic.in/newsite/PrintRelease.aspx?relid=79370.
49. 'India–Saudi Arabia Business Relations', Embassy of India, Riyadh.
50. '15-member Saudi Business Delegation to India', *The Times of India*, 22 November 2012, http://articles.timesofindia.indiatimes.com/2012-11-22/middle-east-news/35302085_1_saudi-indian-business-network-delega-tion-jeddah
51. 'India Keen on Participating in Saudi Arabia's Oil and Gas Sectors', *The Hindu*, 4 January 2012, http://www.thehindubusinessline.com/industry-and-economy/article2774673.ece
52. Ibid.
53. 'Tata Motors-owned JLR Mulls Plant in Saudi Arabia, Signs Letter of Intent', *The Economic Times*, 11 Dec 2012, http://articles.economictimes.indiatimes.com/2012-12-11/news/35749480_1_chief-executive-ralf-speth-jlr-jaguar-land-rover
54. 'Saudi Arabia to Double Exports of Crude Oil to India', *The National*, 6 June 2011, http://www.thenational.ae/business/energy/saudi-arabia-to-double-exports-of-crude-oil-to-india
55. 'India Seeks Additional 5 MT Oil from Saudi Arabia for FY'13', *Zee News*, 24 February 2012, http://zeenews.india.com/business/economy/india-seeks-additional-5-mt-oil-from-saudi-arabia-for-fy13_42669.html
56. Faisal Aboobacker Ponnani, 'Indian Navy Vessels Arrive at Jubail Port', *The Saudi Gazette*, http://www.saudigazette.com.sa/index.cfm?method=home. PrintContent&action=Print&contentID=0000000096739
57. 'The Gulf Forum 2011: The Gulf and the Globe', Press Release, Gulf Research Centre, Saudi Arabia, Riyadh, http://www.grc.ae/index.php?sec=Events&frm_action=event_schedule&frm_useraction=&frm_

module=events&PK_ID=events&frm_event_id=327&sec_type=d&op_la
ng=&override=+%3E+Themes+%26+Schedule&frm_eventid=&frm_
eventday=&frm_eventmonth=&frm_eventyear=

58. 'India and Saudi Arabia Agree to Set Up a Joint Committee on Defence
Cooperation', Press Release, Press Information Bureau, India, 15 February
2012, New Delhi, http://pib.nic.in/newsite/erelease.aspx?relid=80322

59. Ibid.

60. 'First Meeting of India–Saudi Arabia Joint Committee on Defence Cooperation', Press Release, Press Information Bureau, India, 10 September 2012,
New Delhi, http://pib.nic.in/newsite/erelease.aspx?relid=87674

61. Tom Wright, 'Saudi Arabia Uses India to Balance Pakistan', *The Wall Street
Journal*, 23 October 2012, http://blogs.wsj.com/indiarealtime/2012/10/23/
saudi-arabia-uses-india-to-balance-pakistan/

62. Jayanth Jacob, 'Saudi Relation with Saudi Hang between Good, Peculiar:
Officials', *Hindustan Times*, 23 October 2012, http://www.hindustantimes.
com/StoryPage/Print/948752.aspx

63. Wright, 'Saudi Arabia Uses India to Balance Pakistan'.

64. Harsh V. Pant, 'Gulf's Balance of Power Tilts Saudi Arabia towards India', *The National*, 15 July 2012, www.thenational.ae/thenationalcon-
versation/comment/gulfs-balance-of-power-tilts-saudi-arabia-towards-
india#full

65. 'The Global Religious Landscape', Pew Research Center, 18 December
2012, http://www.pewforum.org/global-religious-landscape-muslim.aspx

66. 'Vast Indian Community behind Flourishing Indo–Saudi Relations', *The
Times of India*, 26 January 2012, http://articles.timesofindia.indiatimes.
com/2012-01-26/middle-east-news/30666095_1_indo-saudi-indian-con-
sulate-saudi-arabian

67. 'Imam of Haram to Visit Darul Uloom Deoband Tomorrow', *TwoCircles.net*,
24 March 2011, http://twocircles.net/2011mar24/imam_haram_visit_da-
rul_uloom_deoband_tomorrow.html.

68. 'To Boost Tourism India Likely to Sign MoU with Saudi Arabia', *Holiday
Home Times*, 16 Jan 2012, www.holidayhometimes.com/traveler-and-tour-
ism/boost-tourism-india-sign-mou-saudi-arabia1673.html

69. 'Indian Cultural Week Celebration in KSA from 3rd to 7th November
2012', Embassy of India, Kingdom of Saudi Arabia, Riyadh, http://www.
indianembassy.org.sa/Content.aspx?ID=854

70. 'Indian Cultural Festival Kinks Off in Riyadh', *YaHind.com*, 5 November
2012, http://www.yahind.com/indian-cultural-festival-kicks-off-in-ri-
yadh/

71. ICCR, Exibition Section, http://www.iccrindia.net/exhibitions/exhibition-
slist-dec2012.pdf

72. 'Visit of the Saudi Indian Youth Forum', special issue, *Connect*, May 2012,
http://youngindians.net/img/documents/SaudiIndianYouthForum.pdf

73. MEA, 'Indo–Saudi Relations'.

74. 'Country Brief with Reference to Its People: Saudi Arabia', Ministry of Overseas Indian Affairs (MOIA), New Delhi, http://moia.gov.in/pdf/Saudi%20Arabia.pdf
75. Ibid.
76. *Annual Report*, MOIA, 2011–12 New Delhi, http://moia.gov.in/writereaddata/pdf/Annual_Report_2011-2012.pdf
77. 'India–Saudi Arabia Agree to Discuss Labour Issues', *The Times of India*, 5 November 2012, http://articles.timesofindia.indiatimes.com/2012-11-05/middle-east-news/34926547_1_saudi-arabia-migrant-labourers-saudi-employers
78. Ibid.
79. Ibid.
80. 'Indian Minister Praises Saudi Efforts for Haj', *Arab News*, 30 October 2012, http://www.arabnews.com/indian-minister-praises-saudi-efforts-haj
81. 'Haj VIP Quota Is Bad: Supreme Court', *Hindustan Times*, 18 October 2011, http://www.hindustantimes.com/India-news/NewDelhi/Haj-VIP-quota-is-bad-Supreme-Court/Article1-758672.aspx
82. Vijetha S. N. and Mohammad Ali, 'Eliminate Haj Subsidy in 10 Years: Court', *The Hindu*, 8 May 2012, http://www.thehindu.com/news/national/eliminate-haj-subsidy-in-10-years-court/article3396806.ece
83. 'Nudged by US, India, Saudi Arabia Inch Closer on Terror, Defence', *The Indian Express*, 8 November 2010, http://www.indianexpress.com/news/nudged-by-us-india-s-arabia-inch-closer-on-terror-defence/708028/
84. 'China Presses Saudi Arabia for Oil Access', *The Indian Express*, 15 January 2012, http://www.indianexpress.com/news/china-presses-saudi-arabia-for-oil-access/899900/
85. For details, please refer Naser Al-Tamimi, 'China–Saudi Arabia Relations: Economic Partnership or Strategic Alliance', *HH Sheikh Nasser al-Mohammad al-Sabah Publication Series*, Durham University, No. 2, June 2012, http://www.dur.ac.uk/resources/alsabah/China-SaudiArabiaRelations.pdf
86. 'India Gets Closer to Saudi Arabia', *The Diplomat*, 27 June 2011, http://thediplomat.com/indian-decade/2011/06/27/india-gets-closer-to-saudi-arabia/
87. 'Malik Gives Zardari's Message to Saudi King', *Dawn*, 8 May 2011, http://dawn.com/2011/05/08/malik-gives-zardaris-message-to-saudi-king/
88. 'India Gets Closer to Saudi Arabia'.
89. 'Grenade Attack Hits Saudi Consulate in Karachi', *Arabian Business*, 11 May 2011, http://www.arabianbusiness.com/grenade-attack-hits-saudi-consulate-in-karachi-399263.html
90. 'Gunmen Kill Saudi Diplomat in Karachi', *Dawn*, 16 May 2011, http://dawn.com/2011/05/16/saudi-consulates-car-attacked-in-karachi-driver-killed/
91. Wright, 'Saudi Arabia Uses India to Balance Pakistan'.
92. Stephen Tankel, 'Pakistan's Sticky Wicket: The India–Saudi Link', *Foreign Policy*, 30 July 2012, http://afpak.foreignpolicy.com/posts/2012/07/30/pakistans_sticky_wicket_the_india_saudi_link?wp_login_redirect=0

93. 'India Launches Israeli Spy Satellite', *Al-Bayan*, 21 April 2009, http://www.albayan.ae/across-the-uae/1237400291663- 2009-04-21-1.426353

94. 'Indian "concern" over Saudi Funding for Extremists', *The Hindu*, 17 March 2011, http://www.thehindu.com/news/the-india-cables/article1547622.ece

95. 'India to Take Up Labour Issues with Saudi Arabia', *Business Standard*, 9 May 2006, http://www.business-standard.com/india/news/india-to-takelabour-issuessaudi-arabia/237495/

9

UAE

Jatung Raja Philemon Chiru

Key Indicators

Area: 83,600 sq km; **Population:** 5.47 million; **Native:** 42 per cent; **Expats:** 58 per cent; **Youth population:** 13.8 per cent; **Population growth rate:** 3.055 per cent; **Life expectancy at birth:** 76.7 years; **GDP:** US$271.2 billion; **Per capita income:** US$49,000; **Foreign trade:** US$520.9 billion; **Oil reserves:** 97.8 billion bbl; **Gas reserves:** 6.089 trillion m³; **Ruling family:** Federation of sheikhdoms; **Ruler:** President Khalifa bin Zayed al-Nahyan (since 3 November 2004); **National Day:** 2 December; **Defence budget:** 3.1 per cent of GDP; **HDI rank:** 41; **Literacy rate:** 77.9 per cent; **UN education index:** 0.686; **Gender inequality index:** 0.241.

Source: CIA, *The World Factbook*, https://www.cia.gov/library/publications/the-world-factbook/index.html; UN Human Development Report, Statistics, http://hdr.undp.org/en/statistics/
Note: All data for 2012.

India and the United Arab Emirates (UAE) have a thriving bilateral relationship since historical times. The extensive maritime trade between India and the Persian Gulf region, including the UAE, attracted multitudes of merchants from both sides, dealing in various goods. Trade relations between India and the Gulf region began to be affected with the arrival of European powers such as the Portuguese, English, Dutch, Danish and the French in India since the middle of the fifteenth century. Indian merchants and traders in the Trucial States of Dubai, Sharjah, Abu Dhabi, Ras al-Khaimah, Ajman, Umm al-Qaiwan and Fujairah, which now constitute the UAE, continued to play an important role and made their presence felt even during the British period. Indian merchants, particularly the Gujaratis, Parsees, Sindhis and Khojas, played a crucial role in trade and commerce of Dubai and Abu Dhabi during the early twentieth century. In the latter half of the twentieth century, Indian merchants, professionals and business-people played an important part in the development of Dubai as a trade centre. Since the oil boom of the 1970s, a large number of skilled and unskilled Indian workers who went to Dubai, Sharjah and Abu Dhabi contributed in the growth of different sectors of the economy. This has led to a robust and flourishing trade and commercial relations between India and the UAE today.

Domestic Developments

The UAE is a federation of seven Emirates formed on 2 December 1971 after independence from Britain. Each of the Emirates that constitute the UAE is ruled by a hereditary Emir or Sheikh. The seven Emirs in turn constitute the Federal Supreme Council, the highest policymaking body in the UAE and they elect the President and Prime Minister from among them. However, in reality, the President and the Prime Minister are practically hereditary with the Emir of Abu Dhabi holding the presidency and the Emir of Dubai being the prime minister. There also exists the Federal National Council (FNC) as a permanent part of the country's governing structure. Formed under the criteria of the Provisional Constitution adopted in 1971, it acted as a consultative body to the rulers of the UAE. All the 40 members of the FNC were nominated by the rulers of the Emirates based on the population of each emirate. Abu Dhabi and Dubai have eight seats each, Sharjah and Ras al-Khaimah with six seats and Ajman, Fujairah and Umm al-Qaiwan with four seats each.

As a part of a democratic process to make the FNC more representative, in December 2006 the UAE conducted elections for the first time in which half of the members of the FNC were indirectly elected through electoral bodies from each Emirate. During these elections, the Electoral College consisted of only just over 6,600 members out of a population of 800,000 Emirati citizens, making up less than one per cent of the UAE citizens. In the second election to the FNC held in September 2011, the Electoral College was expanded to 129,274, which was roughly 13 per cent of the UAE's native population, with an aim to encourage the participation of the citizens of the country. However, the voter turnout was a dismal 28 per cent of the electoral college.[1] Out of the 20 seats to the FNC put up for elections, only one seat was won by a woman.[2]

With ample opportunities created by the economic development in the UAE in the past few decades, the role of women in the society has expanded greatly. The government has also played an active role in promoting the rights, welfare and empowerment of women in the country. Today, the women of the UAE have contributed to the development of the Gulf state in various capacities. Women employees formed a huge chunk of the workforce in executive and administrative positions in all professions, public and private, including the police and military. This has been possible due to the encouragement, support and promotion of women's education by the state and society at large. The literacy rate of women is the highest in the UAE among the GCC countries and more than 50 per cent of them continue to pursue higher education and seek employment.[3] The employment of women in the public and governmental sector is also quite high in the UAE. Women continue to be appointed in diplomatic services, administrative positions and ministerial posts as ambassadors, judges, registrars, etc.

Since 2006, when the UAE held limited elections to the FNC, women had participated both as voters and candidates. However, the percentage of women's participation had been low. In the 2011 elections, the number of Electoral College was expanded to 129,274, in which women members numbered 59,991 or 46 per cent of the Electoral College.[4] The number of women candidates contesting for FNC seats increased to 85 out of a total of 469.[5] However, only one seat for the FNC was won by a woman candidate, who hailed from Umm al-Qaiwan.[6] Subsequently six other women were nominated, taking the total number of women to seven. Thus, the number of women in the FNC in 2011 decreased from nine in 2006 to seven, constituting about 18 per cent of the total FNC seats.[7]

Despite women in the UAE making huge strides in the public sphere, the Islamic law, which governs the family and personal spheres, discriminates against them. The law is lopsided in favour of men in matters of divorce, inheritance, child custody, marriages, marriages to non-Muslims, etc.[8] There are also widespread cases of domestic violence and sexual assault against women in the country. However, most of the victims are less likely to report the abuses or violence due to the nature of the law and the apathy of the law-enforcement agencies. In the case of women victims of sexual assault, the law can turn against the victim.[9]

Bilateral Relations

The centuries-old cordial and deep-rooted bilateral relations between India and the UAE continued to flourish in 2012. Political and diplomatic, economic, trade and commerce, and defence and security relations deepened. The year 2012 saw high-level official visits between the two countries and both countries signed various agreements. Trade and economic activities witnessed a new height. Interactions, discussions and consultations on a number of issues, including political, economic, defence and security issues that affected the two countries in particular and the Middle East in general, were dealt with by the two countries.

Political Relations

India and the UAE continued to enhance and cherish their warm bilateral ties. Built on a foundation of mutual respect and goodwill, political, trade and commercial relations have largely been free of trouble. There were close co-operation on issues that are of mutual concern such as narcotics smuggling, human trafficking, terrorism, etc. The two countries have also sealed and implemented various agreements and Memorandum of Understanding (MoU) on a variety of issues since the formation of the UAE in 1971.[10]

Political visits and exchanges continued to take place in 2012. As part of a four-nation visit in January that also took him to Israel, Palestine and Jordan, External Affairs Minister S. M. Krishna paid a brief visit to UAE. In April, he led a 20-member delegation representing various ministries to take part in the 10th session of the India–UAE Joint Commission for Economic Cooperation held in Abu Dhabi. He co-chaired the session with his Emirate counterpart Abdulla Bin Zayed al-Nahyan and discussions were held on 'regional, international and bilateral issues of mutual concerns' and others 'covering diverse areas including co-operation in the fields of Trade, Investments, Customs, Banking, Auditing, Energy, Agriculture, Civil Aviation, Consular, Security, Transport, Tourism, Education, Culture, Manpower and Community Welfare'.[11]

In addition, two important documents were signed by India and the UAE on 16 April 2012, namely, a Protocol to amend the India–UAE Double Taxation Avoidance Agreement and MoU to establish a Joint Committee on Consular Affairs.[12] The Protocol amended the 'article on exchange of information ... updated to bring it at par with internationally accepted standards ... banking information as well as any other information without any domestic tax interest can be shared between the two countries'.[13] The MoU on setting up of Joint Committee on Consular affairs would look into 'concerns on issues related to birth or death registration, quasi-judicial matters like detention or arrest, travel documents like passport and visa etc. affecting Indian or Emirate nationals'.[14]

This was followed by the visit of the Indian Minister of State of External Affairs E. Ahamed to Abu Dhabi to attend the Third India–Arab Partnership Conference[15] held between 22 and 23 May 2012 to expand and 'to explore the opportunities for the Arab world to further deepen and re-define its economic and cultural relations with India'.[16] Minister for Overseas Indian Affairs Vayalar Ravi visited the UAE in November 2012 and held interactions with representatives of Indian Associations, invited the Indian expatriates to attend the Pravasi Bharatiya Divas to be held in Kochi, Kerala, from 7 to 9 January 2013, and handed over the Ministry of Overseas Indian Affairs' contribution of half the amount of US$1.64 million to build a crematorium.[17]

There were reciprocal high-level official visits from the UAE. In January 2012, Minister of Foreign Trade Lubna bint Khalid al-Qasimi came to India to attend the 18th edition of the Confederation of Indian Industry's (CII) Partnership Summit and noted that 'India was one of the

UAE's top trading partners with bilateral trade between the two crossing US$76 billion, accounting for 10.8 per cent of the UAE's total foreign trade'.[18] She also led a UAE delegation to take part in the 19th Partnership Summit in January 2013.[19] Another important visit from the UAE in January 2012 was by that of Hamed bin Zayed al-Nahyan, Managing Director of Abu Dhabi Investment Authority (ADIA), world's largest sovereign wealth fund, to explore and promote investment opportunities in India.[20] Apart from meeting senior Indian leaders which included External Affairs Minister S. M. Krishna, Finance Minister Pranab Mukherjee, Urban Development Minister Kamal Nath, Rural Development Minister J. Ramesh, Communication and Information Technology Minister Kapil Sibal and Commerce, Industry and Textiles Minister Anand Sharma, the two 'countries also agreed to set up a joint working group to facilitate investment ... in the US$90 billion ambitious Delhi Mumbai Industrial Corridor (DMIC) and other infrastructure funds'.[21] The UAE Minister of State for Financial Affairs Obaid Humaid al-Tayer visited India in April 2012 and discussed 'ways of developing financial relations between the two countries and of strengthening joint co-operation efforts in all investment and economic areas' with his Indian counterpart Mukherjee.[22] The following month, UAE's Foreign Minister Abdullah bin Zayed al-Nahyan visited India from 17 to 18 May 2012. During his visit, he held discussions with various leaders of India on bilateral issues and agreed with his Indian counterpart Krishna 'to set up a joint task force to further explore opportunities in investments' and 'the need to increase oil import from UAE'[23] (Table 9.1 and Figure 9.1).

Table 9.1
Share of Oil in India's Imports from UAE (in US$ Million)

Year	Oil imports from UAE	Total oil imports	UAE share in total oil imports	Imports from UAE	Per cent of oil in imports from UAE
2009–10	6,443.36	96,321.16	6.69	19,499.10	33.04
2010–11	9,398.23	115,929.06	8.11	32,753.16	28.69
2011–12	14,599.83	172,753.97	8.45	35,790.39	40.79

Source: Adapted from Director General of Foreign Trade, New Delhi, http://www.dgft.gov.in

Figure 9.1

Share of Oil in India's Total Imports from UAE

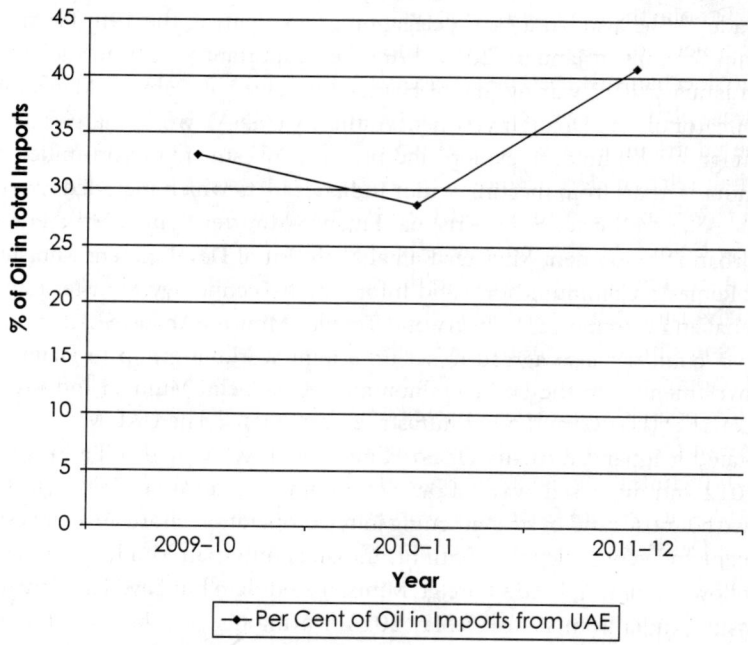

Source: Adapted from Director General of Foreign Trade, New Delhi, http://www.dgft.gov.in

Political relations between India and the UAE were not confined to bilateral reciprocal visits but included some important agreements as well. On 1 April 2012, Central Bureau of Excise Control (CBEC) of India and the UAE's Federal Customs Authority signed the Co-operation and Mutual Assistance in Customs Matter Agreement.[24] A few days later on 4 April 2012, Overseas Indian Affairs Minister Ravi and the UAE's Minister of Labour Saqr Ghobash inked a protocol on electronic contract registration and validation system.[25] This aims to prevent the exploitation of Indian workers in the UAE by mandating that the full and informed consent of the worker, the employer and competent Indian authorities on the terms and conditions of the employment contract shall be registered before the worker is sent to the UAE.[26] Later that month, on 16 April, both countries signed a protocol to amend the India–UAE Double

Taxation Avoidance Agreement and an MoU to set up a joint committee to look into consular affairs between the two.[27]

Despite the fact that the India and the UAE had excellent relations in all spheres of bilateral relations, the setting up of institutional structures and mechanisms that provide a platform to discuss issues, exchange ideas, plan strategies and sort out irritants illustrate the maturity and the efforts undertaken by the two countries to continue to maintain a warm relation. The Second Secretary-level, annual Foreign Office Consultations between India and the UAE were held in February 2012 in New Delhi.[28] Led by India's Foreign Secretary (East) Sanjay Singh of the Ministry of External Affairs and the UAE's Assistant Minister for Foreign Affairs Tariq Ahmed al-Hidan, the two delegations discussed 'wide range of issues including the areas of bilateral and mutual interests, regional developments in the Gulf, Middle East and South Asia and international politics'.[29] In matters related to trade and commerce, the 10th session of the India–UAE Joint Commission Meeting (JCM) for Economic and Technical Cooperation took place in Abu Dhabi in April 2012.[30] In security and defence consultations, the fifth annual meeting of the Joint Defence Cooperation Committee (JDCC) met in New Delhi in May 2012.[31]

Economic Relations

Trade, commerce and economic relations have been the driving and cementing factors in Indo–UAE relationship. Bilateral trade between India and the UAE is not limited to economic and commercial ties, but involves the participation of public and private investors from both countries in diverse sectors such as infrastructure development, information technology (IT), agriculture, pharmaceuticals, etc. The large Indian expatriate community has played a significant role in the development of the UAE and continues to make major contributions to UAE's standing as one of the commercial hubs in Asia. More than 450 weekly flights operate between various destinations in India and the UAE, pointing to the vibrant economic ties between the two countries.

Though a small nation with a population of just over 8 million, for India the UAE is one of the most important trading partners. For three consecutive years in a row, beginning 2008–09, the UAE has been among India's largest trading partners.[32] The bilateral trade between India and UAE grew from US$43.5 billion in 2009–10 to US$71.7 billion in 2011–12. Looking at the data from Tables 9.2 and 9.3 and Figure 9.2, some important observations can be made. First, there was a slight increase in the total volume of trade from US$66.6 billion in 2010–11 to US$71.7 billion in 2011–12. Second, the balance of trade in India's favour had shrunk significantly from US$1.07 billion in 2010–11 to US$.014 billion in 2011–12. Third, in 2011–12, the UAE was reduced to the second place after China as India's largest trading partner. Fourth, the UAE continued to be India's largest export destination.

Another important fact is that unlike other Persian Gulf countries India-UAE trade is not dependent on energy which comprises only eight per cent of India's imports from the UAE (Table 9.4).

Table 9.2
India–UAE Bilateral Trade (in US$ Million)

	2009–10	2010–11	2011–12
India's total exports to UAE	23,970.40	33,822.39	35,925.52
India's total imports from UAE	19,499.10	32,753.16	35,790.39
Total trade	43,469.50	66,575.55	71,715.91
Share of UAE in total trade	9.31	10.72	9.02

Source: Adapted from Director General of Foreign Trade, New Delhi, http://www.dgft.gov.in

Table 9.3
India's Five Largest Trading Partners in 2011–12 (in US$ Million)

Country	Exports	Imports	Total trade
China	18,076.55	57,517.88	75,594.44
United Arab Emirates	35,925.52	35,790.39	71,715.91
United States	34,741.60	24,470.16	59,211.75
Saudi Arabia	5,683.29	31,060.10	36,743.40
Switzerland	1,095.34	32,404.95	33,500.29

Source: Adapted from 'Export Import Data Bank, Country-wise', Department of Commerce, Government of India, http://commerce.nic.in/eidb/iecntq.asp

Figure 9.2
India–UAE Bilateral Trade

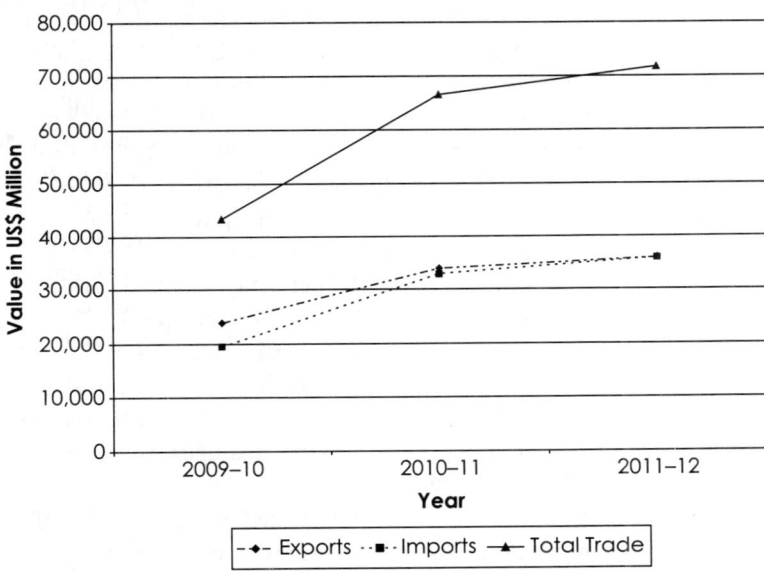

Source: Adapted from Director General of Foreign Trade, New Delhi, http://www.dgft.gov.in

Table 9.4
India's Energy Imports from UAE (in US$ Million)

	2009–10	2010–11	2011–12
Energy imports from UAE	6,443.36	9,398.23	14,599.83
Total energy imports	96,321.16	115,929.06	172,753.97
Total imports from Persian Gulf	55,904.14	66,688.4	103,915.24
Share in total imports (in per cent)	6.69	8.11	8.45
Share in imports from Persian Gulf (in per cent)	11.53	14.09	14.05

Source: Adapted from Director General of Foreign Trade, New Delhi, http://www.dgft.gov.in

One major area of co-operation between India and the UAE is investments in each others' economies. Investment by public and private
enterprises from the two countries flows both ways. The UAE is the

10th-largest source of Foreign Direct Investment (FDI) for India and is the top investor among the countries of the Persian Gulf region. India, as an emerging and one of the fastest growing economies of the world, has become an attractive destination for FDI from the UAE. There is a huge demand for investments in infrastructure, energy, communications, IT and other sectors that promise high returns. The UAE's total investment in India is estimated at US$8 billion, of which about US$2.36 billion is through FDI mode.[33] Though diverse, the preferred sectors of destinations for the UAE investors are energy and power (15 per cent), metallurgical industries (12 per cent), infrastructure and construction development (11 per cent), services (10 per cent), computer hardware and software (5 per cent) and tourism and hotel (6 per cent).

Some of the UAE companies that have sizable investments in India are the Dubai government-owned Emaar which specializes in real estate and property development; Dubai Ports World (DP World), a leading international marine terminal operator; tile manufacturing company Ras al-Khaimah (RAK) Ceramics; Abu Dhabi National Energy Company (TAQA) in power generation and transmission projects; the ADIA involved mostly in portfolio investments in India. Likewise, many eminent and reputable Indian companies and banks, belonging to the public and private sectors invest and operate in UAE. They are active in fields such as manufacturing, IT, education, tourism and hospitality, health, retail, entertainment, etc. In recent years, the UAE has attracted a considerable number of Indian business interests.

The creation of world-class infrastructure facilities and the provisions for largely tax-free regimes by the UAE has attracted Indian companies. Further, Abu Dhabi and Dubai have successfully positioned themselves as an important centre of international trade and finance in the region. With huge projects like the Academic City, Internet City and Media City, Dubai is regarded as an important centre for the service sectors in IT, education and entertainment. It has also been a re-export centre which the Indian business community has utilized to enhance trade with the Persian Gulf nations and others. Many Indian companies have invested in free trade zones in the UAE such as Abu Dhabi Industrial City, Hamiriya Free Trade Zone, Jebel Ali Free Trade Zone, Sharjah Airport, Ajman and RAK Fujairah Free Trade Zones. Some of the prominent Indian companies that conduct businesses in the UAE are Hinduja Group's Ashok Leyland, Taj Group of Hotels, Emke Group, Amarek Chemicals, Al-Fara'a

Group, J.K. Cement, Mahindra, Dabur, Essar Steel, Apollo Tyres, Zee Entertainment, Birla Institute of Technology and Science (BITS) Pilani, Larson and Toubro, Dodsal, Punj Lloyd, Bank of Baroda and Engineers India Ltd.

In the year 2012, contacts and negotiations between the two governments resulted in signing some important agreements related to further facilitating trade between the two countries. On 1 April 2012, the two sides signed a bilateral Co-operation and Mutual Assistance on Custom Matters (CMACM) Agreement.[34] Among others, the Agreement would enable the two parties for 'exchanging experiences, boosting economic co-operation, increasing mutual trade, as well as protecting the society against illicit commercial practices by exchanging information on mutual customs shipments' and strengthen

> the fight against practices that jeopardize the security, economy and safety of the society, development of customs awareness and culture by exchanging experiences and information and offering joint training courses ... the emphasis on the role of customs as a major economic partner and the basic rules of information protection, including a legal access to information ...[35]

India and the UAE also sought to increase their co-operation in economic, scientific, information and other fields. The 10th session of the JCM for Economic, Scientific and Technical Cooperation was held in Abu Dhabi in which the two countries exchanged ideas on various issues in order to promote mutual co-operation in fields such as 'trade and investment; education, culture, youth and sports; health, science and technology, agriculture and environment; manpower; and energy, hydrocarbons, petrochemicals and fertilizers'.[36]

With growing bilateral trade, in addition to huge opportunities and potential for investments, India and the UAE are in the process of negotiating a bilateral Free Trade Agreement. As India's largest trading partner for a number of years, a bilateral Free Trade Agreement with the UAE makes perfect sense. This need was compounded by the fact that the negotiations for the India–Gulf Cooperation Council (GCC) Free Trade Agreement that began in 2006 made no headway even after three rounds of talks[37] due to various reasons.[38] Therefore, the Indian business community in the UAE, led by the Indian Business Leaders Forum (IBLF) has been keen on making the bilateral Free Trade Agreement a reality by impressing on the various ministries of the Government of India for such a need.[39]

However, as per information available in public domain, both countries did not appear to have floated the idea of a bilateral Free Trade Agreement and were instead focusing on working together within the context of India–GCC Free Trade Agreement.[40] In recent years, talks on the India–GCC Free Trade Agreement have continued between India and representatives from the GCC.[41] Both India[42] and the UAE[43] had also called for quicker and rapid negotiations to bring about India–GCC Free Trade Agreement into reality. In this endeavour, India's Minister for Commerce and Industry Anand Sharma urged the UAE's Minister of Foreign Trade Lubna Bint Khalid al-Qasimi that 'the UAE should take the lead in re-energizing the negotiations for concluding the India–GCC FTA talks'[44] which had not made any headway. In July 2012, the former Chairman of CII, K. K. M. Kutty expressed confidence that the India–GCC Free Trade Agreement could be concluded within a year[45] and order to further trade, commerce and investment.

Defence Relations

Another vital area of the India–UAE relationship is the military and security sector. The two countries have a mutual interest in securing the trade routes and keeping the Sea Lines of Communication (SLOC) open as the bulk of the trade between India and the UAE are conducted through sea routes. Further need for security co-operation arose to counter nefarious activities such as terrorism, arms, narcotics and drug smuggling, etc. Though steps were taken to widen defence co-operation in the 1990s, it was not until June 2003 that the two countries signed an MoU on Defence Cooperation which envisaged 'development of defence co-operation, import and export of arms and coordination in the fields of military training, military medical services, cultural and sports activities, environmental issues and pollution caused by the military particularly at sea ... defence industry, scientific research, humanitarian and peace-keeping operations'.[46] The signatories also agreed to a strategic dialogue on a regular basis and set up the JDDC to discuss security and defence-related issues of importance to them. Another milestone was achieved by the two countries on 23 November 2011, when they signed the Agreement on Security Cooperation.[47] The agreement sought to 'strengthen

and develop the existing bilateral framework/mechanism to enhance security co-operation in the areas such as combating terrorism in all forms,
addressing activities of organized criminal groups, drug trafficking, illicit
trafficking in weapons, ammunition, explosives etc., and initiatives on
training of personnel'.[48]

With an aim to shore up military partnership, India and the UAE had,
from time to time, conducted joint exercises and Indian Naval Ships
had visited UAE ports. In September 2008, the two countries conducted
their first joint air force exercises at the al-Dhabra air force base in Abu
Dhabi.[49] Joint naval exercises took place as early as 2003 and a number of UAE military personnel began taking training courses in India.[50]
In March 2011, three Indian Naval Ships—INS Teer, INS Krishna and
ICGS Veera—made calls at Abu Dhabi.[51] This visit was in continuation
of the routine goodwill visits by Indian ships to the Emirates.

In the past few years, the bilateral military partnership had focused
on imparting training to military personnel, co-operation in military
medical services, supply of defence inventory and regular exchange
programmes. Besides these, co-operation can be notably improved in
manufacturing and development of military arsenals, joint exercises of
the armed forces of the two countries, sharing of expertise on strategy
and doctrines, technical co-operation in various aspects, etc.[52] India has
also regularly participated in the biennial International Defence Exhibition (IDEX) held in Abu Dhabi.

Despite the wide spectrum of bilateral defence co-operation in the
India–UAE relationship, one important aspect that stands out is the insti-
tutionalization of the partnership at various levels. The steps taken have
shown the commitment of the two parties in furthering their defence
relations to higher levels. With the setting up of the JDCC through the
provisions of the agreement on Defence Cooperation signed in 2003,
India and UAE finally embarked on a new era in bilateral defence ties.
The JDCC was established to serve as a platform for the two countries
to conduct strategic dialogue, exchange views and an arena of mutual
consultation on a variety of issues that touched upon the defence ties
between India and UAE. The first meeting of India–UAE JDCC was held
in April 2006.[53] In the course of time, another four meetings took place,
the last one between 1 and 3 May 2012 in New Delhi.[54] Apart from
the JDCC meetings, India and UAE also 'inaugurated naval staff talks in

January 2007 following a series of high-level naval visits dating back to 2004'.[55]

Cultural Relations

In modern times, the presence of a large number of expatriate Indian communities lends credence to the historic ties and continues to be the driving factor behind the robust Indo–UAE cultural relations. There are an estimated 1.75 million Indians residing in the UAE, constituting nearly 30 per cent of the resident UAE population, outnumbering migrants from other countries as well as the Emirati citizens. The Indian community in the UAE has not only contributed to the evolution of the UAE, but also to the strong economic and cultural ties between India and the UAE. Indian culture is prominent in the UAE through Indian music, dances and festivals not only among the Indian diaspora and migrants, but is also widely accepted and popular amongst migrants from other countries and the native population. As the language of the single largest expatriate community and spoken by the majority of Indian workers, Indian languages such as Hindi and Malayalam have been found to have linguistic influences on the local Arabic dialects.

In the past, many agreements had been signed between India and UAE for regular cultural exchanges at various levels. Organizations like Abu Dhabi Authority for Culture and Heritage (ADACH) and the UAE's Ministry of Culture had helped organize Indian cultural events such as film festivals, painting exhibitions, translation of Indian books into Arabic, etc. The Indian Council for Cultural Relations (ICCR) with its objective to 'foster mutual understanding between India and other countries and to promote cultural exchanges with other peoples'[56] opened a cultural centre within the Indian Embassy in Abu Dhabi in December 2009 to 'foster and strengthen cultural relations and mutual understanding between India and the United Arab Emirates and to promote cultural exchanges with the United Arab Emirates and its people'.[57] In 2012, the Indian Film Society of UAE organized a three-day (19–21 April) Indian Film Festival at the Embassy of India Auditorium, a Seminar and Open Discussion at the India Social and Cultural Centre and a three-day (27–30 September) retrospective of the films of Shyam Benegal at the Embassy Auditorium.[58]

External Players

While India has good relations with the United States (US), the same cannot be said about Pakistan and China. India has a number of outstanding bilateral issues with Pakistan and China. On the other hand, the UAE has friendly relations with the US, Pakistan and China. In the near and long-term future, these three countries could have a major impact on the Indo–UAE relations.

The US: The US and the UAE have a broad and close bilateral relationship primarily focused on security co-operation, oil and energy supply, trade and counter-terrorism efforts to name a few. The strategic alliance between the two countries goes back to the formation and independence of the UAE in December 1971 from Britain. As the UAE was a small and weak country, the US provided security to the government or ruling elites of the Gulf country. After the 1990 Iraqi invasion of Kuwait, the UAE sought closer security ties with the US which led to the Defence Co-operation Agreement of 1994. The primary reason that determined UAE's decision was that the US, being a super-power and an important actor in the region, was needed to maintain the security and stability of the region. Further important factor in this regard was the protection of sea routes for safe energy trade with the outside world. Secondly, the presence and close ties with the US was necessary to balance the Iranian influence in the region. Thus, the US–UAE Defence Co-operation Agreement was mutually beneficial as it provided regime security to the UAE, safeguarded the oil routes and contained the Iranian ambitions. The Agreement allows for the stationing of US military personnel and equipments in al-Dhafra air base and other bases and the use of Jebel Ali port by US warships. Today, the strategic relation between the US and the UAE has taken various forms: stationing of US troops in UAE, training of the Emirates' armed forces by the US, purchase of US-made F-16s, missiles and missile systems, etc.

The second important agenda that drives the US–UAE ties is the supply of energy and bilateral trade. The UAE is an important source of energy as the US imported 3.645 billion barrels of crude oil and other petroleum products from the UAE in 2011.[59] Another major area of co-operation between the US and the UAE was in counter-terrorism. In the past, the US was concerned about the presence of terrorists in the

UAE, the exploitation of the UAE's financial system to wire money by the terrorists through hawala, and the shadowy manner in which the UAE controlled and enforced export, import and border security, which could be used by terrorists to ship arms and explosives. However, after the 11 September 2001 terrorist attacks, the US–UAE began co-operating more closely in 'arrests of senior al-Qaeda operatives; denouncing terror attacks; improving border security; prescribing guidance for Friday prayer leaders to criticize extremist ideology; investigating suspect financial transactions; criminalizing use of the internet by terrorist groups, and strengthening its bureaucracy and legal framework to combat terrorism'.[60] The UAE also hosted the third Ministerial meeting of Global Counter-Terrorism Forum (GCTF) on 14 December 2012 in Abu Dhabi.[61] The forum is 'an informal, multilateral counterterrorism (CT) platform that focuses on identifying critical civilian CT needs, mobilizing the necessary expertise and resources to address such needs and enhance global cooperation'.[62] The UAE had volunteered to build the International Centre of Excellence for Countering Violent Extremism (CVE)[63] at Abu Dhabi and was inaugurated during the third ministerial.[64]

China: The primary focus of China–UAE relationship has been trade and commercial ties. China has been paying attention to the region's market in general, and the Arab market in particular, both for export of manufactured goods and as a source of much-needed energy. As per 2011 data, China is the fourth-largest trading partner of the UAE after India, the European Union and Japan,[65] and for China, the UAE is the 18th-largest trading partner in the world.[66] In January 2012, Chinese Premier Wen Jiabao visited the UAE in an effort to bolster economic ties. The two nations also signed a pact for the establishment of a long-term energy policy and agreed on a currency swap worth 35 billion yuan or US$5.5 billion, with a clear intention to boost bilateral economic relationship. The Chinese effort at forging closer partnership should be seen in the light of its requirement for energy needs for its booming economy. Though China's oil import from the UAE is relatively low at present, it is expected to rise in the future. According to the International Energy Agency, 'China is expected to become the world's biggest oil importer by 2020.'[67] Therefore, the Chinese policy of courting the UAE in particular and the GCC countries in general, could enhance its energy security and increase its economic clout in the region. In the past few years, the UAE's oil supply to China has been increasing steadily and has registered as the fastest growing among the GCC nations. The UAE is also becoming increasingly important for China's export-oriented economy because the 'Chinese economy depends on the UAE as a trade outlet for Chinese exporters in the region, as nearly 70 per cent of Chinese exports to the UAE are re-exported to the GCC countries, Africa and even Europe'.[68]

Apart from bilateral economic relations, the most substantial event brought about by the Chinese Premier's visit was in the willingness of China and the UAE to establish greater strategic co-operation.[69] This would reinforce the partnership between China and UAE in 'areas like law-enforcement, security, anti-terrorism and elimination of crime, and commitment to strengthening coordination and cooperation within international organizations for safeguarding their mutual interests'.[70] Thus, it becomes clear that China's objective is to seek closer strategic and security relations with UAE and other Gulf states—in light of the premier's visit to Saudi Arabia, Qatar and UAE[71]—with a view to playing a more active role in the security of the Persian Gulf region. Keeping these developments in mind, India would have to watch China's moves in the Persian Gulf in general and the UAE in particular, as its interests in trade and commerce and defence and security could be negatively affected.

Pakistan: Pakistan has friendly political, economic, cultural and people-to-people relations with the UAE which has been described by Pakistan's President Asif Ali Zardari as 'close and cordial'[72] and by Pakistan's ambassador to the UAE Jamil Ahmad Khan as 'cordial and brotherly'.[73] The number of Pakistani expatriate population in the UAE stands around 1.4 million,[74] which is the second largest expatriate community after India. The remittances sent by the Pakistani expatriate workers and diaspora in the UAE touched US$3 billion in 2912.[75] Pakistan's Foreign Minister Hina Rabbani Khar met her counterpart Abdullah Bin Zayed al-Nayhan at the 10th meeting of the Pakistan–UAE Joint Ministerial Commission held in Abu Dhabi in February 2012, during which the UAE's Foreign Minister 'assured Pakistan of the UAE's full support for the Pakistan-GCC FTA'.[76] On 2 December 2012, the President of Pakistan, Asif Ali Zardari also graced a function hosted by the UAE's Ambassador to

Pakistan Essa Abdulla al-Noaimi in Islamabad, celebrating the Emirates 41st National Day.[77] The volume of bilateral trade between Pakistan and the UAE was estimated at US$8 billion for the year 2011–12.[78] The UAE is the highest[79] source of FDI for Pakistan amounting to US$2.8 billion, and is mainly concentrated in the airlines, telecommunications, financial business, oil and gas, and real estate sectors.[80]

As far as bilateral trade and commerce is concerned, Pakistan lags far behind India–UAE trade volumes and does not pose any challenge. However, when it comes to terrorism and organized crime, there could be tensions between the two countries if terrorist groups from Pakistan use UAE soil to plan and carry out violent activities against targets in India. On top of this, criminals, fugitives and terrorists wanted in India could also take refuge in the UAE. Pakistani terrorist groups pose a challenge not only to India but also to the UAE government. In light of the 2008 Mumbai terror attacks, which was carried out using the sea routes in the international waters, extremist groups could exploit the UAE territory and used international waters to strike and carry out acts of terror in India.

Challenges

There are a number of problems and challenges that the Indo–UAE relationship faces. Problems such as terrorism, drug smuggling, human trafficking, exploitation and ill-treatment of the Indian labour are just a few of them. The scourge of terrorism is a major problem that affects the security of both the countries. The two nations have faced terrorist attacks in the past, though the UAE to a lesser extent. Because of this mutual concern, the two countries had signed agreements in the past to jointly tackle the issue of terrorism. India's main concern is that the extremist elements from Pakistan would use the UAE to raise funds, take shelter and as a staging area for subversive activities against India. The UAE as a major transit point for goods could be used by anti-Indian elements to smuggle arms, explosives and transfer money through hawala to India. Another concern in this respect is that terrorists, criminals and individuals wanted by the law could get refuge in the UAE. Again connected to this is the issue of money laundering by underworld elements in the UAE. Therefore, with respect to the issue of terrorism and criminal activities, both the countries need to keep a close watch on extremist ideology and elements that emanate from Pakistan. Sharing of intelligence, joint training of law-enforcement forces, sharing strategy and experiences on this issue could help effectively combat this problem.

Some other problems that the two countries are dealing with are unauthorized staying, overstaying the permitted work period and illegal unemployment. To solve this problem to a certain extent, the government of the UAE announced a two-month amnesty from 4 December 2012 till 3 February 2013, for foreign 'illegal residents who overstayed their visas ... to obtain outpasses and leave the country without penalties or regularize their visas, after payment of fines ...'[81] or face prosecution by the UAE government. According to Minister for Overseas Indian Affairs Vayalar Ravi, 'as many as 45,000 Indians staying illegally in the United Arab Emirates (UAE) are expected to seek amnesty announced by the Gulf country.'[82] He also wrote to various chief ministers, 'requesting them to make provisions for free air tickets to poor and deserving workers from respective states held up in UAE'.[83] India also decided to waive the application fee applicable to issue of emergency exit certificate or pass to those who decide to avail the opportunity provided by the amnesty[84] and provide free air tickets to those poor and deserving such as 'women, those who have been in jail, people who are bankrupt and the like'.[85]

Though the bilateral relations between India and the UAE are warm and ties have grown by leaps and bounds, there are still prospects and potential for enhancement. India could initiate various policies in this regard. Some vital areas in which the two countries can help each other is in the field of food security, agriculture, science and technology, better management of land and natural resources in the UAE, diversification of UAE's economy, education, IT, biotechnology, etc. In many of the fields cited above, India has advantages and could help the UAE. Co-operation would be easier due to friendly relations, cultural affinity and geographical proximity of the two countries.

Conclusion

The cordial and warm relations between India and the UAE continued during 2012 without any major hiccups. Trade and commerce between the two countries reached an all-time high of US$72 billion. Bilateral relations in other field such as investments, political co-operation, defence and security partnership, and cultural ties saw major improvements and growth. In short, India–UAE relations remained free from any tension and did not come under the influence of any major regional or international actor. The two sides not only enhanced their relationship, but are expected to see improvement in the future.

Notes

1. '36,277 out of 130,000 Voters Voted: Gargash', *Khaleej Times*, 25 September 2011, http://www.khaleejtimes.com/displayarticle. asp?xfile=data/theuae/2011/September/theuae_September591. xml&section=theuae&col=
2. Ibid.
3. 'Dubai Women's Establishment Launches UAE Women's Index Report', *Zawya*, 27 November 2012, http://www.zawya.com/story/Dubai_Womens_Establishment_Launches_UAE_Womens_Index_Report-ZA-WYA20121127105635/
4. National Election Committee, 'Percentage of Women and Men in Electoral Colleges', United Arab Emirates, 12 July 2011, http://www.uaenec.ae/en/statistics-and-figures.aspx
5. National Election Committee, '469 Candidates on the Preliminary List for Federal National Council elections', United Arab Emirates, 20 August 2011, http://www.uaenec.ae/en/media-centre/news-updates/20/8/2011/469-candidates-on-the-preliminary-list-for-federal-national-council-elections.aspx
6. 'A Vote for the Country's Future', *Gulf News*, 25 September 2011, http://gulfnews.com/news/gulf/uae/government/a-vote-for-the-country-s-future-1.876321
7. Samir Salama, 'Mohammad Ahmad Al Murr Elected Uncontested as FNC Speaker', *Gulf News*, 15 November 2011, http://gulfnews.com/news/gulf/uae/government/mohammad-ahmad-al-murr-elected-uncontested-as-fnc-speaker-1.931061
8. Human Rights Watch, 'United Arab Emirates', in *World Report 2013*, http://www.hrw.org/world-report/2013/country-chapters/united-arab-emirates?page=3
9. For further details, please refer to 'Women's Rights in the United Arab Emirates (UAE)', International Federation for Human Rights, http://www.fidh.org/IMG/pdf/UAE_summaryreport_for_CEDAW.pdf
10. For further details, P. R. Kumaraswamy (ed.), *Persian Gulf 2012: India's Relations with the Region* (Kindle Direct Publishing, 2012).

11. Press Release, Embassy of India, United Arab Emirates, Abu Dhabi, 21 April 2012, http://www.indembassyuae.org/drupal/node/769

12. Ibid.

13. 'India UAE Sign Agreements on FTAA', *CurrentEventsWorld.com*, 24 April 2012, http://www.currenteventsworld.com/categories/details/world-news/india-uae-sign-agreements-on-ftaa.html

14. Ibid.

15. 'Key Note Address by Minister of State for External Affairs Shri E. Ahmed at the 3rd Arab India Partnership Conference, Abu Dhabi 2012', Press Release, Consulate General of India, Dubai, 22 May 2012, http://www.cgidubai.com/key-note-address-by-minister-of-state-for-external-affairs-shri-e-ahamed-at-the-3rd-arab-india-partnershi%E2%80%8Bp-conference%E2%80%8B-abu-dhabi-2012/

16. 'Indo–Arab Partnership Conference to Be Held in Abu Dhabi on May 22', *Emirates 24/7*, 16 May 2012, http://www.emirates247.com/business/economy-finance/indo-arab-partnership-conference-to-be-held-in-abu-dhabi-on-may-22-2012-05-16-1.459099

17. Joseph George, 'UAE Indian Expat Alert: NRI Minister "kills" Air India, "opens" Sharjah Cemetery', *Emirates 24/7*, 13 November 2012, http://www.emirates247.com/news/emirates/uae-indian-expat-alert-nri-minister-kills-air-india-opens-sharjah-cemetery-2012-11-13-1.482868; 'I'm Just a Call Away for Overseas Indians: Valayar Ravi', *The Times of India*, 12 November 2012, http://articles.timesofindia.indiatimes.com/2012-11-12/middle-east-news/35067747_1_gulf-indians-gulf-nations-overseas-indian-affairs-minister

18. 'India Has Huge Potential, Feels Singapore Minister; Warns of Recession', *Business Line*, 12 January 2012, http://www.thehindubusinessline.com/industry-and-economy/article2795975.ece; Ashraf Padanna, 'India Partnership Summit to Explore Innovations That Can Drive Global Growth', *Gulf Today*, 4 January 2012, http://gulftoday.ae/portal/ec165915-6c82-4485-8676-5cfa252c2a8a.aspx

19. 'Lubna Takes Part in "The Partnership Summit 2013" in India', *Khaleej Times*, 27 January 2013, http://www.khaleejtimes.com/kt-article-display-1.asp?xfile=data/uaebusiness/2013/January/uaebusiness_January374.xml&section=uaebusiness

20. 'Abu Dhabi Investment Authority Looks for Investment Opportunities in India; ADIA and Indian Government to Form Joint Working Group to Finalize Projects', Press Release, Ministry of Commerce and Industry, New Delhi, 16 January 2012, http://commerce.nic.in/pressrelease/pressrelease_detail.asp?id=2884; 'ADIA Chief to Visit India to Explore Investments', *The Economic Times*, 15 January 2012, http://articles.economictimes.indiatimes.com/2012-01-15/news/30629758_1_uae-zayed-al-nahyan-m-k-lokesh

21. 'Abu Dhabi Investment Authority Head Visits India', Press Release, Embassy of the United Arab Emirates, New Delhi, India, http://www.uaeembassy-newdelhi.com/theembassy_press-releases_ADIA2012.asp

22. 'HE Obaid Humaid Al Tayer on an Official Visit to India', *Zawya*, 3 April 2012, http://www.zawya.com/story/ZAWYA20120403125432/

23. 'UAE Foreign Minister Sheikh Abdullah bin Zayed Al Nahyan Visits India', *The Week in Review* (Institute for Defence Studies and Analyses) 5, no. 3 (May 2012), http://www.idsa.in/TWIR/5_3_2012_UAE

24. WAM, 'UAE and India Sign Mutual Assistance in Customs Matters Agreement', 1 April 2012, http://www.wam.org.ae/servlet/Satellite?c=WamLocEnews&cid=1289998326249&p=1135099400124&pagename=WAM%2FWamLocEnews%2FW-T-LEN-FullNews

25. 'UAE and India to Activate an Electronic Contract Registration and Validation System to Streamline the Employment of Indian Contract Workers', Press Release, Press Information Bureau, New Delhi, India, 4 April 2012, http://pib.nic.in/newsite/erelease.aspx?relid=82092

26. 'Indian Authorities' Clearance Must for Work Contract in UAE', *The Times of India*, 4 April 2012, http://articles.timesofindia.indiatimes.com/2012-04-04/india/31286984_1_indian-workers-uae-s-ministry-uae-and-india; Rayeesa Absai, 'New System Aims to Protect Workers,' *Gulf News,* 5 April 2012, http://gulfnews.com/news/gulf/uae/employment/new-system-aims-to-protect-workers-1.1004345; Anwar Ahmad, 'New E-system in Place to Recruit Indian Workers', *Khaleej Times,* 4 April 2012, http://www.khaleejtimes.com/DisplayArticle09.asp?xfile=data/theuae/2012/April/theuae_April149.xml&section=theuae

27. Atul Aneja, 'India, UAE Discuss Roadmap for Future', *The Hindu,* 16 April 2012, http://www.thehindu.com/news/international/india-uae-discuss-roadmap-for-future/article3320637.ece; 'India Signs Taxation, Consular Agreements with the UAE', *The Economic Times,* 16 April 2012, http://articles.economictimes.indiatimes.com/2012-04-16/news/31349682_1_uae-investment-uae-counterpart-zayed-al-nahyan

28. 'Second India–UAE Foreign Office Consultations', Press Release, Ministry of External Affairs, New Delhi, 8 February 2012, http://www.mea.gov.in/press-releases.htm?dtl/18291/Second+India+UAE+Foreign+Office+Consultations

29. 'India–UAE Relations', Ministry of External Affairs, New Delhi, February 2012, http://www.mea.gov.in/Images/pdf/india-uae-relations-16-05-2012-press-release.pdf

30. 'Visit of External Affairs Minister to United Arab Emirates', Press Release, Ministry of External Affairs, New Delhi, 14 February 2012, http://www.mea.gov.in/press-releases.htm?dtl/19313/Visit+of+External+Affairs+Minister+to+United+Arab+Emirates

31. Ibid.

32. 'India's Cumulative Export Growth in April–Dec 2010–11 Stood at 29.5% with US$ 164.7 Billion of Exports ₹2,23,132.31 Crore Exports from SESs During First Three Quarters with Total Employment at 6,44,073', Press Release, Press Information Bureau, New Delhi, India, 25 February 2011 http://pib.nic.in/newsite/erelease.aspx?relid=70155

33. Estimate as of November 2012. 'India–UAE Relations', Ministry of External Affairs, New Delhi, January 2013.

34. 'India, UAE Sign Deal on Customs Cooperation', Abu Dhabi News.Net, 1 April 2012, http://www.abudhabinews.net/story/204575449

35. 'Customs Cooperation Agreement Between India and UAE', Press Release, Consulate General of India, United Arab Emirates, Dubai, http://www.cgidubai.com/india-and-uae-signs-bilateral-agreement-on-mutual-assistance-in-customs-matters/; 'UAE and India Sign Mutual Assistance in Customs Matters agreement', AMEinfo.com, 1 April 2012, http://www.ameinfo.com/295414.html

36. Anwar Ahmad, 'Indo–UAE Joint Panel Meeting Tomorrow', Khaleej Times, 14 April 2012, http://www.khaleejtimes.com/DisplayArticle11.asp?xfile=data/theuae/2012/April/theuae_April431.xml&section=theuae

37. These negotiations were all held in Riyadh in March 2006, September 2008 and January 2009. For more details, see Free Trade Negotiations, Ministry of Foreign Trade, United Arab Emirates, http://www.moft.gov.ae/wto/index.php?option=com_content&view=article&id=35&Itemid=62&lang=en; Gulf Cooperation Council (GCC), Ministry of External Affairs, New Delhi, April 2012, http://mea.gov.in/Portal/ForeignRelation/gulf-cooperation-council-april-2012.pdf

38. Some of the causes were the refusal by Saudi Arabia and the UAE to include petroleum and petroleum products in the negative list, India's desire for safeguards against its petrochemical and chemicals sector, non-existence of common customs union among GCC countries, disagreement on protective items list among the GCC nations specifying certain items which will attract higher rate of duty, and uncertainty due to the global economic recession. For further details, see Huma Siddiqui, 'India–GCC FTA Hangs Fire as UAE, S Arabia Oppose Petro Products in Negative List', The Financial Express, 21 August 2009, http://www.financialexpress.com/news/indiagcc-fta-hangs-fire-as-uae-s-arabia-oppose-petro-products-in-negative-list/504677/2; Huma Siddiqui, 'Ministries to Revisit GCC Free Trade Area Plan', The Financial Express, 3 January 2011, http://www.financialexpress.com/news/ministries-to-revisit-gcc-free-trade-area-plan/732241/2

39. 'IBLF to Push for India–UAE Free Pact', Business Line, 17 June 2011, http://www.thehindubusinessline.com/industry-and-economy/iblf-to-push-for-indiauae-free-trade-pact/article2112413.ece; 'Indian Business Forum to Push for FTA with UAE', The Economic Times, 17 June 2011, http://articles.economictimes.indiatimes.com/2011-06-17/news/29670072_1_fta-uae-investment-opportunities

40. The UAE is one of the six-member GCC countries. The other five being Oman, Bahrain, Kuwait, Qatar and Saudi Arabia.

41. Huma Siddiqui, 'India, GCC Discuss FTA', *The Financial Express,* 16 August 2011, http://www.financialexpress.com/news/india-gcc-discuss-fta/832318/0

42. 'Reenergize Negotiations for Concluding India–GCC FTA Talks: Anand Sharma', Press Release, Press Information Bureau, New Delhi, India, 17 February 2013, http://pib.nic.in/newsite/erelease.aspx?relid=92273

43. 'UAE Trade Minister Calls for Arab–Indian FTA', *Global Trade Review,* 18 June 2012, http://www.gtreview.com/trade-finance/global-trade-review-news/2012/June/UAE-trade-minister-calls-for-Arab-Indian-FTA_10013.shtml

44. 'Reenergize Negotiations for Concluding India–GCC FTA Talks: Anand Sharma', Press Information Bureau.

45. 'GCC, India Seen to Sign FTA with a Year', *The Saudi Gazette,* 28 June 2012, http://www.saudigazette.com.sa/index.cfm?method=home.regcon&conten tid=20120628128352; 'India, Gulf Cooperation Council to Ink Free Trade Agreement within a Year: CII', *The Economic Times,* 27 June 2012, http://articles.economictimes.indiatimes.com/2012-06-27/news/32441212_1_gcc-oman-and-india-trade-agreement

46. 'India, UAE Sign Defence Cooperation', *The Times of India,* 1 July 2003, http://articles.timesofindia.indiatimes.com/2003-07-01/india/27205796_1_defence-cooperation-defence-industry-subir-dutta

47. 'India, UAE Step Up Security Cooperation', *The Hindu,* 23 November 2011, http://www.thehindu.com/news/national/india-uae-step-up-security-cooperation/article2653594.ece

48. 'UAE, India Sign Security Agreements', *India Strategic,* November 2011, http://www.indiastrategic.in/topstories1269_UAE_India_sign_agreement.htm

49. 'India–UAE Relations', Ministry of External Affairs, New Delhi, August 2012, http://www.mea.gov.in/Portal/ForeignRelation/uae-august-2012.pdf

50. Geoffrey Kemp, *The East Moves West: India, China and Asia's Growing Presence in the Middle East* (Washington, DC: Brookings Institution Press, 2010), 49.

51. Imran Mojib, 'Indian Naval Ships Dock in Capital', *Gulf Today,* 18 March 2011, http://gulftoday.ae/portal/7cd387ac-a092-4cb0-8bba-381f6e4aaa88.aspx

52. 'India–UAE Relations', Ministry of External Affairs.

53. Kemp, *The East Moves West,* 49.

54. 'India–UAE Relations', Ministry of External Affairs.

55. Kemp, *The East Moves West,* 49.

56. Indian Council for Cultural Relations, http://www.iccrindia.net/

57. About the Cultural Wing, Embassy of India, United Arab Emirates, Abu Dhabi, http://www.indembassyuae.org/drupal/AboutCulturalWing

58. Past Events Archive, Indian Film Society of United Arab Emirates, http://www.ifsuae.com/Screeningsevents.aspx

59. Petroleum and Other Liquids, US Imports by Country of Origin, United Arab Emirates, US Energy Information Administration, http://www.eia.gov/dnav/pet/pet_move_impcus_a1_NTC_ep00_im0_mbbl_a.htm. The total US imports of Crude Oil and Products from all countries in 2011 is 4,198.806 billion barrels annually. http://www.eia.gov/dnav/pet/pet_move_impcus_a1_Z00_ep00_im0_mbbl_a.htm

60. Kenneth Katzman, 'The United Arab Emirates (UAE): Issues for U.S. Policy', CRS Report for Congress, 4 October 2012, 15, http://www.fas.org/sgp/crs/mideast/RS21852.pdf

61. Co-chairs Summary, Third Ministerial Plenary Meeting, 14 September 2012, http://www.thegctf.org/documents/10162/30110/Co-Chairs+Summary-Third+Ministerial+Plenary

62. Co-chairs Factsheet: About the GCTF, http://www.thegctf.org/documents/10162/30110/12Dec11_Co-Chairs+Fact+Sheet-About+the+GCTF

63. Also known as Hedayah Center for Countering Violent Extremism.

64. 'Center to Counter Extremism Opens in Abu Dhabi', Al Alarab Online, 15 December 2012, http://www.alarab.co.uk/english/display.asp?fname=%5C2012%5C12%5C12-15%5Czsubz%5C910.htm&dismode=x&ts=15-12-2012%2010:49:05; Philip Kurata, 'United Arab Emirates Hosts World Center to Fight Extremism', IIP Digital, 14 December 2012, http://iipdigital.usembassy.gov/st/english/article/2012/12/20121214140002.html#axzz2M28dR4Hg

65. 'United Arab Emirate's Trade with Main Partners 2011', 'United Arab Emirates–EU Bilateral Trade and Trade with the World', 29 November 2012, http://trade.ec.europa.eu/doclib/docs/2006/september/tradoc_113458.pdf

66. 'China's Trade with Main Partners 2011', 'China–EU Bilateral Trade and Trade with the World', 29 November 2012, http://trade.ec.europa.eu/doclib/docs/2006/september/tradoc_113366.pdf

67. Katherine Spenley, 'From Strength to Strength: New Boost for UAE—China Relations', Vision: Fresh Perspective from Dubai, January 2012, http://vision.ae/en/business/articles/from_strength_to_strength_new_boost_for_uae_china_relations

68. 'The UAE and China: A Strategic Partnership', The Emirates Center for Strategic Studies and Research, 26 January 2012, http://www.ecssr.ac.ae/ECSSR/print/ft.jsp?lang=en&ftId=/FeatureTopic/ECSSR/FeatureTopic_1500.xml

69. 'China, UAE Issue Joint Statement on Establishing Strategic Partnership', Xinhua, 17 January 2012, http://news.xinhuanet.com/english/china/2012-01/17/c_122598697.htm, accessed on 21 February 2013.

70. 'The UAE and China: A Strategic Partnership', The Emirates Centre for Strategic Studies and Research, 26 January 2012.

71. 'China, UAE Issue Joint Statement on Establishing Strategic Partnership'.

72. 'President Hails Pakistan's Ties with UAE', *The Daily Times,* 3 December 2012, http://www.dailytimes.com.pk/default.asp?page=2012%5C12%5C0 3%5Cstory_3-12-2012_pg7_27

73. 'Officials Open High-level UAE–Pakistan Meeting in Abu Dhabi', *Gulf Daily,* 26 February 2012, http://www.gulfdaily.net/officials-open-high-level-uae-pakistan-meeting-in-abu-dhabi/

74. Pakistan–UAE Relations, Embassy of the United Arab Emirates, Pakistan, Islamabad, http://uae-embassy.ae/Embassies/pk/Content/3489

75. Tahir Khan, 'Pakistanis in UAE Remit $3 Billion: Envoy', *News Pakistan,* 13 December 2012, http://www.newspakistan.pk/2012/12/13/pakistanis-uae-remit-3-billion-envoy/

76. Imran Sherif, 'UAE to Back Pakistan's Quest for Free Trade Agreement with the GCC', *Gulf News,* 28 February 2012, http://gulfnews.com/news/gulf/uae/government/uae-to-back-pakistan-s-quest-for-free-trade-agreement-with-the-gcc-1.987280

77. Mehmood Ul Hassan Khan, 'President Zardari Graced 41st UAE National Day Celebrations', *Overseas Pakistani Friends,* http://www.opfblog.com/13469/president-zardari-graced-41th-uae-national-day-celebrations/

78. 'UAE, Pakistan Discuss Boosting Trade Cooperation', *Khaleej Times,* 9 January 2013, http://www.khaleejtimes.com/kt-article-display-1.asp?xfile= data/nationgeneral/2013/January/nationgeneral_January140.xml& section=nationgeneral; 'Economic Relations: UAE Invites Pakistani Invest-ment', *The Express Tribune,* 10 January 2012, http://tribune.com.pk/sto-ry/491846/economic-relations-uae-invites-pakistani-investment/

79. 'UAE Biggest Foreign Investor in Pakistan, Says Envoy', *The Nation,* 11 February 2013, http://www.nation.com.pk/pakistan-news-newspaper-dai-ly-english-online/business/11-Feb-2013/uae-biggest-foreign-investor-in-pakistan-says-envoy

80. 'Bilateral, Trade and Investment Relations between Pakistan and UAE', Embassy of Pakistan, United Arab Emirates, Abu Dhabi, UAE, http:// www.pakistanembassyuae.org/view/bilateral-trade—investment-relations. aspx; 'Country Wise FDI Inflows', Board of Investment, Prime Minister's Secretariat, Government of Pakistan, http://www.pakboi.gov.pk/index. php?option=com_content&view=article&id=180&Itemid=137

81. Samir Salama, 'Two-month Amnesty to Illegal Residents', *Gulf News,* 13 November 2012, http://gulfnews.com/news/gulf/uae/visa/two-month-am-nesty-to-illegal-residents-1.1104133; Atul Aneja, 'UAE Amnesty for Expa-triates', *The Hindu,* 14 November 2012, http://www.thehindu.com/news/international/uae-amnesty-for-expatriates/article4095627.ece

82. '45,000 Indians Staying Illegally in UAE Will Return: Vayalar Ravi', *The Economic Times,* 4 December 2012, http://articles.economictimes.india-times.com/2012-12-04/news/35594818_1_uae-amnesty-scheme-illegal-immigrants

83. '45,000 Indians Staying Illegally in UAE Will Return: Govt.', *APN News*, 4 December 2012, http://apnnews.com/2012/12/04/45000-indians-staying-illegally-in-uae-will-return-govt/

84. 'Indian Amnesty Seekers in UAE to Get Financial Assistance', *Business Standard*, 24 December 2012, http://www.business-standard.com/article/pti-stories/indian-amnesty-seekers-in-uae-to-get-financial-assistance-112122400290_1.html

85. 'Indian Embassy in UAE Would Provide Financial Help to Amnesty Seekers', *Siasat Daily*, 20 January 2012, http://www.siasat.com/english/news/indian-embassy-uae-would-provide-financial-help-amnesty-seekers

10
Yemen

Dipanwita Chakravortty

Key Indicators
Area: 527,968 sq km; **Population:** 25.40 million; **Youth population:** 21.1 per cent; **Population growth rate:** 2.575 per cent; **Life expectancy at birth:** 65.9 years; **GDP:** US$54.85 billion; **Per capita income:** US$2,200; **Foreign trade:** US$16.85 billion; **Oil reserves:** 2.88 billion bbl (2013); **Gas reserves:** 478.5 billion m³; **Ruling party:** General People's Congress; **Ruler:** President Abd Rabuh Mansur al-Hadi (since 25 February 2012); **National Day:** 22 May; **Defence budget:** 6.6 per cent of GDP; **HDI rank:** 160; **Literacy rate:** 63.9 per cent; **Gender inequality index:** 0.747.
Source: CIA, *The World Factbook*, https://www.cia.gov/library/publications/the-world-factbook/index.html UN Human Development Report, Statistics, http://hdr.undp.org/en/statistics/   *Note:* All data for 2012.

Traditionally, India and Yemen have maintained a strong bilateral relation because of close people-to-people contact and similar security concerns. Yemen has the least proved reserves of hydrocarbons amongst the Persian Gulf countries and plays a minor yet important role in India's energy trade and security. Under the rule of President Ali Abdullah Saleh, the focus of the bilateral relation was on the energy trade. India provided huge investments to explore and produce oil in the oil blocks of Yemen.

Domestic Developments

The year 2012 saw Yemen making a tangible transition towards democracy as demanded by its citizens during the 2011 uprising which was a part of the wider popular protests that were taking place in the Arab world. In early 2011, people came out on to streets protesting against rising food prices, unemployment, corruption and deteriorating economic conditions. Due to the apathy shown by the government, the protests soon turned against President Saleh.[1] The common demand of the people was the ouster of the president along with the formation of a new government. In due course of time, the protests turned violent when the military was brought in to crack down on the protestors. By the end of 2011 several hundred people were killed in clashes between the protesters and the security forces.[2] In an attack at the presidential palace on 3 June 2011, the president was severely injured and was rushed to Saudi Arabia for emergency medical treatment. His prolonged convalescence in Riyadh did not bring about an immediate end to violence in Yemen.

Towards resolving the crisis, the Gulf Cooperation Council (GCC) proposed an initiative that sought a transition of power from Saleh to his deputy Abdrabuh Mansour Hadi in an orderly manner. On 23 November 2011, President Saleh signed the GCC deal that, among other things, guaranteed immunity to him and to his family from persecution or retribution and allowed him to remain as honorary president for three months.[3] As a result of the initiative, early presidential elections were called on 21 February 2012. Saleh's deputy, Abdrabuh Mansour Hadi became the president in this uncontested election. A new coalition cabinet consisting 35 members was formed which was divided equally between the former ruling party, General People's Congress (GPC) and the opposition party, the Joint Meeting Parties (JMP). According to the understanding reached by all the parties, President Hadi and the government would implement an inclusive national dialogue within two years towards drafting of a new constitution before fresh elections are held in 2014.[4]

After signing the GCC deal, Saleh left for the United States (US) on 22 January 2012 for medical treatment. He returned to Yemen on 25 February 2012. On 27 February 2012, he formally ceded power to Mansour Hadi. However, he continued as the president of Yemen's largest political party, the GPC which he founded in 1982. The United Nations Security Council (UNSC) reports have blamed Saleh of interfering in the National Dialogue Conference (NDC) and creating roadblocks to the same. According to the UNSC report for May 2012, Saleh threatened to pull out his loyalists from the Unity cabinet on 20 March 2012 so as to call for early elections before the NDC. According to the UNSC report for September 2012, UN Secretary General's Special Adviser on Yemen Jamal Benomar, appointed on 1 August 2012, reported that Saleh along with his key loyalists had repeatedly interfered in the process for hosting NDC and has become a key obstacle to the same.

The transition of power was followed by a series of continuing protests that created a situation swiftly deteriorating into a civil war. Protestors loyal to the Saleh family sporadically attacked several government institutions that were violently responded by the pro-government forces. A Shia group known as the Houthis, who live in the north-western part of the country, runs a parallel government in three provinces of Yemen, namely al-Jawf, Hajjah and Sa'ada.[5] This group consolidated its position, exploiting the power vacuum created by the uprisings in 2011. The Houthis have constantly clashed with the Salafis, who are associated with the Islamist party, Islah, which has resulted in loss of several civilian lives and of public property. Approximately, 600 people were killed between November 2011 and December 2012 due to the heavy fighting between the Houthis and the Salafis in Hajjah Governorate, mainly in Kushar and Mustaba districts. They also boycotted the presidential elections.[6] The Hadi government gave several concessions to the group, such as allowing the group to carry their own weapons, continue having their own candidates in the governorates they are dominant in, and also provided them with monetary aid from the centre. Hadi also assured them positions in the new government. On 31 May 2012, the Houthis agreed to take part in the Dialogue. Many political analysts believe that these concessions helped in avoiding an imminent civil war.[7] In the southern part of the country, separatist sentiment regained currency due to the political chaos at the centre. The secessionist movement Hirak rebels boycotted the elections and demanded freedom. It stated that the Sana'a governments have always ignored the plight of the southern Yemenis and was only interested in the revenue garnered from the oilfields.[8] They accused President Hadi for becoming a 'Western Agent' and ignoring the demands of his own people.

The UN Security Council Report prepared in May 2012 by Secretary General Ban Ki-Moon's Special Adviser to Yemen, Jamal Benomar, noted that the security and humanitarian situation had worsened since 2011 and remained a major concern for the reforms undertaken by President Hadi.[9] The report noted that the rise of al-Qaeda and similar outfits like Ansar al-Sharia led to kidnappings, suicide bombings and terrorist attacks aimed at compelling the new government to bow to their demands which were usually for the release of several militants who were imprisoned during the reign of Saleh. Due to the lack of political stability as well as the complete failure of the military structure in Yemen, the terrorist groups have taken over several provinces and run parallel governments in most of them. The capital city of Sana'a itself is divided amongst the Republican Guard troops, armed Shia tribesmen from the north-west and armed cadres of al-Qaeda in the Arab peninsula (AQAP).[10] These groups are in constant clash with each other over territory and conveniences like electricity, water, etc. The proliferation of armed tribesmen and AQAP is a constant threat over the political process in Yemen.

As part of its ongoing war against terrorism, American drone attacks against suspected terrorists are common in southern part of Yemen. These attacks not only killed alleged terrorists but also several civilians. In 2012, these drones killed Fahd al-Quso, the leader of AQAP as well as Said al-Sihri, the second-in-command of AQAP.[11] Apart from these two successful drone attacks, several innocent civilians too were killed, which brought people on to the streets to protest against the indiscriminate killings by the drones and the reluctance of the present government to take up the issue with America.[12]

On 14 August 2012, the Republican Guard troops under the command of Brig. Gen. Ahmed Ali Abdullah Saleh—the former president's son—attacked the office of the Defence Ministry in Sana'a which resulted in the death of more than five people. President Hadi took immediate action and disbanded the troops. He also removed most of the army officials who were loyal to Saleh as part of his attempt to restructure and centralize the military.[13] According to the Human Rights Watch's *World Report 2013*, the involvement of former officials was implicit in various terrorist attacks in Yemen that killed more than 2,000 innocent civilians.

The report stated that the immunity given to Saleh and his family in exchange for stepping down has turned him into a tyrant. The immunity law that was passed in January 2012 has become the major obstacle in the peaceful political transition.[14]

Another issue that affected Yemen was the violation of human rights. During the last few months of President Saleh's rule, many Yemeni youth were jailed for protesting against the government. These youth continued to stay behind the bars even after the change of government. In March 2012, the United Nations Human Rights Council adopted a resolution that called upon all parties in Yemen to release persons arbitrarily detained and to end practices of unlawful detention.[15] On 24 July 2012, the government and United Nations Development Programme signed an agreement to undertake a project aimed at strengthening human rights during the transition period in Yemen.[16]

As a result of political turmoil, the economy of Yemen has suffered a setback. The main reasons behind the 2011 uprising were the dismal economic conditions that prompted the people to protest against the government. Despite the change in the government, there is no significant improvement in the economic situation of Yemen. The lack of availability of food has led to food insecurity in the society. Malnutrition levels across the country have deteriorated.[17] Most of the foreign companies have closed their offices due to prevailing insecure environment which has made many Yemeni youth unemployed. Due to constant terror threat in Southern Yemen, schools and colleges have stopped functioning on a daily basis which in turn has affected the education standards of many young Yemeni children.[18] Despite foreign aid, the situation has not improved.

In January 2010, 39 countries and international organizations came together to form *Friends of Yemen* to aid and assist the country in its political transition as well as to tackle the underlying causes of instability and emerging terrorism in the country.[19] This group is co-chaired by the United Kingdom, Saudi Arabia and Yemen and included India as a participant. The three priorities of this group are to ensure progress on the NDC, help in the preparation for presidential and parliamentary elections in 2014 and to pledge US$7.8 billion by the group for improving the living standards in Yemen. By the end of 2012, the group has met four times and has constantly supported the efforts of President Hadi.[20]

Bilateral Relations

India and Yemen share historical ties that can be dated back to the Roman Empire and Yemeni traders came to India to trade horses and weapons in exchange of spices. On the other hand, the Indian merchants found Aden as the gateway to Middle East and Europe.[21] In 1839, Aden became part of the British Empire and was administered by the Bombay Presidency. Several families from Aden came and settled in India for economic purposes. Majority of them settled in southern India, especially in the present-day Andhra Pradesh under the Nizam of Hyderabad and decided to stay back even after the independence of India. On the other hand, during the late nineteenth century, many Indians belonging to the Bohra, Kachchi and Khoja communities migrated to Aden and decided to remain there and they gradually became Yemeni citizens.[22]

After India got independence, several merchant families, especially from Gujarat, migrated to Yemen as it offered economic opportunities for investments as well as for trade. The strait of Bab-al-Mandab became an important passage for trade that connected India to the rest of Middle East and Europe. Once oil was discovered in South Yemen in late 1950s, Aden became an important port because of increased economic activity. The oil trade sparked growth in other sectors of the economy as well, especially in the infrastructure sector and trade. Many Indians migrated as labourers to the newly discovered oil port of Aden. Even after the independence of South Yemen, many Indians decided to stay back. However, during 1990–94, many of them returned to India following the outbreak of civil war.

India was one of the first countries to establish diplomatic ties with the Yemen Arab Republic (YAR) in 1962 and People's Democratic Republic of Yemen (PDRY) in 1967. In 1990, following the unification of both a new Republic of Yemen was formed. India recognized the newly unified Yemen and set up diplomatic ties with it. Since then, the bilateral relations between India and Yemen have strengthened. India has stood steadfast in its support for the territorial integrity of Yemen and has supported Yemen as a non-member of Organization of Petroleum Exporting Countries. Yemen, on the other hand, has supported India's candidature for permanent membership in the United Nations.[23] Both the countries are members of several international forums like Indian

Ocean Rim Association for Regional Cooperation (IOR-ARC) and Convention on Bio-diversity (CBD).[24]

Political Relations

The year 2012 saw a number of ministerial visits from Yemen to participate in various political forums. The most significant visit was by Dr Abu Bakr al-Qirbi, Minister of Foreign Affairs of Yemen, to attend the 12th Meeting of the Council of Ministers of the Indian IOR-ARC, which was held on 2 November in Gurgaon. Dr Qirbi raised the issue of piracy in the Indian Ocean and said that piracy has led to the loss of lives of several fishermen and over US$200 million of revenue loss for Yemen. He proposed the establishment of a traditional fishing resource unit in Yemen that would promote and enhance the abilities of a fisherman.[25]

Other visits included that of Abdo Razza Saleh Khaled, Minister of Water and Environment, who participated in the 11th Conference of Parties to the Convention of Biological Diversity that was held in Hyderabad during 17–19 October.[26] Dr Saleh Sumae, Minister of Electricity, participated in the International Seminar on Energy Access that was organized by the Indian Ministry of New and Renewable Energy in October.[27] The only visit of a bilateral nature was by Dr Ali Muthana Hassan, Vice-Minister of Foreign Affairs, for the Foreign Office consultations held in June 2012. Despite many proposals for new memorandums of understanding, none were signed during the consultations.[28] There were no major political visits from India in 2012. However, India has continued to engage with Yemen and the international community, on various multilateral forums for the peaceful resolution of the crisis in Yemen.

India has actively participated in *Friends of Yemen* group since its inception in 2010. Taking part in the third meeting of the Group in Riyadh on 23 May 2012, Minister of State for External Affairs E. Ahamed said that India supports peace, security, stability and territorial integrity of Yemen. He further stated that India has an elaborate programme of capacity-building and training for Yemeni citizens and such programmes would be extended to include more Yemeni citizens.[29] In the fourth ministerial meeting of the Friends of Yemen in New York held on 27 September 2012, Additional Secretary in the Ministry of External Affairs Navtej Sarna said that India was ready to bilaterally help Yemen outside the framework of the group by looking at specific proposals for assistance, particularly in the field of entrepreneurship development, education and IT.[30] The improvement in the bilateral relations between India and Yemen since the change of government was clearly articulated by the Ambassador of Yemen to India, Dr Khadija Radman Ghanem, in a media interview. She said that the constant support of India to Yemen during the recent crisis has further strengthened the bilateral relations between the two.[31]

Economic Relations

In 2012, the Yemeni economy got a huge setback when several of its oil pipelines were attacked by the militant groups operating in the country.[32] The price of rice and cereals skyrocketed due to their unavailability which led to several food riots in the north-eastern part of the country.[33] Due to the dire straits of its economy, several countries and international organizations came forward with monetary support and aid. India too sent a consignment of rice worth US$2 million to assist Yemen to overcome the food shortage.[34]

Due to the crisis-ridden economy, the total trade of Yemen declined dramatically in 2012 compared to the previous years.[35] India's imports from Yemen, which stood at US$1.57 billion in 2009–10, had increased to US$1.74 billion in 2010–11, but fell to US$973.6 million in 2011–12 (Table 10.1 and Figure 10.1). India's exports to Yemen have, however, increased in comparison to 2010–11. It stood at US$514.1 million in 2010–11 and increased to US$730.62 million in 2011–12 (Table 10.2 and Figure 10.2). The total bilateral trade in 2009–10 stood at US$2.3 billion and declined to US$2.25 billion the following year. The total trade further declined in 2011–12 with the total value at US$1.7 billion. In terms of its share, the bilateral trade with Yemen accounts for a marginal share in India's overall foreign trade; it was 0.49 per cent in 2009–10, 0.36 per cent in 2010–11 and 0.21 per cent in 2011–12 (Table 10.3 and Figure 10.2). Amid the continuing decline in trade, and economic relations being held hostage to the political situation in Yemen, there were a

Table 10.1
India–Yemen Bilateral Trade (in US$ Million)

	2009–10	2010–11	2011–12
Exports	727.39	514.10	730.62
Imports	1,575.55	1,743.90	973.65
Total trade	2,302.95	2,258.00	1,704.27
Share of Yemen in total trade	0.55	0.47	0.20

Source: Adapted from Director General of Foreign Trade, http://www.dgft.gov.in

Figure 10.1
India–Yemen Bilateral Trade

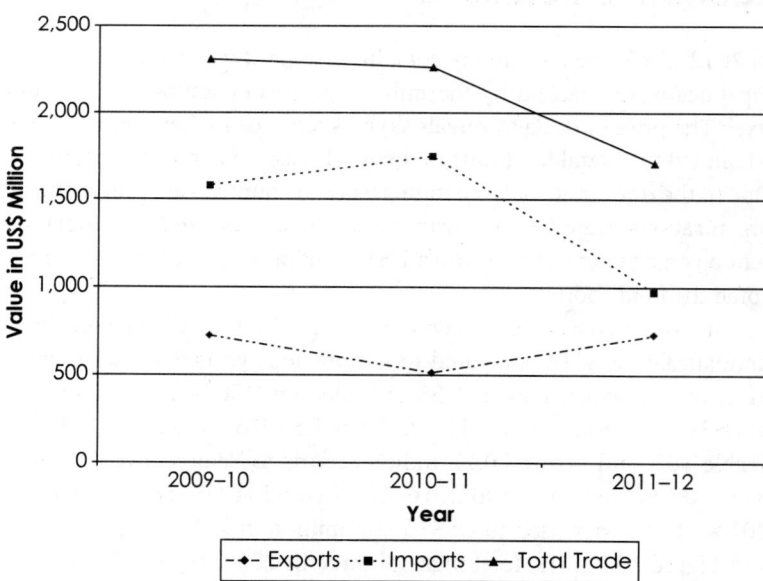

Source: Adapted from Director General of Foreign Trade, http://www.dgft.gov.in

few encouraging signs as well. The state-owned Bharat Heavy Electricals Ltd. won a US$436 million contract for setting up the Marib gas-based power project in Yemen. The project is being funded by the Arab Fund for Economic and Social Development and the Saudi Fund for Development.[36] However, despite such occasional collaboration in infrastructure

Table 10.2
Share of Oil in India's Imports from Yemen (in US$ Million)

Year	Oil imports from Yemen	Total oil imports	Yemen's share in total oil imports	Imports from Yemen	Per cent of oil in imports from Yemen
2009–10	1,563.15	96,321.16	1.62	1,575.55	99.21
2010–11	1,722.95	115,929.06	1.49	1,743.90	98.80
2011–12	955.26	172,753.97	0.55	973.65	98.11

Source: Adapted from Director General of Foreign Trade, http://www.dgft.gov.in

Figure 10.2
Share of Oil in India's Total Imports from Yemen

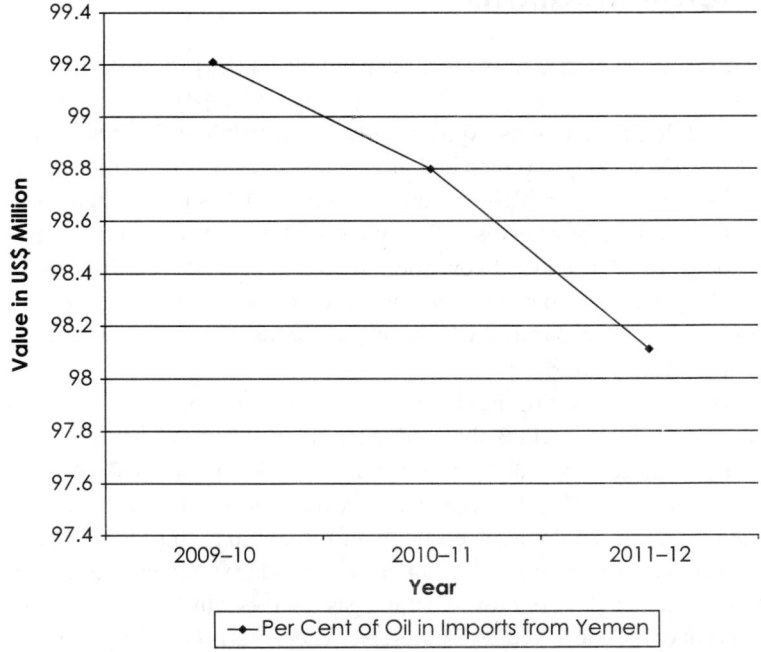

Source: Adapted from Director General of Foreign Trade, New Delhi, http://www.dgft.gov.in

and other fields, India's economic relations with Yemen continue to be dominated by energy and agricultural products.

Table 10.3
India's Energy Imports from Yemen (in US$ Million)

	2009–10	2010–11	2011–12
Energy imports from Yemen	1,563.15	1,722.95	955.26
Total energy imports	96,321.16	115,929.06	172,753.97
Total imports from Persian Gulf	55,904.14	66,688.40	103,915.24
Share in total imports (in per cent)	1.62	1.49	0.55
Share in imports from Persian Gulf (in per cent)	2.80	2.58	0.92

Source: Adapted from Director General of Foreign Trade, http://www.dgft.gov.in

Energy Relations

The economy of Yemen is highly dependent on the production and export of oil and natural gas, with the country's oil exports accounting for around 90 per cent of its export revenues. According to *BP Statistical Review of World Energy*, Yemen had proven oil reserves of 2.7 billion barrels at the end of 2011 which accounts for almost 0.2 per cent share of the entire Middle East reserves.[37] Though it has the least proven oil reserves amongst the Persian Gulf countries, Yemen has several huge oilfields or blocks that are yet to be explored or brought into production. At present there are 87 blocks out of which only 12 produce oil to break even the cost of production.[38]

Due to the ongoing instability in Yemen, the production of oil has steadily declined. In 2008, the production stood at 316,000 barrels per day which declined to 306,000 barrels per day in 2009 and 301,000 barrels per day in 2010. In 2011, the declining curve took a sharp bend further due to the turmoil in the domestic economy of the country, and the production in that year was a mere 228,000 barrels per day.[39] Yemen also has 0.5 trillion cubic metres of proven natural gas reserves which accounts for 0.2 per cent of the entire Middle East reserve. There was no substantial production of natural gas in Yemen before 2009. In 2009, 0.8 billion cubic metres was produced which increased to 6.2 billion cubic metres in 2010 and 9.4 billion cubic metres in 2011.[40] Given the over-dependence of Yemeni economy on oil and natural gas, it is no surprise that India's bilateral trade with Yemen is also dominated by import of oil and natural gas.

More than 98 per cent of India's imports from Yemen are oil related. Owing to the political turmoil in Yemen, this trade has suffered in last two years. The total import of mineral oil and its products from Yemen sharply declined in the financial year 2011–12.[41] In 2010–11, the import of mineral oil and its products was worth US$1,722.95 million which came down to US$955.26 million in 2011–12. The percentage decline in the import was 44.56 in 2011–12, as compared to the previous year. In contrast, the total import of mineral oil and its products by India increased from US$115.9 billion in 2010–11 to US$172.7 billion in 2011–12. The share of the crude oil and gas in the total trade with Yemen has decreased from 1.49 per cent to 0.55 per cent in 2011–12 as compared to the previous year. The only positive trend in energy imports was registered in the import of Liquefied Natural Gas (LNG). The total import of LNG from Yemen to India was US$37.14 million in 2010–11 which increased to US$75.76 million in 2011–12.

In case of investments in Yemen's oil blocks, three Indian oil companies play an important role. They are Reliance India Limited, Indian Oil Corporation and Gujarat State Petroleum Corporation. After 2006, under President Saleh's new oil and gas policy, the above three Indian companies were given the rights of exploration and production in more than 10 oil blocks.[42] On 5 December 2012, Reliance India Limited sold off its rights in one of the three oil blocks it had a stake in. At present, it has stake in just two oil blocks in Yemen, namely, Block 34 and 37, in eastern part of the country.[43] The other two companies, Indian Oil Corporation and Gujarat State Petroleum Corporation too have steadily decreased their shares.

The primary reason for the declining trend in production as well as in export is the growing insecurity in the provinces near the oilfields, especially in Hadramaut which has 84 per cent of known oil reserves of Yemen. The oil production as well as export infrastructure is under constant attack by the terrorist outfits like AQAP. Pipelines are the easiest targets as they cannot be given complete security. The Marib–Red Sea oil pipeline network was bombed over a dozen times by the armed tribesmen and was declared closed after a lot of oil went to waste.[44] Apart from the infrastructures, the armed tribesmen and the terrorist groups also target the employees of the oil company. Very frequently, they kidnap them for ransoms or lay siege to the offices. This has compelled several oil companies to shut oil explorations and shift their offices outside Yemen.[45]

Cultural Relations

At present, there are approximately 300,000 people of Yemeni origin residing in India, out of which 150,000 reside in Andhra Pradesh alone. On the other hand, there are approximately 100,000 people of Indian origin who are Yemeni citizens and reside near Aden and Hadramaut.[46] The close cultural ties between the people can be observed through various common customs and expressions. Several families of Yemeni origin from Hyderabad have forged family ties with Yemenis through the marriage of their children and vice versa.[47] In June 2012, the Indian Ambassador to Yemen Dr Ausaf Sayeed said that an honorary consulate was being considered in Hyderabad to boost the bilateral relations. Apart from the consulate in Mumbai, the proposed honorary consulate in Hyderabad would not only ease the visa application process but also further closer cultural ties.[48]

In 2011, there were approximately 14,000 Indian workers in Yemen, most of them in the oil blocks in eastern part of the country. As the domestic situation deteriorated at an alarming pace in Yemen, the Ministry of External Affairs issued several travel advisories[49] and asked its nationals to leave Yemen, while considering special flights to evacuate willing citizens back to India.[50] However, a mere hundred Indian workers returned to India in early 2012 while majority continued to stay back in Yemen as their meagre salaries from the oil industry of Yemen was significantly larger than what they would have got in India.[51]

At the educational level, India has been providing opportunities to Yemeni students under the General Cultural Scholarship Scheme (GCSS) of the Indian Council for Cultural Relations for pursuing higher studies in various Indian universities. In 2012, the number of scholarships offered was 36, which were increased to 54 in 2013.[52] Apart from such scholarships, India also provides 65 slots to Yemeni citizens for training and capacity-building in different fields under the Indian Technical and Economic Cooperation programme. The numbers of slots were increased to 80 for the year 2012–13. A new cultural exchange programme is under consideration which would be signed and brought to effect not later than 2014.[53]

To boost people-to-people contact, a new Visa Issuance System for online submission of visa applications was started in Sana'a. During the inauguration, the Indian Ambassador to Yemen said that this system comes as a part of enhancing Yemeni–Indian bilateral co-operation.[54]

On 8 April 2012, Nobel laureate Tawakkol Karman visited India to deliver the fifth Babu Jagjivan Ram Memorial Lecture in New Delhi. She won the Nobel Peace Prize for her efforts during the 2011 Arab uprising in Yemen. She interacted with several academicians, experts and school children. In an interview, she said, 'I am here to listen, learn and visit the country that gave the most important value to the world which is non-violence.... I expect to learn a lot here and give this expertise to Arab countries and especially to the people of Yemen.'[55]

The Indian Council of World Affairs (ICWA) organized a seminar on Yemen in collaboration with the Sheba Centre for Strategic Studies (SCSS) in April 2012. Strategic experts and academicians from both the countries discussed various aspects of the bilateral relations and prospects of improvement of the same. The issue of piracy which affects both the countries was discussed extensively. ICWA and SCSS signed a memorandum of understanding (MoU) 'to explore mutual areas of interests and to help engage knowledge communities of the two countries'.[56]

External players

The US: Under the rule of President Saleh, bilateral relations between the US and Yemen were an extension of Saleh's desire to be close to the former. After 2001, Yemen under Saleh became a staunch ally of the US and its war against terrorism.[57] However, Yemen's lax policy towards the militants of AQAP as well as its apathy towards the rise of new terror outfits in its territories made the US–Yemeni relations strained. During the second term of President George W. Bush, Yemen was declared as a front runner in the 'war on terror'.[58] In 2009, President Barack Obama initiated a major review of US policy towards Yemen, particularly after the attempted airline bombing over Detroit in December 2009. The new review known as the National Security Council's Yemen Strategic Plan was essentially a three-fold plan which focuses on combating AQAP in the short term, increasing development assistance to meet long-term challenges and to garner support for global efforts to stabilize Yemen.[59] However, the priority for the US President was the end of war against terror and to do so, the US deployed drone attacks in Yemen against suspected militants and terrorists. The 2011 uprisings in Yemen that compelled President Saleh to step down created a power vacuum which was seized by the terrorist outfits like AQAP to capture provinces in southern Yemen. They also began kidnapping as well as bombing foreign institutions in and outside the country. The changing nature of the AQAP compelled a steadfast US involvement in Yemen.[60] The number of drone attacks increased in 2012 which led to the killing of the leader as well as the second-in-command of AQAP. Seven more alleged terrorists were also killed by the attacks.[61] Apart from these, approximately 443 civilians were killed and properties were destroyed during these drone attacks. This has created a very strong anti-American sentiment amongst the people in Southern Yemen who have accused President Hadi of 'selling' the interests of his own people to the US.[62]

China: The bilateral relation between China and Yemen is a part of former's larger policy towards the Middle East which is based on two main pillars: increasing Chinese investment in the Middle East and avoiding interference in the domestic issues of these countries.[63] Yemen is of high strategic importance to China because of its geographical position near Bab-al Mandab, which is a strait that connects the Red Sea to the Persian Gulf.

Yemen also plays an important role in China's efforts to diversify its energy sources and increase its energy security. Despite being a moderate producer of oil and natural gas, Yemen lacks investments for better research and production of hydrocarbons.[64] This, along with the present domestic crisis in Yemen, has decreased the production of hydrocarbons drastically in Yemen. In 2012, Yemeni Minister of Oil and Minerals, Hisham Sharaf, asked the Chinese ambassador to Yemen, Liu Denglin, to enhance Chinese investment in the hydrocarbon sector in Yemen.[65] As a part of the growing ties, China reduced 95 per cent of the custom duties on Yemeni exports. Apart from the economic investments, China also promised to send doctors and medical equipments to Yemen for aiding the crisis ridden society.[66]

Yemen is important to China's foreign policy as it has become an important front for the US-led war against terror. The constant drone attacks have not only devastated the economic conditions of the country but have also given rise to popular opposition against the US. This has provided China an opportunity to diplomatically tackle the American influence in the country as well as in the region.

Pakistan: As members of the Organisation of Islamic Cooperation (OIC), Pakistan and Yemen share a very cordial bilateral relation. Both the countries have supported each other in different forums like Yemen's support for Pakistan's bid to win the non-permanent UNSC membership in 2011.[67] After 2001, both the countries supported the US-initiated war against terror. But soon after, they became the front for the war which devastated their economy and society. The constant drone attacks and the presence of the US military personnel have challenged their territorial integrity and have created popular opposition against the US despite close relations between the two governments.[68] In an effort to tackle the increasing interference by the US in the domestic issues of the country, both countries look towards China for support and aid. Though Pakistan is not a member of the *Friends of Yemen* group, it continues to support Yemen in its political transition phase through OIC, which is a common forum.[69]

After September 11 attacks, both Pakistan and Yemen were seen as countries that provided refuge to al-Qaeda. While being active supporters of the US-led 'war on terror', both countries faced drone attacks from 2003 to 2004 as well as covert actions by US that challenged their sovereignty. The common fate of both the countries has brought them close in experience and values. Though they are not significant trade partners, they depend on each other for crucial items, like hydrocarbons from Yemen; rice and cereals from Pakistan and so on. Both the countries have signed several MoUs regarding military tie-ups and capacity-building programmes.[70] Pakistan has invested heavily in building infrastructures in Yemen like hospitals, roads, schools, etc. There are several thousand Pakistani expatriates who live in Yemen and work in the oilfields, hospitals, construction industries and so forth.[71]

Conclusion

India's bilateral relation with Yemen is governed by various issues such as concern for the welfare of the Indian expatriate community living in Yemen, protection of Indian investments, standing by its principles of state sovereignty and non-intervention and inclination towards expanding its influence in the region. With such important issues, India has to take cautious steps in strengthening the bilateral relations with Yemen. The lack of political stability and increasing power of al-Qaeda has made it difficult for India to engage politically with Yemen. However, India has made efforts to consolidate economic as well as cultural ties with the country. During 2012, India reinforced its bilateral relations by participating in various common international forums like IOC-ARC. The changing political climate in Yemen would impact the bilateral relations but whether it would be positive or adverse is uncertain.

Notes

1. Laura Kasinoff, 'Yemeni Youth Square Off with Forces', *The New York Times*, 13 February 2011, http://www.nytimes.com/2011/02/14/world/middleeast/14yemen.html?_r=0
2. Uri Friedman, '40 Per Cent of Casualties in Yemen Uprising Came in Last Ten Days', *The Atlantic Wire*, 3 July 2011, http://www.theatlanticwire.com/global/2011/06/40-casualties-yemen-uprising-came-last-ten-days/38468/
3. 'Yemen', *United Nations Security Council Report*, March 2012, http://www.securitycouncilreport.org/monthly-forecast/2012-03/lookup_c_glKWLeMTIsG_b_7996437.php
4. Ibid.
5. April Longley Alley, 'Triage for a Fracturing Yemen', *Foreign Policy,* 31 October 2012, http://mideast.foreignpolicy.com/posts/2012/10/31/triage_for_a_fracturing_yemen?wp_login_redirect=0
6. 'Yemen', *United Nations Security Council Report*, March 2012.
7. Alley, 'Triage for a Fracturing Yemen'; Atiaf Zaid Alwazir, 'Yemen: Time for Hadi to Move Beyond Managing Power Struggles', *The Guardian,* 13 October 2012, http://www.guardian.co.uk/commentisfree/2012/oct/13/hadi-power-yemen
8. Ibid.
9. 'Yemen', *United Nations Security Council Report*, May 2012, http://www.securitycouncilreport.org/monthly-forecast/2012-05/lookup_c_glKWLeMTIsG_b_8075189.php
10. Alley, 'Triage for a Fracturing Yemen'.
11. 'Yemen', *United Nations Security Council Report*, July 2012, http://www.securitycouncilreport.org/monthly-forecast/2012-07/lookup_c_glKWLeMTIsG_b_8192003.php; See also 'Yemen', *United Nations Security*

Council Report, November 2012, http://www.securitycouncilreport.org/monthly-forecast/2012-11/yemen_1.php

12. Alley, 'Triage for a Fracturing Yemen'.

13. 'Yemen', *United Nations Security Council Report,* September 2012, http://www.securitycouncilreport.org/monthly-forecast/2012-09/yemen.php. See also 'Yemen', *United Nations Security Council Report,* January 2013, http://www.securitycouncilreport.org/monthly-forecast/2013-01/yemen_2.php

14. Human Rights Watch, *World Report 2013,* http://www.hrw.org/world-report/2013

15. 'Yemen', *United Nations Security Council Report,* May 2012.

16. 'Yemen', *United Nations Security Council Report,* September 2012, http://www.securitycouncilreport.org/monthly-forecast/2012-09/yemen.php

17. Alley, 'Triage for a fracturing Yemen'.

18. Ibid.

19. 'Friends of Yemen: Question and Answers', The Government of United Kingdom, 1 February 2013, https://www.gov.uk/government/news/friends-of-yemen-q-a

20. Ibid.

21. 'India–Yemen Relations', Ministry of External Affairs, New Delhi, February 2013, http://www.mea.gov.in/Portal/ForeignRelation/Yemen_brief_for_MEA_s_website.pdf

22. Ibid

23. Ibid.

24. Ibid.

25. 'Dr. Al-Qirbi Discuss Yemen Partnership on 12th Meeting of the Council Of Ministers IOR-ARC', *National Yemen,* 2 November 2012, http://nationalyemen.com/2012/11/02/dr-al-qirbi-discuss-yemen-partnership-on-12th-meeting-of-the-council-of-ministers-meeting/

26. 'India–Yemen Relations', Ministry of External Affairs.

27. Ibid.

28. Ibid.

29. 'Intervention by Shri E Ahamed, Minister of State for External Affairs at the Third Ministerial Meeting of the Friends of Yemen in Riyadh', Ministry of External Affairs.

30. 'Intervention by Ambassador Navtej Sarna, Additional Secretary, on Forth Ministerial Meeting of the Friends of Yemen Group New York on 27 September 2012', *Statements at the United Nations,* Permanent Mission of India to the United Nations, New York, 27 September 2012, http://www.un.int/india/2012/ind2070.pdf

31. Fakhri Al-Arashi, 'Interview: Yemeni Ambassador to India. Dr. Khadija Radman Ghanem', *National Yemen,* 18 November 2012, http://nationalyemen.com/2012/11/18/interview-yemeni-ambassa0dor-to-india-dr-khadija-radman-ghanem/

32. 'Yemen's Main Oil Pipeline Shut after Bombings', *Al Jazeera,* 12 November 2012, http://www.aljazeera.com/news/middleeast/2012/11/20121112938 39600663.html
33. Kelly Gillbride, 'The Crisis in Yemen is Food, Not Terror', *CNN,* 24 May 2012, http://edition.cnn.com/2012/05/24/opinion/yemen-hunger-crisis
34. 'India's Humanitarian Food Assistance to the Republic of Yemen', Press Release, Ministry of External Affairs, New Delhi, 9 July 2012, http://www.mea.gov.in/press-releases.htm?dtl/20092/Indias+Humanitarian+Food+Assistance+to+Republic+of+Yemen
35. All data given in Economic section are from Ministry of Commerce and Industry, India, http://commerce.nic.in/eidb/default.asp
36. 'BHEL Bags USD 436 mn Contract for Power Project in Yemen', *The Economic Times,* 14 February 2011, http://articles.economictimes.indiatimes.com/2011-02-14/news/28540130_1_bhel-gas-turbine-based-power-plant-mn-contract
37. 'Statistical Review of World Energy, 2012', British Petroleum, http://www.bp.com/sectionbodycopy.do?categoryId=7500&contentId=7068481
38. Ibid.
39. Ibid.
40. Ibid.
41. All data pertaining to the bilateral trade between India and Yemen are from Ministry of Commerce and Industry, India, http://commerce.nic.in/eidb/default.asp
42. Press Information Bureau, 'Indian Oil Companies Sign Agreements for Oil Blocks in Yemen', http://pib.nic.in/newsite/erelease.aspx?relid=37513
43. 'Reliance Industries Completes Sale of 25% Stake in Yemen Oil Block to Medco Energi', *The Indian Express,* 5 December 2012, http://www.indianexpress.com/news/reliance-industries-completes-sale-of-25—stake-in-yemen-oil-block-to-medco-energi/1040792/0
44. 'Yemen's Main Pipeline Attacked, Pumping Halted', *Reuters,* 8 February 2013, http://www.reuters.com/article/2013/02/08/us-yemen-oil-pipeline-idUSBRE9170GO20130208
45. Haykal Bafana, 'Dark Days Loom Ahead for Yemen Oil and Gas', *Yemen Times,* 28 May 2012, http://www.yementimes.com/en/1576/report/906/Dark-days-loom-ahead-for-Yemen-oil-and-gas.htm
46. 'Country Brief—Yemen, 2012', Ministry of Overseas Indian Affair, New Delhi, http://moia.gov.in/pdf/Yemen.pdf
47. Ibid.
48. 'Yemen's Consulate to Boost Historic Ties with Hyderabad', *NDTV,* 7 June 2012, http://www.ndtv.com/article/cities/yemen-s-consulate-to-boost-historic-ties-with-hyderabad-228591
49. 'Helpline of Indian Embassy in Yemen and Travel Advisory', Ministry of External Affairs, New Delhi, 20 February 2011, http://meaindia.

nic.in/mystart.php?id=530217202. See also, 'Indian Nationals, Whose Presence Is Not Essential Advised to Leave Yemen', Ministry of External Affairs, New Delhi, 11 March 2011, http://meaindia.nic.in/mystart.php?id=530217376

50. 'Govt. Mulls Special Flights to Bring in Indians from Yemen', *The Economic Times*, 14 June 2011, http://articles.economictimes.indiatimes.com/2011-06-14/news/29656997_1_special-flights-indian-nationals-indian-embassy

51. Adith Charlie, 'Decoding India's Response to the Arab Spring', *USAK*, 24 January 2013, http://www.usak.org.tr/EN/haber.asp?id=2084

52. Iscander al-Mammari, 'Indian Embassy in Sana'a Launches Online Visa Issuance System', *Yemen Fox*, 7 February 2013, http://www.yemenfox.net/news_details.php?sid=5732

53. 'Intervention by Shri E Ahamed, Minister of State for External Affairs at the Third Ministerial Meeting of the Friends of Yemen in Riyadh', Ministry of External Affairs.

54. Al-Mammari, 'Indian Embassy in Sana'a Launches Online Visa Issuance System'.

55. Kaushal Lakotia, 'Interview with Tawakkol Karman', *Yemen Post*, 8 April 2012, http://www.yemenpost.net/Detail123456789.aspx?ID=3&SubID=5063&MainCat=4

56. 'India Can Help Yemen in Energy, Education, Say Experts', *The Daily News*, 18 April 2012, http://india.nydailynews.com/business/56a50c6d20d180241a0714d6f6124952/india-can-help-yemen-in-energy-education-say-experts

57. Jeremy M. Sharp, 'Yemen: Background and U.S. Relations', Congressional Research Service, 1 November 2012, http://www.fas.org/sgp/crs/mideast/RL34170.pdf

58. Ibid.

59. Ibid.

60. Ibid.

61. Ibid.

62. Alley, 'Triage for a Fracturing Yemen'.

63. Ben Simpfendorfer, 'Yemen's Security Challenge Tests China's Foreign Policy', *South China Morning Post*, 7 March 2013, http://www.scmp.com/article/976877/yemens-security-challenge-tests-chinas-foreign-policy

64. Ibid.

65. 'Yemen Seeks to Increase Chinese Oil, Gas Investments', *Yemen News Agency*, 14 April 2012, http://www.gulfoilandgas.com/webpro1/MAIN/Main-news.asp?id=20082

66. 'Yemen China Sign US$5 Million Agreement, Discuss Aid for Change', *Yemen Fox*, 29 January 2013, http://www.yemenfox.net/news_details.php?sid=5659

67. Huma Imtiaz, 'Pakistan Wins Temporary UN Council Seat', *The Express Tribune*, 21 October 2011, http://tribune.com.pk/story/279024/pakistan-just-manages-to-win-non-permanent-member-seat-on-un-security-council/

68. Glenn Greenwald, 'New Town Kids vs Yemenis and Pakistanis: What Explains the Disparate Reactions?', *The Guardian,* 19 December 2012, http://www.guardian.co.uk/commentisfree/2012/dec/19/newtown-drones-children-deaths

69. 'OIC Envoy: Changes in Yemen Amazing', *Yemen Fox,* 10 February 2013, http://www.yemenfox.net/news_details.php?sid=5741

70. 'Pakistan–Yemen Relations', Embassy of Pakistan in Yemen, Yemen, Sana'a, http://www.mofa.gov.pk/yemen/contents.aspx?type=statements&id=1

71. Ibid.

11

Gulf Cooperation Council (GCC)

Mushtaq Hussain

The Gulf Cooperation Council (GCC), officially called the Cooperation Council for the Arab States of the Gulf, is a regional organization which has tremendous significance for India. As discussed in this volume, India shares close historical ties with the six constituent countries of this group, namely, Bahrain, Kuwait, Oman, Qatar, Saudi Arabia and the United Arab Emirates (UAE) and the formation of the GCC in 1981 added another facet to India's relations with the region. In recent times, the Persian Gulf region has been viewed in the Indian foreign policy circles as part of its 'immediate' neighbourhood, separated only by the Arabian Sea, hence investing huge stakes in the stability, security and prosperity of the region.[1]

Internal Developments

By early 2011, the regional upheaval and protests had reached Bahrain and Oman, thereby forcing the GCC to come to terms with the Arab Spring. While almost all GCC countries witnessed some sort of public demonstrations, Bahrain and Oman witnessed prolonged street protests and violence, with the former facing the worst crisis which is still unresolved. The popular unrest in Oman and Bahrain put the GCC in a spotlight, especially after it had, some would say reluctantly, supported reforms and political changes in other Arab countries in North Africa. In some cases, key GCC countries were more active. Qatar took the lead in supporting the opposition to Muammar Qaddafi in Libya and in the subsequent military intervention by North Atlantic Treaty Organization (NATO). It had also taken the lead role in supporting the Syrian opposition and issued calls for the resignation of President Bashar al-Assad.[2] Saudi Arabia was instrumental in convincing President Ali Abdullah Saleh of Yemen to step down in face of prolonged and violent protests. The reactions to developments in Tunisia and Egypt were also similar, though muted initially.

However, when similar popular protests began in the Gulf region, the response of the GCC was strikingly different. It was natural that the organization was accused of practicing 'double standards'[3] when it came to the public protests, demonstrations, violence and killings in its own backyard.

When protests broke out at the Pearl Roundabout on 14 February 2011 and Bahraini security forces moved to clear the protesters, the GCC held an emergency meeting the same night and pledged to support the ruling al-Khalifa family.[4] Similar protests were simmering in Oman against Sultan Qaboos. The GCC felt threatened by unprecedented protests against monarchies in Bahrain and Oman, and was afraid that the instability would spread to the other Gulf countries. Hence, it took the extraordinary step of sending armed troops to Bahrain in support of the beleaguered al-Khalifa rule. The 1,200-strong Saudi contingent along with 600 armed policemen from UAE entered Bahrain on 14 March 2011 to help quell the protests.[5] Simultaneously, the GCC tried to pacify aggrieved populace through economic handouts. Just before the armed intervention, on 10 March 2011, after a meeting of GCC Foreign Ministers in Riyadh, a massive US$20 billion aid package was announced for Bahrain and Oman.[6] The Saudi-led GCC forces eventually started withdrawing from Bahrain on 2 July 2011,[7] thereby signalling relative internal stability under al-Khalifa.

This security–economic response was accompanied by some signs of political accommodation. In June 2011, Bahrain established a fact-finding commission to look into the causes of the protests and the allegations of excessive use of force and torture by the security forces.[8] The government also started a National Dialogue, the recommendations of which were sought to be implemented towards meeting some of the key demands of the Shia opposition groups.[9] Similarly, citing inefficiency, the Omani Sultan dismissed 12 cabinet ministers in March 2011.[10] In response to widespread criticisms over the unemployment situation, he ordered the government to hire 50,000 Omanis and pay US$390 a month to jobseekers, and also agreed to cede some power to the partially elected council.[11] This mix of repression, economic package and moderate political reform characterized the response of GCC to the protests in its member states.

One dominant fear among the GCC states regarding the popular protests was the spectre of widespread Shia–Sunni strife, especially in Saudi Arabia and Bahrain with their sizable, and generally marginalized, Shia populations living under Sunni rule. There was the looming threat of Iran exploiting the situation for its political goals. In order to pre-empt any Iranian move and to signal unconditional support for the embattled monarchies, on 14 May 2011, Saudi Arabia and Bahrain announced that they supported a plan to form a close political and military union among the GCC states. At a GCC leadership meeting in Riyadh that day, the other four GCC states opposed such a union and the GCC as a whole formally deferred a decision on the Saudi–Bahraini plan. Sharp reaction from Iran also contributed in shelving the plan.[12]

Howsoever ill-devised the plans might have been, the Arab Spring did bring the ruling Gulf monarchies closer and paved a way for more coordination, especially in matters of security. In a surprise move seen as an attempt to enhance GCC's political standing in the region, the organization initiated first steps towards broadening its membership. In May 2011, the GCC decided to expand its membership to include Morocco and Jordan,[13] a step viewed by some as an attempt to make a joint stand for the safeguarding of Arab monarchies against further existential threats. In September 2011, as a first tangible move, the GCC agreed to fund a five-year development aid programme for the two monarchies.[14] However, the GCC is yet to initiate the process for membership of Jordan and Morocco under its fold.

On 25 December 2012, Bahrain announced that it would host the first-ever GCC United Military Command aimed at deterring threats against the region and further strengthening the military ties between the six-member states.[15] The 33rd GCC Summit, which concluded in Manama on 25 December 2012, passed resolutions on mutual action to boost full GCC citizenship and deepening economic integration among the member states. During the Summit, the GCC Heads of State also ratified the Joint Defence Council (which created the Unified Military Command) and the security agreement aimed at sharing of intelligence among the security departments of the member states.[16]

In the wake of the popular protests in the region, Bahrain proved to be the weakest link in the GCC in terms of its vulnerability to sectarian strife. Oman was the second weakest, but was able to peacefully manage the reformist demands. The same can be said for Kuwait as well, where the elections of November 2011 gave a democratic opening to the opposition parties, thereby containing the limited protests that had preceded during the year. Recent events made it clear that while not being immune to popular protests and defiance against authority, the GCC states were willing to act in unison against any existential threat, either internal or external. In this show of unity, Saudi Arabia enhanced its stature of being the leader of the GCC, owing to its military and economic weight.

The strongest link within GCC appeared to be Qatar owing to its political stability, economic clout, diplomatic finesse and, perhaps most decidedly, its sway over the region with Al-Jazeera representing 'the depth of Qatar's influence on the Arab Spring'.[17] Another strong link in the regional coalition was UAE, which along with Qatar, was the only other GCC state that did not witness popular demonstrations, and continued to be the economic powerhouse of the grouping. Saudi Arabia, however, is straddled between these two scenarios as it would have to balance the growing restlessness among its youth, women and marginalized Shia population with the conservative clergy which bestows legitimacy to the al-Saud rule. These were complicated by the octogenarian nature of the principle Saudi rulers and questions over succession.

Bilateral Relations

Towards the last quarter of the twentieth century, changing geopolitical circumstances required re-examining of India's policy towards the Persian Gulf region as historical relations could no longer ensure continued goodwill. To secure its growing interests in the region—from energy security to welfare of burgeoning number of expatriates and counter-terrorism—India had to frame a more cohesive approach. This change of approach culminated in what has been dubbed as India's 'Look West Policy'. One of the first official indications of this policy came during the July 2005 meeting of the Prime Minister's Trade and Economic Relations Committee (TERC). The launching of negotiations for a Free Trade Agreement (FTA) with the GCC and Comprehensive Economic Cooperation Agreement (CECA) with individual member countries were announced. In the course of the meeting, Prime Minister Manmohan Singh said,

> The Gulf region, like South-East and South Asia, is part of our natural economic hinterland. We must pursue closer economic relations with all our neighbours in our wider Asian neighbourhood. India has successfully pursued a 'Look East' policy to come closer to the countries of South-East Asia. We must, similarly, come closer to our western neighbours in the Gulf.[18]

Political Relations

Relevance of the GCC countries has to be viewed in terms of India's wider strategic interests. The Persian Gulf is an inseparable part of India's foreign policy interests in terms of counter-terrorism, energy security, remittances and capital investments. There is also the factor of religious and psychological affinity felt towards this region by India's more than 138 million Muslims.[19] All these factors have led to growing political contacts between India and the GCC countries. There have been numerous visits by political dignitaries from both sides, the last being the visit of the Crown Prince of Bahrain Salman bin Hamad al-Khalifa, in May 2012.[20] India's Deputy National Security Advisor Vijaya Latha Reddy visited the region to take part in the 'Manama Dialogue' in December 2012 where she spoke on the issue of counter-terrorism.[21]

In recent years, however, there have been no major political contacts between India and the GCC as a separate collective entity. The last high-level visit took place in February 2004 when GCC Secretary General Abdulrahman bin Hamad al-Attiyah visited India and met then Home Minister and Deputy Prime Minister L. K. Advani, Minister of External

Affairs Yashwant Sinha and Deputy Chairperson of the Rajya Sabha Najma Heptullah.[22] However, both sides have been regularly holding ministerial-level political dialogues. The first India–GCC Political Dialogue at the level of the External Affairs Minister and GCC Secretary General and GCC ambassadors/representatives was held on the sidelines of the United Nations General Assembly (UNGA) session in September 2003.[23] Since then, such dialogues have become an annual feature during the UNGA sessions. The sixth round of this Dialogue was held in New York on 26 September 2011. The Indian side was led by the External Affairs Minister S. M. Krishna while the GCC was represented by the Secretary General of GCC Abdul Latif bin Rashid al-Zayani; the Foreign Minister of UAE as current Chair of GCC Ministerial Council, and the Deputy Foreign Minister of Saudi Arabia.[24] During the dialogue, wide-ranging issues were discussed including strengthening of economic co-operation, tackling terrorism and UN reforms.

Economy and Energy

India's economic linkages with the GCC countries have increased steadily since the 1980s, principally due to growth in oil imports.[25] These relations enabled by geographical proximity have been supplemented by growing trade and investment ties between the two sides. With the GCC states embarking on ambitious development projects and India espousing a new shift in its foreign policy, by way of 'Look West' there was a new momentum in the economic ties.

This renewed focus on the region came as no surprise. That the Gulf region in general and the GCC countries in particular hold tremendous economic importance for India cannot be emphasized enough.

Following India's economic liberalization since 1991 and the GCC starting to 'look East', trade between the two economies started to flourish and has been steadily increasing in the past decade (Table 11.1 and Figure 11.1). Both are members of the World Trade Organization and have granted each other 'Most Favoured Nation' status.[26] Merchandise trade between the two economies increased from a mere US$5.6 billion in 2001 to US$88.8 billion in 2010,[27] US$117.4 billion in 2011 and

Table 11.1

India–GCC Bilateral Trade (in US$ Million)

Country	2009–10	2010–11	2011–12
Bahrain	753.07	1,293.08	1,316.28
Kuwait	9,031.95	12,169.65	17,556.78
Oman	4,532.82	5,088.55	4,651.45
Qatar	5,185.49	7,195.27	13,731.77
Saudi Arabia	21,004.57	25,069.68	36,743.40
UAE	43,469.50	66,575.55	71,715.91
Total GCC	83,977.40	117,391.78	145,715.59
India's total trade	467,124.31	620,905.32	795,283.41
Share in total trade	17.98	18.91	18.32

Source: Adapted from Director General of Foreign Trade, New Delhi, http://www.dgft.gov.in

Figure 11.1

India–GCC Bilateral Trade

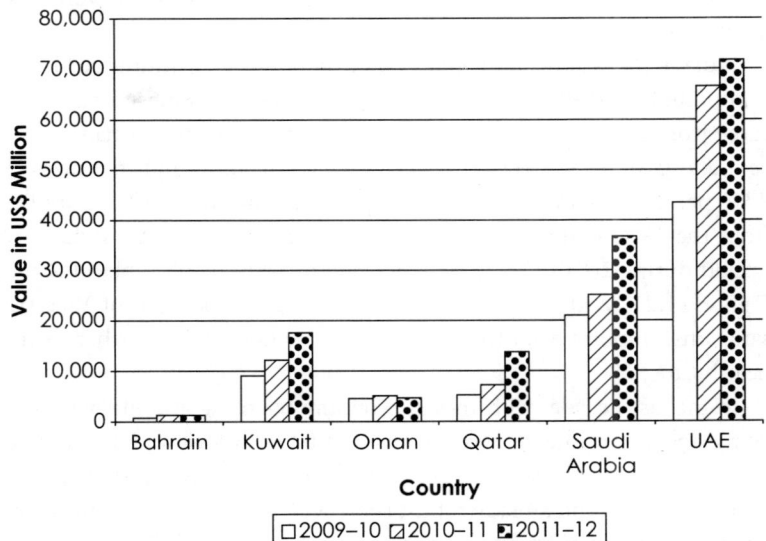

Source: Adapted from Director General of Foreign Trade, New Delhi, http://www.dgft.gov.in

US$145.7 billion in 2012.[28] The UAE was the single largest trading partner of India in 2010,[29] accounting for 10.4 per cent of India's total global trade, and currently the second largest after China, with total trade reaching US$71.5 billion.[30] Recently, Indian Minister of Commerce and Industry predicted that the UAE would continue to drive two-way economic relations between India and GCC, with total trade including import of crude and petroleum products, expected to reach US$175 billion in 2013.[31] this would be a significant rise over the figures for 2011–12 which stood at US$145.7 billion.[32]

To give a further boost to trade and economic relations, India and GCC signed a Framework Agreement on Economic Cooperation to explore the possibility of a Free Trade Area between the two sides.[33] Despite the non-fruition of FTA talks, different avenues have been constantly explored to promote further trade and investment opportunities. Under the aegis of the India–Arab Cooperation Forum, the second India–Arab Investment Projects Conclave was held in New Delhi in February 2010 with delegates from all the GCC countries attending.[34] However, negotiations on an FTA are still continuing and the Confederation of Indian Industries (CII) has expressed optimism that an agreement would be concluded by 2013.[35]

India is the world's fourth-largest oil importer and during 2011–12, it imported US$140 billion worth of oil;[36] out of this, almost 19 per cent came from Saudi Arabia, with Kuwait accounting for more than 10 per cent and UAE for 9.2 per cent. The GCC as a whole supplied a massive 43.7 per cent of India's total oil imports during 2011–12.[37] Supplies from the GCC countries constituted 39.5 per cent of total Indian oil import during 2010–11 and 38.5 per cent in 2009–10[38] (Table 11.2 and Figure 11.2). With imports from Iran decreasing because of Western sanctions, imports from the GCC countries would grow further in the near future.

In the last decade, with Indian economy booming and many sectors being opened to foreign investments, the GCC was viewed as a potential source of much-needed capital investments. Complementarities in both economies and already robust trade were seen as an enabling factor for promoting investments on both sides. Even though Foreign Direct Investment (FDI) from GCC to India has picked up pace in recent years,

Table 11.2

India's Energy Imports from GCC (in US$ Million)

	2009–10	2010–11	2011–12
Total energy imports	96,321.12	115,929.02	172,753.92
Energy imports from GCC	36,997.63	46,632.91	72,582.75
Total imports from Persian Gulf	55,904.14	66,688.4	103,915.24
GCC share in total imports (in per cent)	38.41	40.23	42.02
GCC share in imports from Persian Gulf (in per cent)	66.18	69.93	69.85

Source: Adapted from Director General of Foreign Trade, New Delhi, http://www.dgft.gov.in

Figure 11.2

Share of GCC in India's Total Oil Imports

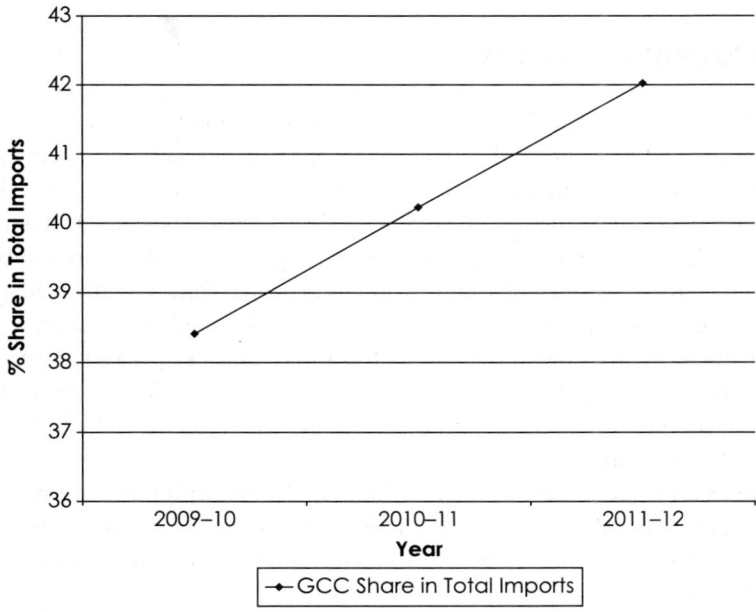

Source: Adapted from Director General of Foreign Trade, New Delhi, http://www.dgft.gov.in

it remains negligible relative to trade flows, and represents just a small percentage of total FDI from the region to the world. Cumulative FDI from GCC to India, from April 2000 to January 2012, was a meagre US$2.6 billion accounting for only 1.7 per cent of total FDI inflows into India.[39] Clearly there is much scope for improvement in this area.

Another important factor in the economic relations between India and GCC is the inflow of remittances from the region. Currently, the number of Indians living in the GCC countries is estimated to be around 6 million, making them the largest expatriate community in the region.[40] In 2008, this huge expatriate population remitted a little over US$3 billion to India.[41] According to the World Bank, of the US$55 billion India received in remittances in 2010, US$24.5 billion came from the GCC.[42] In 2012, total remittances to India were expected to be US$70 billion, highest for any developing country.[43] With the overall increase in the amount of remittances, the share of GCC countries set to grow even further.

External Players

The GCC countries have multidimensional relations with the United States (US), Pakistan and China—countries that can have an impact on India's relations with the GCC. The US has strategic, economic, political, commercial and defence interests in the GCC states. Pakistan has fraternal relations with the GCC constituents owing to geographical proximity and cultural and religious affinity. In recent years, China has emerged as one of the leading trade partners of the GCC. Although India has pragmatic bilateral ties with the GCC, these three countries pose some challenge to India's policy in the Council. China, for example, has emerged as a competitor for energy imports from the GCC, forcing India to look for diversification. On the other hand, Pakistan has the potential to play a negative role in development of India's relations with the GCC in the Persian Gulf. All three sides are in the process of negotiations to sign an FTA with the GCC; however, not much headway has been made in any of the cases.

The US: Since the outbreak of popular protests in the Middle East, relations between the US and GCC countries remained strained owing to what was seen as harsh and unfriendly stand taken by Washington on issues such as human rights, political reforms and the rule of law. A shift in US strategic thinking, with its disengagement from Iraq and Afghanistan and 'pivot to Asia', raised concerns regarding US commitments to the Gulf. Although some have argued that the GCC is no longer limiting its options to its traditional security guarantor and seeking alternatives, including India,[44] the US continues to be the region's bulwark against perceived Iranian threats. Differences over many issues did not deter the two sides form forging operational ties in matters of security and counter-terrorism.

For decades, US–GCC relations were asymmetrical when it came to dealing with the GCC states bilaterally. In recent times, the US had elevated its strategic relationship with Kuwait and Bahrain, branding them 'Major non-NATO Allies' while keeping its ties unchanged with the four other GCC states. In the economic sector, US had better bilateral ties, through its FTAs signed with Bahrain (2005) and UAE (2009). But in March 2012, relations evolved to a new level of partnership with the launching of the US–GCC Strategic Cooperation Forum (SCF). This was the first such initiative with the regional organization aimed at centralizing and streamlining counter-terrorism efforts.[45] Trade also continued to be robust between the two economies, crossing the US$100 billion mark in 2011–12 and US FDI in GCC countries reaching US$23.5 billion in 2010.[46]

Under pressure to use its leverage with the Gulf monarchies towards promoting political reforms, the US had to take a public stand on the issues emanating from the Arab Spring, thereby straining its relations with the GCC states to some extent. However, overriding strategic, security and political considerations ensured that domestic issues did not interfere with the cordial bilateral and multilateral relations. Speaking during the inaugural meeting of US–GCC SCF on March 2012, US Secretary of State Hillary Clinton put all doubts to rest with an assertion that, 'I underscore the rock-solid commitment of the US to the people and nations of the Gulf'.[47]

China: While India has been trying to speed up its efforts to forge better economic ties with the GCC, China has made significant progress in strengthening its co-operation with the GCC states. While there has been no top-level political interaction between India and GCC in past several years, in January 2012 Chinese Premier Wen Jiabao met the GCC Secretary General during his three-nation tour of Saudi Arabia, UAE and Qatar. Premier Wen and Secretary General al-Zayani agreed to speed up negotiations on a FTA.[48] In Sharjah, Wen Jiabao attended the fourth Arab–Chinese Business Conference.[49] The disparity in Chinese and Indian engagements can be realised from the fact that India only had one high-level political dialogue with the GCC in the last two years while China has had nearly a dozen high-level meetings and dialogues during 2011 and 2012.[50]

Pakistan: Pakistan enjoys strong ties with the GCC, which are based on historic, geographic, economic and cultural affinities. Aiming to take the traditional relations to the strategic level, Pakistani Foreign Minister Mahmoud Quraishi proposed the setting up of a formal 'security bloc' with the GCC states.[51] Consequently, the First Joint Ministerial Meeting of the GCC–Pakistan Strategic Dialogue was held on 8 March 2011 where the two sides discussed forging a 'comprehensive partnership'.[52] During his visit to Kuwait in October 2012 for the Asian Cooperation Dialogue (ACD) Summit, Pakistani Prime Minister Raja Parvez Ashraf also expressed desire for closer defence ties with GCC,[53] a development which could pose new challenges to India's relations with the GCC.

Conclusion

Following a trend of past several years, India's interactions with the GCC countries primarily remained a bilateral rather than regional affair. Progress during 2012 was very limited and the much-discussed FTA has not made any headway. The Arab Spring and the resultant domestic uncertainty in some of these countries further prevented any meaningful progress. The regional upheaval has put to test the resolve of the GCC states to survive and create coping mechanisms against existential threats. Partly to overcome the challenges, in May 2011, the GCC decided to expand and include two other monarchies—Jordan and Morocco. Discussions for formalizing their memberships are currently under way. With the exception of Bahrain, most other members of the GCC have weathered the upheaval. However, the regional upheaval of 2011 does raise the possibility of instability in the region, thereby posing a challenge for progress in India–GCC relations.

Notes

1. 'India–GCC Relations', Embassy of India, Kingdom of Saudi Arabia, Riyadh, 9 October 2012, http://www.indianembassy.org.sa/Content.aspx?ID=708
2. 'Arab League Calls for Transitional Government in Syria–Qatar', *Jordan Times*, 23 July 2012, http://jordantimes.com/arab-league-calls-for-transition-government-in-syria—qatar
3. Silvia Colombo, 'Unpacking the GCC's Response to the Arab Spring', *Sharaka Commentaries*, 2012, http://www.iai.it/pdf/mediterraneo/Sharaka/Sharaka_C_01.pdf
4. Silvia Colombo, *The GCC Countries and the Arab Spring: Between Outreach, Patronage and Repression*, Instituto Affari Internazionali, IAI Working Papers 12, 2012, 5, http://www.iai.it/pdf/DocIAI/iaiwp1209.pdf
5. Kenneth Katzman, 'Bahrain: Reform, Security and U.S. Policy', *Congressional Research Service Report for Congress*, 12 February 2013, 8, http://www.fas.org/sgp/crs/mideast/95-1013.pdf
6. 'GCC to Set Up $20 bn Bailout Fund for Bahrain and Oman', *The National*, 11 March 2011, http://www.thenational.ae/news/world/middle-east/gcc-to-set-up-20bn-bailout-fund-for-bahrain-and-oman
7. 'Saudi Troops Begin to Pull Out of Bahrain', *The National*, 29 June 2011, http://www.thenational.ae/news/world/middle-east/saudi-troops-begin-to-pull-out-of-bahrain
8. 'Bahrain's King Orders Investigation into Human Rights Abuses at Protests', *The Guardian*, 29 June 2011, http://www.guardian.co.uk/world/2011/jun/29/bahrain-king-human-rights-protests
9. 'Committee to Execute Dialogue Outcomes', *Gulf Daily News*, 1 August 2011, http://www.gulf-daily-news.com/NewsDetails.aspx?storyid=310911
10. 'Sultan Fires Ministers amid Oman Unrest', *The Financial Times*, 7 March 2011, http://www.ft.com/cms/s/0/95626aec-48ea-11e0-af8c-00144feab49a.html#axzz2PCEQN4qj
11. 'Omani Protestors Torch Government Building', *Press TV*, 13 March 2011, http://edition.presstv.ir/detail/169796.html
12. 'Gulf Unity Plan on Hold Amid Iranian Warning', *The Guardian*, 14 May 2011, http://www.guardian.co.uk/world/2012/may/14/gulf-unity-plan-on-hold?INTCMP=SRCH
13. 'Welcome for "Enlarged GCC" that would Include Morocco and Jordan', *The National*, 12 May 2011, http://www.thenational.ae/news/world/middle-east/welcome-for-enlarged-gcc-that-would-include-morocco-and-jordan

14. 'GCC Agrees Five-Year Aid Plan for Morocco and Jordan', *The National*, 13 September 2011, http://www.thenational.ae/news/world/middle-east/gcc-agrees-five-year-aid-plan-for-morocco-and-jordan

15. 'Bahrain to Host GCC Unified Military Command', *Xinhua*, 26 December 2012, http://news.xinhuanet.com/english/world/2012-12/26/c_132063212.htm

16. 'The 33rd GCC Summit Concludes Today in the Kingdom of Bahrain', *Bahrain News Agency*, 25 December 2012, http://www.bna.bh/portal/en/news/539240

17. Abdulkhaleq Abdullah 'Repercussions of the Arab Spring on GCC States', *Arab Center for Research and Policy Studies*, 17 May 2012, http://english.dohainstitute.org/release/050a254b-e013-4060-9aab-32238f34cf47

18. Sanjaya Baru, 'Look West Policy', *Business Standard*, 8 March 2010, http://www.business-standard.com/article/opinion/sanjaya-baru-look-west-policy-110030800029_1.html

19. India Online, 'Population by Religion in India', http://www.indiaonlinepages.com/population/religious-population-in-india.html

20. 'Official Visit of Crown Prince of Bahrain to India', Embassy of India, Kingdom of Bahrain, Ghudaibiya, 1 June 2012, http://www.indianembassybahrain.com/cp_bah_visits_india.html

21. 'Manama Dialogue 2012: Speaker Agenda', International Institute of Strategic Studies, 7 December 2012, http://www.google.co.in/url?sa=t&rct=j&q=india%20manama%20dialogue%20december%20 2012&source=web&cd=1&cad=rja&ved=0CDEQFjAA&url=http%3A%2 F%2Fwww.iiss.org%2FEasySiteWeb%2FGatewayLink.aspx%3FalId%3D7 1864&ei=8BE3UerUJOby4QTA-IBw&usg=AFQjCNEbK00CxHqVUhz3K YC70mfuE7Flyw&bvm=bv.43287494,d.bGE

22. 'Gulf Cooperation Council', Ministry of External Affairs, Government of India, April 2012, http://meaindia.nic.in/staticfile/gccmarch2011.pdf

23. Ibid.

24. Ibid.

25. 'Visit of Gulf Cooperation Council (GCC) Secretary General to India, 15–18 February 2004', MEA, Government of India, 14 February 2004, http://www.mea.gov.in/press-releases.htm?dtl/7755/Visit+of+Gulf+Cooperation+Council+GCC+Secretary+General+to+India+1518+February+2004

26. Samir Ranjan Pradhan, *India, GCC and the Global Energy Regime: Exploring Interdependence and Outlook for Collaboration* (New Delhi: Academic Foundation, 2008), 312.

27. 'Trade and Capital Flows—GCC and India', Alpen Capital, 2 May 2012, 8, http://www.alpencapital.com/downloads/Trade%20and%20Capital%20 Flows%20-%20GCC%20and%20India_Final_May%2002%202012.pdf

28. 'India–GCC Relations', Embassy of India.

29. Alpen Capital, 'Trade and Capital Flows'.

30. 'UAE Seen to Drive GCC and India Trade to $175 bn in 2013', *Khaleej Times*, 18 February 2013, http://www.khaleejtimes.com/kt-article-display-1.asp?xfile=data/uaebusiness/2013/February/uaebusiness_February303.xml&section=uaebusiness

31. Ibid.

32. 'India–GCC Relations', Embassy of India.

33. 'Gulf Cooperation Council', Ministry of External Affairs, http://meaindia.nic.in/staticfile/gccmarch2011.pdf

34. Ibid.

35. 'India, Gulf Cooperation Council to Ink Free Trade Agreement within a Year', *The Economic Times,* 27 June 2012, http://articles.economictimes.indiatimes.com/2012-06-27/news/32441212_1_gcc-oman-and-india-trade-agreement

36. 'India's Crude Oil Import Bill Jumps 40% to $140 bn in FY 12', *Business Line*, 13 June 2012, http://www.thehindubusinessline.com/industry-and-economy/article3523827.ece

37. 'Table—India's Country-Wise Crude Oil Imports since 2001/02', *Reuters*, 6 August 2012, http://in.reuters.com/article/2012/08/06/india-crude-import-idINL4E8IU4HI20120806

38. Ibid.

39. 'Investments from GCC to India Remain Negligible: Report', *The Economic Times*, 3 May 2012, http://articles.economictimes.indiatimes.com/2012-05-03/news/31558875_1_gcc-capital-flows-bilateral-merchandise-trade

40. Alpen Capital, 'Trade and Capital Flows'.

41. Samir Pradhan, 'India's Economic and Political Presence in the Gulf: A Gulf Perspective', in Gulf Research Center, *India's Growing Role in the Gulf: Implication for the Region and the United States* (2009), 23, http://www.cftni.org/Monograph-Indias-Growing-Role-in-the-Gulf.pdf

42. Kumar Rishabh and Rajiv Ranjan, 'Evolution of Indo–GCC Trade Relations: The Last Two Decades', *International Journal of Economics, Commerce and Research (IJECR)* 2, No. 4 (2012), http://www.google.co.in/url?sa=t&rct=j&q=remittances%20to%20india%20from%20gcc%20statistics&source=web&cd=14&cad=rja&ved=0CE0QFjADOAo&url=http%3A%2F%2Fessential.metapress.com%2Fcontent%2F435h44pg3742h362%2Ffulltext.pdf&ei=7zI3Ud-OGuqM4ATf7YD4Bg&usg=AFQjCNH3pPkkZeVOdckFsW7MiQ74gk4PNg

43. 'India to Receive Record $$70 Billion Remittances in 2012: World Bank', *The Economic Times*, 21 November 2012, http://articles.economictimes.indiatimes.com/2012-11-21/news/35256192_1_remittance-flows-private-capital-flows-world-bank

44. N. Janardhan, 'Fatigue in GCC–US Ties', *Khaleej Times*, 1 March 2013, http://www.khaleejtimes.com/kt-article-display-1.asp?xfile=data/opinion/2013/March/opinion_March3.xml&section=opinion

45. 'The US–GCC Strategic Cooperation Forum: A Multilateral Approach to Counter-Terrorism', *IISS Voices*, 12 September 2012, http://iissvoicesblog. wordpress.com/2012/12/09/the-us-gcc-strategic-cooperation-forum-a-multilateral-approach-to-counter-terrorism/

46. 'US, GCC Agree to Boost Trade, Investment Ties', *The Saudi Gazette*, 28 September 2012, http://www.saudigazette.com.sa/index.cfm?method=home. regcon&contentid=20120928137709

47. 'Remarks by Secretary Clinton, March 2012: Remarks with Saudi Arabian Foreign Minister Saud Al-Faisal', *U.S. Department of State*, 31 March 2012, http://www.state.gov/secretary/rm/2012/03/187245.htm

48. 'China, GCC Agree to Accelerate FTA Negotiations', *China Daily*, 16 January 2012, http://www.chinadaily.com.cn/china/2012-01/16/content_14449569.htm

49. 'Chinese Premier Calls for GCC Free Trade Agreement', *Khaleej Times*, 19 January 2012, http://www.khaleejtimes.com/DisplayArticle.asp?xfile=data/business/2012/January/business_January334.xml&section=business&col=

50. 'GCC News 2011', Secretariat General, Gulf Co-operation Council, http://www.gcc-sg.org/index9718.html?action=News&Sub=Archive-ShowResult&Y=2011; and 'GCC News 2012', http://www.gcc-sg.org/index5fc6.html?action=News&Sub=Archive-ShowResult&Y=2012

51. 'Pakistan–GCC Security Bloc Proposed', *Gulf News*, 7 February 2011, http://gulfnews.com/news/world/pakistan/pakistan-gcc-security-bloc-proposed-1.758165

52. 'Pakistan–GCC Issue Joint Statement on Strategic Dialogue', Ministry of Foreign Affairs, Government of Pakistan, 8 March 2011, http://www.mofa. gov.pk/press_releases/2011/Mar/Pr_086.htm

53. 'Pakistan Desires Stringer Defence Ties with GCC: PM Ashraf', *Pak Tribune*, 18 October 2012, http://paktribune.com/news/Pakistan-desires-stronger-defence-ties-with-GCC-PM-Ashraf-254274.html

12

Policy Options for India

MEI@ND

1. **Prioritize the Persian Gulf:** In terms of political, economic, strategic and cultural ties, the Persian Gulf is far more critical for India than its immediate South Asian neighbourhood. The stability of the Gulf region is critical for global tranquillity and economic progress. The Persian Gulf presents both challenges and opportunities. Time has come for India to move out of its obsession with South Asia and pay more attention to the Gulf. Indeed, India's future lies in a stable and progressing Persian Gulf.

2. **Engage politically:** Political contacts between India and the Persian Gulf countries have dwindled considerably during 2012. There were no state visits from India to the region. Prime Minister Manmohan Singh's visit to Tehran in August for the 16th summit meeting of the Non-aligned Movement was converted into a bilateral visit. Visits of Defence Minister A. K. Antony to Saudi Arabia in February and of External Affairs Minister S. M. Krishna to Israel, Palestine, Jordan and UAE were the senior most visits from India. From the region Qatari Emir (April) and Bahraini Crown Prince (May) visited India in 2012. Otherwise, there were no high-level political contacts between the two sides; indeed, the president, the vice president or the prime minister had not visited the Gulf countries since the visit of President Pratibha Patil to the UAE in November 2010.

3. **Counter-terrorism cooperation:** The willingness of Saudi Arabia to deport three wanted persons for terror-related charges marks a new beginning in the Indo-Gulf relations. Similar requests in the past were ignored due to these countries' closer ties with Pakistan. India should capitalize on this new trend and tighten the possible flow of hawala and other forms of financial transfers from the Gulf to various terror groups within the country. Such measure would also require a stronger legal basis for Indian request than political statements.

4. **Recognize regional tensions:** India will not be able to escape from the Arab–Persian tensions being played out more visibly in Bahrain and Iraq. While taking sides is not an option, India would not be able to stay indifferent to a potential confrontation, especially if the controversies surrounding the Iranian nuclear programme is not resolved peacefully.

5. **Managing the United States (US):** Because the US has become a de facto Persian Gulf power, India would have to learn to manage relations with the US regarding the Persian Gulf. Some of American policies are helpful to India while others harmful. Hence, greater foresight is required if India is to avoid ambushes such as oil sanctions against Iran.

6. **Accept internal cleavages:** In political sense, the wider Middle East, especially the Gulf region is in a flux. The popular protests in many Arab countries have not produced a viable road map or an attractive response to the Arab Spring. Even within particular countries there are multiplicity of players and pressures. India needs to recognize competing political and social forces in various countries. Without seeking to intervene in the internal affairs of the Gulf countries, India needs to recognize, understand and closely follow various internal fault lines, cleavages and minority groups that exist in the region and their sociopolitical function and importance.

7. **Restore closer ties with Oman:** The close historical ties between India and Oman have come under strain. The double honour planned for the Sultan in January 2013 did not materialize. Besides being the Chief Guest of the Republic Day celebrations, he was slated to receive the Jawaharlal Nehru Award for 2004. There

are signs that some tension and misunderstanding have cropped up and it is in India's interest that the issues are resolved and the Sultan's visit is rescheduled at the earliest possible date.

8. **Prepare for Arabization:** For a long time, the oil-rich Gulf Arab countries have been seeking increased employment opportunities for their citizens over expatriates. While the progress has been slow, the Arab Spring and economic hardships have intensified the calls for the Arabization of the workforce. This trend would be more visible in Bahrain and Oman, which have limited resources to pursue welfare mechanism. Towards the end of 2012, Saudi Arabia began implementing its Nitaqat policy, originally outlined in 2010, whereby Saudi companies which do not adhere to the quota of local employees would face severe fines and punishment. This had already resulted in panic among the Indian expatriate community and their families in India. While the Arabization process would unfold over time, India would have to prepare itself for a gradual reduction in the flow of Indian people to the Persian Gulf and its economic consequences.

9. **Inaccurate data:** Official figures regarding the number of Indian expatriates in the Gulf region are nothing more than educated guesses. The number of expatriate workers who sought Emigration Clearance is the only reliable data on the subject. Even here the post of disembarkation indicates not that the person is a resident of that particular state, but merely the airport from where he or she took the flight. With the likelihood of large-scale return of migrants due to Arabization of the workforce, India requires a more accurate data to prepare any contingency plan for their evacuation or rehabilitation.

10. **Refocus bilateral trade:** India's economic relations with the Gulf are highly skewed in favour of oil and gas imports. Not only they dominate the bilateral trade, in some countries they account for almost the entire Indian imports. The oil imports also contribute to high trade imbalance which is adding to India's payment problems with Iran. With exports accounting a tenth of its imports from Iran, for example, India is finding it difficult to settle the oil bill through rupee payment.

11. **Dispelling concerns:** Some of the controversies surrounding India's economic policy are causing anxiety and concerns among the Arab countries. The decision of the Supreme Court in February 2012 to strike down the 2G spectrum allocation resulted in Emirati firm Etisalat pulling out of the Indian telecom section. Similar fears have also delayed the willingness of the Ethihad Airliner to investing in the Indian aviation sector. While it cannot assure non-intervention by the judiciary, the Indian government would have to provide sufficient guarantees and assurances to the Gulf countries, if it were to be an attractive destination for Gulf investments.

12. **Economic engagement:** Economic difficulties are the root causes of popular protests, especially in poorer countries like Bahrain and Yemen. This situation offers new opportunities for long-term Indian investments. Although they carry significant risks, Indian investments have the potential to help these societies and fetch long-term advantages for the country.

13. **Bilateral Free Trade Agreements (FTAs):** With the FTA negotiations with the GCC not making any headway, India should consider FTAs with individual countries such as Oman while working for a comprehensive regional arrangement.

14. **Explore joint ventures:** Although the region is energy-rich, most countries do not allow foreign ownership of energy assets. This policy is a result of colonialism and prolonged western exploitation of oil resources and is unlikely to change. Hence, India would have to replicate its joint venture model, such as the Oman India Fertilizer Company, in other countries.

15. **Continued neglect:** The Indian media and non-official circles continue to ignore the importance of the Persian Gulf region. Mainstream media do not find visits by Gulf leaders worthy enough for primetime coverage. The sudden replacement of Bhutanese King as the chief guest for the 2013 Republic day celebrations, for example, did not evoke any attention. None asked as to why Omani ruler was replaced at the last minute.

16. **Nomenclature:** Etymologically, the name 'India' is a foreign construct. If that name is adopted for self-identity, the region must also be recognized by its historic and widely accepted international

names, namely, Middle East and the Persian Gulf. Middle East is a term of self-identity for the region. Like other geographic terms such as Arabian Sea, Indian Ocean and the South China Sea, the expression Persian Gulf does not denote Iranian ownership of the said waters.

About the Editor and Contributors

Editor

P. R. Kumaraswamy teaches contemporary Middle East at Jawaharlal Nehru University, New Delhi and is the Honorary Director of Middle East Institute, New Delhi (MEI@ND).

Contributors

Dipanwita Chakravortty is a doctoral candidate at the Centre for West Asian Studies, School of International Studies, Jawaharlal Nehru University, New Delhi.

Jatung Raja Philemon Chiru is a doctoral candidate at the Centre for West Asian Studies, School of International Studies, Jawaharlal Nehru University, New Delhi.

Mushtaq Hussain is a doctoral candidate at the Centre for West Asian Studies, School of International Studies, Jawaharlal Nehru University, New Delhi.

Alvite Singh Ningthoujam is a doctoral candidate at the Centre for West Asian Studies, School of International Studies, Jawaharlal Nehru University, New Delhi.

Md. Muddassir Quamar is a doctoral candidate at the Centre for West Asian Studies, School of International Studies, Jawaharlal Nehru University, New Delhi.

Sonia Roy is a doctoral candidate at the Centre for West Asian Studies, School of International Studies, Jawaharlal Nehru University, New Delhi.

Paulami Sanyal is a doctoral candidate at the Centre for West Asian Studies, School of International Studies, Jawaharlal Nehru University, New Delhi.

Manjari Singh is a doctoral candidate at the Centre for West Asian Studies, School of International Studies, Jawaharlal Nehru University, New Delhi.

Marimuthu Ulaganathan is a doctoral candidate at the Centre for West Asian Studies, School of International Studies, Jawaharlal Nehru University, New Delhi.

About MEI@ND

Middle East Institute (MEI) is a forward-looking, policy-oriented non-governmental research institution, striving for academic openness. Non-partisan, non-nationalistic and non-ideological, the MEI has no agenda of its own. The aim is to facilitate a professional and comprehensive understanding of the Middle East.

We at MEI intend to do so by actively engaging with all regional actors and great powers with stakes in the region. The MEI would function as a forum for debate, dialogue and discourse concerning the Middle East.

The MEI is India-based but not Indo-centric. Web address: www. mei.org.in

Index